Grimm Fairy Tales
Myths & Legends

zenescope

Grimm Fairy Tales
MYTHS & LEGENDS

CREATED AND STORY BY
RAVEN GREGORY
JOE BRUSHA
RALPH TEDESCO

TRADE DESIGN BY
CHRISTOPHER COTE

TRADE EDITED BY
RALPH TEDESCO

THIS VOLUME REPRINTS THE COMIC
SERIES GRIMM FAIRY TALES MYTHS &
LEGENDS ISSUES #8-11 AND GRIMM
FAIRY TALES ISSUES #25-26 PUBLISHED
BY ZENESCOPE ENTERTAINMENT.

WWW.ZENESCOPE.COM

FIRST EDITION, MARCH 2012
ISBN: 978-1-937068-31-8

zenescope
WWW.ZENESCOPE.COM
FACEBOOK.COM/ZENESCOPE

ZENESCOPE ENTERTAINMENT, INC.

Joe Brusha • President & Chief Creative Officer
Ralph Tedesco • Editor-in-Chief
Jennifer Bermel • Director of Licensing & Business Development
Raven Gregory • Executive Editor
Anthony Spay • Art Director
Christopher Cote • Production Manager
Dave Franchini • Direct Market Sales & Customer Service
Stephen Haberman • Marketing Manager

Grimm Fairy Tales™ Myths & Legends

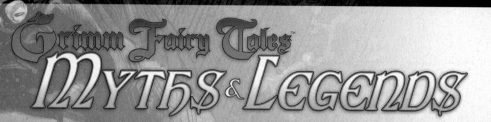

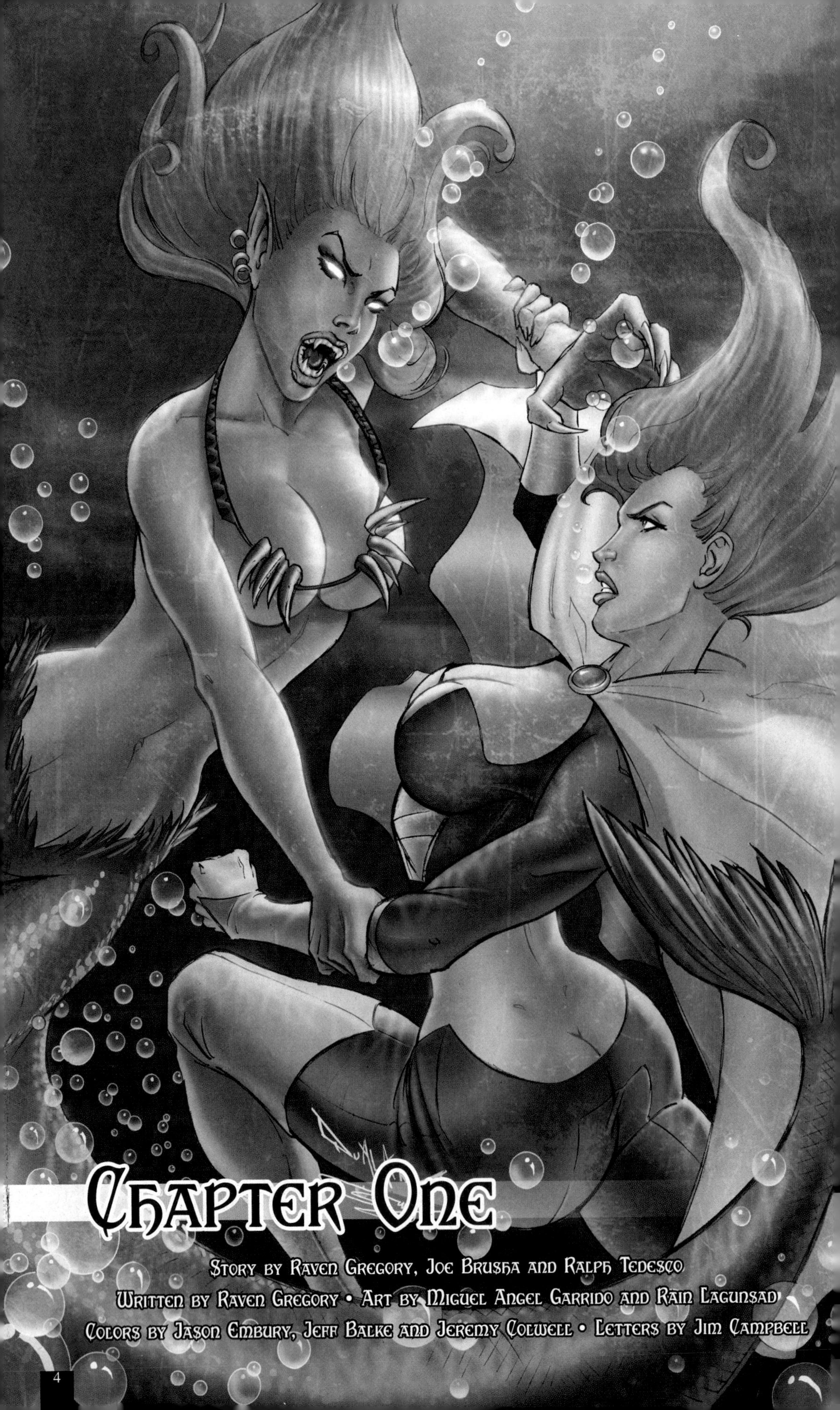

Chapter One

Story by Raven Gregory, Joe Brusha and Ralph Tedesco

Written by Raven Gregory • Art by Miguel Angel Garrido and Rain Lagunsad

Colors by Jason Embury, Jeff Balke and Jeremy Colwell • Letters by Jim Campbell

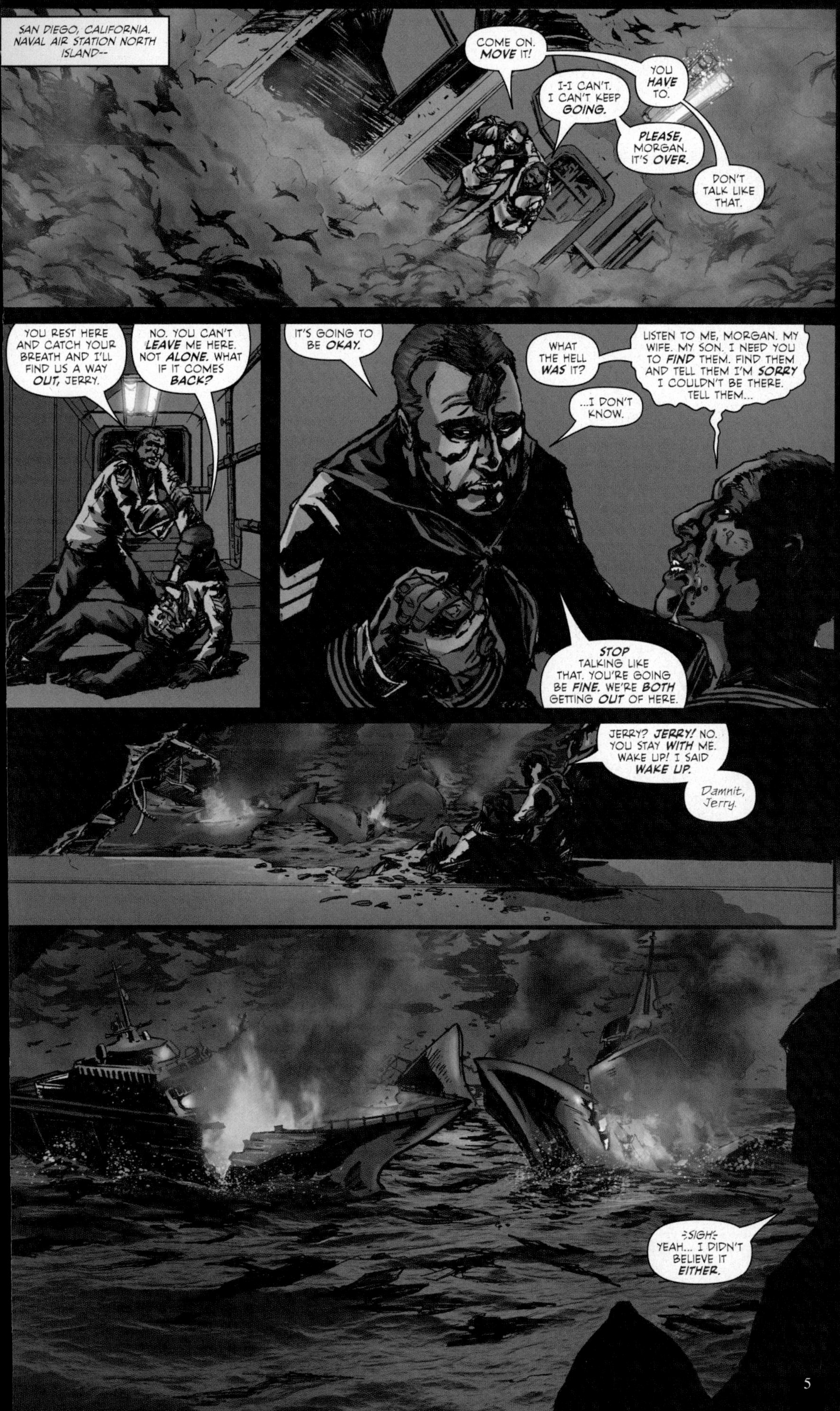
SAN DIEGO, CALIFORNIA. NAVAL AIR STATION NORTH ISLAND--
COME ON. MOVE IT!
YOU HAVE TO.
I-I CAN'T. I CAN'T KEEP GOING.
PLEASE, MORGAN. IT'S OVER.
DON'T TALK LIKE THAT.
YOU REST HERE AND CATCH YOUR BREATH AND I'LL FIND US A WAY OUT, JERRY.
NO. YOU CAN'T LEAVE ME HERE. NOT ALONE. WHAT IF IT COMES BACK?
IT'S GOING TO BE OKAY.
WHAT THE HELL WAS IT?
...I DON'T KNOW.
LISTEN TO ME, MORGAN. MY WIFE. MY SON. I NEED YOU TO FIND THEM. FIND THEM AND TELL THEM I'M SORRY I COULDN'T BE THERE. TELL THEM...
STOP TALKING LIKE THAT. YOU'RE GOING BE FINE. WE'RE BOTH GETTING OUT OF HERE.
JERRY? JERRY! NO. YOU STAY WITH ME. WAKE UP! I SAID WAKE UP.
Damnit, Jerry.
SIGH
YEAH... I DIDN'T BELIEVE IT EITHER.

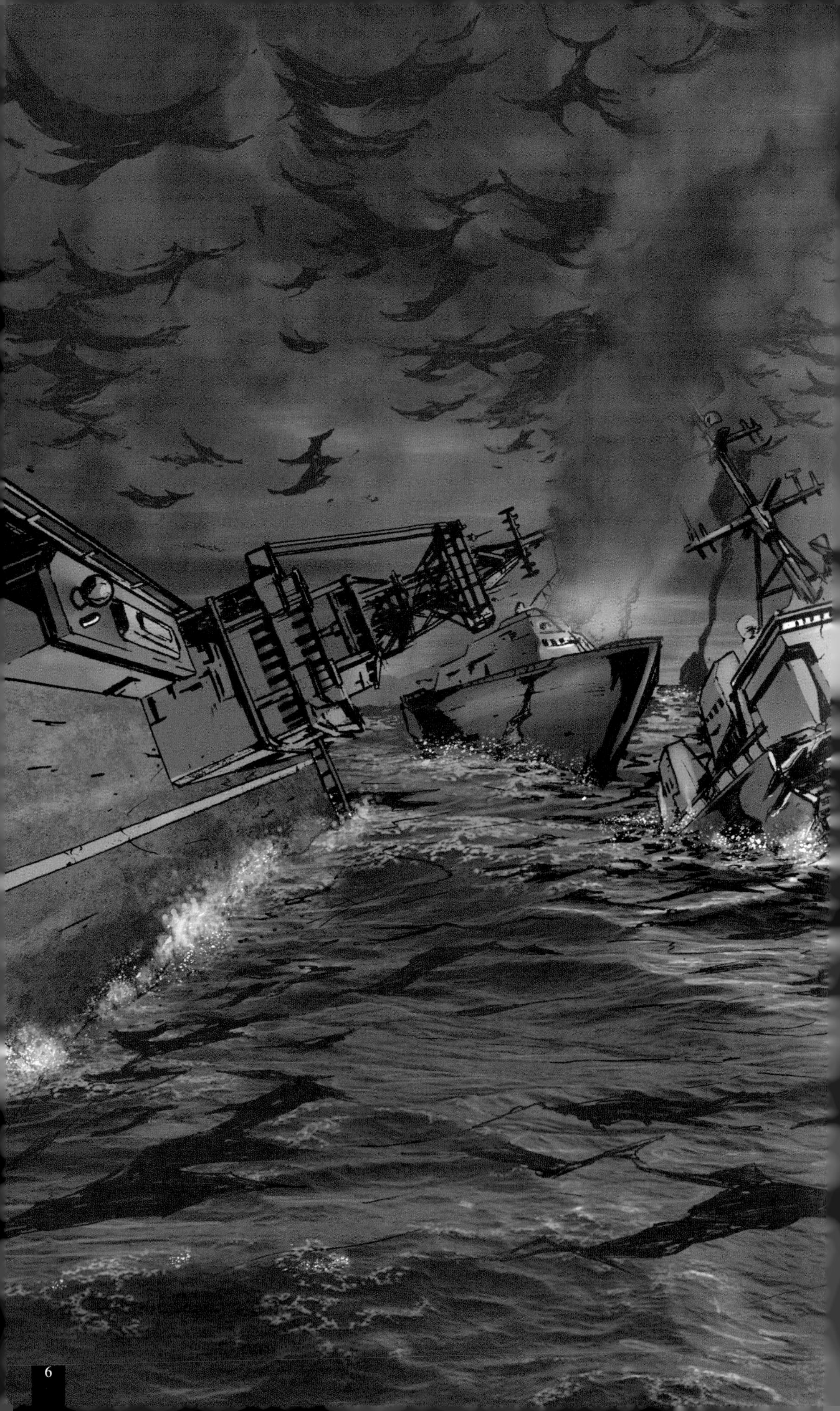

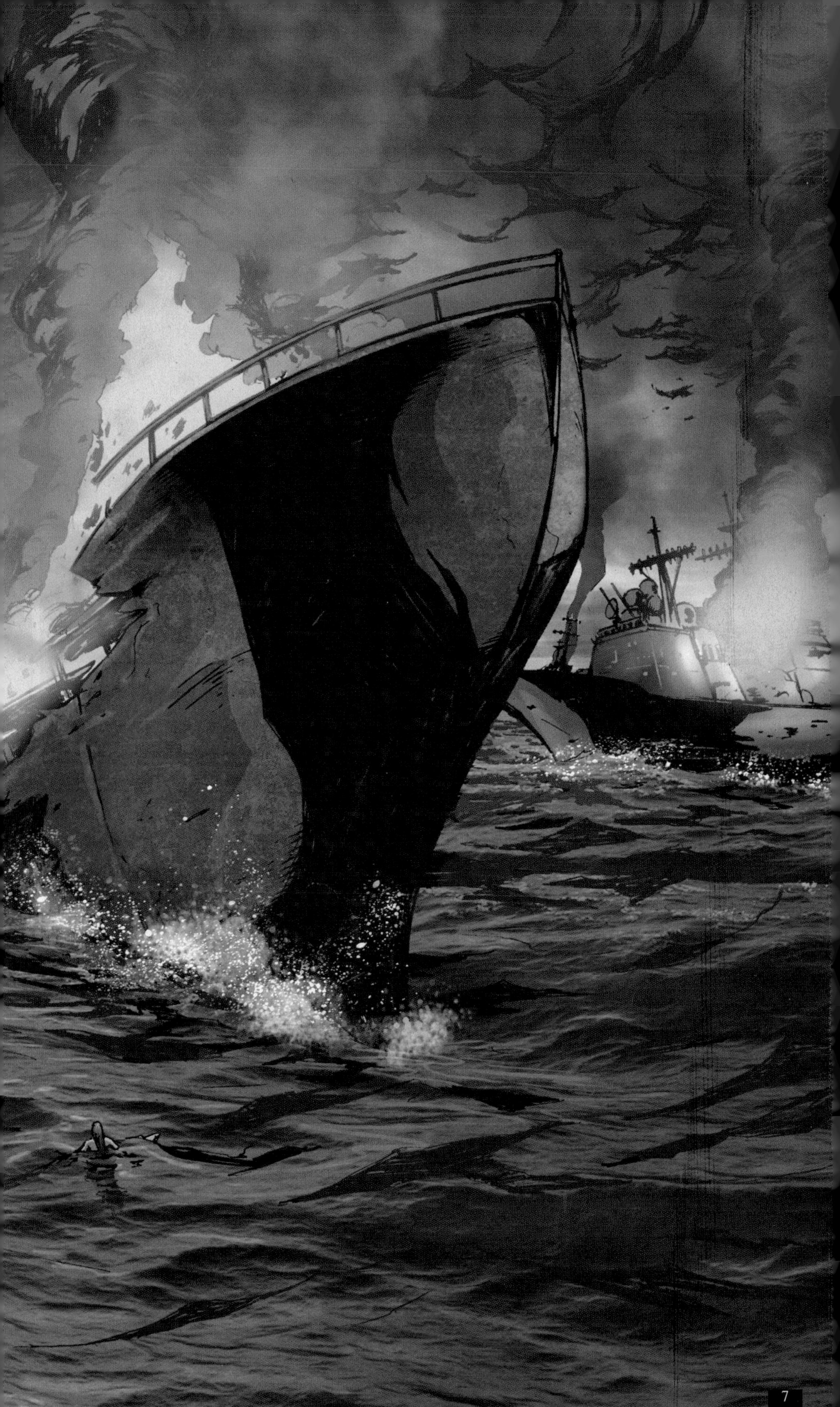

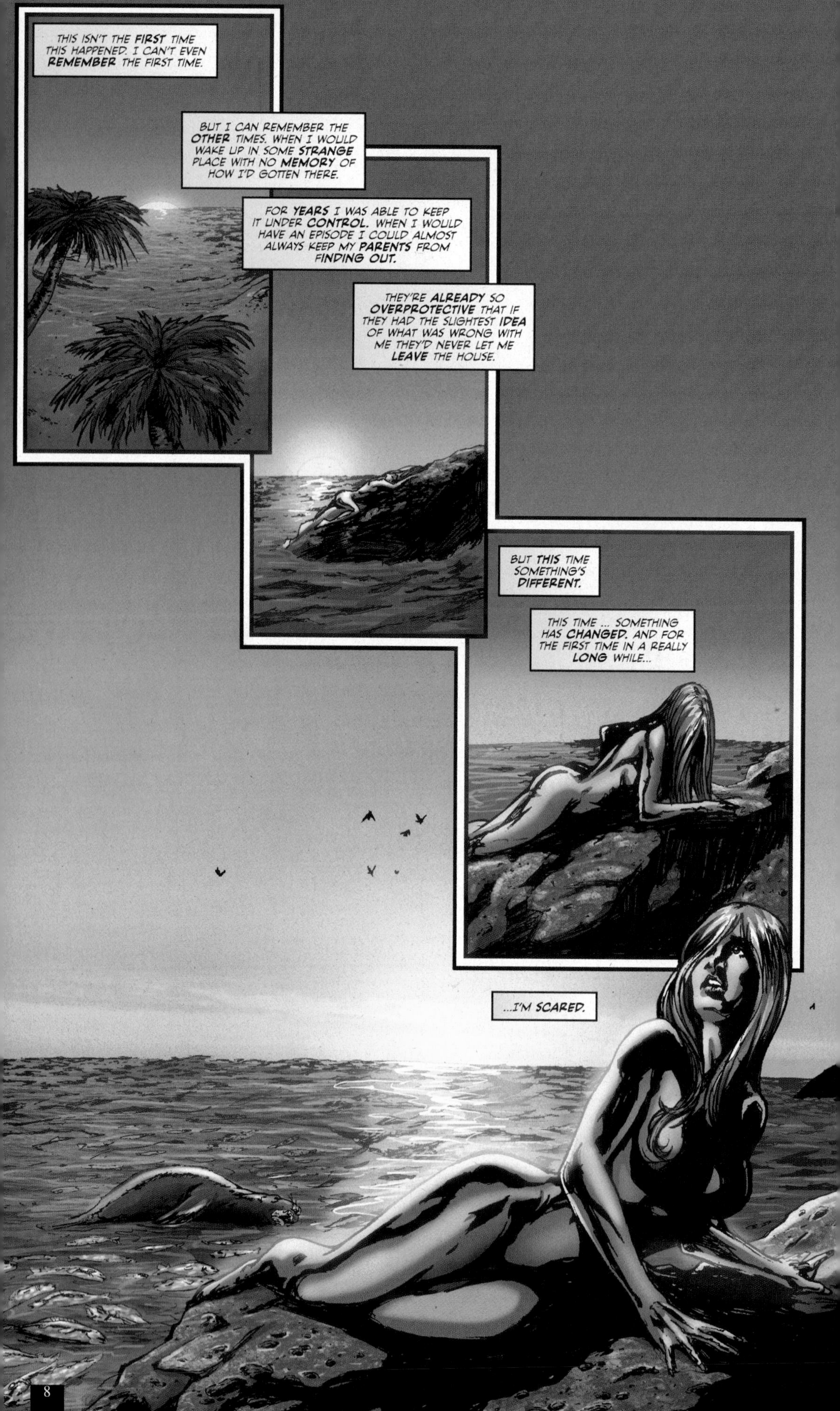
THIS ISN'T THE FIRST TIME THIS HAPPENED. I CAN'T EVEN REMEMBER THE FIRST TIME.
BUT I CAN REMEMBER THE OTHER TIMES. WHEN I WOULD WAKE UP IN SOME STRANGE PLACE WITH NO MEMORY OF HOW I'D GOTTEN THERE.
FOR YEARS I WAS ABLE TO KEEP IT UNDER CONTROL. WHEN I WOULD HAVE AN EPISODE I COULD ALMOST ALWAYS KEEP MY PARENTS FROM FINDING OUT.
THEY'RE ALREADY SO OVERPROTECTIVE THAT IF THEY HAD THE SLIGHTEST IDEA OF WHAT WAS WRONG WITH ME THEY'D NEVER LET ME LEAVE THE HOUSE.
BUT THIS TIME SOMETHING'S DIFFERENT.
THIS TIME ... SOMETHING HAS CHANGED. AND FOR THE FIRST TIME IN A REALLY LONG WHILE...
...I'M SCARED.

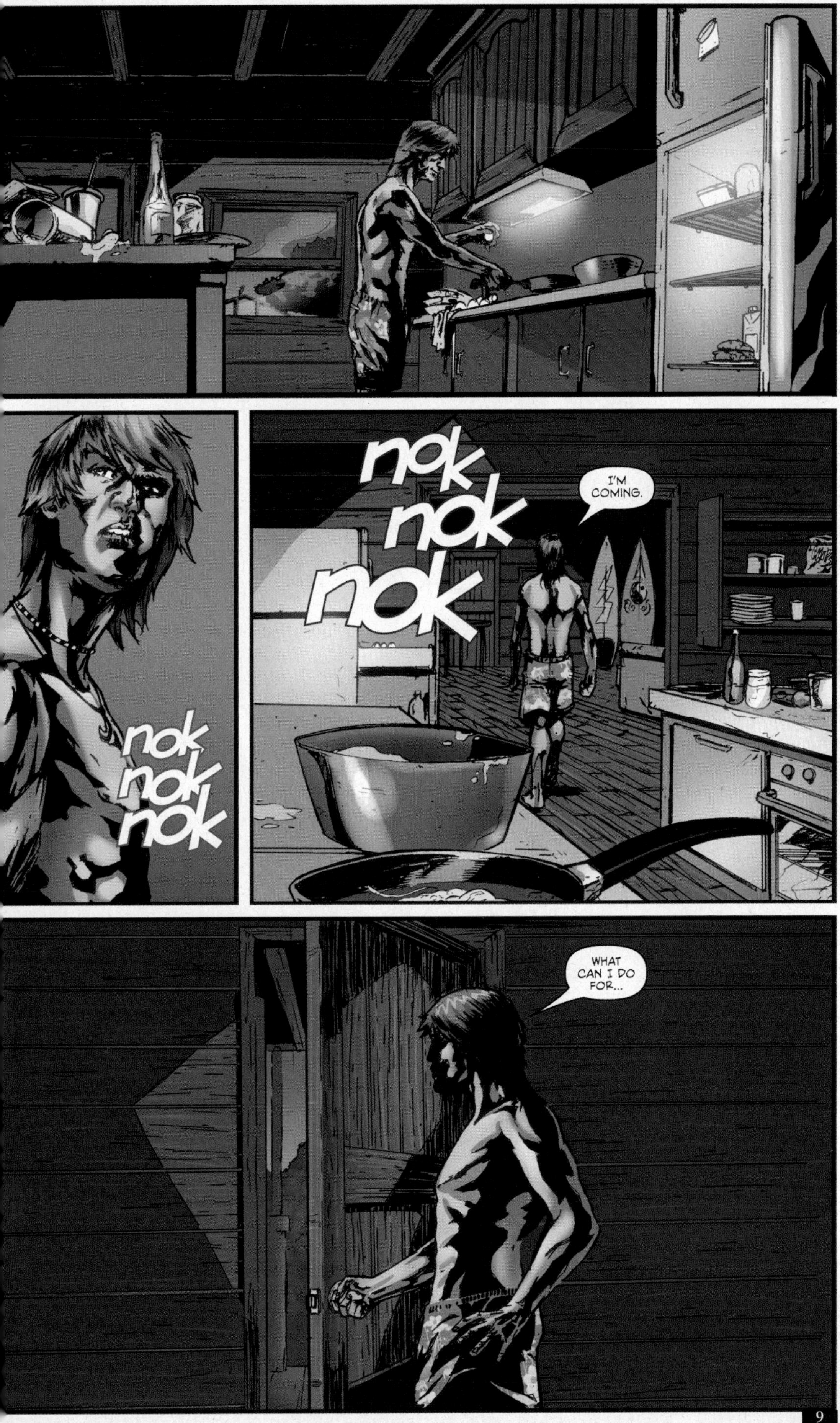
nok nok nok
nok nok nok
I'M COMING.
WHAT CAN I DO FOR...

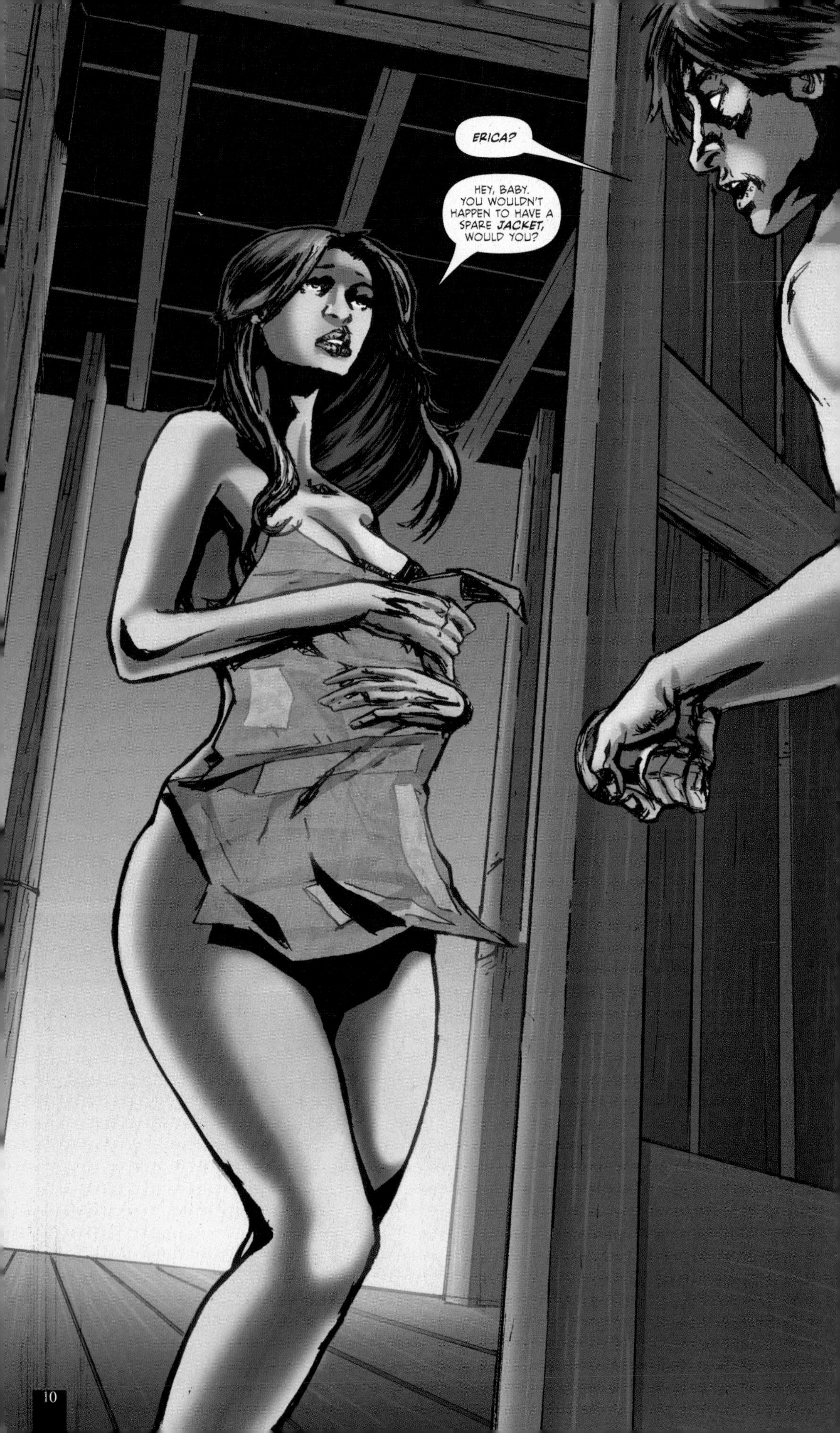
ERICA?
HEY, BABY. YOU WOULDN'T HAPPEN TO HAVE A SPARE JACKET, WOULD YOU?

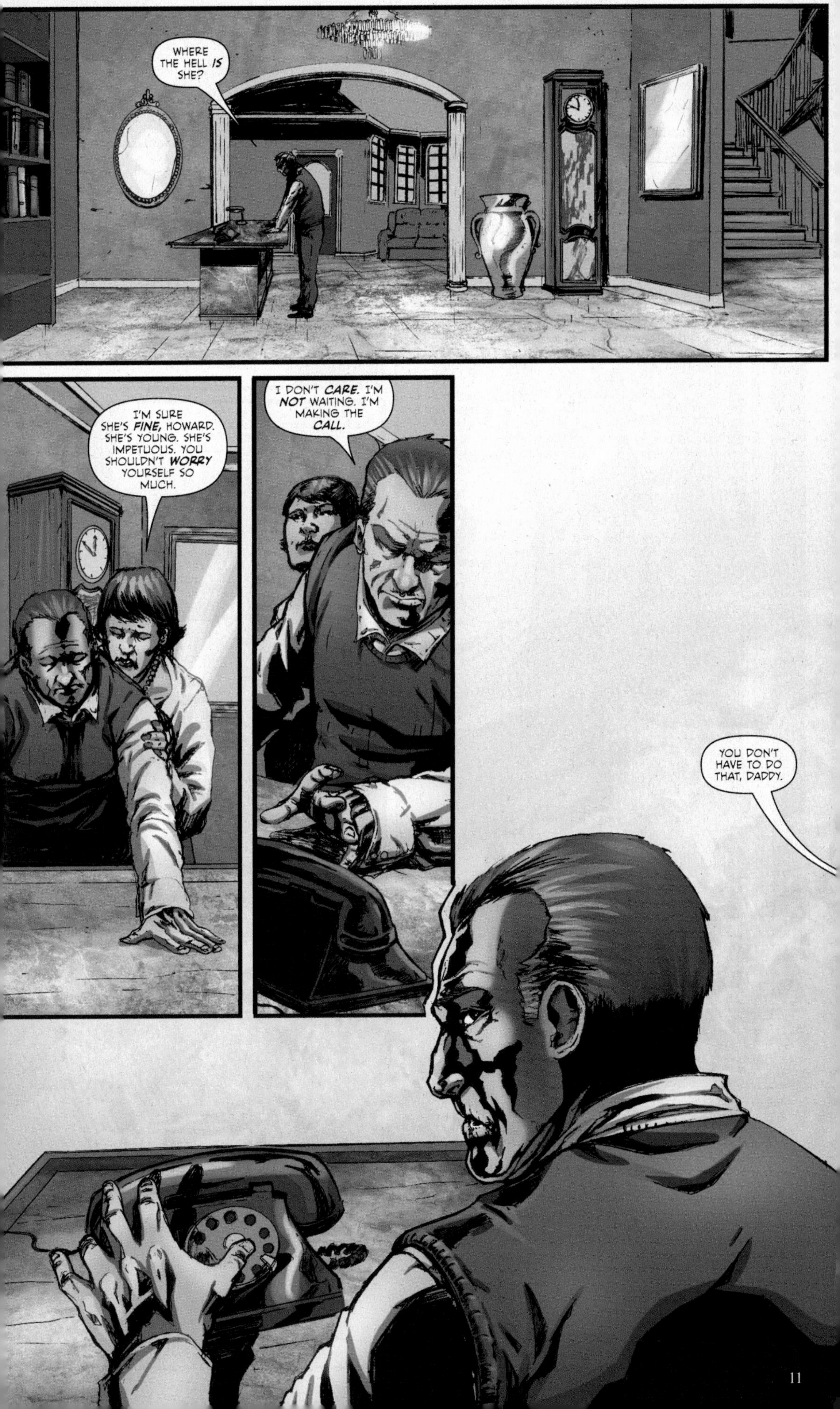

WHERE THE HELL *IS* SHE?
I'M SURE SHE'S *FINE,* HOWARD. SHE'S YOUNG. SHE'S IMPETUOUS. YOU SHOULDN'T *WORRY* YOURSELF SO MUCH.
I DON'T *CARE.* I'M *NOT* WAITING. I'M MAKING THE *CALL.*
YOU DON'T HAVE TO DO THAT, DADDY.

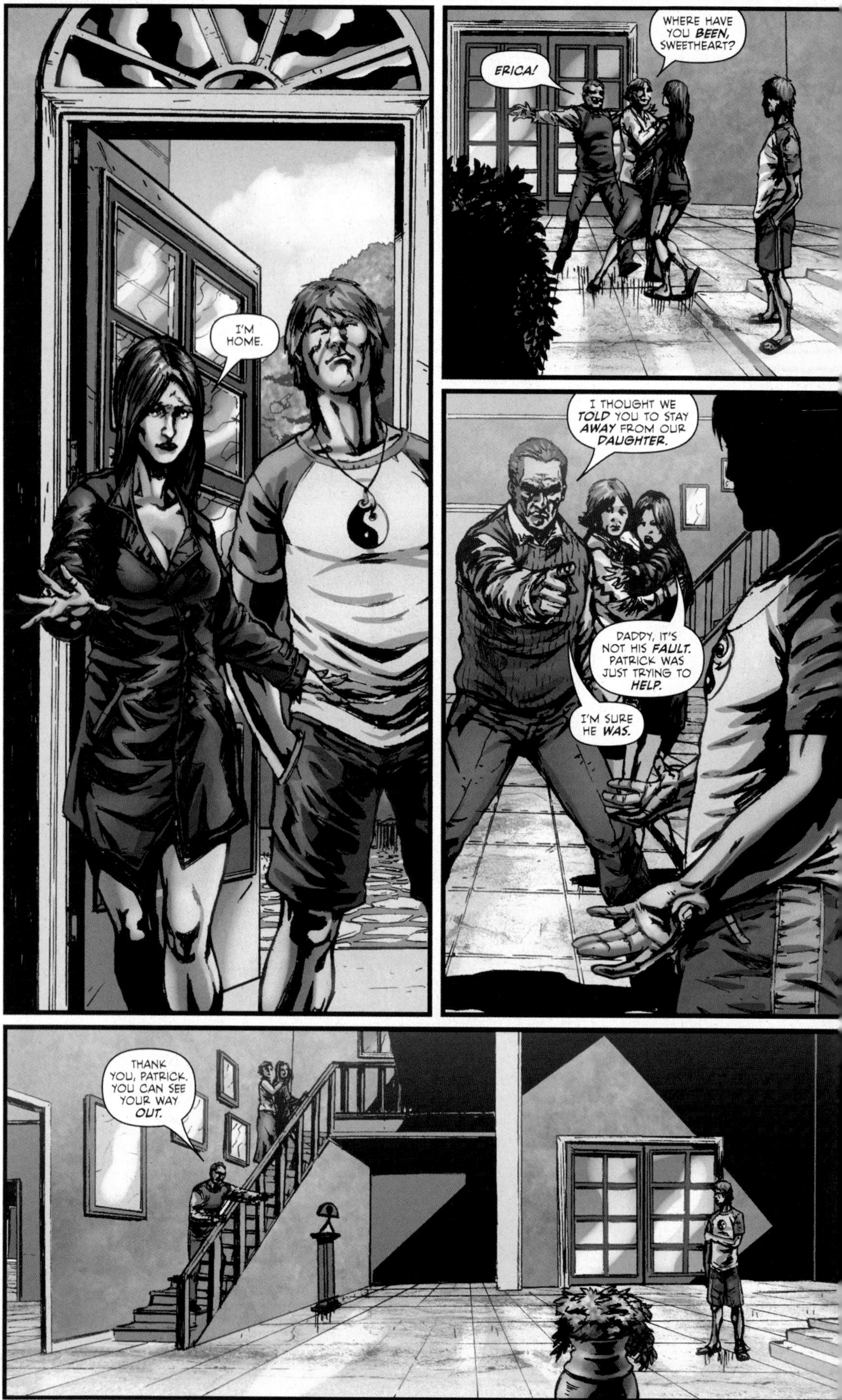
I'M HOME.
ERICA!
WHERE HAVE YOU BEEN, SWEETHEART?
I THOUGHT WE TOLD YOU TO STAY AWAY FROM OUR DAUGHTER.
DADDY, IT'S NOT HIS FAULT. PATRICK WAS JUST TRYING TO HELP.
I'M SURE HE WAS.
THANK YOU, PATRICK. YOU CAN SEE YOUR WAY OUT.

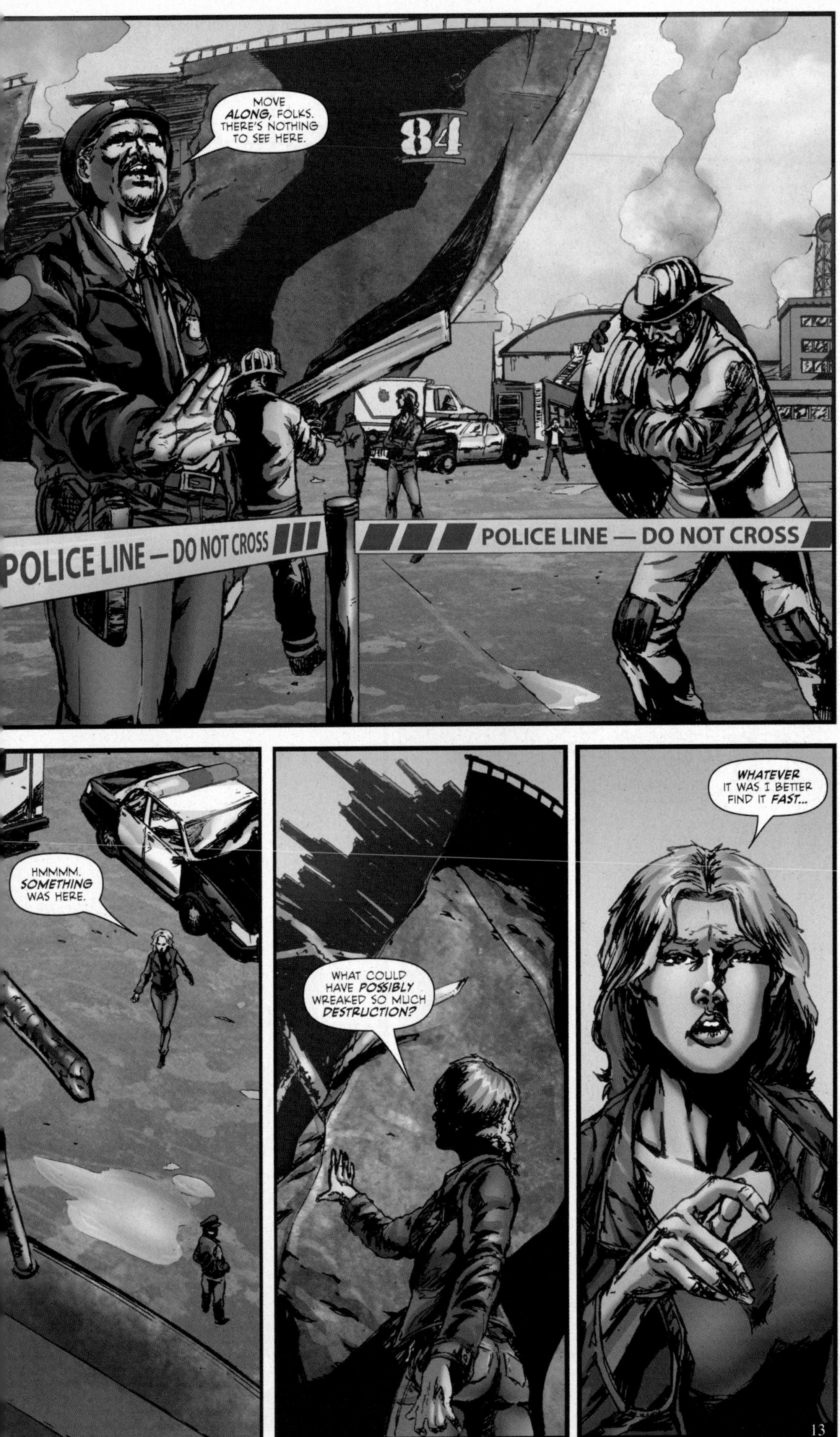
MOVE ALONG, FOLKS. THERE'S NOTHING TO SEE HERE.
84
POLICE LINE — DO NOT CROSS
POLICE LINE — DO NOT CROSS
HMMMM. SOMETHING WAS HERE.
WHAT COULD HAVE POSSIBLY WREAKED SO MUCH DESTRUCTION?
WHATEVER IT WAS I BETTER FIND IT FAST...

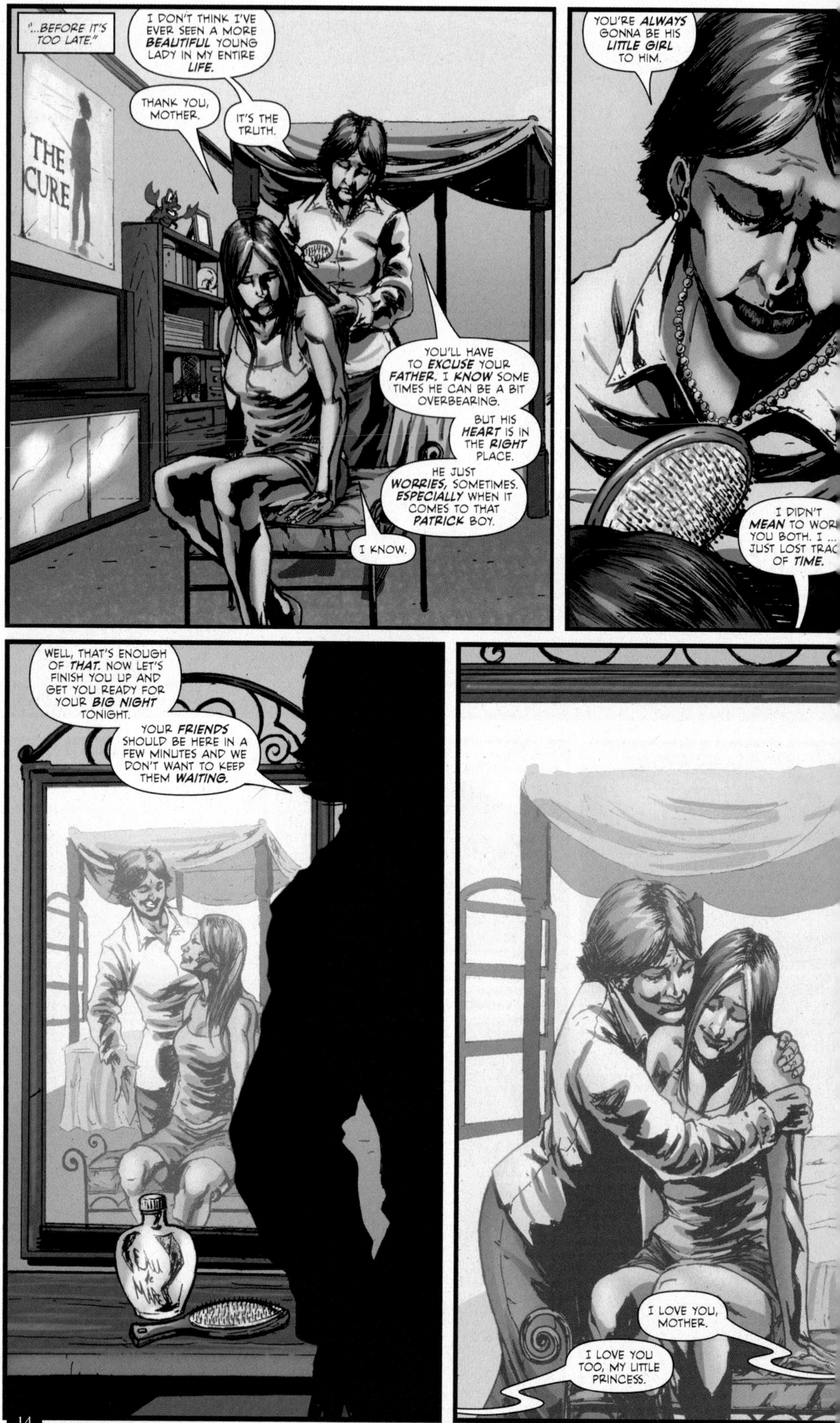
"...BEFORE IT'S TOO LATE."
I DON'T THINK I'VE EVER SEEN A MORE BEAUTIFUL YOUNG LADY IN MY ENTIRE LIFE.
THANK YOU, MOTHER.
IT'S THE TRUTH.
THE CURE
YOU'LL HAVE TO EXCUSE YOUR FATHER. I KNOW SOME TIMES HE CAN BE A BIT OVERBEARING.
BUT HIS HEART IS IN THE RIGHT PLACE.
HE JUST WORRIES, SOMETIMES. ESPECIALLY WHEN IT COMES TO THAT PATRICK BOY.
I KNOW.
YOU'RE ALWAYS GONNA BE HIS LITTLE GIRL TO HIM.
I DIDN'T MEAN TO WOR YOU BOTH. I ... JUST LOST TRAC OF TIME.
WELL, THAT'S ENOUGH OF THAT. NOW LET'S FINISH YOU UP AND GET YOU READY FOR YOUR BIG NIGHT TONIGHT.
YOUR FRIENDS SHOULD BE HERE IN A FEW MINUTES AND WE DON'T WANT TO KEEP THEM WAITING.
I LOVE YOU, MOTHER.
I LOVE YOU TOO, MY LITTLE PRINCESS.

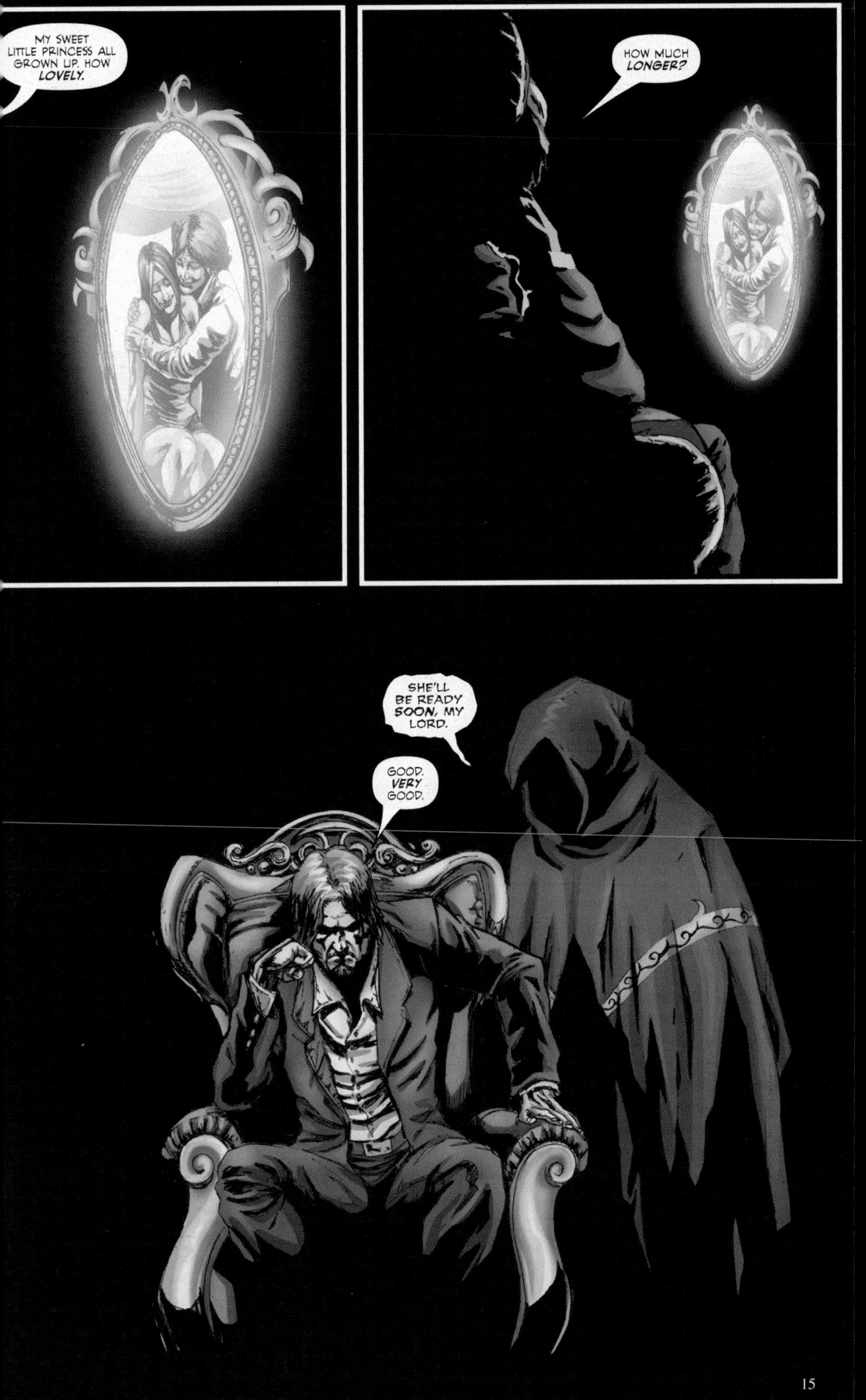
MY SWEET LITTLE PRINCESS ALL GROWN UP. HOW *LOVELY.*
HOW MUCH *LONGER?*
SHE'LL BE READY *SOON*, MY LORD.
GOOD. *VERY* GOOD.

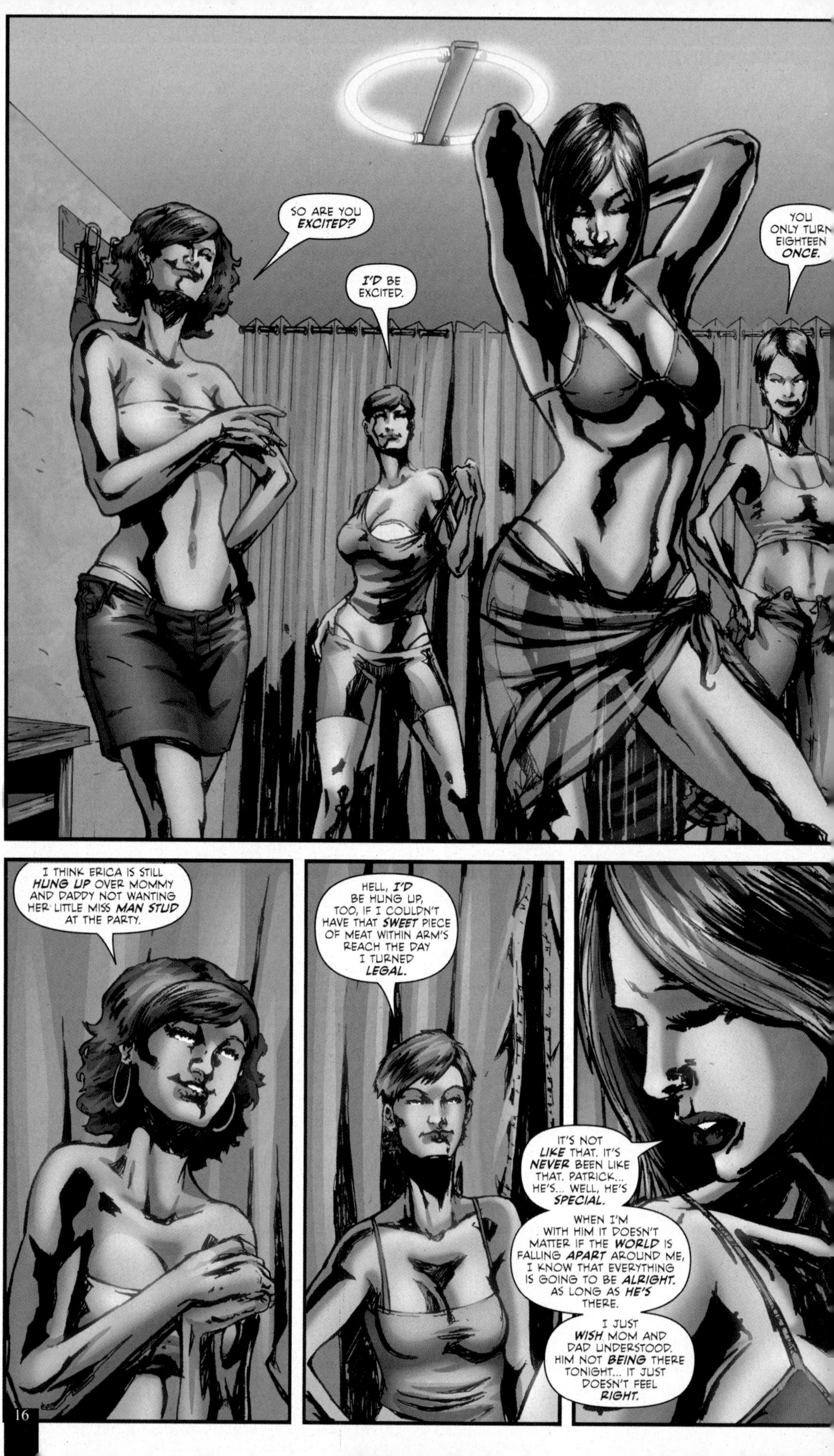

SO ARE YOU EXCITED?
I'D BE EXCITED.
YOU ONLY TURN EIGHTEEN ONCE.
I THINK ERICA IS STILL HUNG UP OVER MOMMY AND DADDY NOT WANTING HER LITTLE MISS MAN STUD AT THE PARTY.
HELL, I'D BE HUNG UP, TOO, IF I COULDN'T HAVE THAT SWEET PIECE OF MEAT WITHIN ARM'S REACH THE DAY I TURNED LEGAL.
IT'S NOT LIKE THAT. IT'S NEVER BEEN LIKE THAT. PATRICK... HE'S... WELL, HE'S SPECIAL.
WHEN I'M WITH HIM IT DOESN'T MATTER IF THE WORLD IS FALLING APART AROUND ME, I KNOW THAT EVERYTHING IS GOING TO BE ALRIGHT. AS LONG AS HE'S THERE.
I JUST WISH MOM AND DAD UNDERSTOOD. HIM NOT BEING THERE TONIGHT... IT JUST DOESN'T FEEL RIGHT.

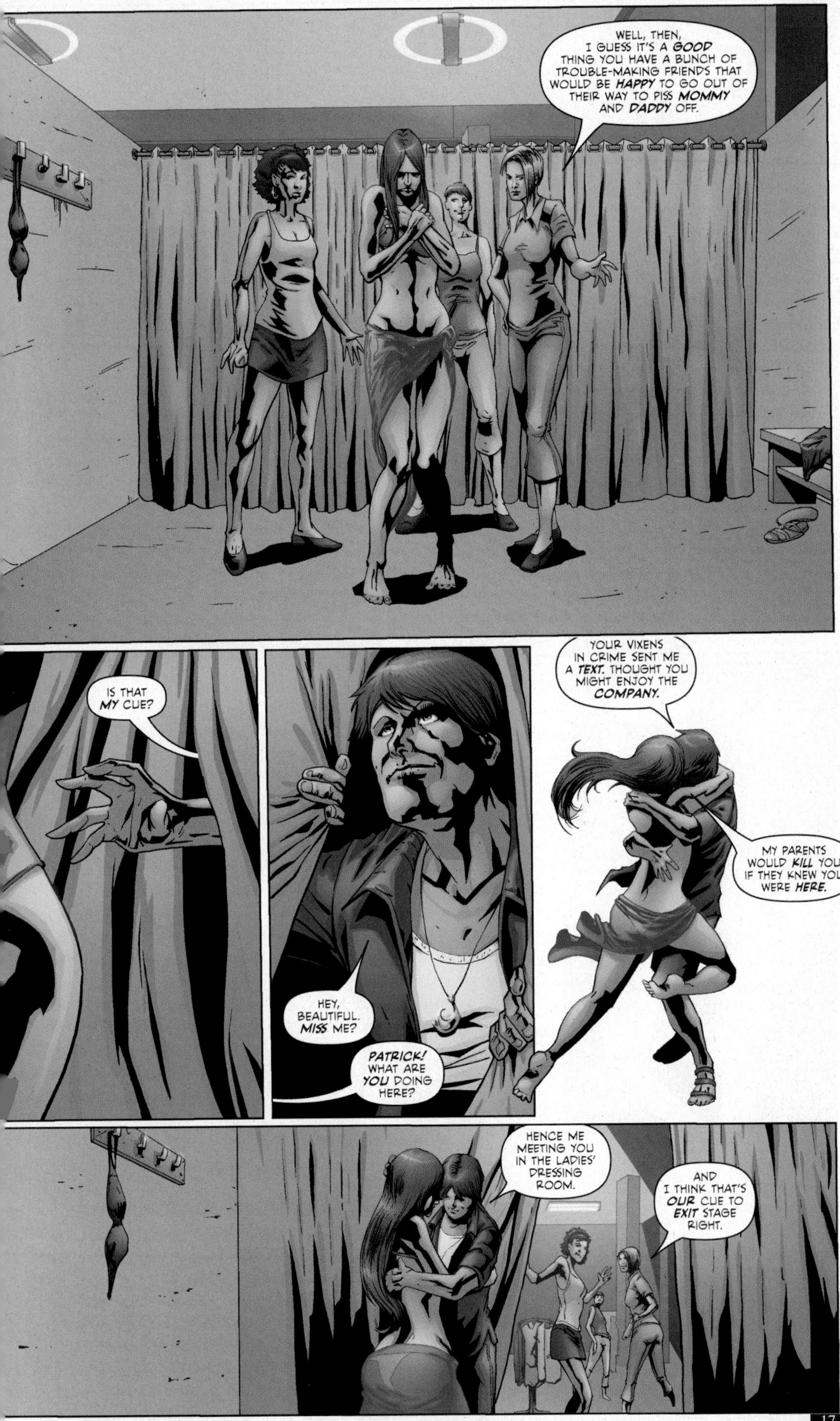
WELL, THEN, I GUESS IT'S A GOOD THING YOU HAVE A BUNCH OF TROUBLE-MAKING FRIENDS THAT WOULD BE HAPPY TO GO OUT OF THEIR WAY TO PISS MOMMY AND DADDY OFF.
IS THAT MY CUE?
HEY, BEAUTIFUL. MISS ME?
PATRICK! WHAT ARE YOU DOING HERE?
YOUR VIXENS IN CRIME SENT ME A TEXT. THOUGHT YOU MIGHT ENJOY THE COMPANY.
MY PARENTS WOULD KILL YOU IF THEY KNEW YOU WERE HERE.
HENCE ME MEETING YOU IN THE LADIES' DRESSING ROOM.
AND I THINK THAT'S OUR CUE TO EXIT STAGE RIGHT.

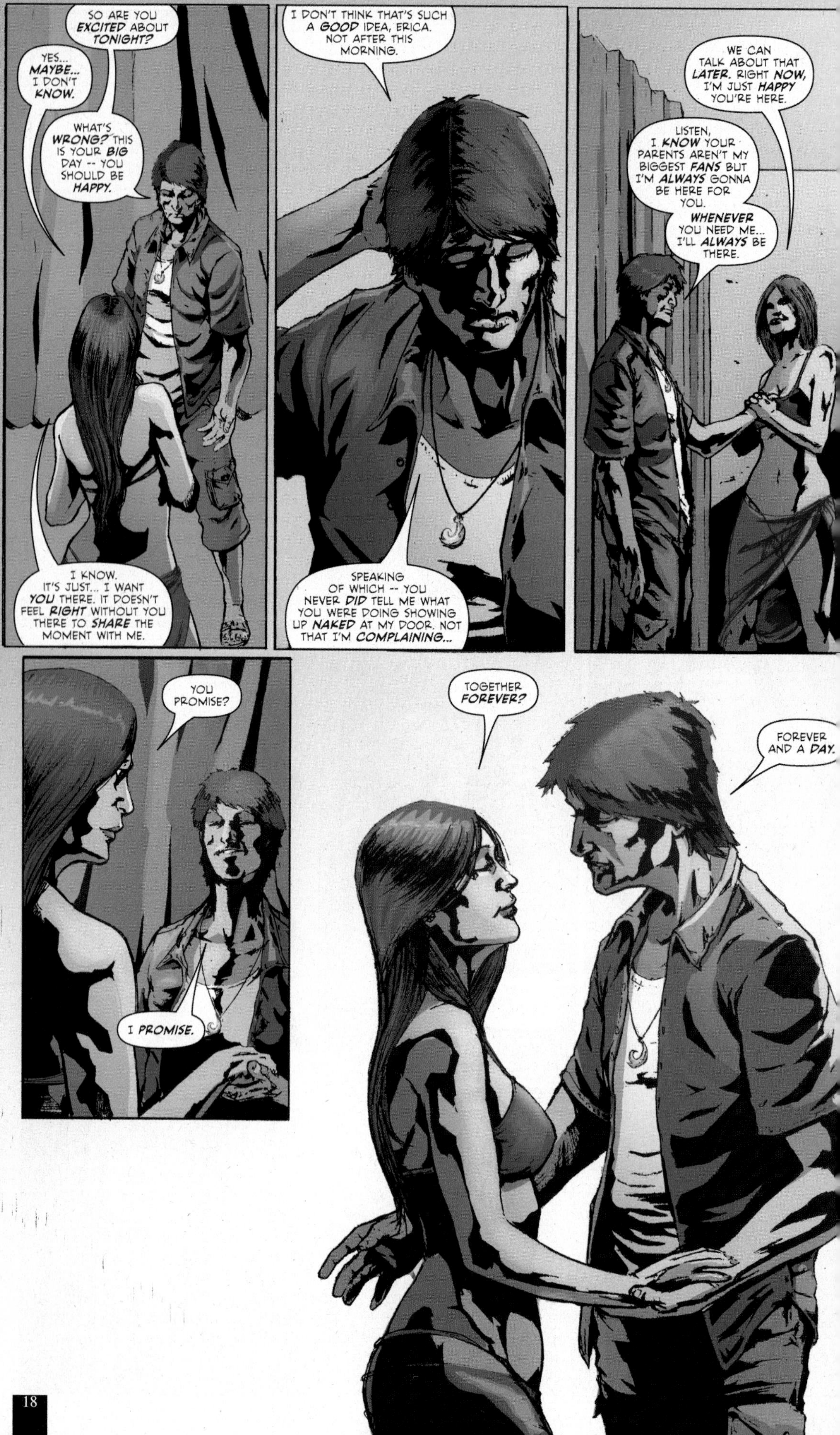
SO ARE YOU EXCITED ABOUT TONIGHT?
YES... MAYBE... I DON'T KNOW.
WHAT'S WRONG? THIS IS YOUR BIG DAY -- YOU SHOULD BE HAPPY.
I KNOW. IT'S JUST... I WANT YOU THERE. IT DOESN'T FEEL RIGHT WITHOUT YOU THERE TO SHARE THE MOMENT WITH ME.
I DON'T THINK THAT'S SUCH A GOOD IDEA, ERICA. NOT AFTER THIS MORNING.
SPEAKING OF WHICH -- YOU NEVER DID TELL ME WHAT YOU WERE DOING SHOWING UP NAKED AT MY DOOR. NOT THAT I'M COMPLAINING...
WE CAN TALK ABOUT THAT LATER. RIGHT NOW, I'M JUST HAPPY YOU'RE HERE.
LISTEN, I KNOW YOUR PARENTS AREN'T MY BIGGEST FANS BUT I'M ALWAYS GONNA BE HERE FOR YOU.
WHENEVER YOU NEED ME... I'LL ALWAYS BE THERE.
YOU PROMISE?
I PROMISE.
TOGETHER FOREVER?
FOREVER AND A DAY.

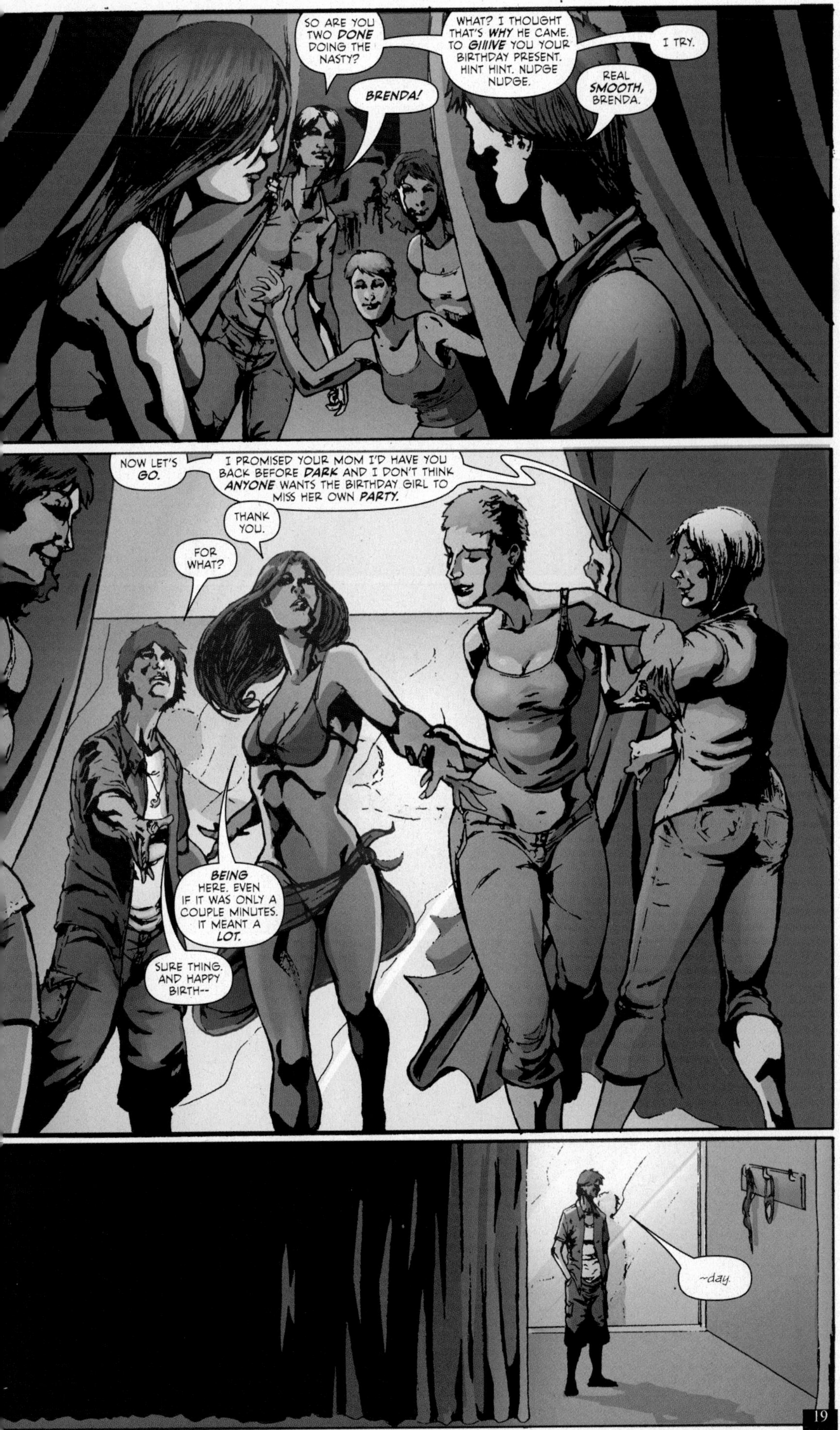
SO ARE YOU TWO DONE DOING THE NASTY?
BRENDA!
WHAT? I THOUGHT THAT'S WHY HE CAME. TO GIIIVE YOU YOUR BIRTHDAY PRESENT. HINT HINT. NUDGE NUDGE.
I TRY.
REAL SMOOTH, BRENDA.
NOW LET'S GO.
I PROMISED YOUR MOM I'D HAVE YOU BACK BEFORE DARK AND I DON'T THINK ANYONE WANTS THE BIRTHDAY GIRL TO MISS HER OWN PARTY.
THANK YOU.
FOR WHAT?
BEING HERE. EVEN IF IT WAS ONLY A COUPLE MINUTES. IT MEANT A LOT.
SURE THING. AND HAPPY BIRTH--
~day.

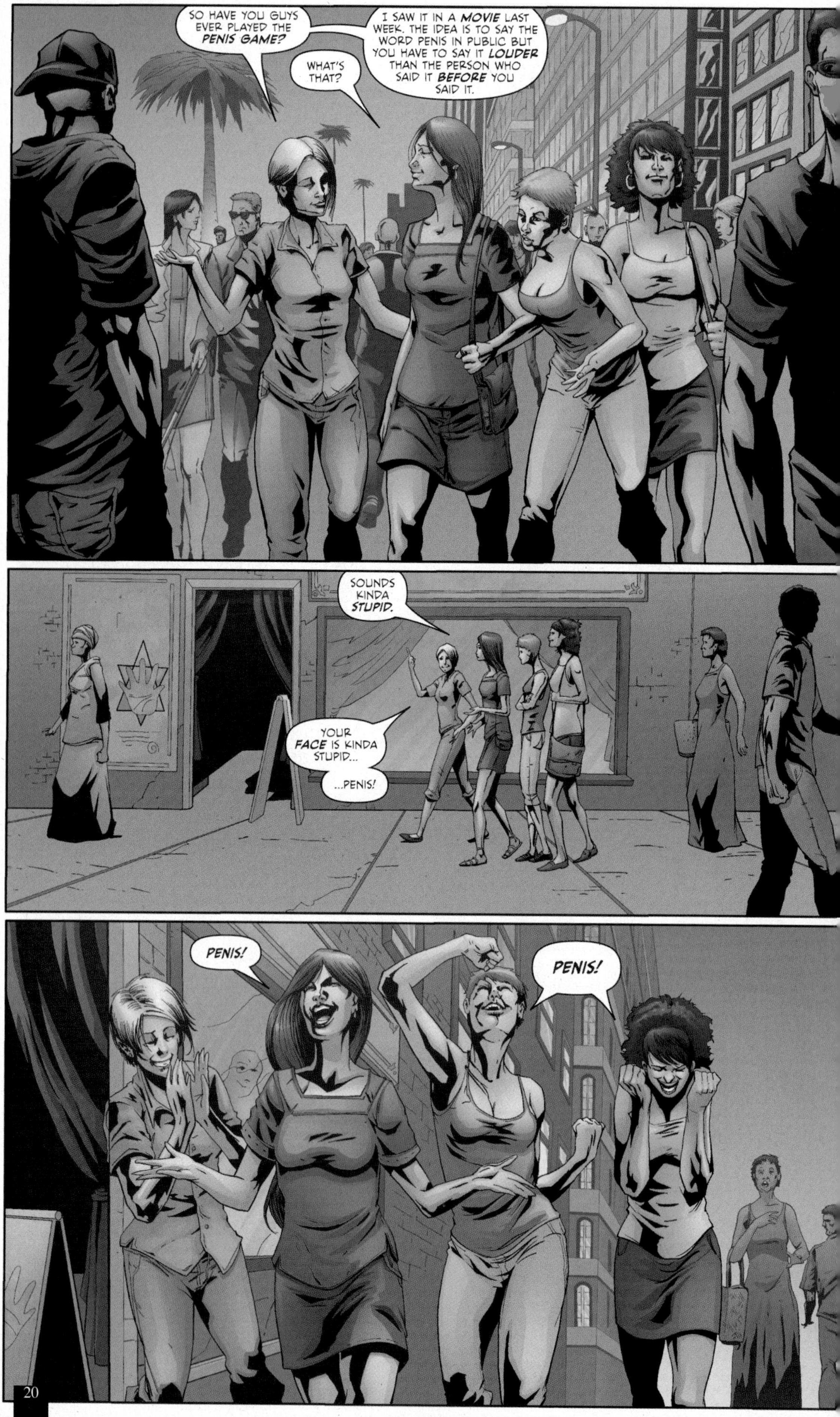
SO HAVE YOU GUYS EVER PLAYED THE PENIS GAME?
WHAT'S THAT?
I SAW IT IN A MOVIE LAST WEEK. THE IDEA IS TO SAY THE WORD PENIS IN PUBLIC BUT YOU HAVE TO SAY IT LOUDER THAN THE PERSON WHO SAID IT BEFORE YOU SAID IT.
SOUNDS KINDA STUPID.
YOUR FACE IS KINDA STUPID...
...PENIS!
PENIS!
PENIS!

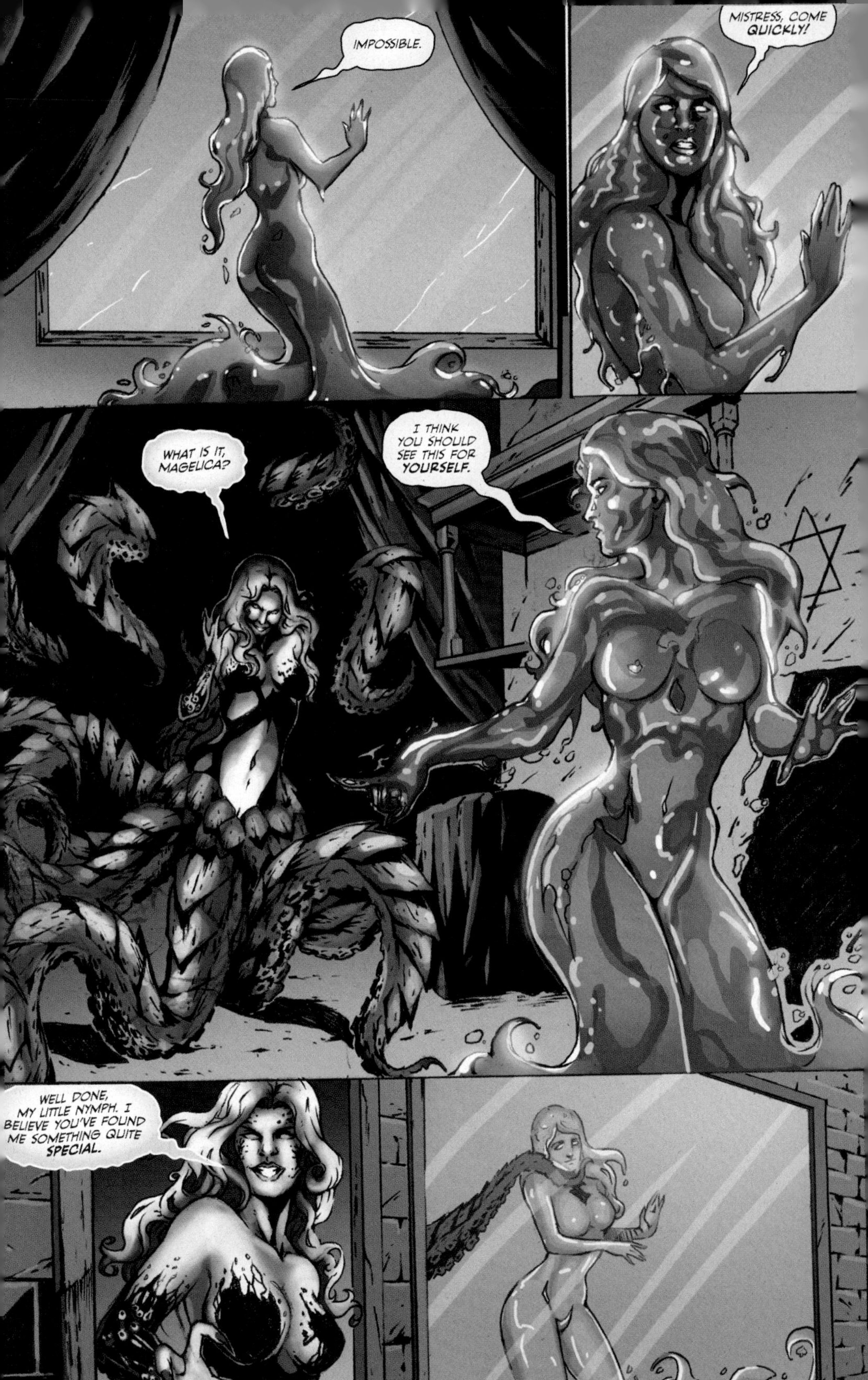
IMPOSSIBLE.
MISTRESS, COME QUICKLY!
WHAT IS IT, MAGELICA?
I THINK YOU SHOULD SEE THIS FOR YOURSELF.
WELL DONE, MY LITTLE NYMPH. I BELIEVE YOU'VE FOUND ME SOMETHING QUITE SPECIAL.

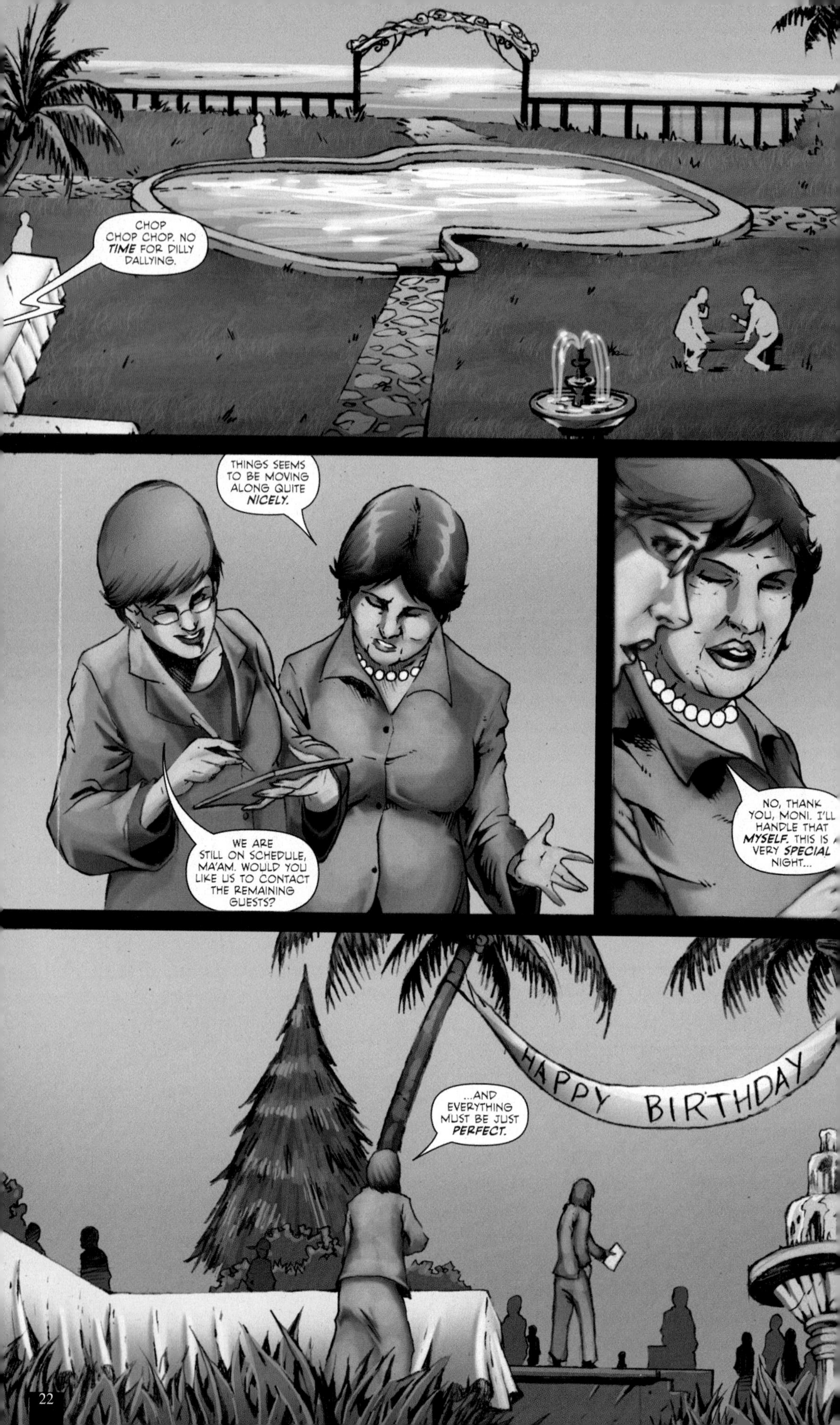
CHOP CHOP CHOP. NO TIME FOR DILLY DALLYING.
THINGS SEEMS TO BE MOVING ALONG QUITE NICELY.
WE ARE STILL ON SCHEDULE, MA'AM. WOULD YOU LIKE US TO CONTACT THE REMAINING GUESTS?
NO, THANK YOU, MONI. I'LL HANDLE THAT MYSELF. THIS IS A VERY SPECIAL NIGHT...
HAPPY BIRTHDAY
...AND EVERYTHING MUST BE JUST PERFECT.

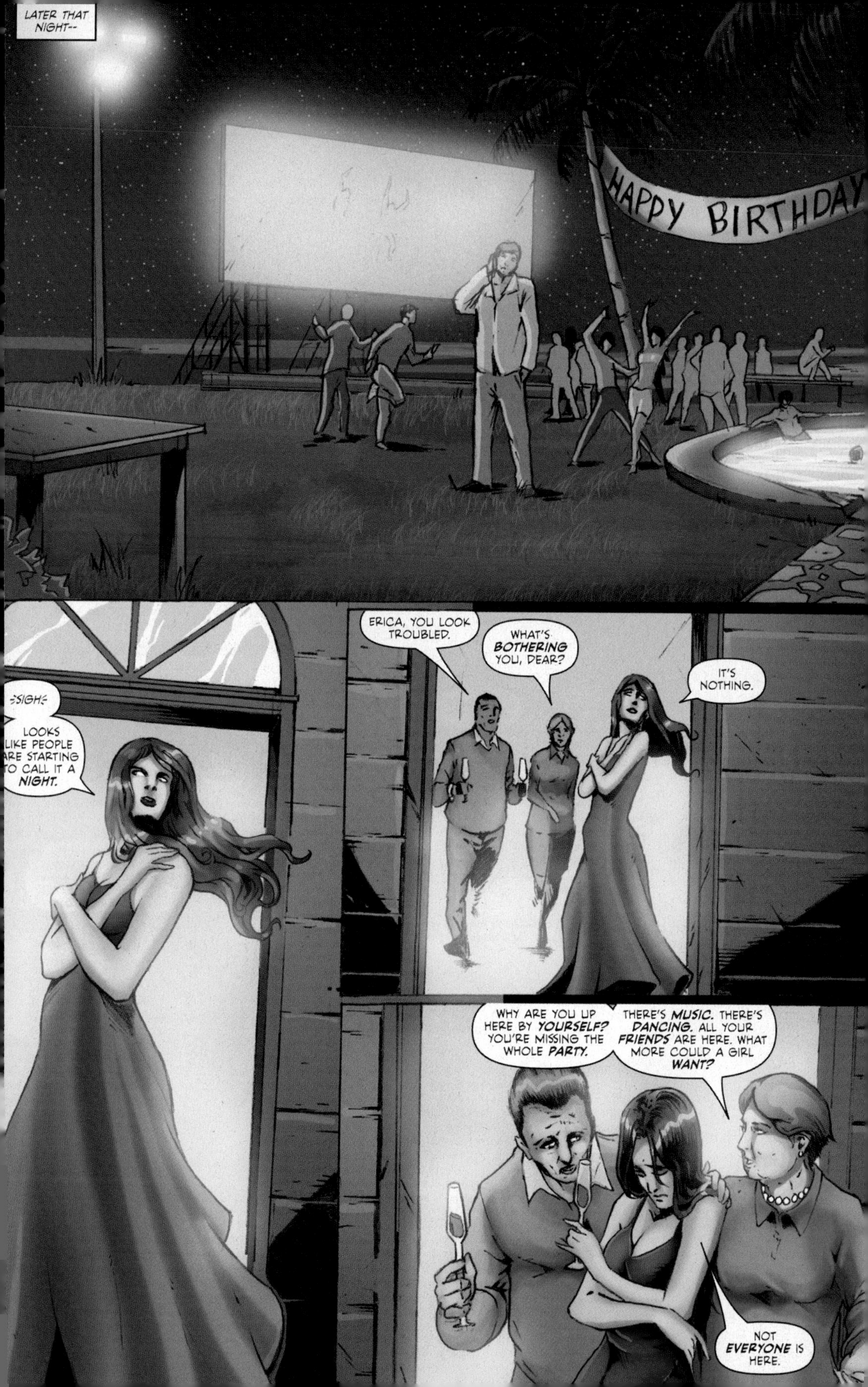
LATER THAT NIGHT--
HAPPY BIRTHDAY
=SIGH=
LOOKS LIKE PEOPLE ARE STARTING TO CALL IT A NIGHT.
ERICA, YOU LOOK TROUBLED.
WHAT'S BOTHERING YOU, DEAR?
IT'S NOTHING.
WHY ARE YOU UP HERE BY YOURSELF? YOU'RE MISSING THE WHOLE PARTY.
THERE'S MUSIC. THERE'S DANCING. ALL YOUR FRIENDS ARE HERE. WHAT MORE COULD A GIRL WANT?
NOT EVERYONE IS HERE.

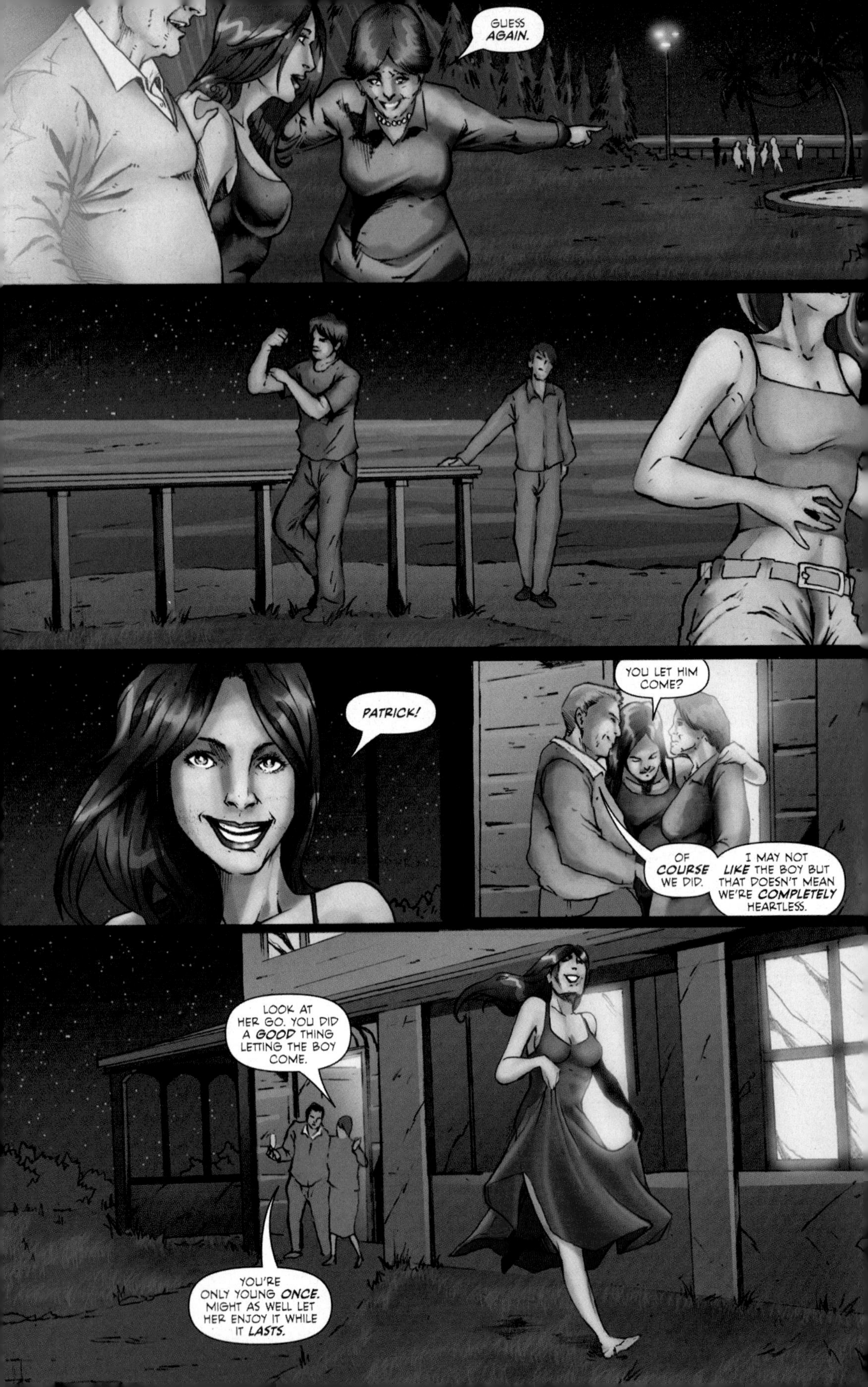
GUESS AGAIN.
PATRICK!
YOU LET HIM COME?
OF COURSE WE DID.
I MAY NOT LIKE THE BOY BUT THAT DOESN'T MEAN WE'RE COMPLETELY HEARTLESS.
LOOK AT HER GO. YOU DID A GOOD THING LETTING THE BOY COME.
YOU'RE ONLY YOUNG ONCE. MIGHT AS WELL LET HER ENJOY IT WHILE IT LASTS.

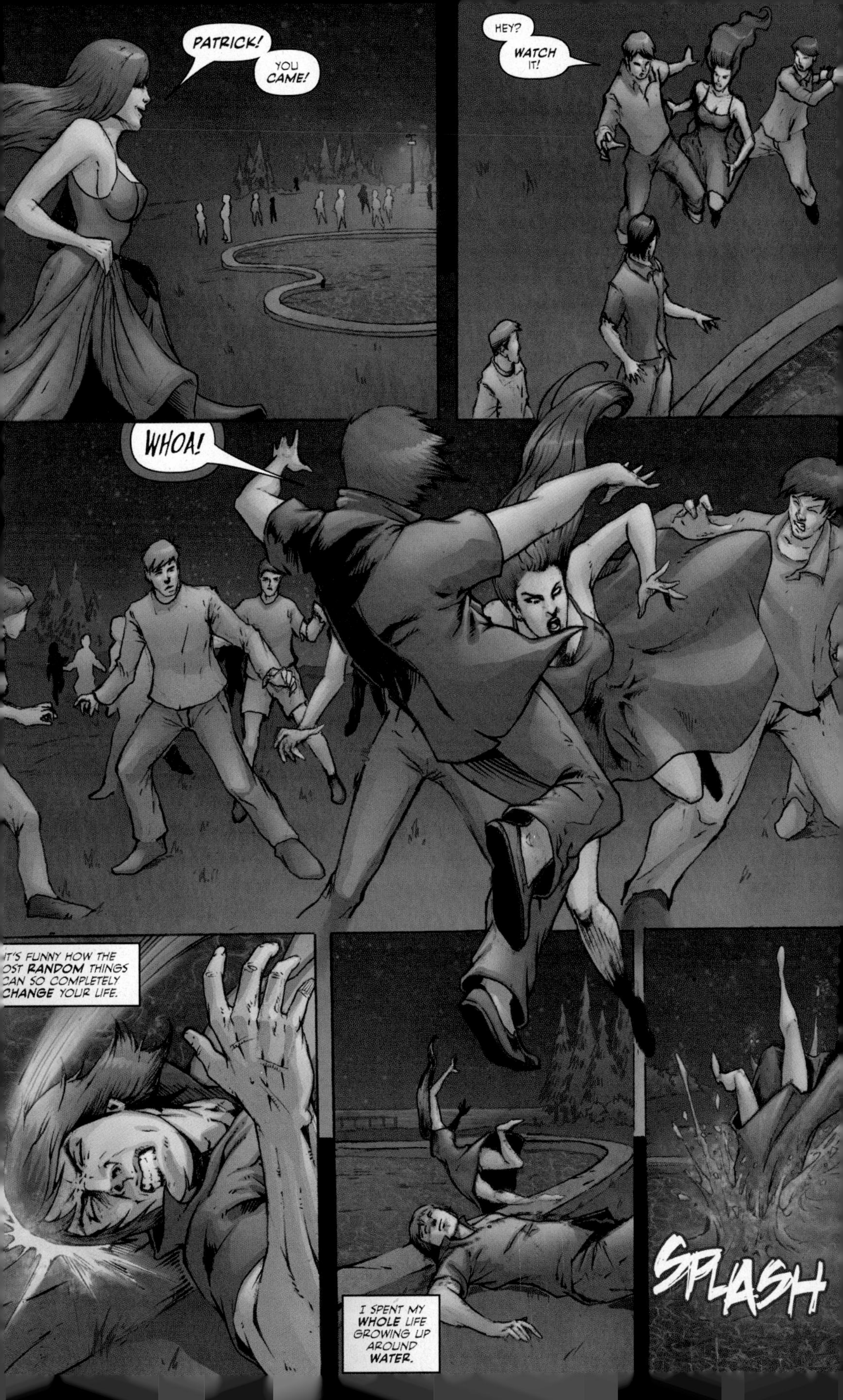
PATRICK!
YOU CAME!
HEY?
WATCH IT!
WHOA!
IT'S FUNNY HOW THE OST RANDOM THINGS CAN SO COMPLETELY CHANGE YOUR LIFE.
I SPENT MY WHOLE LIFE GROWING UP AROUND WATER.
SPLASH

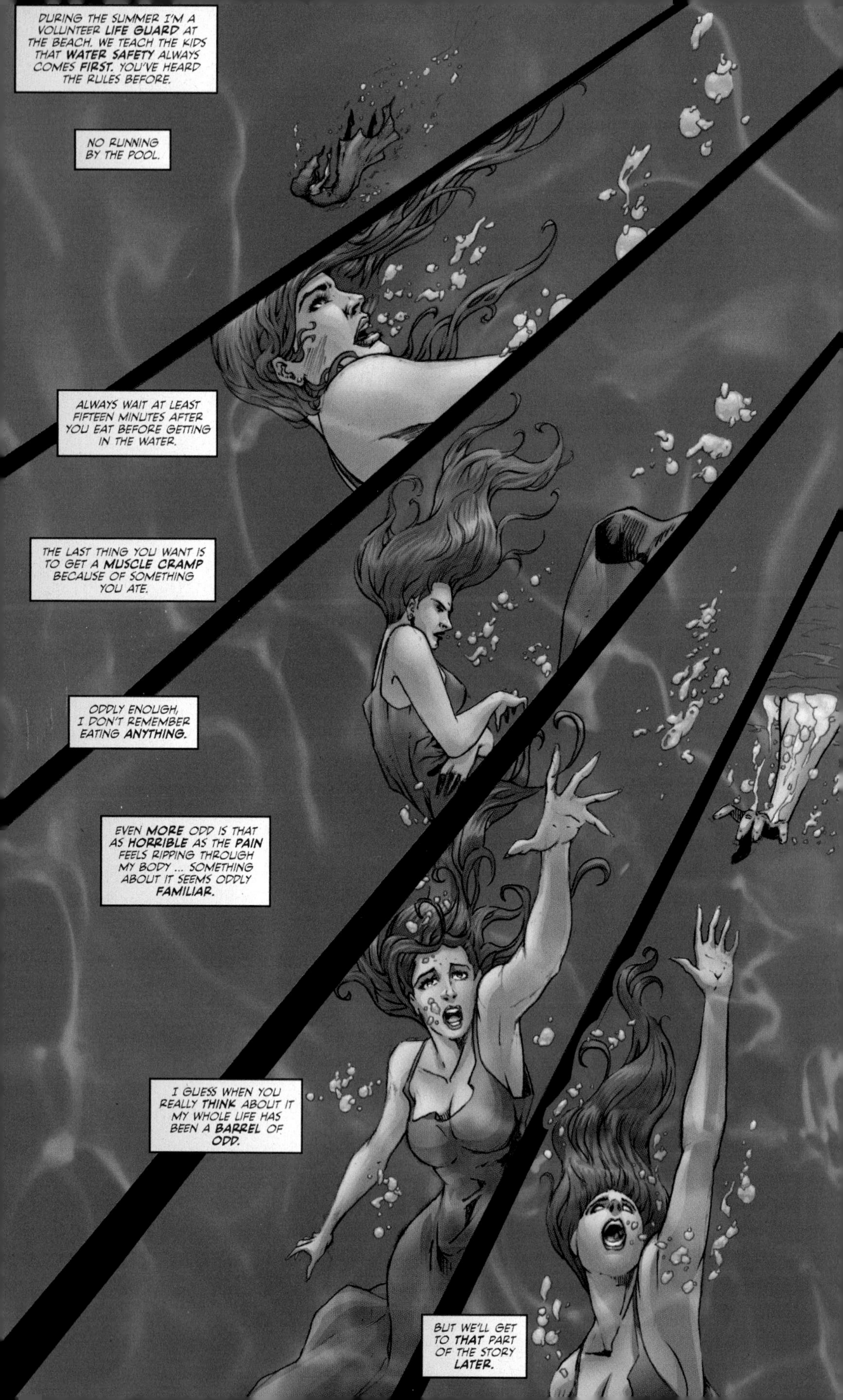
DURING THE SUMMER I'M A VOLUNTEER LIFE GUARD AT THE BEACH. WE TEACH THE KIDS THAT WATER SAFETY ALWAYS COMES FIRST. YOU'VE HEARD THE RULES BEFORE.
NO RUNNING BY THE POOL.
ALWAYS WAIT AT LEAST FIFTEEN MINUTES AFTER YOU EAT BEFORE GETTING IN THE WATER.
THE LAST THING YOU WANT IS TO GET A MUSCLE CRAMP BECAUSE OF SOMETHING YOU ATE.
ODDLY ENOUGH, I DON'T REMEMBER EATING ANYTHING.
EVEN MORE ODD IS THAT AS HORRIBLE AS THE PAIN FEELS RIPPING THROUGH MY BODY ... SOMETHING ABOUT IT SEEMS ODDLY FAMILIAR.
I GUESS WHEN YOU REALLY THINK ABOUT IT MY WHOLE LIFE HAS BEEN A BARREL OF ODD.
BUT WE'LL GET TO THAT PART OF THE STORY LATER.

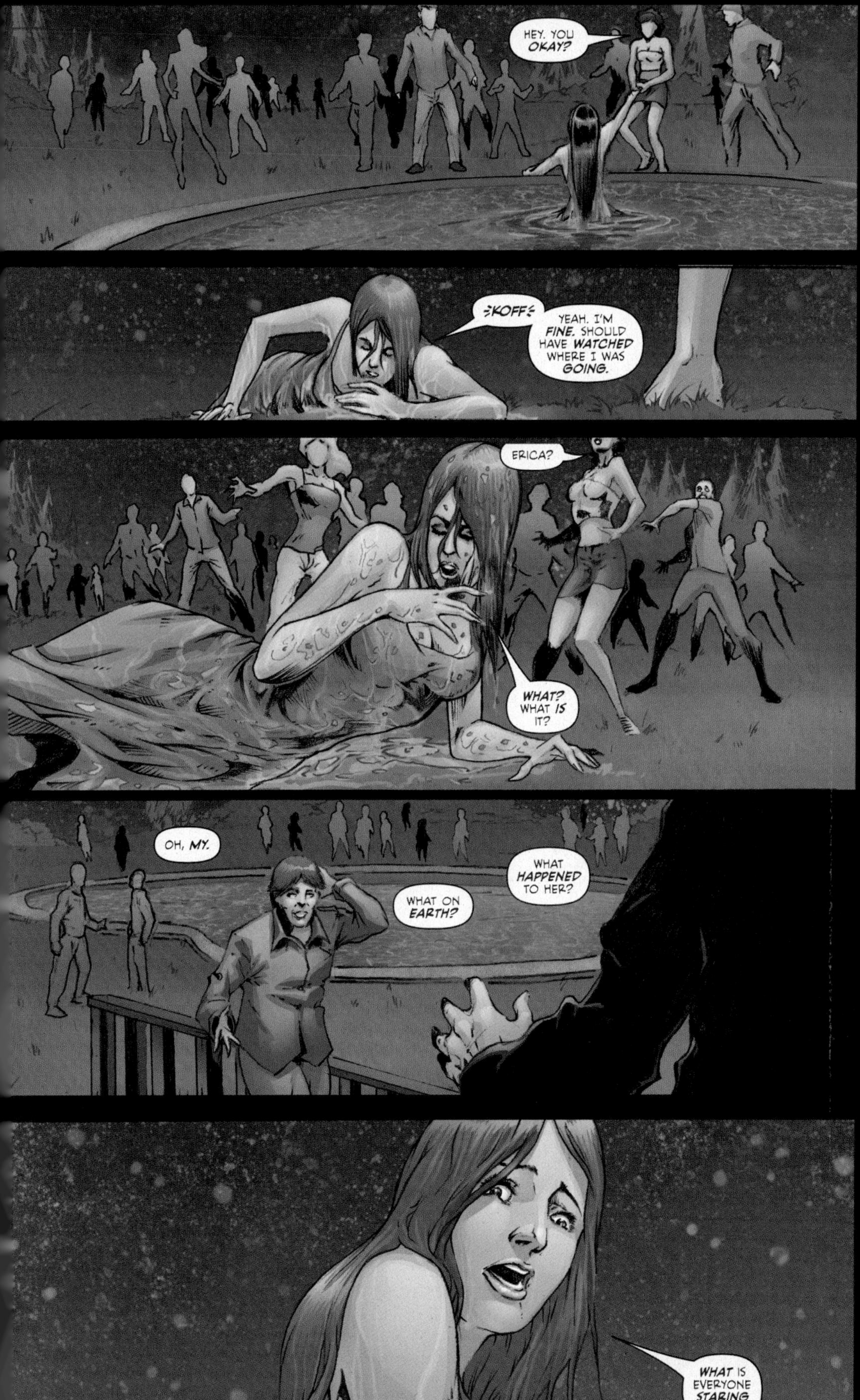
HEY. YOU OKAY?
KOFF
YEAH. I'M FINE. SHOULD HAVE WATCHED WHERE I WAS GOING.
ERICA?
WHAT? WHAT IS IT?
OH, MY.
WHAT ON EARTH?
WHAT HAPPENED TO HER?
WHAT IS EVERYONE STARING AT?

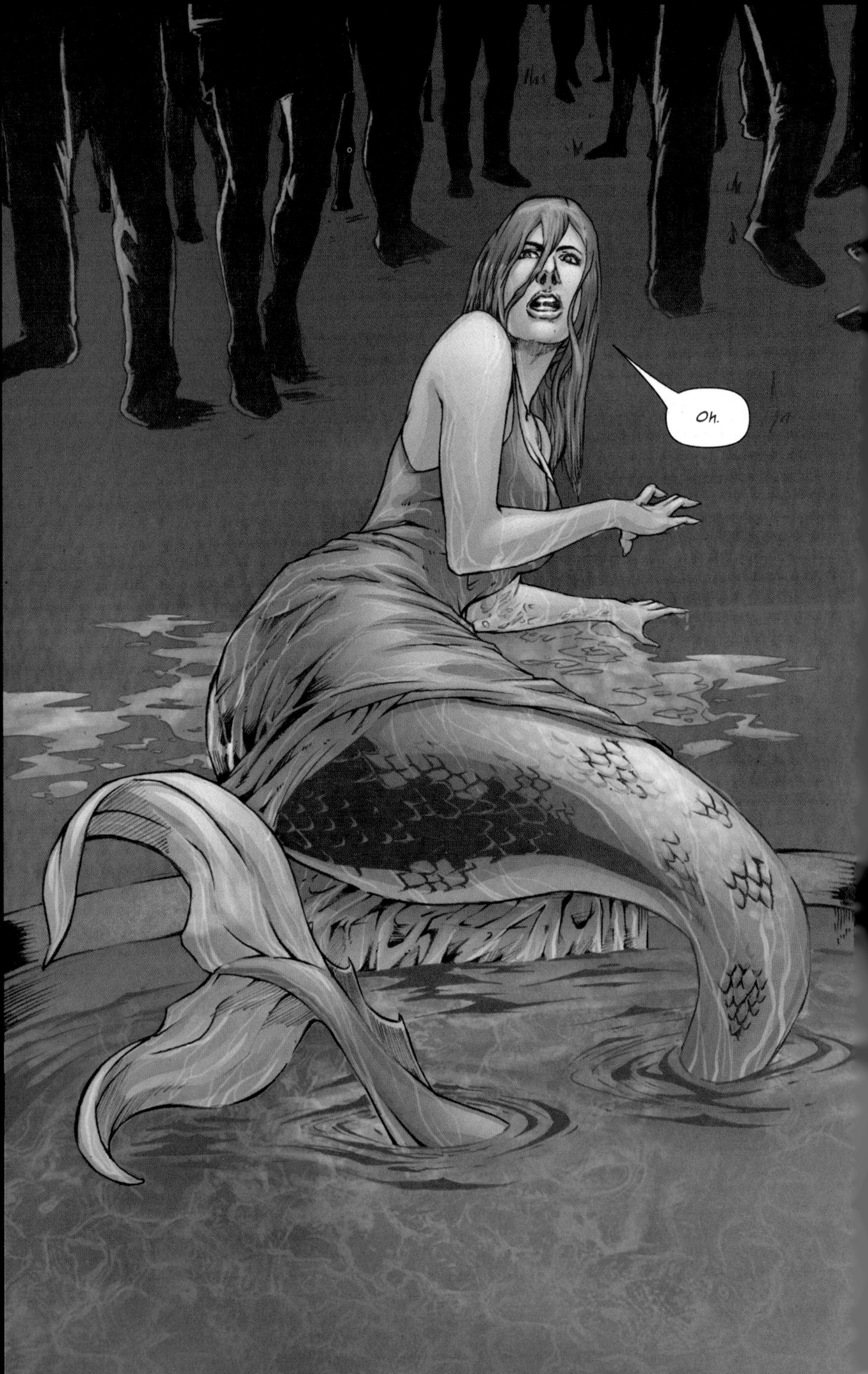
Oh.
TO BE CONTINUED

Grimm Fairy Tales
MYTHS & LEGENDS

Chapter Two

Story by Raven Gregory, Joe Brusha and Ralph Tedesco

Written by Raven Gregory • Art by Marlin Shoop

Colors by Jeremy Colwell, Andrew Elder and Jason Embury • Letters by Jim Campbell

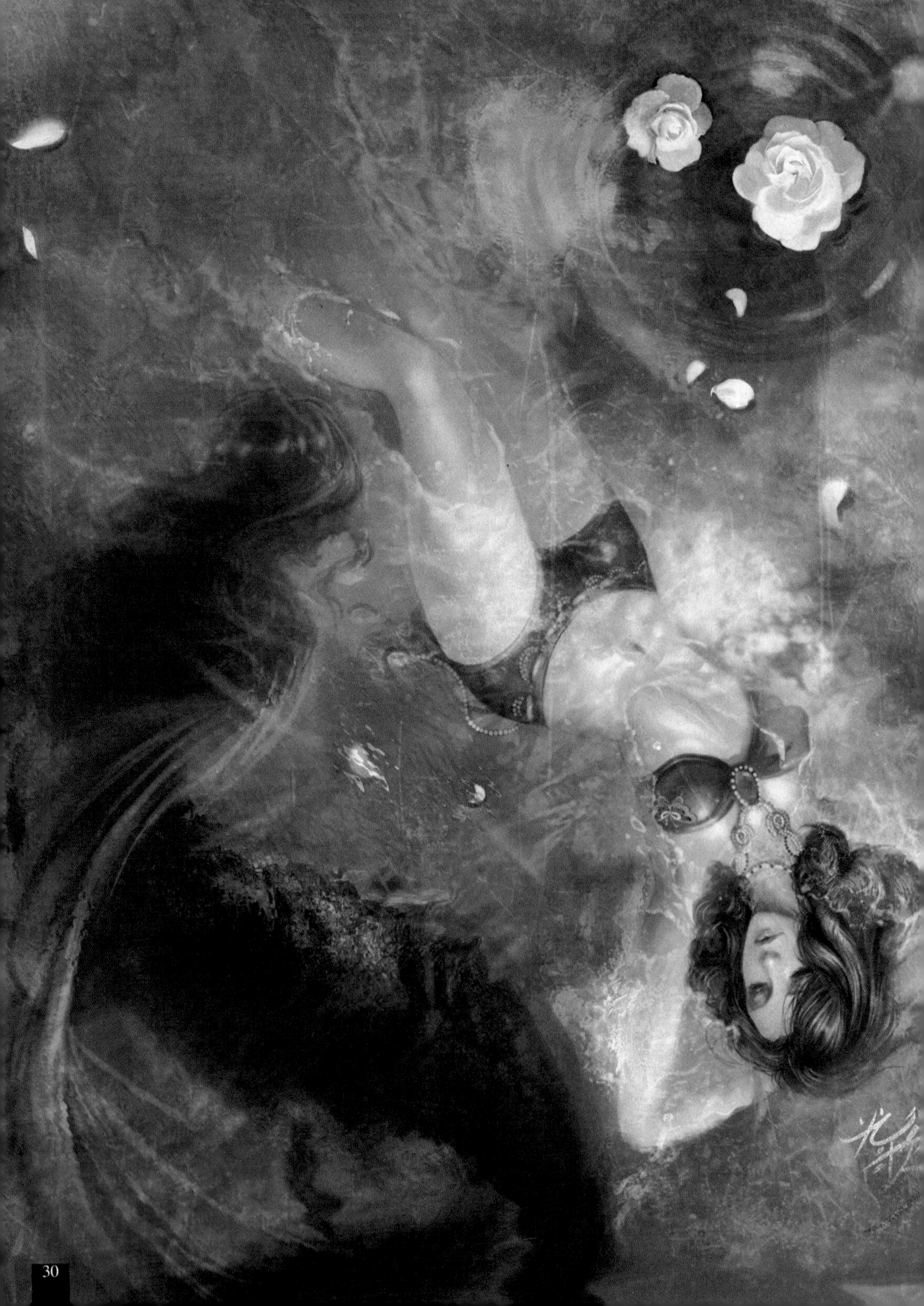

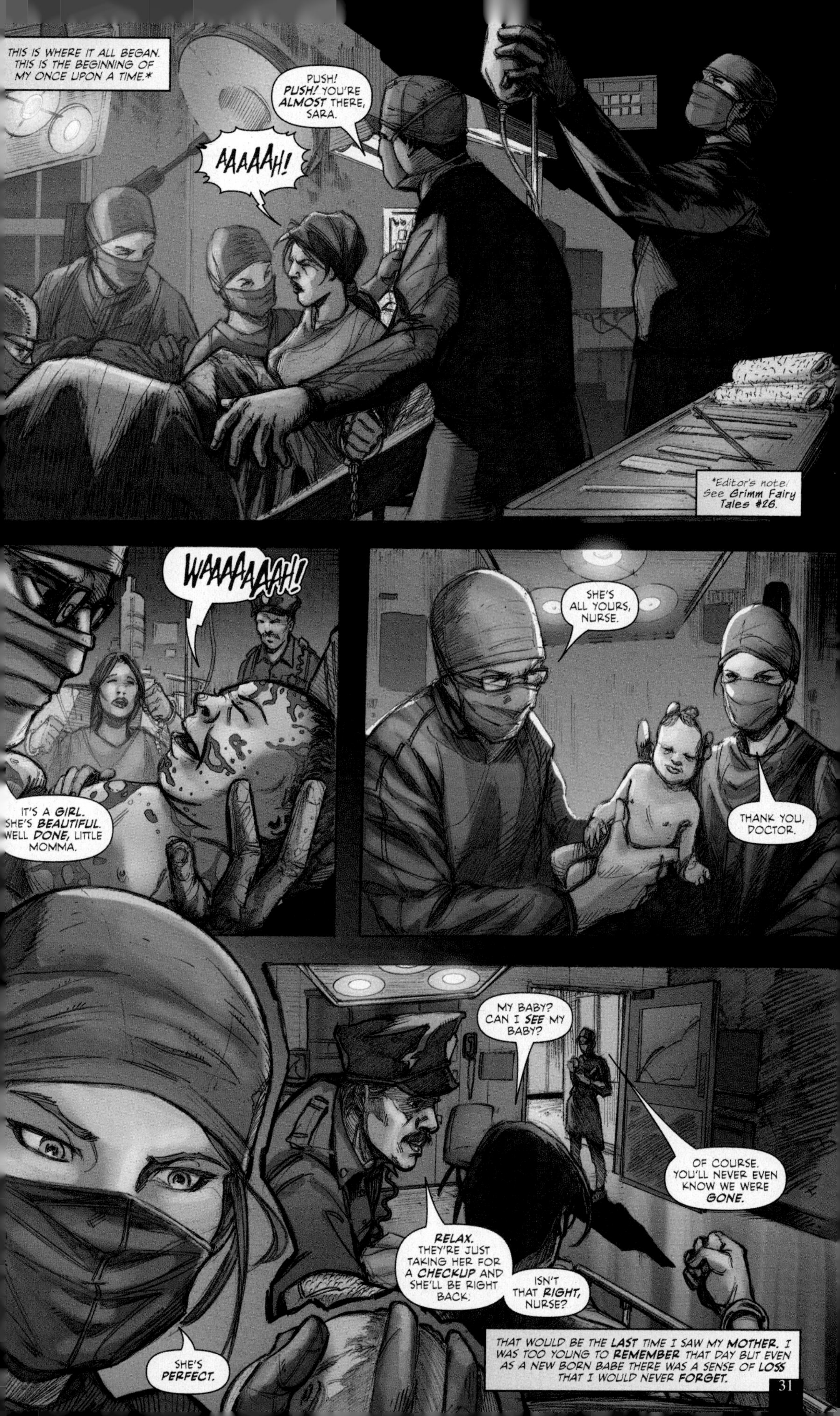
THIS IS WHERE IT ALL BEGAN. THIS IS THE BEGINNING OF MY ONCE UPON A TIME.*
PUSH! PUSH! YOU'RE ALMOST THERE, SARA.
AAAAAH!
*Editor's note: See Grimm Fairy Tales #26.
WAAAAAAAH!
IT'S A GIRL. SHE'S BEAUTIFUL. WELL DONE, LITTLE MOMMA.
SHE'S ALL YOURS, NURSE.
THANK YOU, DOCTOR.
SHE'S PERFECT.
MY BABY? CAN I SEE MY BABY?
RELAX. THEY'RE JUST TAKING HER FOR A CHECKUP AND SHE'LL BE RIGHT BACK.
ISN'T THAT RIGHT, NURSE?
OF COURSE. YOU'LL NEVER EVEN KNOW WE WERE GONE.
THAT WOULD BE THE LAST TIME I SAW MY MOTHER. I WAS TOO YOUNG TO REMEMBER THAT DAY BUT EVEN AS A NEW BORN BABE THERE WAS A SENSE OF LOSS THAT I WOULD NEVER FORGET.

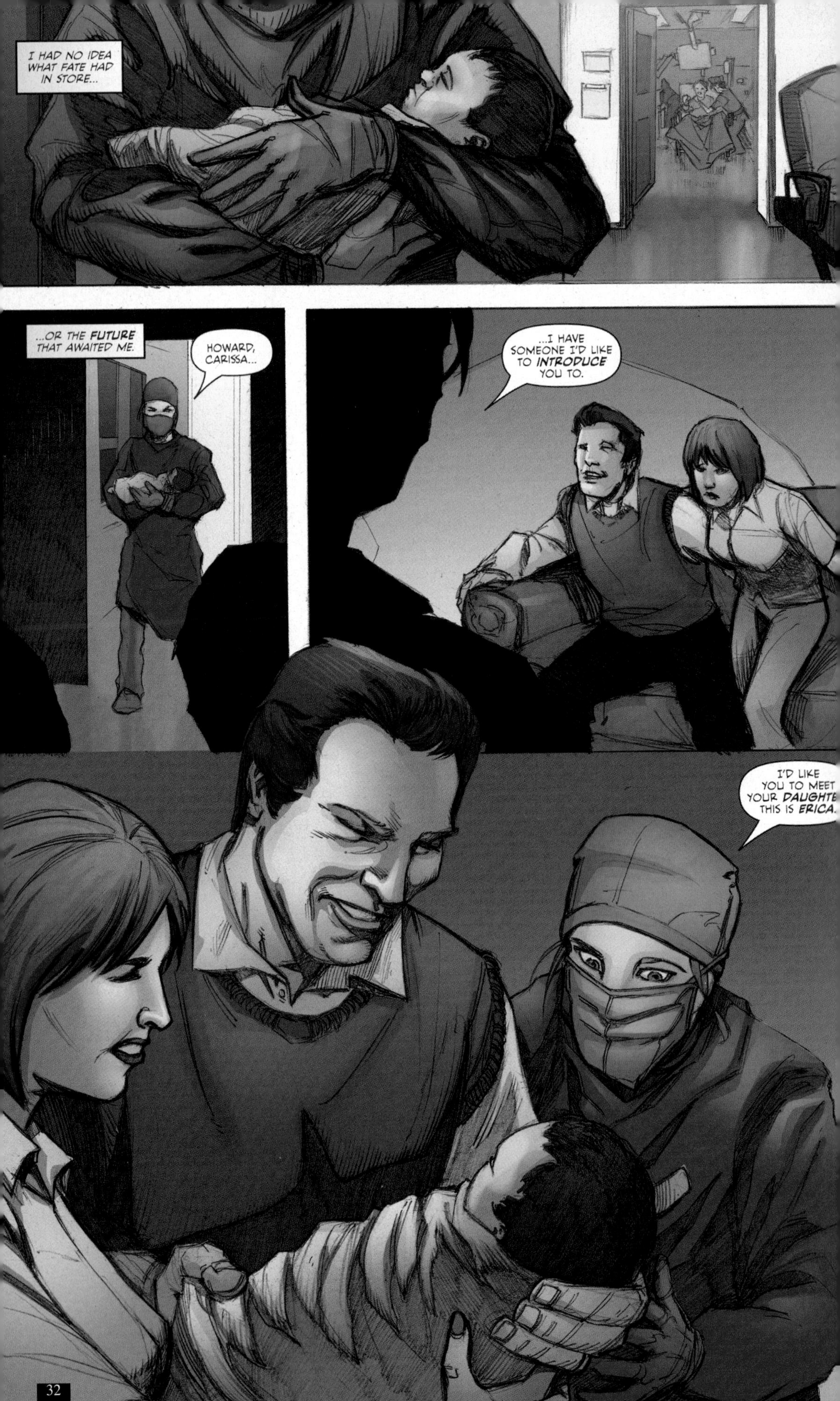
I HAD NO IDEA WHAT FATE HAD IN STORE...
...OR THE FUTURE THAT AWAITED ME.
HOWARD, CARISSA...
...I HAVE SOMEONE I'D LIKE TO INTRODUCE YOU TO.
I'D LIKE YOU TO MEET YOUR DAUGHTE THIS IS ERICA.

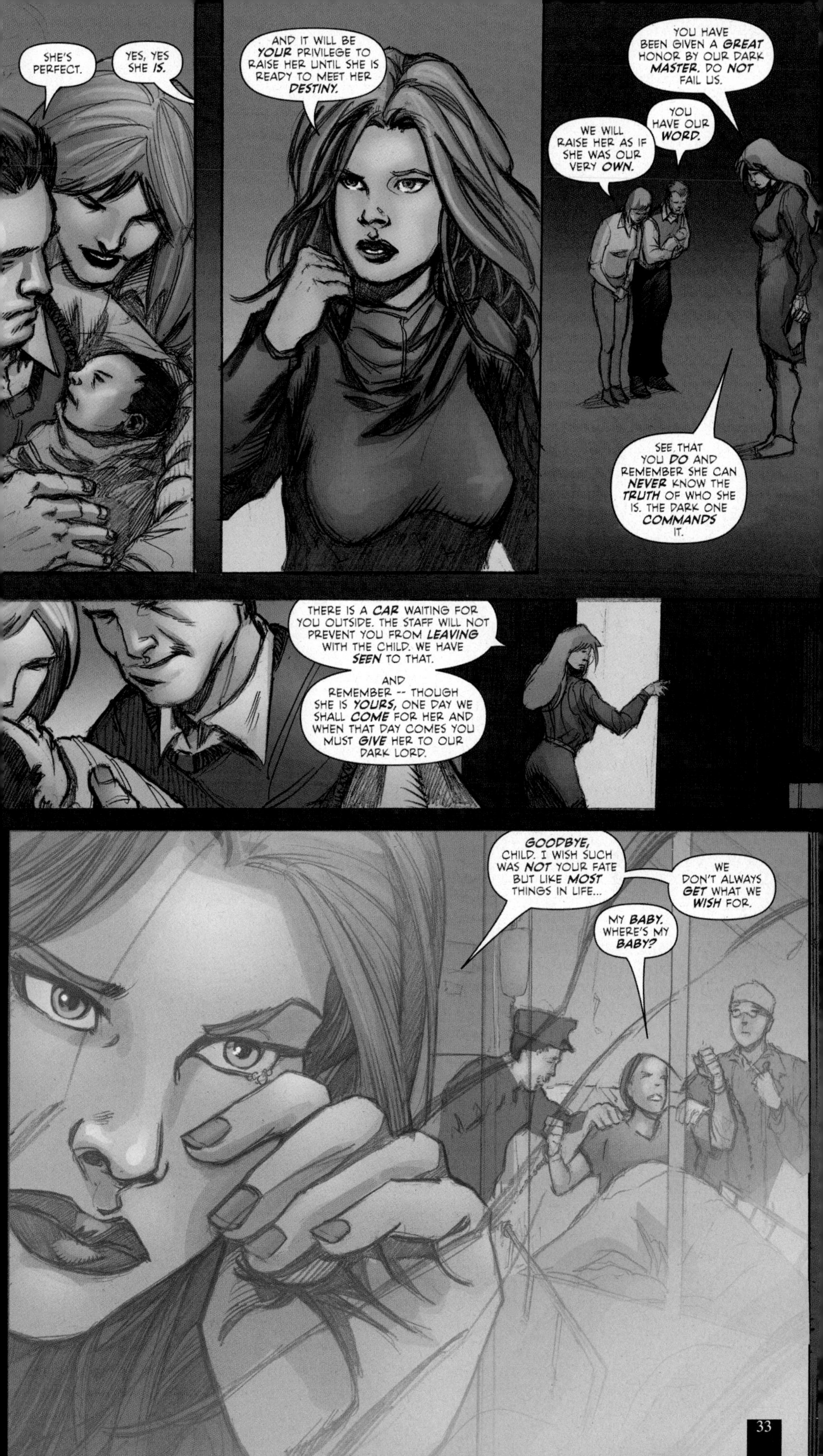
SHE'S PERFECT.
YES, YES SHE IS.
AND IT WILL BE YOUR PRIVILEGE TO RAISE HER UNTIL SHE IS READY TO MEET HER DESTINY.
YOU HAVE BEEN GIVEN A GREAT HONOR BY OUR DARK MASTER. DO NOT FAIL US.
WE WILL RAISE HER AS IF SHE WAS OUR VERY OWN.
YOU HAVE OUR WORD.
SEE THAT YOU DO AND REMEMBER SHE CAN NEVER KNOW THE TRUTH OF WHO SHE IS. THE DARK ONE COMMANDS IT.
THERE IS A CAR WAITING FOR YOU OUTSIDE. THE STAFF WILL NOT PREVENT YOU FROM LEAVING WITH THE CHILD. WE HAVE SEEN TO THAT.
AND REMEMBER -- THOUGH SHE IS YOURS, ONE DAY WE SHALL COME FOR HER AND WHEN THAT DAY COMES YOU MUST GIVE HER TO OUR DARK LORD.
GOODBYE, CHILD. I WISH SUCH WAS NOT YOUR FATE BUT LIKE MOST THINGS IN LIFE...
WE DON'T ALWAYS GET WHAT WE WISH FOR.
MY BABY. WHERE'S MY BABY?

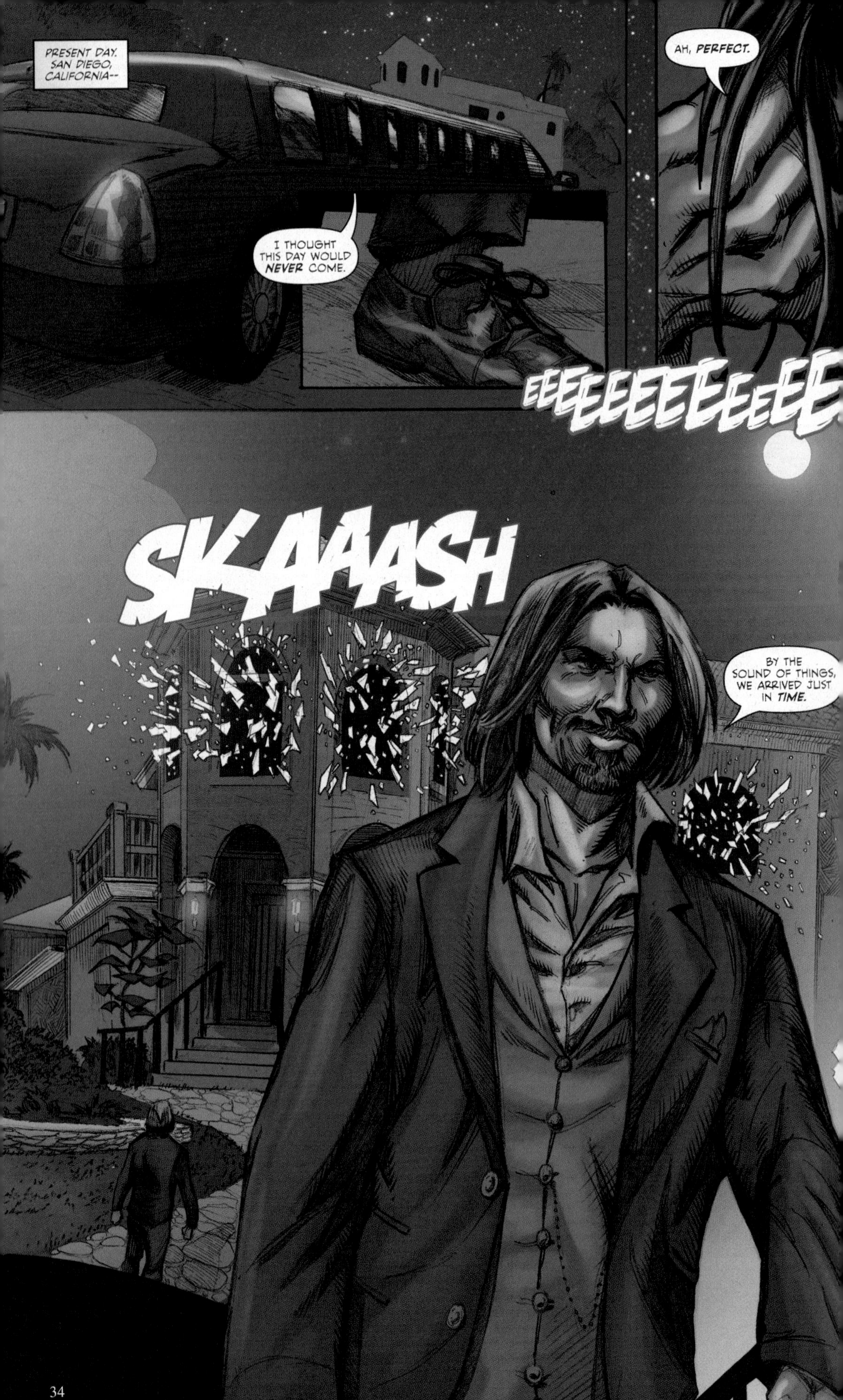
PRESENT DAY. SAN DIEGO, CALIFORNIA--
I THOUGHT THIS DAY WOULD NEVER COME.
AH, PERFECT.
EEEEEEEEEEEE
SKAAASH
BY THE SOUND OF THINGS, WE ARRIVED JUST IN TIME.

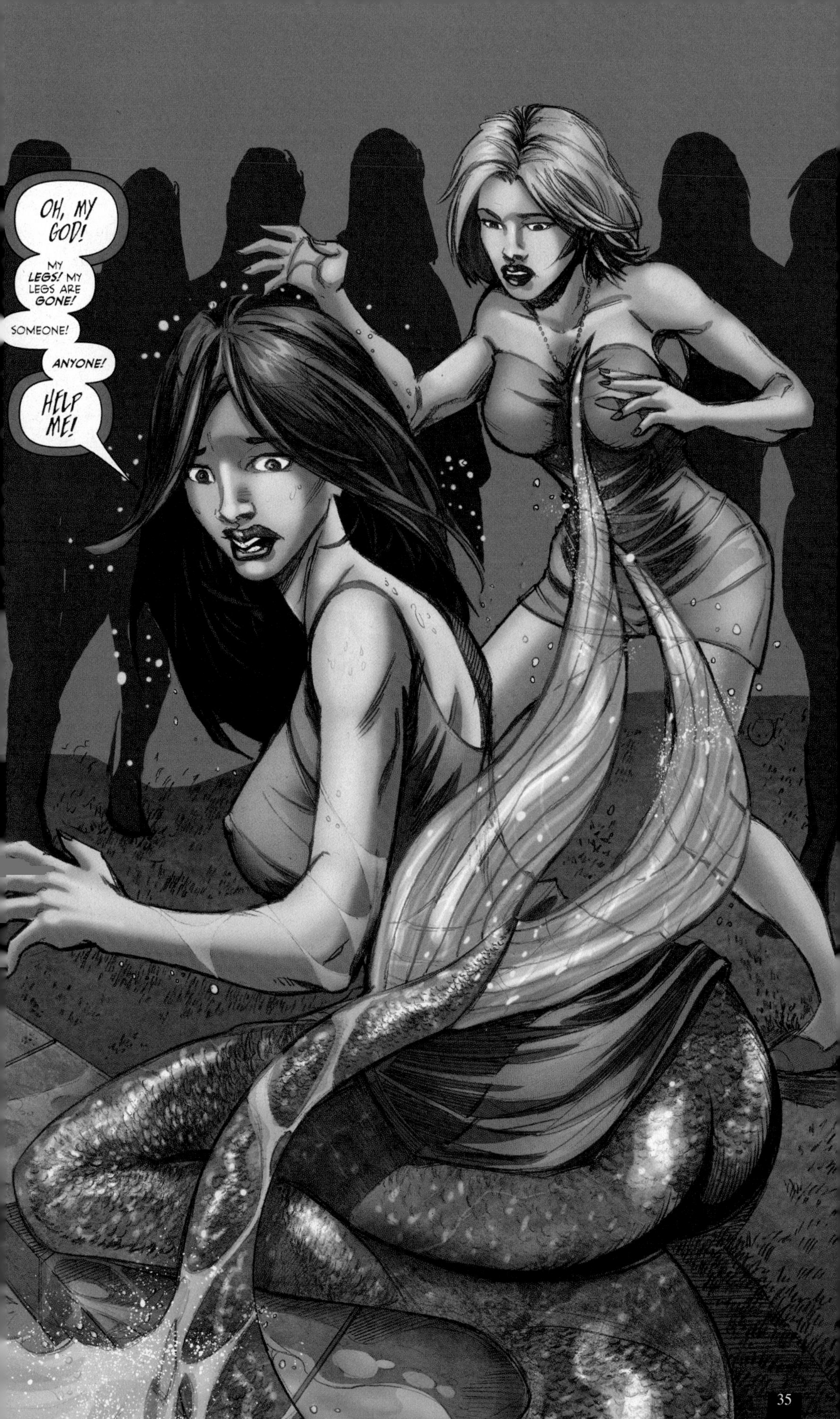
OH, MY GOD!
MY LEGS! MY LEGS ARE GONE!
SOMEONE!
ANYONE!
HELP ME!

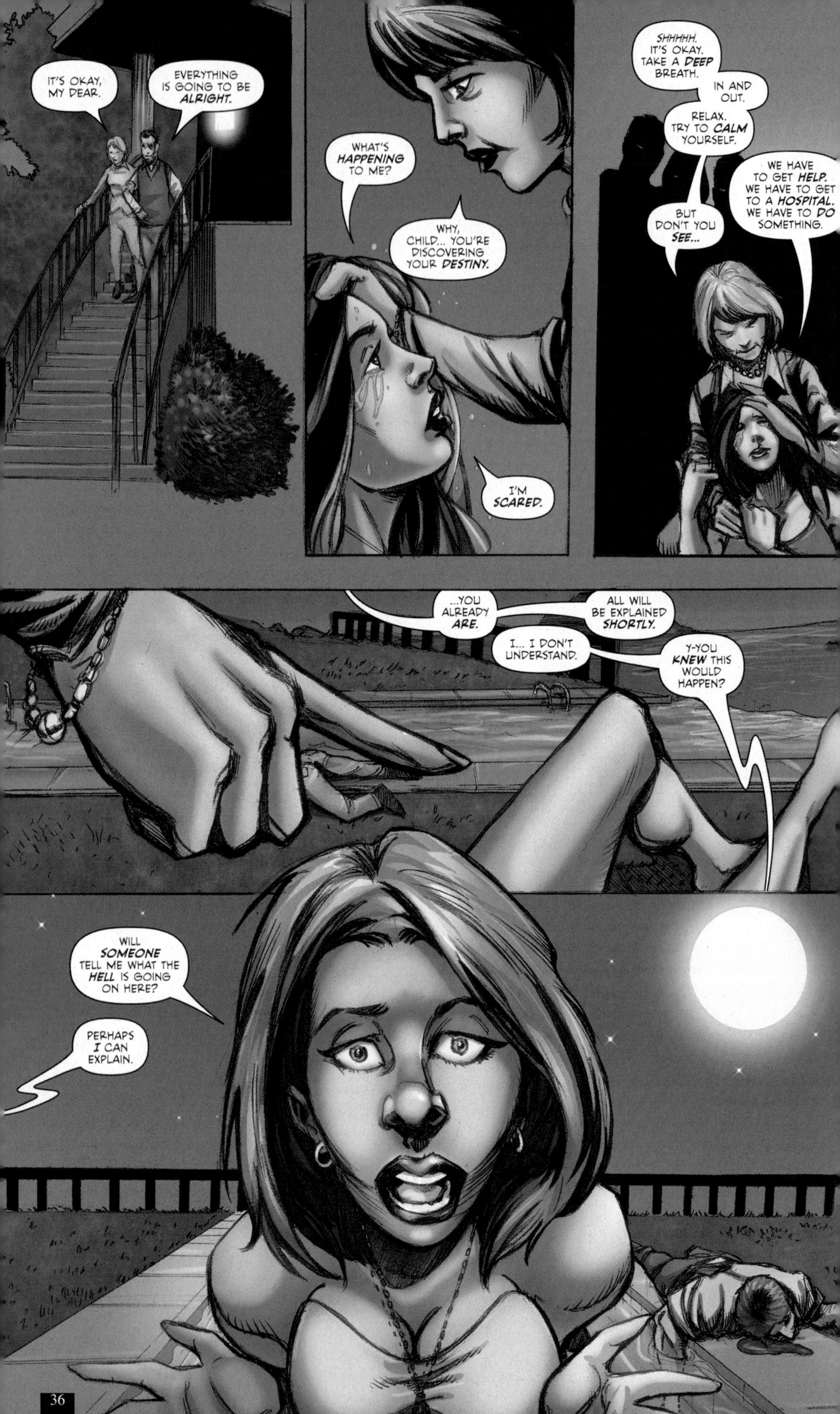
IT'S OKAY, MY DEAR.
EVERYTHING IS GOING TO BE ALRIGHT.
WHAT'S HAPPENING TO ME?
WHY, CHILD... YOU'RE DISCOVERING YOUR DESTINY.
I'M SCARED.
SHHHHH. IT'S OKAY. TAKE A DEEP BREATH.
IN AND OUT.
RELAX. TRY TO CALM YOURSELF.
BUT DON'T YOU SEE...
WE HAVE TO GET HELP. WE HAVE TO GET TO A HOSPITAL. WE HAVE TO DO SOMETHING.
...YOU ALREADY ARE.
ALL WILL BE EXPLAINED SHORTLY.
I... I DON'T UNDERSTAND.
Y-YOU KNEW THIS WOULD HAPPEN?
WILL SOMEONE TELL ME WHAT THE HELL IS GOING ON HERE?
PERHAPS I CAN EXPLAIN.

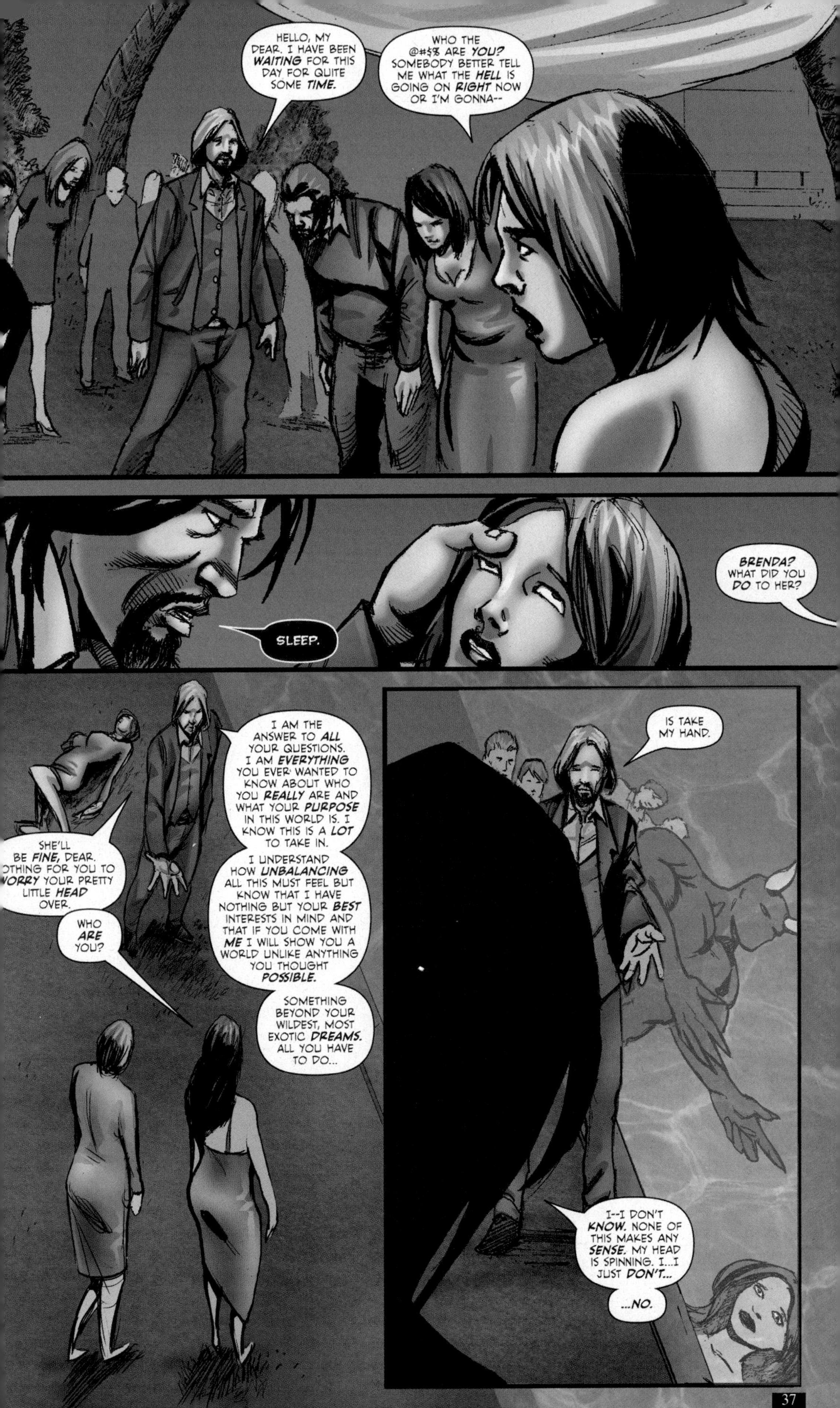
HELLO, MY DEAR. I HAVE BEEN WAITING FOR THIS DAY FOR QUITE SOME TIME.
WHO THE @#$% ARE YOU? SOMEBODY BETTER TELL ME WHAT THE HELL IS GOING ON RIGHT NOW OR I'M GONNA--
SLEEP.
BRENDA? WHAT DID YOU DO TO HER?
SHE'LL BE FINE, DEAR. OTHING FOR YOU TO ORRY YOUR PRETTY LITTLE HEAD OVER.
WHO ARE YOU?
I AM THE ANSWER TO ALL YOUR QUESTIONS. I AM EVERYTHING YOU EVER WANTED TO KNOW ABOUT WHO YOU REALLY ARE AND WHAT YOUR PURPOSE IN THIS WORLD IS. I KNOW THIS IS A LOT TO TAKE IN.
I UNDERSTAND HOW UNBALANCING ALL THIS MUST FEEL BUT KNOW THAT I HAVE NOTHING BUT YOUR BEST INTERESTS IN MIND AND THAT IF YOU COME WITH ME I WILL SHOW YOU A WORLD UNLIKE ANYTHING YOU THOUGHT POSSIBLE.
SOMETHING BEYOND YOUR WILDEST, MOST EXOTIC DREAMS. ALL YOU HAVE TO DO...
IS TAKE MY HAND.
I--I DON'T KNOW. NONE OF THIS MAKES ANY SENSE. MY HEAD IS SPINNING. I...I JUST DON'T...
...NO.

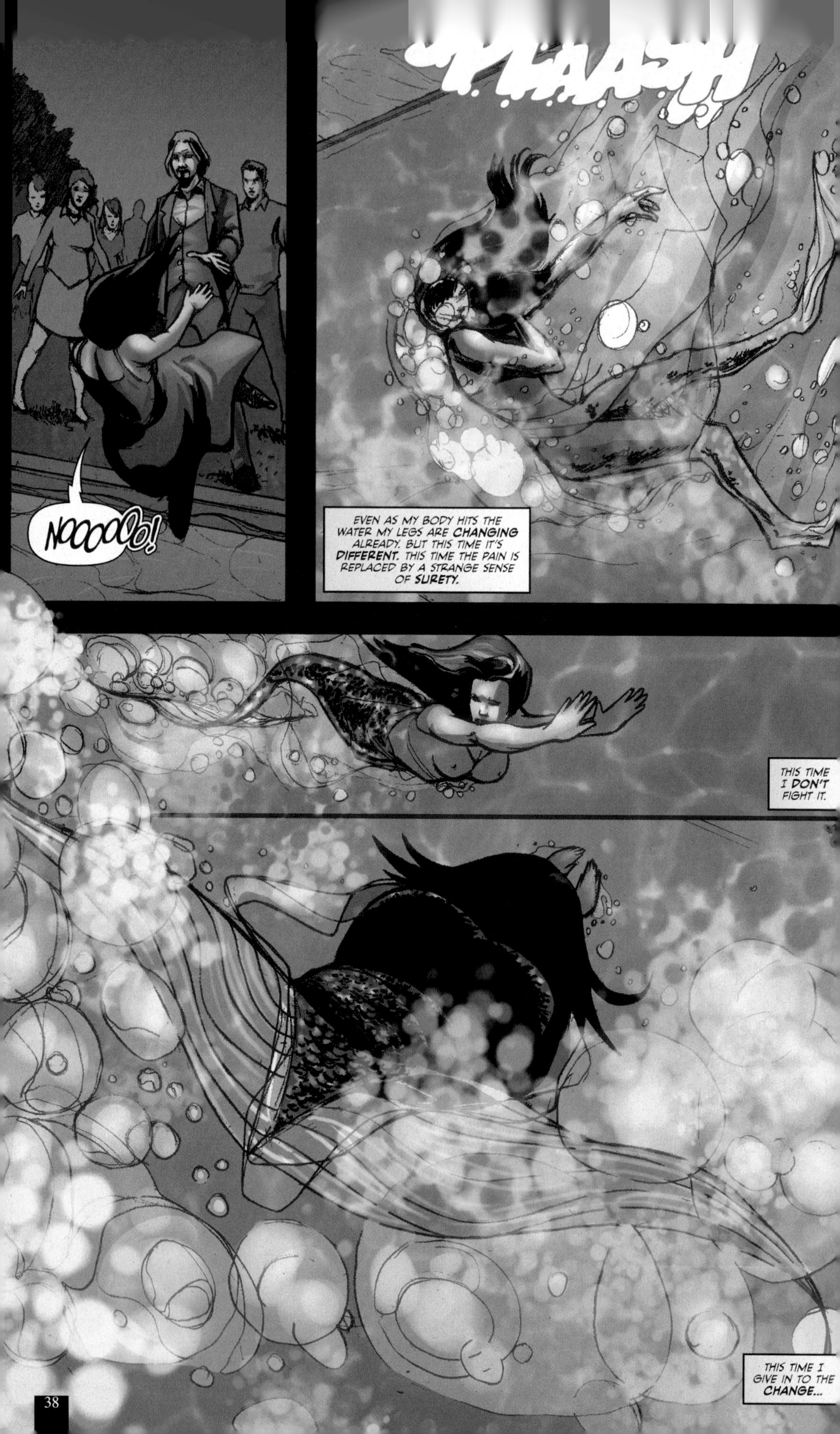

NOOOOOO!
EVEN AS MY BODY HITS THE WATER MY LEGS ARE **CHANGING** ALREADY. BUT THIS TIME IT'S **DIFFERENT**. THIS TIME THE PAIN IS REPLACED BY A STRANGE SENSE OF **SURETY**.
THIS TIME I **DON'T** FIGHT IT.
THIS TIME I GIVE IN TO THE **CHANGE**...

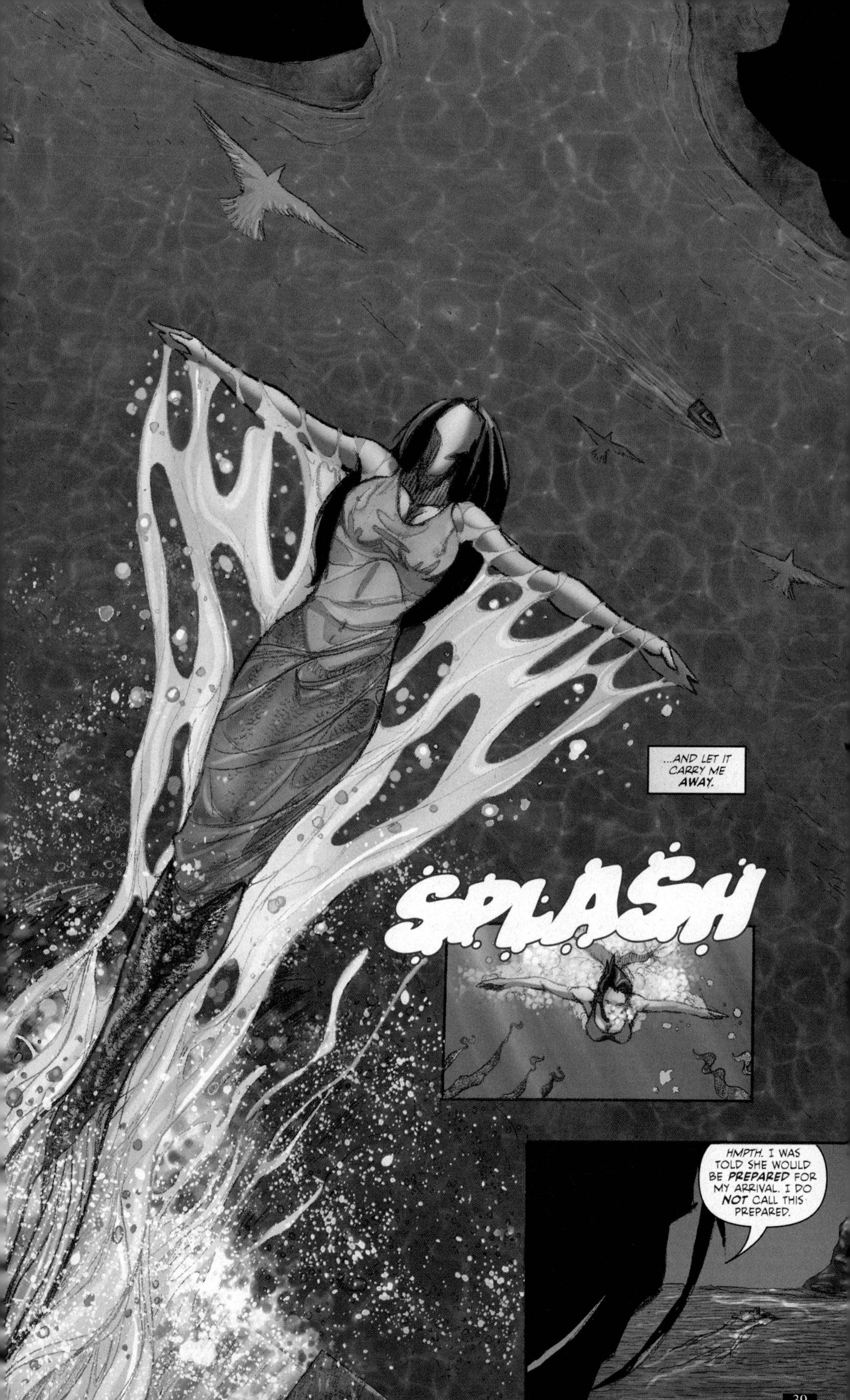
...AND LET IT CARRY ME AWAY.
SPLASH
HMPTH. I WAS TOLD SHE WOULD BE PREPARED FOR MY ARRIVAL. I DO NOT CALL THIS PREPARED.

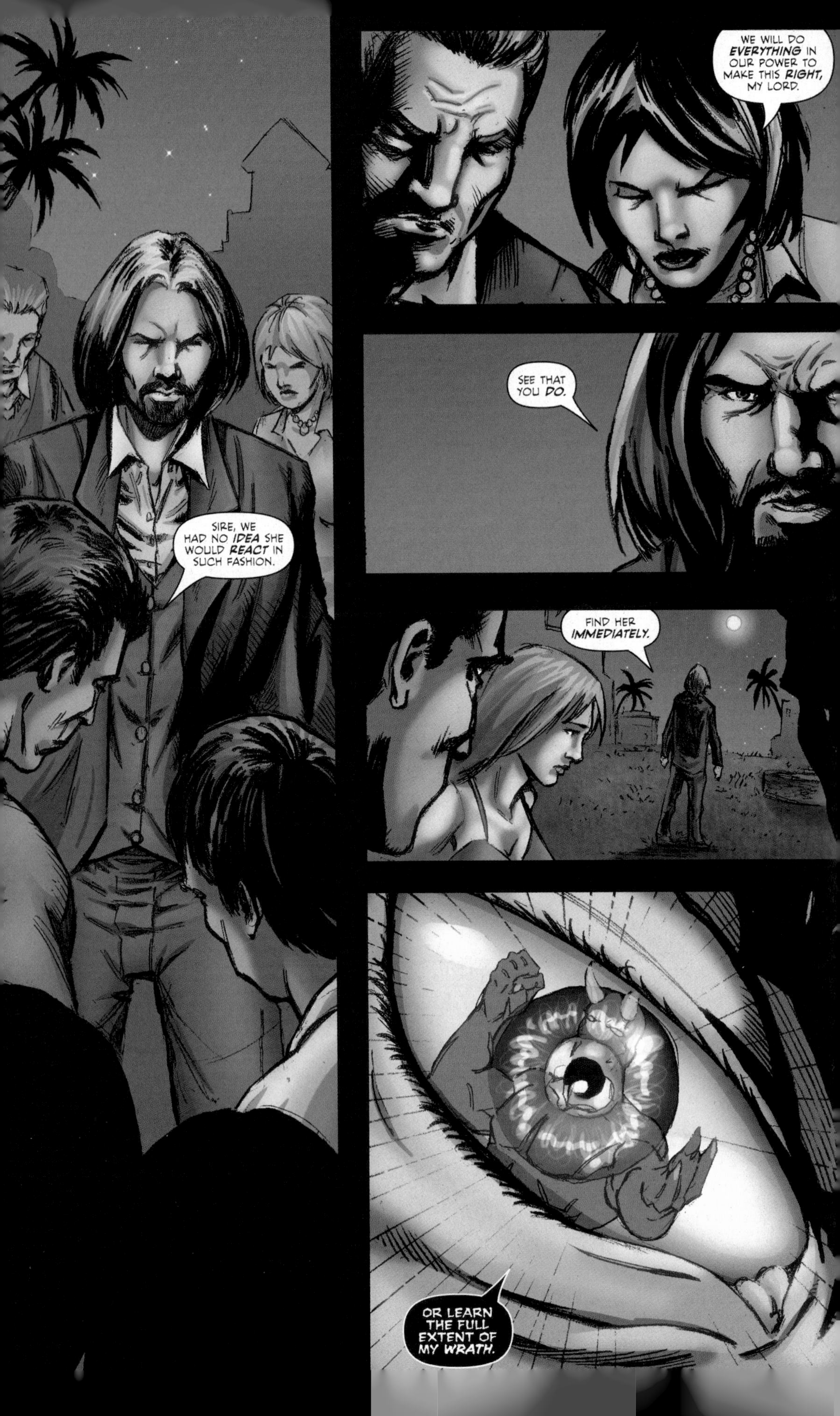
SIRE, WE HAD NO IDEA SHE WOULD REACT IN SUCH FASHION.
WE WILL DO EVERYTHING IN OUR POWER TO MAKE THIS RIGHT, MY LORD.
SEE THAT YOU DO.
FIND HER IMMEDIATELY.
OR LEARN THE FULL EXTENT OF MY WRATH.

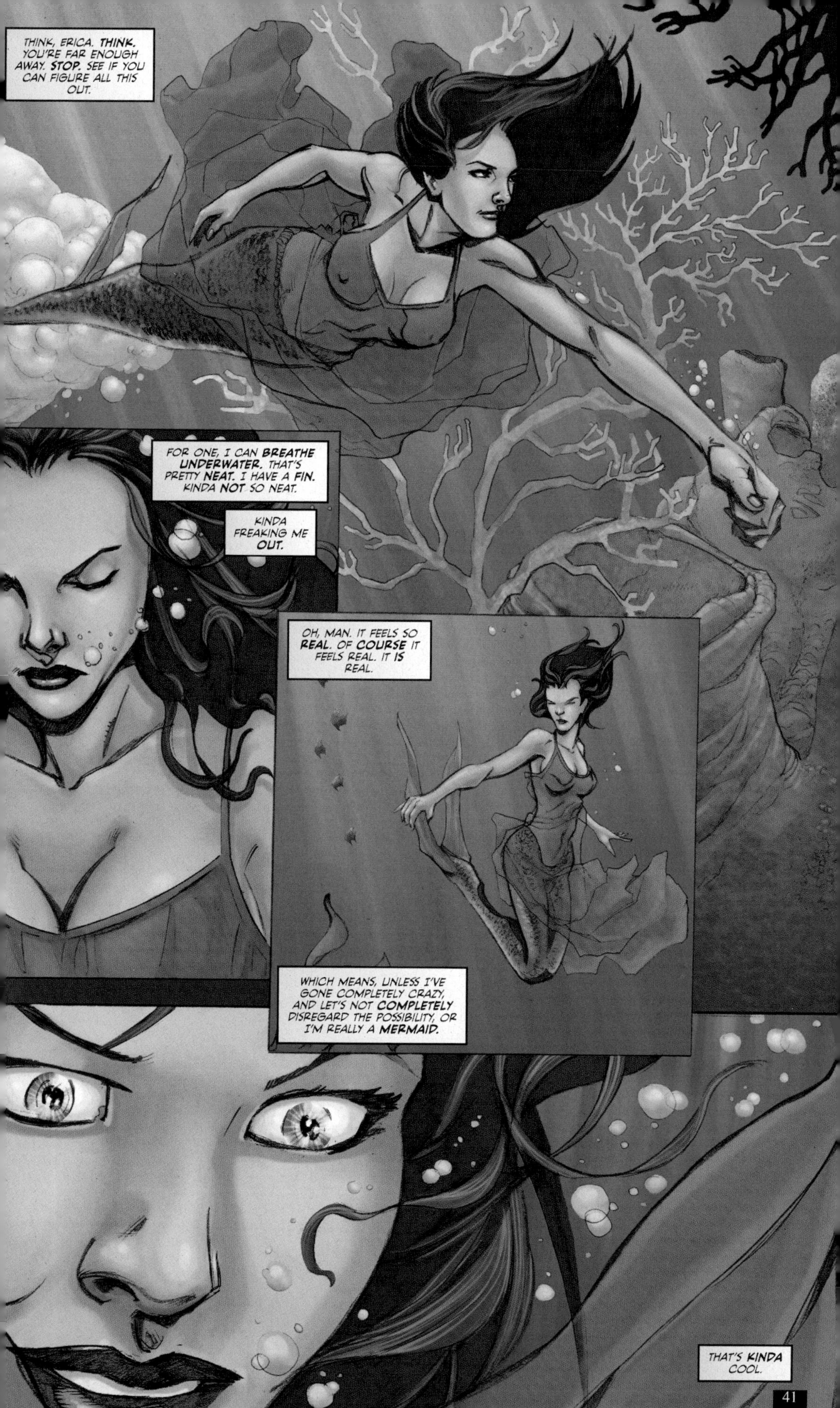
THINK, ERICA. THINK. YOU'RE FAR ENOUGH AWAY. STOP. SEE IF YOU CAN FIGURE ALL THIS OUT.
FOR ONE, I CAN BREATHE UNDERWATER. THAT'S PRETTY NEAT. I HAVE A FIN. KINDA NOT SO NEAT.
KINDA FREAKING ME OUT.
OH, MAN. IT FEELS SO REAL. OF COURSE IT FEELS REAL. IT IS REAL.
WHICH MEANS, UNLESS I'VE GONE COMPLETELY CRAZY, AND LET'S NOT COMPLETELY DISREGARD THE POSSIBILITY, OR I'M REALLY A MERMAID.
THAT'S KINDA COOL.

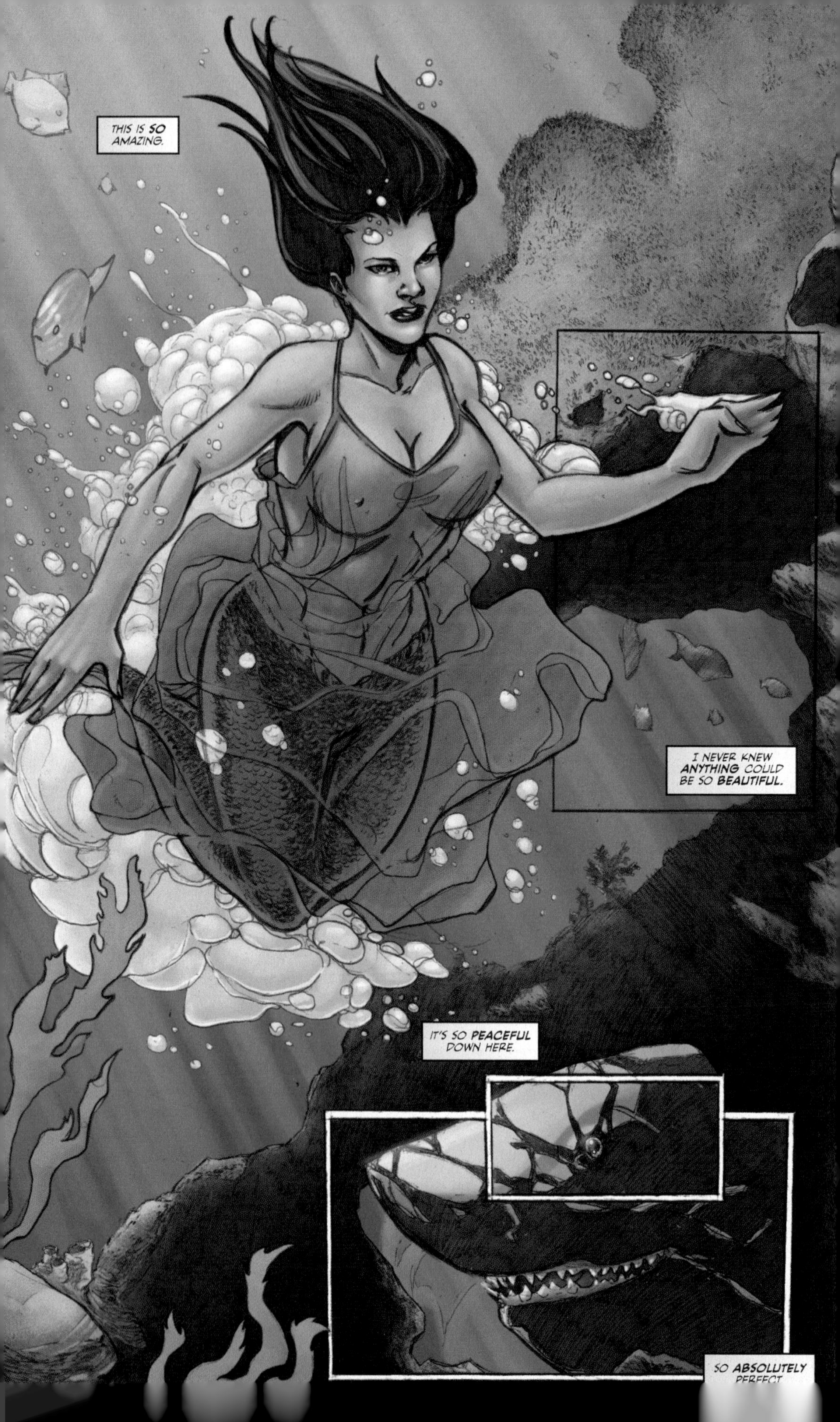
THIS IS **SO** AMAZING.
I NEVER KNEW **ANYTHING** COULD BE SO **BEAUTIFUL**.
IT'S SO **PEACEFUL** DOWN HERE.
SO **ABSOLUTELY** PERFECT

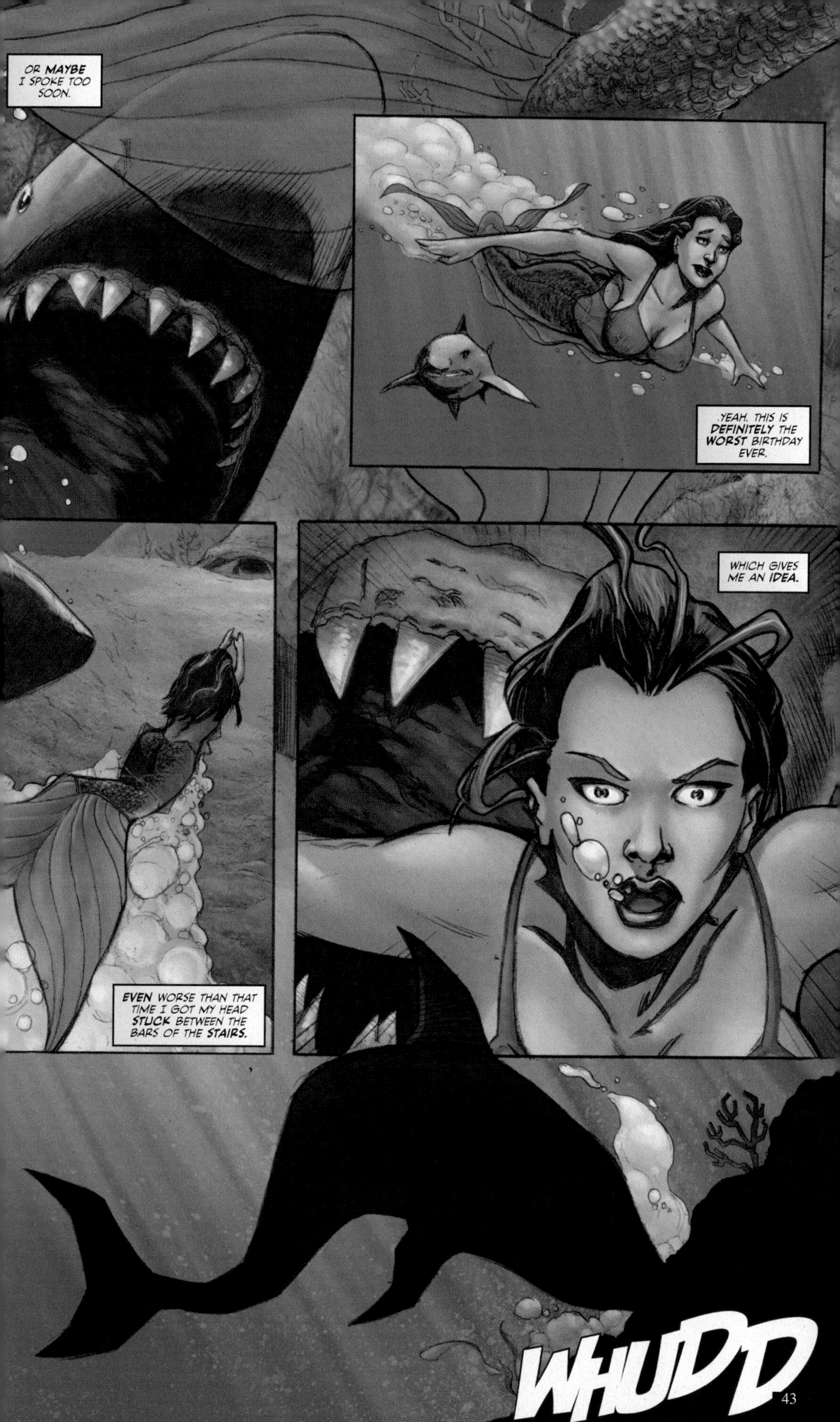

OR MAYBE I SPOKE TOO SOON.
...YEAH. THIS IS DEFINITELY THE WORST BIRTHDAY EVER.
EVEN WORSE THAN THAT TIME I GOT MY HEAD STUCK BETWEEN THE BARS OF THE STAIRS.
WHICH GIVES ME AN IDEA.
WHUDD

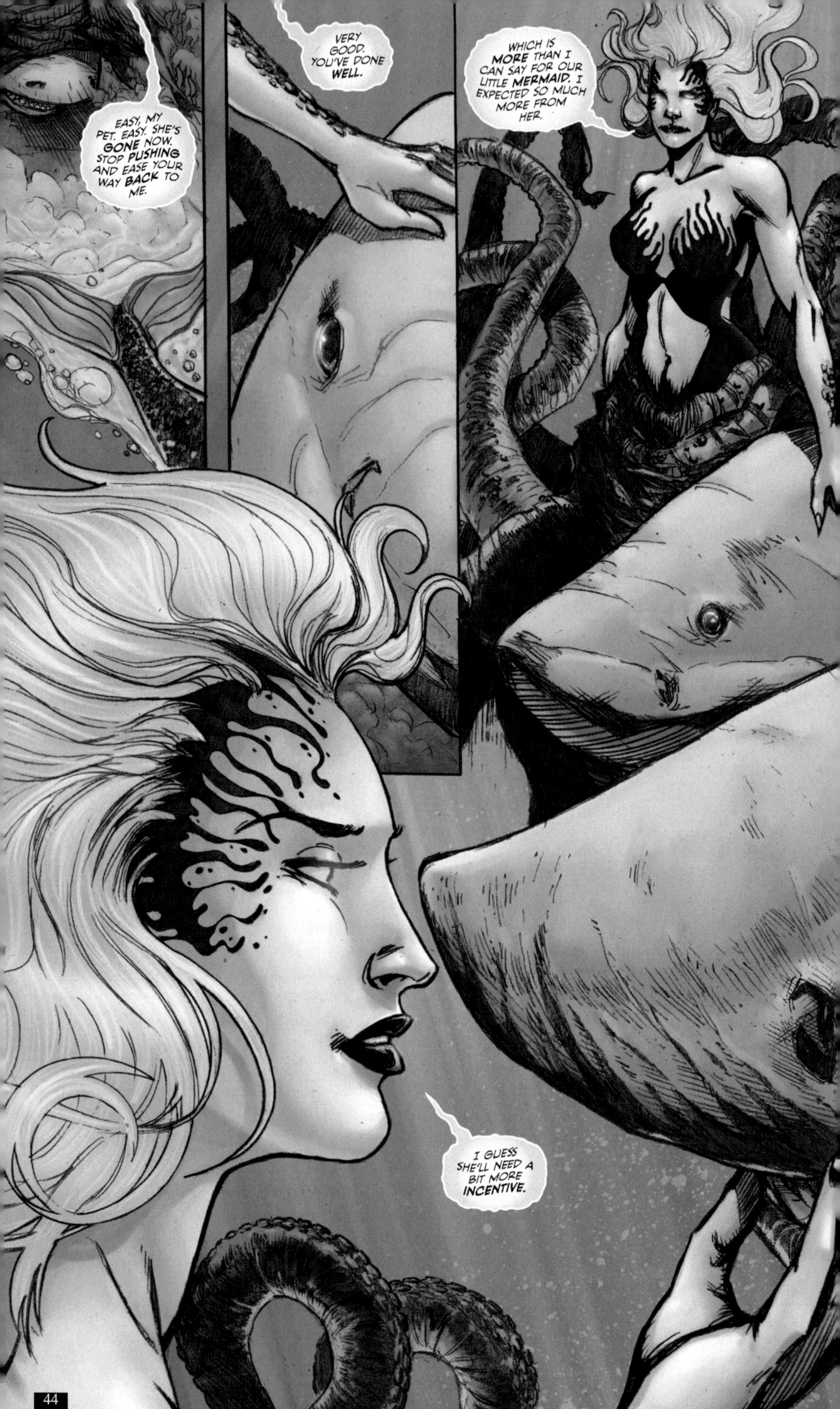
EASY, MY PET. EASY. SHE'S GONE NOW. STOP PUSHING AND EASE YOUR WAY BACK TO ME.
VERY GOOD. YOU'VE DONE WELL.
WHICH IS MORE THAN I CAN SAY FOR OUR LITTLE MERMAID. I EXPECTED SO MUCH MORE FROM HER.
I GUESS SHE'LL NEED A BIT MORE INCENTIVE.

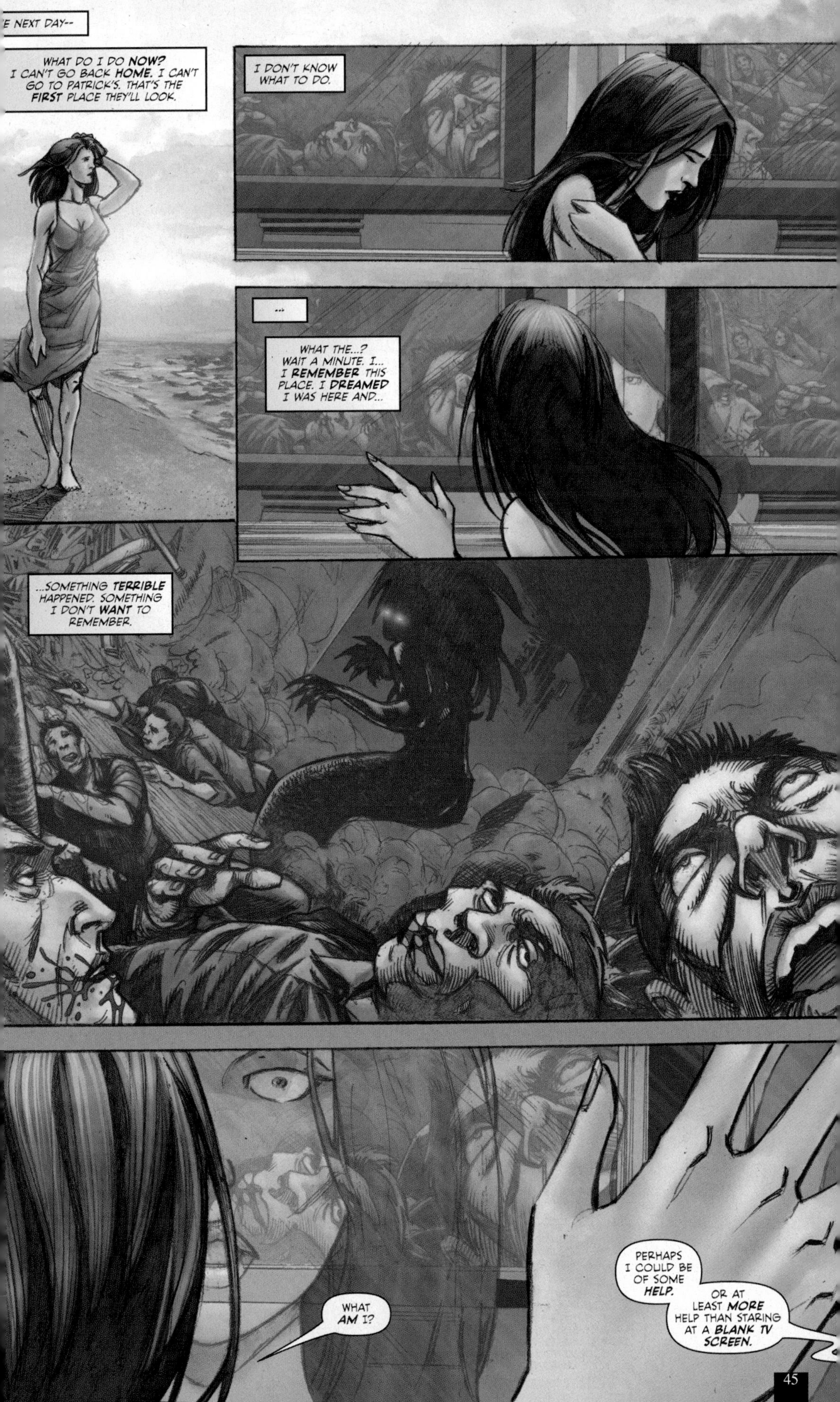
E NEXT DAY--
WHAT DO I DO NOW? I CAN'T GO BACK HOME. I CAN'T GO TO PATRICK'S. THAT'S THE FIRST PLACE THEY'LL LOOK.
I DON'T KNOW WHAT TO DO.
...
WHAT THE...? WAIT A MINUTE. I... I REMEMBER THIS PLACE. I DREAMED I WAS HERE AND...
...SOMETHING TERRIBLE HAPPENED. SOMETHING I DON'T WANT TO REMEMBER.
WHAT AM I?
PERHAPS I COULD BE OF SOME HELP.
OR AT LEAST MORE HELP THAN STARING AT A BLANK TV SCREEN.

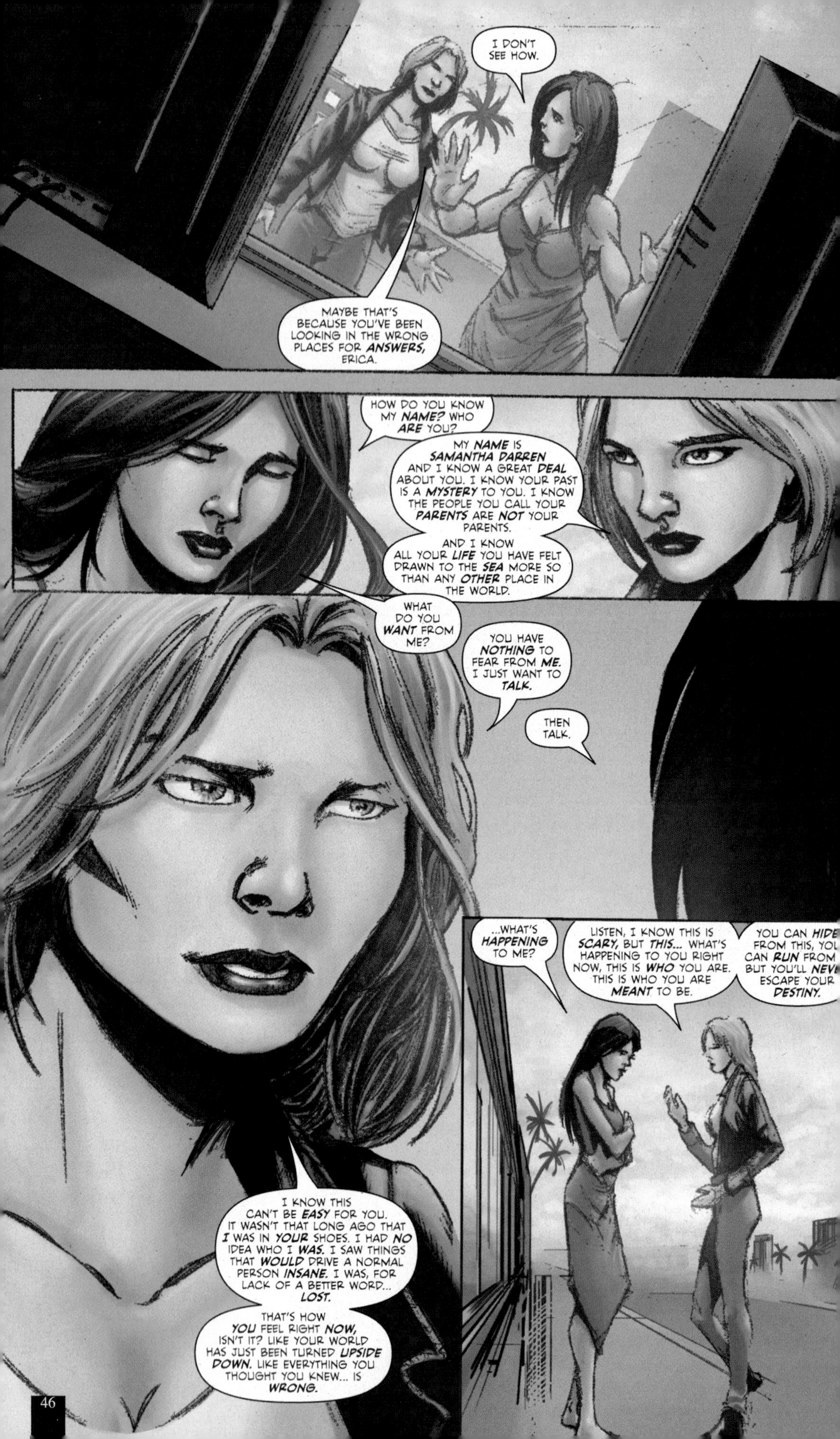
I DON'T SEE HOW.
MAYBE THAT'S BECAUSE YOU'VE BEEN LOOKING IN THE WRONG PLACES FOR ANSWERS, ERICA.
HOW DO YOU KNOW MY NAME? WHO ARE YOU?
MY NAME IS SAMANTHA DARREN AND I KNOW A GREAT DEAL ABOUT YOU. I KNOW YOUR PAST IS A MYSTERY TO YOU. I KNOW THE PEOPLE YOU CALL YOUR PARENTS ARE NOT YOUR PARENTS.
AND I KNOW ALL YOUR LIFE YOU HAVE FELT DRAWN TO THE SEA MORE SO THAN ANY OTHER PLACE IN THE WORLD.
WHAT DO YOU WANT FROM ME?
YOU HAVE NOTHING TO FEAR FROM ME. I JUST WANT TO TALK.
THEN TALK.
I KNOW THIS CAN'T BE EASY FOR YOU. IT WASN'T THAT LONG AGO THAT I WAS IN YOUR SHOES. I HAD NO IDEA WHO I WAS. I SAW THINGS THAT WOULD DRIVE A NORMAL PERSON INSANE. I WAS, FOR LACK OF A BETTER WORD... LOST.
THAT'S HOW YOU FEEL RIGHT NOW, ISN'T IT? LIKE YOUR WORLD HAS JUST BEEN TURNED UPSIDE DOWN. LIKE EVERYTHING YOU THOUGHT YOU KNEW... IS WRONG.
...WHAT'S HAPPENING TO ME?
LISTEN, I KNOW THIS IS SCARY, BUT THIS... WHAT'S HAPPENING TO YOU RIGHT NOW, THIS IS WHO YOU ARE. THIS IS WHO YOU ARE MEANT TO BE.
YOU CAN HIDE FROM THIS, YOU CAN RUN FROM BUT YOU'LL NEV ESCAPE YOUR DESTINY.

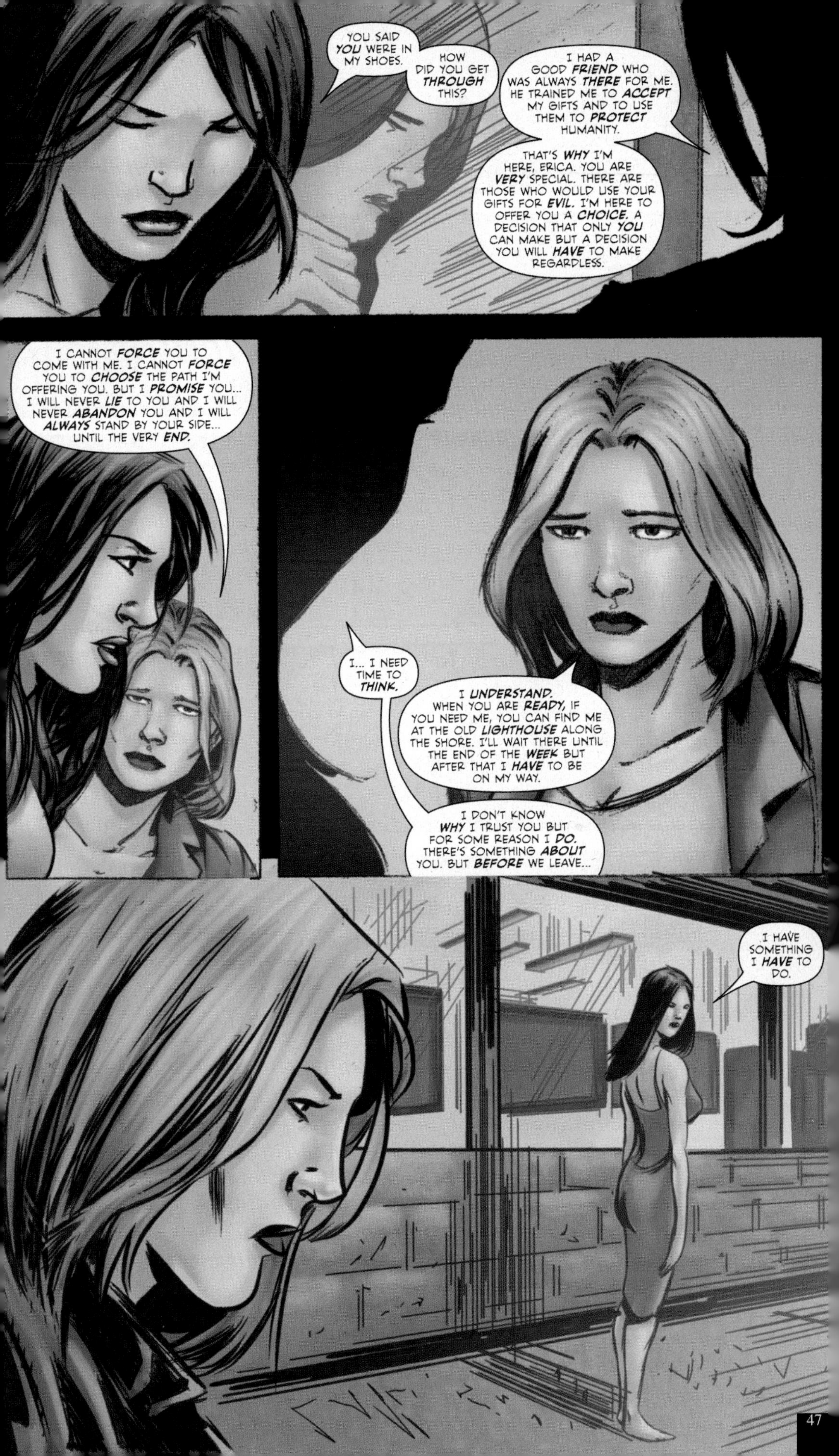
YOU SAID YOU WERE IN MY SHOES.
HOW DID YOU GET THROUGH THIS?
I HAD A GOOD FRIEND WHO WAS ALWAYS THERE FOR ME. HE TRAINED ME TO ACCEPT MY GIFTS AND TO USE THEM TO PROTECT HUMANITY.
THAT'S WHY I'M HERE, ERICA. YOU ARE VERY SPECIAL. THERE ARE THOSE WHO WOULD USE YOUR GIFTS FOR EVIL. I'M HERE TO OFFER YOU A CHOICE. A DECISION THAT ONLY YOU CAN MAKE BUT A DECISION YOU WILL HAVE TO MAKE REGARDLESS.
I CANNOT FORCE YOU TO COME WITH ME. I CANNOT FORCE YOU TO CHOOSE THE PATH I'M OFFERING YOU. BUT I PROMISE YOU... I WILL NEVER LIE TO YOU AND I WILL NEVER ABANDON YOU AND I WILL ALWAYS STAND BY YOUR SIDE... UNTIL THE VERY END.
I... I NEED TIME TO THINK.
I UNDERSTAND. WHEN YOU ARE READY, IF YOU NEED ME, YOU CAN FIND ME AT THE OLD LIGHTHOUSE ALONG THE SHORE. I'LL WAIT THERE UNTIL THE END OF THE WEEK BUT AFTER THAT I HAVE TO BE ON MY WAY.
I DON'T KNOW WHY I TRUST YOU BUT FOR SOME REASON I DO. THERE'S SOMETHING ABOUT YOU. BUT BEFORE WE LEAVE...
I HAVE SOMETHING I HAVE TO DO.

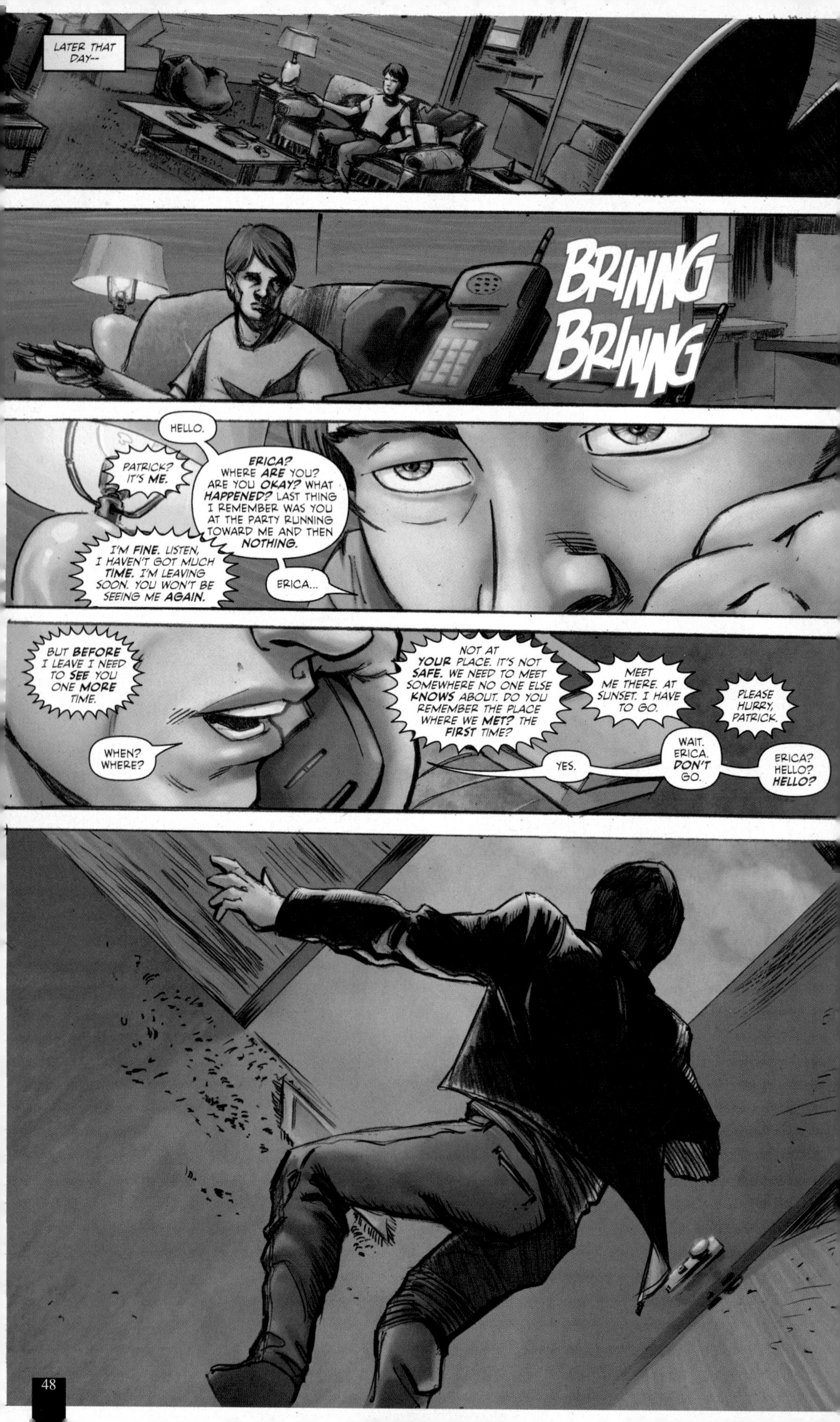
LATER THAT DAY--
BRINNG BRINNG
HELLO.
PATRICK? IT'S ME.
ERICA? WHERE ARE YOU? ARE YOU OKAY? WHAT HAPPENED? LAST THING I REMEMBER WAS YOU AT THE PARTY RUNNING TOWARD ME AND THEN NOTHING.
I'M FINE. LISTEN, I HAVEN'T GOT MUCH TIME. I'M LEAVING SOON. YOU WON'T BE SEEING ME AGAIN.
ERICA...
BUT BEFORE I LEAVE I NEED TO SEE YOU ONE MORE TIME.
WHEN? WHERE?
NOT AT YOUR PLACE. IT'S NOT SAFE. WE NEED TO MEET SOMEWHERE NO ONE ELSE KNOWS ABOUT. DO YOU REMEMBER THE PLACE WHERE WE MET? THE FIRST TIME?
YES.
MEET ME THERE. AT SUNSET. I HAVE TO GO.
WAIT. ERICA. DON'T GO.
PLEASE HURRY, PATRICK.
ERICA? HELLO? HELLO?

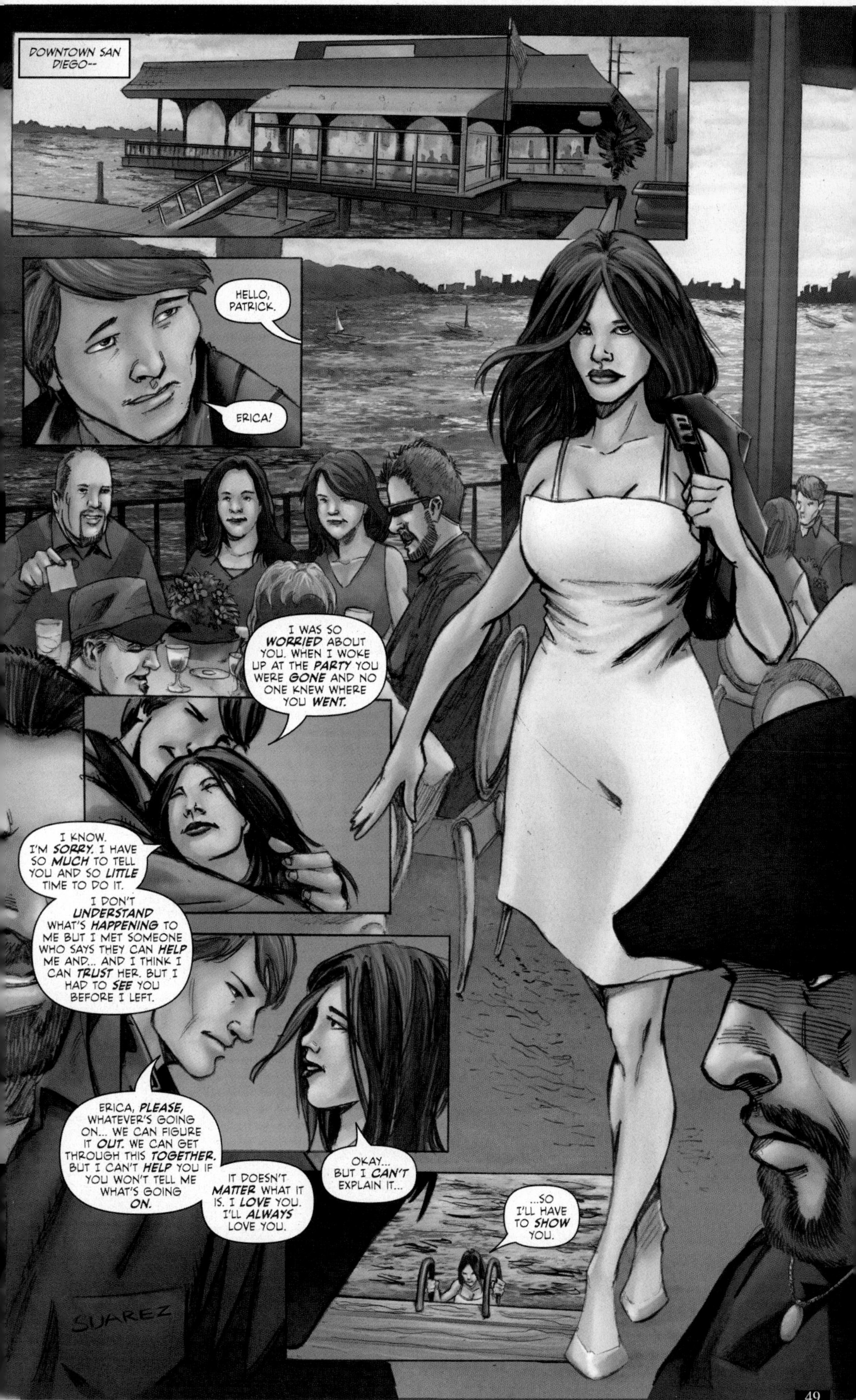
DOWNTOWN SAN DIEGO--
HELLO, PATRICK.
ERICA!
I WAS SO WORRIED ABOUT YOU. WHEN I WOKE UP AT THE PARTY YOU WERE GONE AND NO ONE KNEW WHERE YOU WENT.
I KNOW. I'M SORRY. I HAVE SO MUCH TO TELL YOU AND SO LITTLE TIME TO DO IT.
I DON'T UNDERSTAND WHAT'S HAPPENING TO ME BUT I MET SOMEONE WHO SAYS THEY CAN HELP ME AND... AND I THINK I CAN TRUST HER. BUT I HAD TO SEE YOU BEFORE I LEFT.
ERICA, PLEASE, WHATEVER'S GOING ON... WE CAN FIGURE IT OUT. WE CAN GET THROUGH THIS TOGETHER. BUT I CAN'T HELP YOU IF YOU WON'T TELL ME WHAT'S GOING ON.
IT DOESN'T MATTER WHAT IT IS. I LOVE YOU. I'LL ALWAYS LOVE YOU.
OKAY... BUT I CAN'T EXPLAIN IT...
...SO I'LL HAVE TO SHOW YOU.
SUAREZ

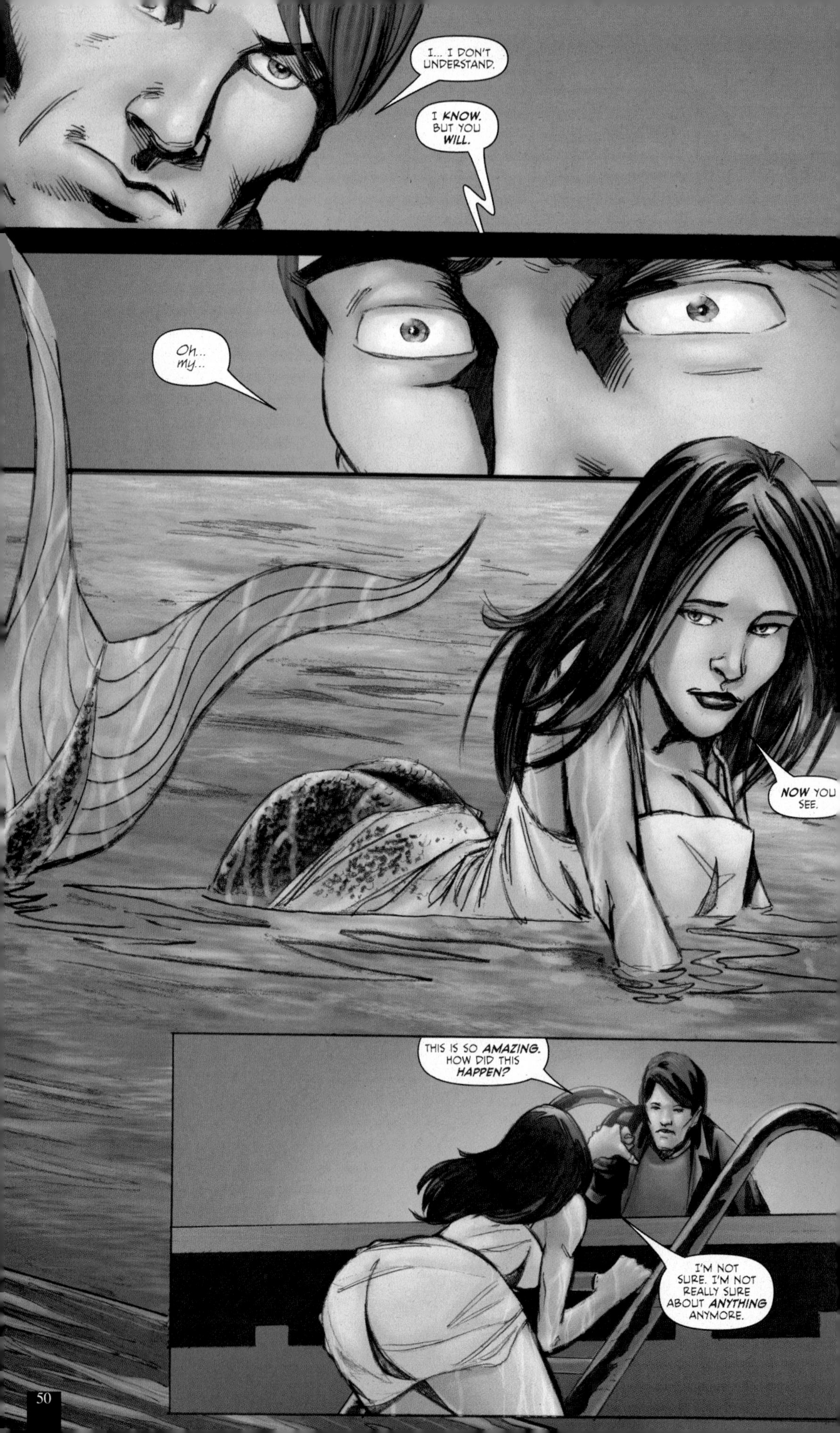
I... I DON'T UNDERSTAND.
I KNOW. BUT YOU WILL.
Oh... my...
NOW YOU SEE.
THIS IS SO AMAZING. HOW DID THIS HAPPEN?
I'M NOT SURE. I'M NOT REALLY SURE ABOUT ANYTHING ANYMORE.

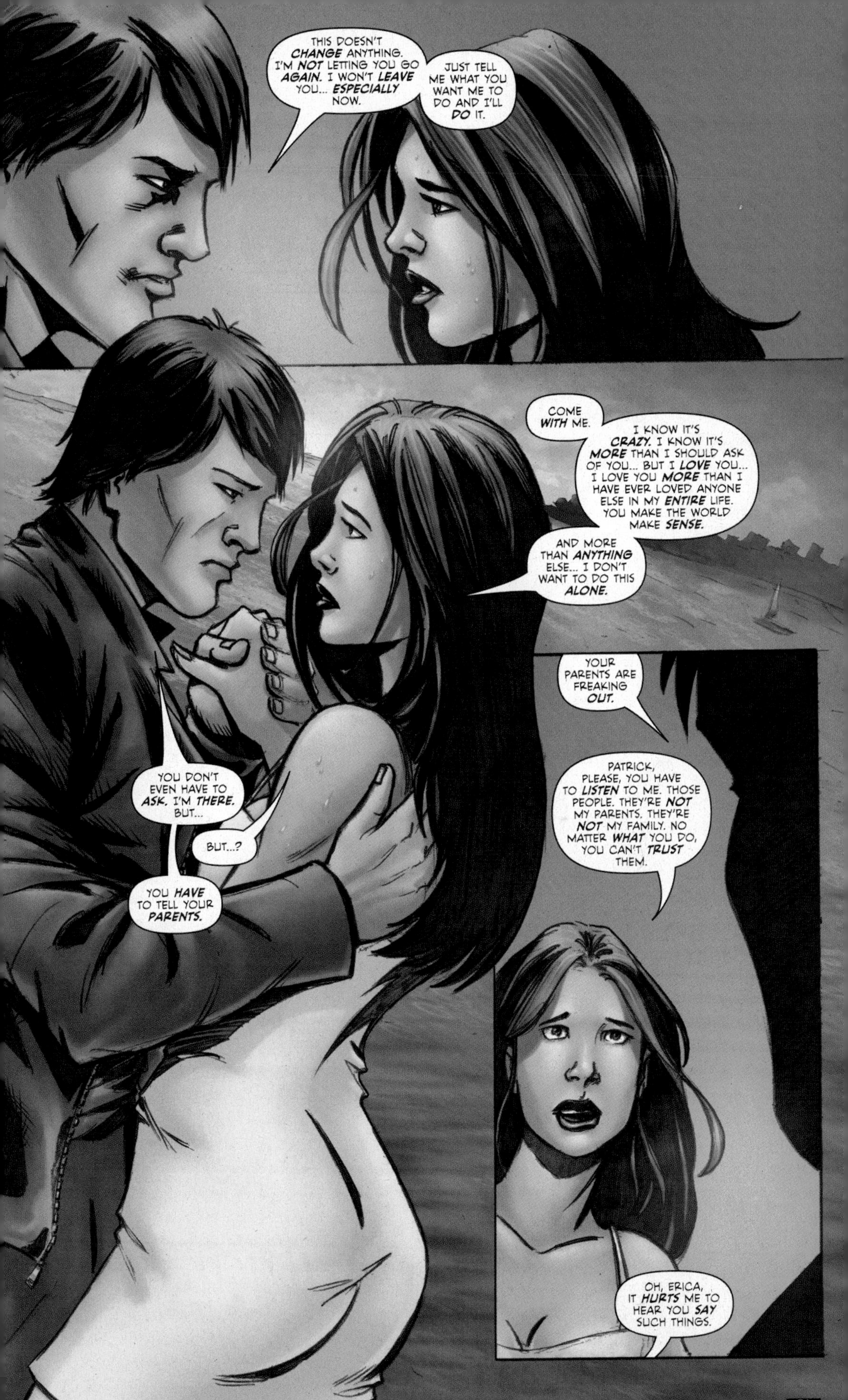
THIS DOESN'T CHANGE ANYTHING. I'M NOT LETTING YOU GO AGAIN. I WON'T LEAVE YOU... ESPECIALLY NOW.
JUST TELL ME WHAT YOU WANT ME TO DO AND I'LL DO IT.
COME WITH ME.
I KNOW IT'S CRAZY. I KNOW IT'S MORE THAN I SHOULD ASK OF YOU... BUT I LOVE YOU... I LOVE YOU MORE THAN I HAVE EVER LOVED ANYONE ELSE IN MY ENTIRE LIFE. YOU MAKE THE WORLD MAKE SENSE.
AND MORE THAN ANYTHING ELSE... I DON'T WANT TO DO THIS ALONE.
YOU DON'T EVEN HAVE TO ASK. I'M THERE. BUT...
BUT...?
YOU HAVE TO TELL YOUR PARENTS.
YOUR PARENTS ARE FREAKING OUT.
PATRICK, PLEASE, YOU HAVE TO LISTEN TO ME. THOSE PEOPLE. THEY'RE NOT MY PARENTS. THEY'RE NOT MY FAMILY. NO MATTER WHAT YOU DO, YOU CAN'T TRUST THEM.
OH, ERICA, IT HURTS ME TO HEAR YOU SAY SUCH THINGS.

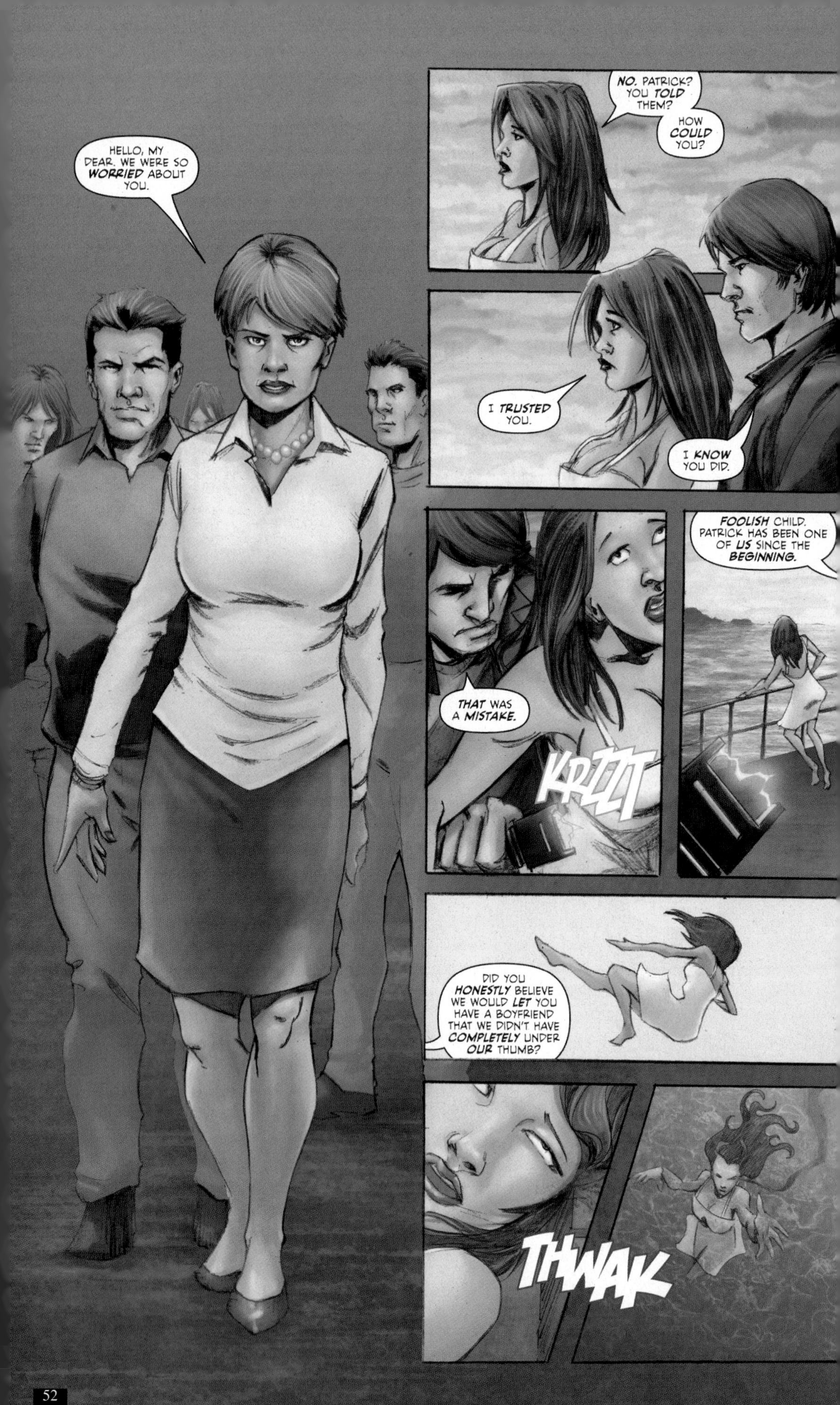

HELLO, MY DEAR. WE WERE SO WORRIED ABOUT YOU.
NO. PATRICK? YOU TOLD THEM?
HOW COULD YOU?
I TRUSTED YOU.
I KNOW YOU DID.
THAT WAS A MISTAKE.
KRZZZT
FOOLISH CHILD. PATRICK HAS BEEN ONE OF US SINCE THE BEGINNING.
DID YOU HONESTLY BELIEVE WE WOULD LET YOU HAVE A BOYFRIEND THAT WE DIDN'T HAVE COMPLETELY UNDER OUR THUMB?
THWAK

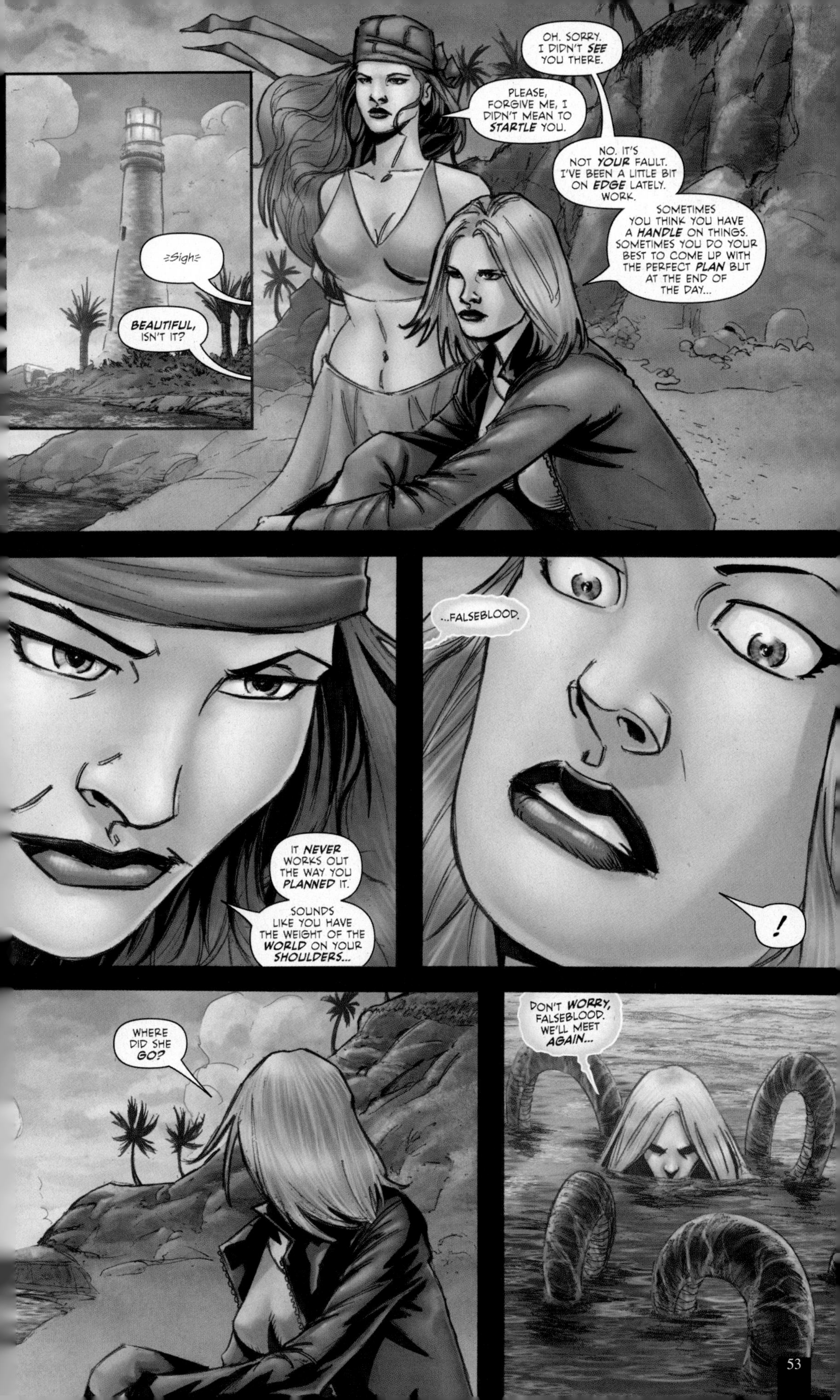

=Sigh=
BEAUTIFUL, ISN'T IT?
PLEASE, FORGIVE ME, I DIDN'T MEAN TO STARTLE YOU.
OH. SORRY. I DIDN'T SEE YOU THERE.
NO. IT'S NOT YOUR FAULT. I'VE BEEN A LITTLE BIT ON EDGE LATELY. WORK.
SOMETIMES YOU THINK YOU HAVE A HANDLE ON THINGS. SOMETIMES YOU DO YOUR BEST TO COME UP WITH THE PERFECT PLAN BUT AT THE END OF THE DAY...
IT NEVER WORKS OUT THE WAY YOU PLANNED IT.
SOUNDS LIKE YOU HAVE THE WEIGHT OF THE WORLD ON YOUR SHOULDERS...
...FALSEBLOOD.
!
WHERE DID SHE GO?
DON'T WORRY, FALSEBLOOD. WE'LL MEET AGAIN...

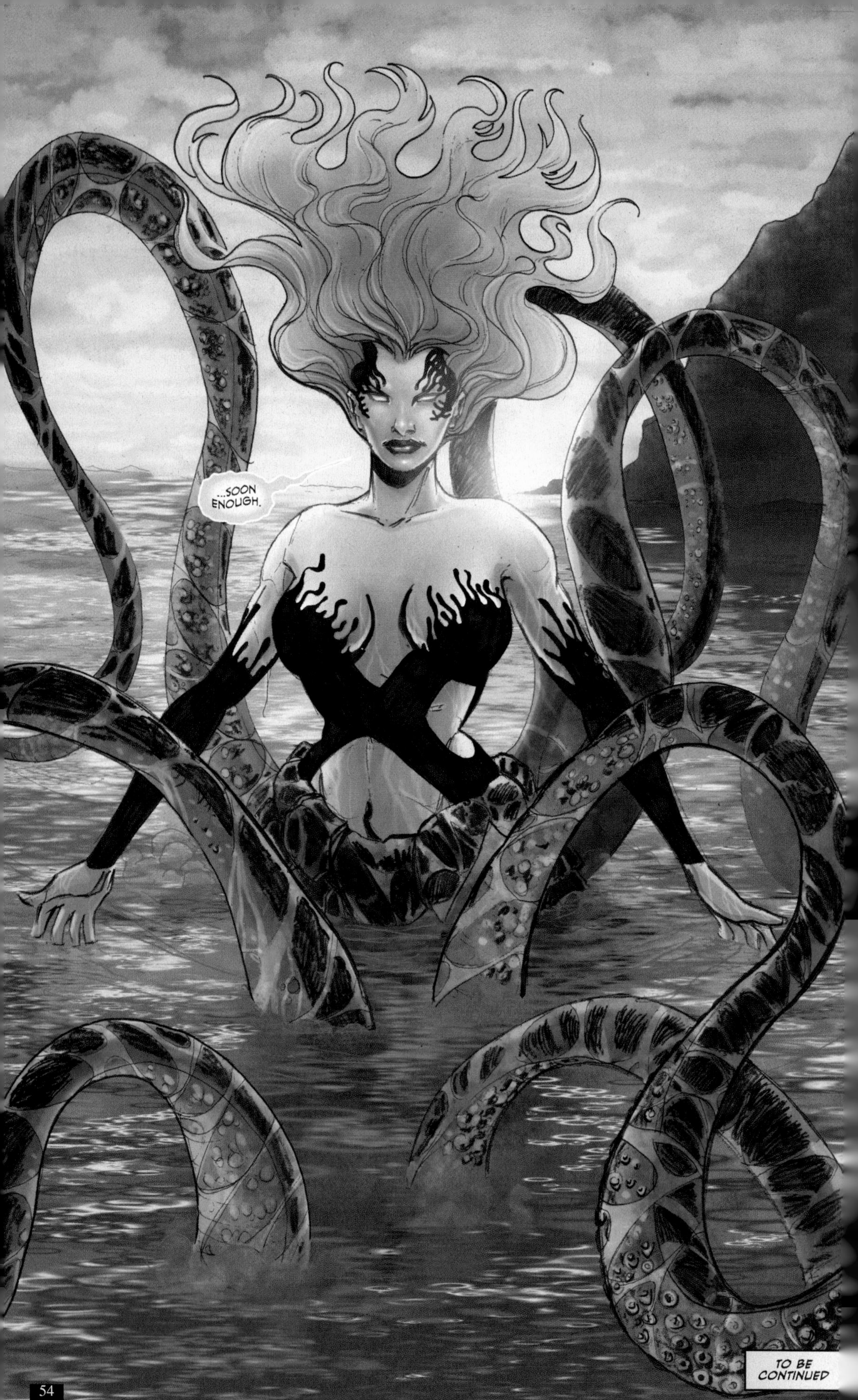
...SOON ENOUGH.
TO BE CONTINUED

Grimm Fairy Tales
Myths & Legends

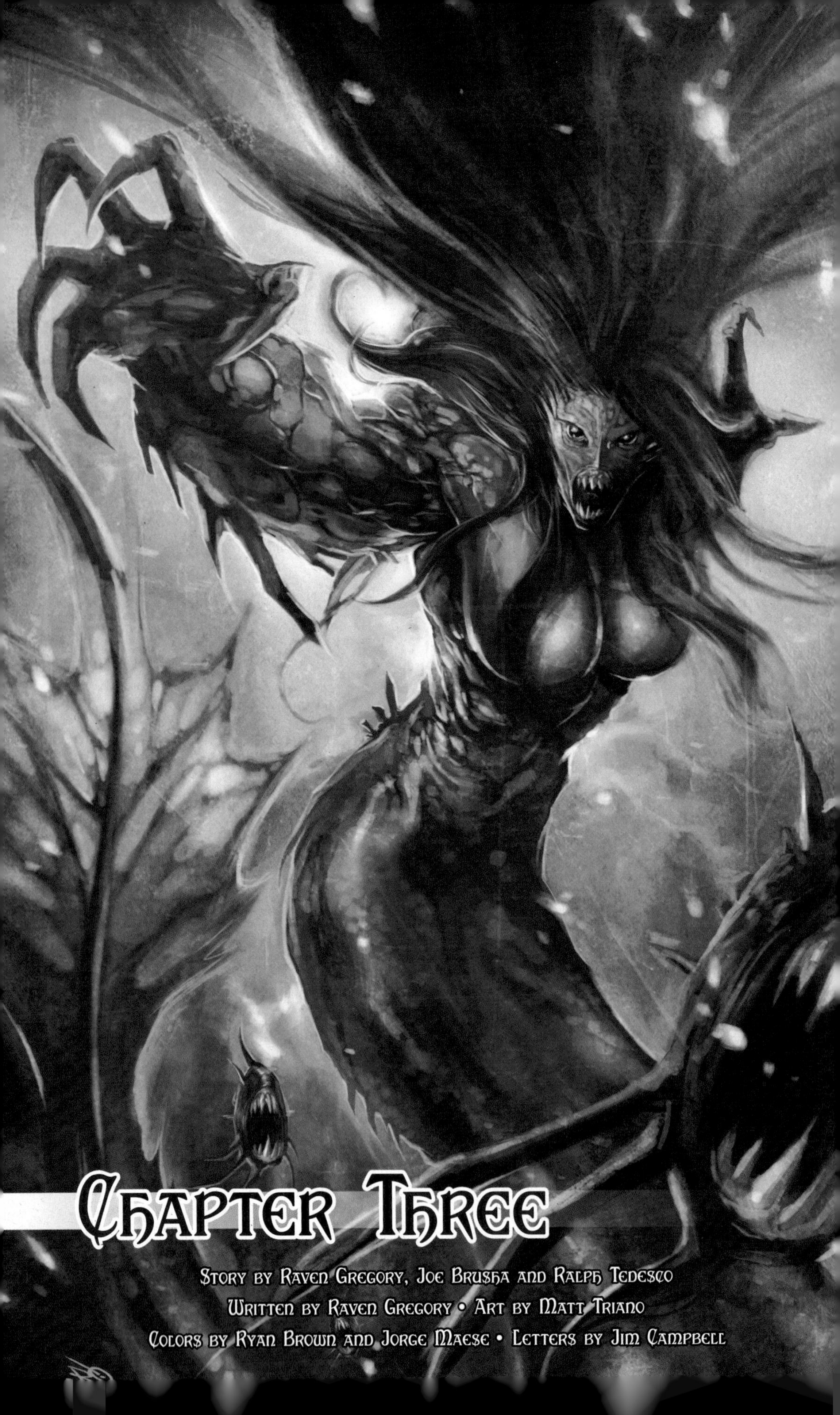

Chapter Three

Story by Raven Gregory, Joe Brusha and Ralph Tedesco
Written by Raven Gregory • Art by Matt Triano
Colors by Ryan Brown and Jorge Maese • Letters by Jim Campbell

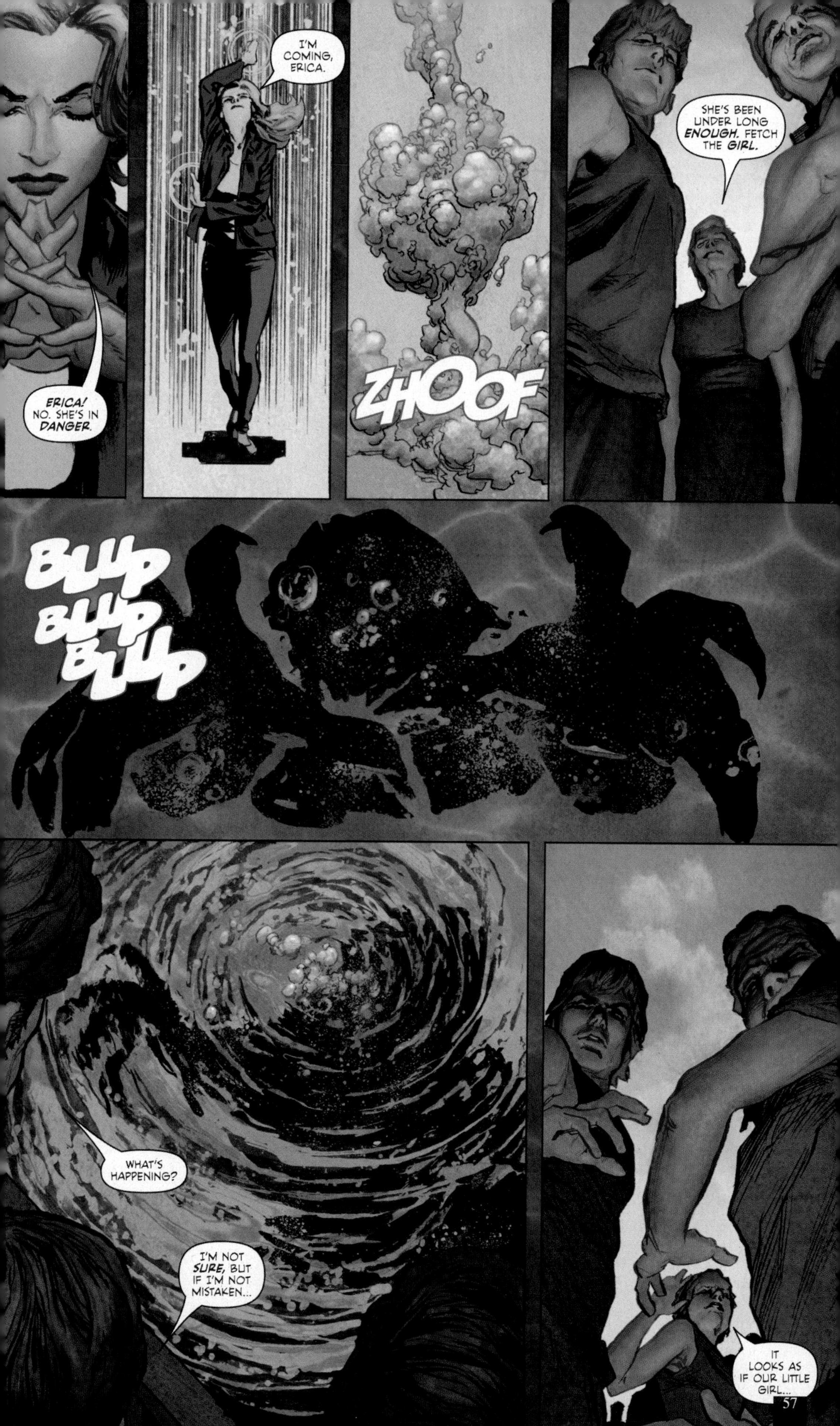
ERICA! NO. SHE'S IN DANGER.
I'M COMING, ERICA.
ZHOOF
SHE'S BEEN UNDER LONG ENOUGH. FETCH THE GIRL.
BLUP BLUP BLUP
WHAT'S HAPPENING?
I'M NOT SURE, BUT IF I'M NOT MISTAKEN...
IT LOOKS AS IF OUR LITTLE GIRL...

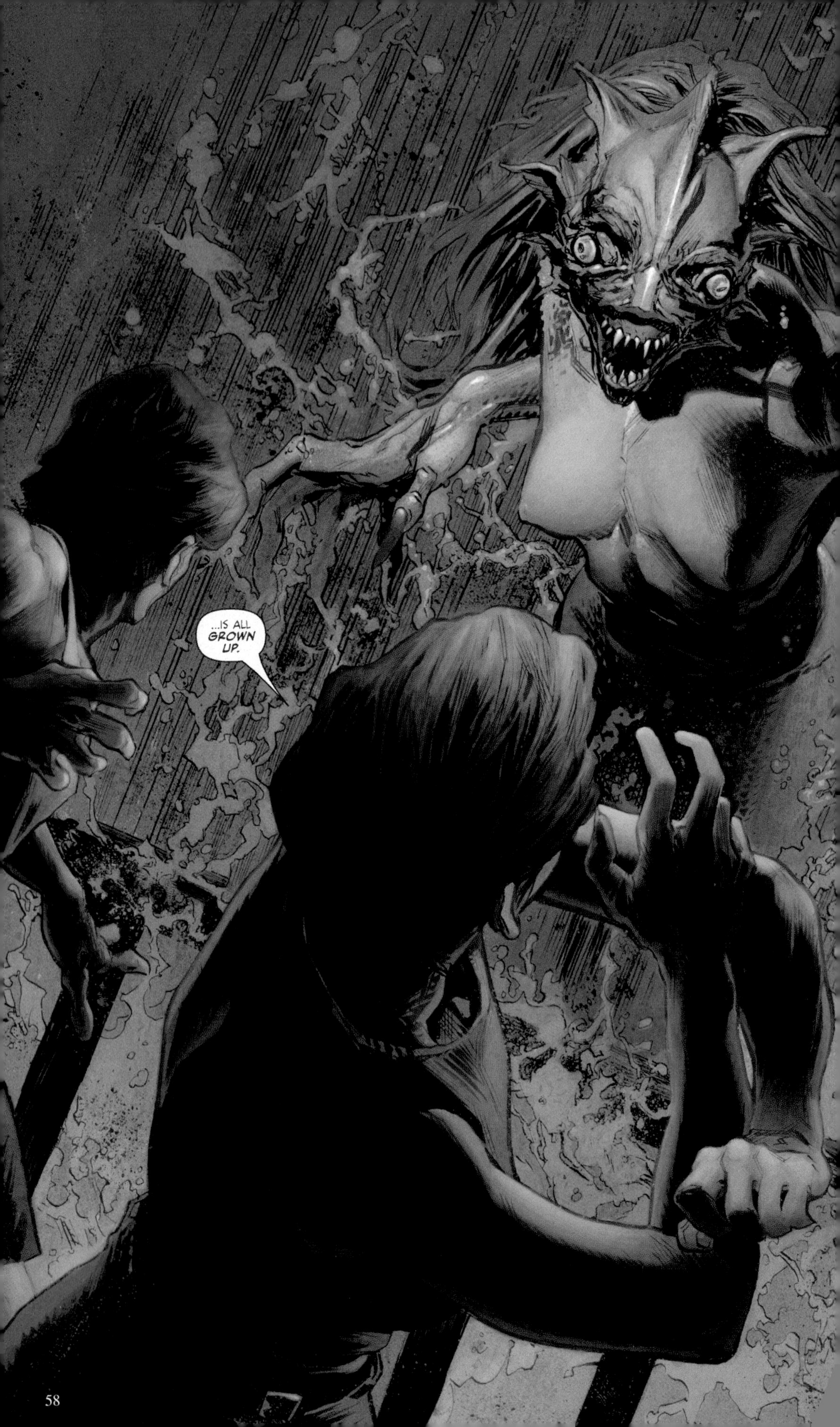
...IS ALL GROWN UP.

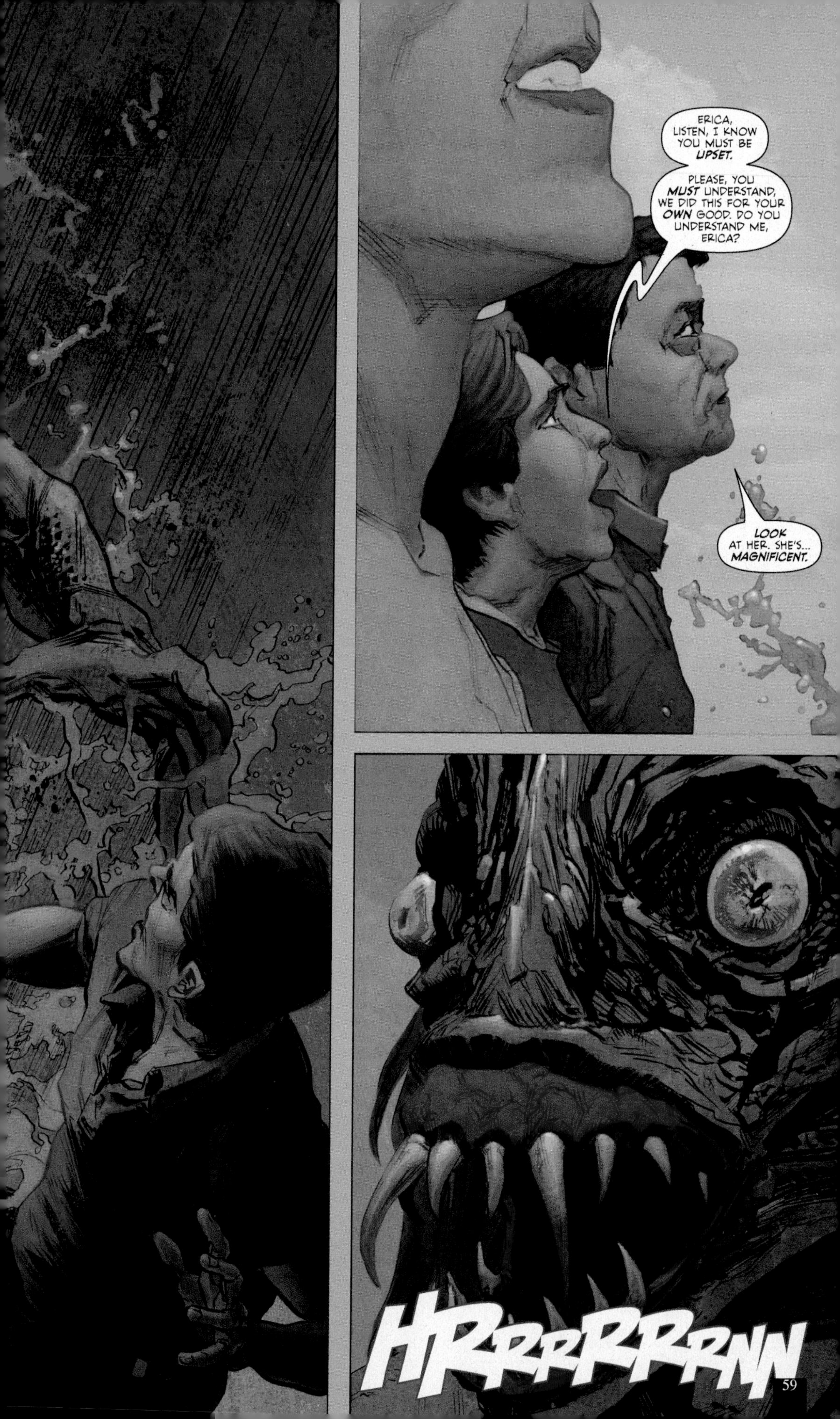
ERICA, LISTEN, I KNOW YOU MUST BE UPSET.
PLEASE, YOU MUST UNDERSTAND, WE DID THIS FOR YOUR OWN GOOD. DO YOU UNDERSTAND ME, ERICA?
LOOK AT HER. SHE'S... MAGNIFICENT.
HRRRRRRNN

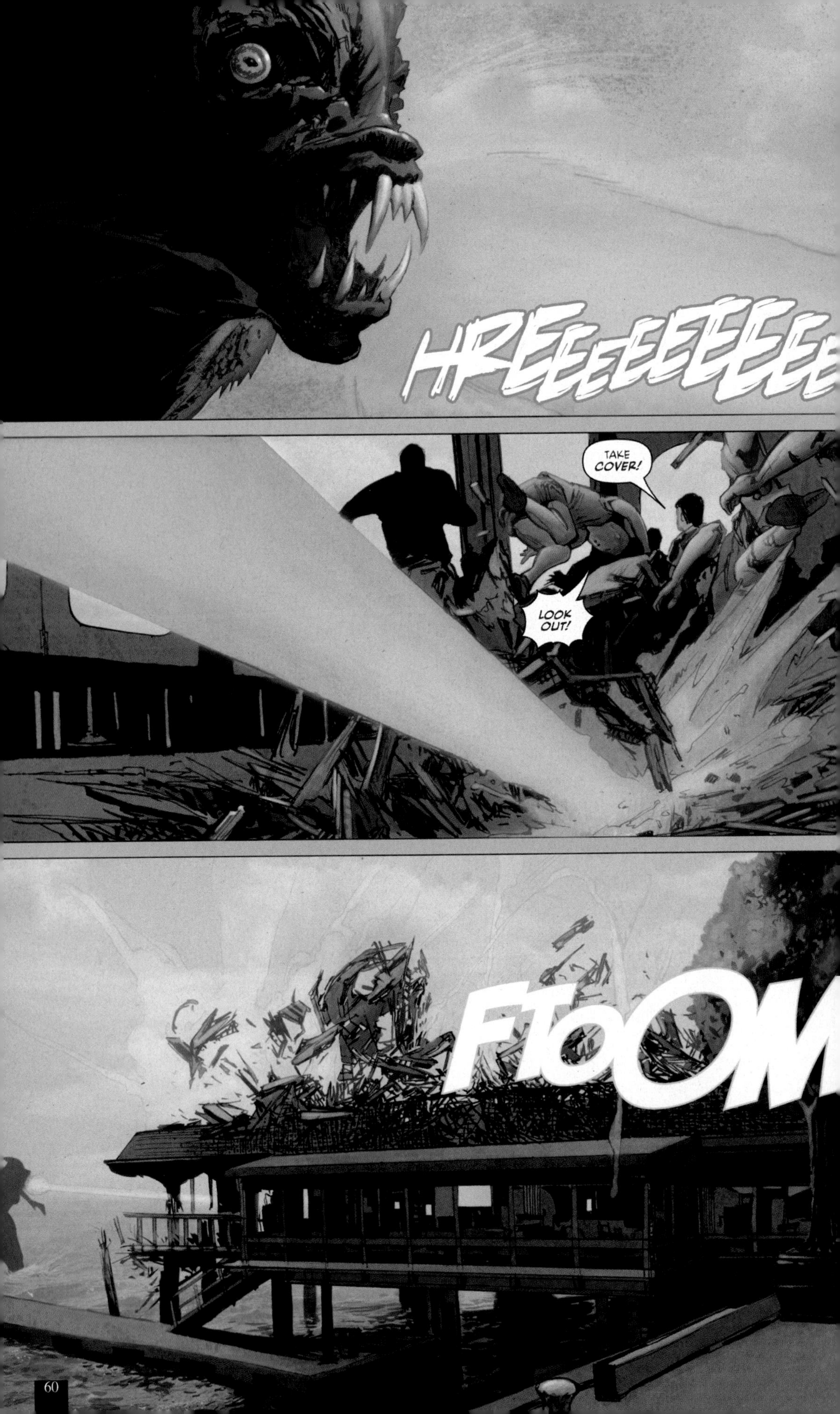
HREEEEEEEEEEE
TAKE COVER!
LOOK OUT!
FTOOM

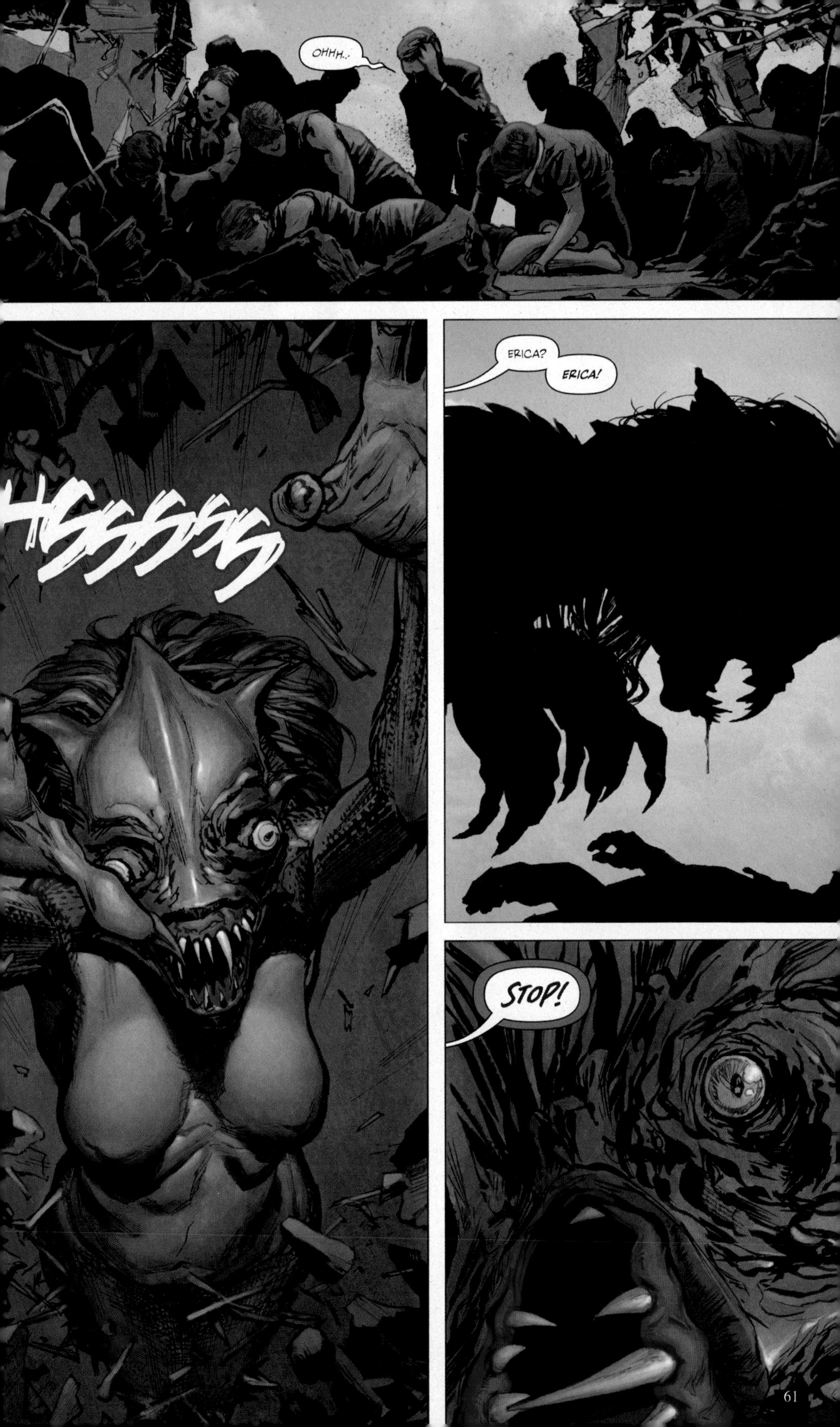
OHHH...
HSSSSS
ERICA?
ERICA!
STOP!

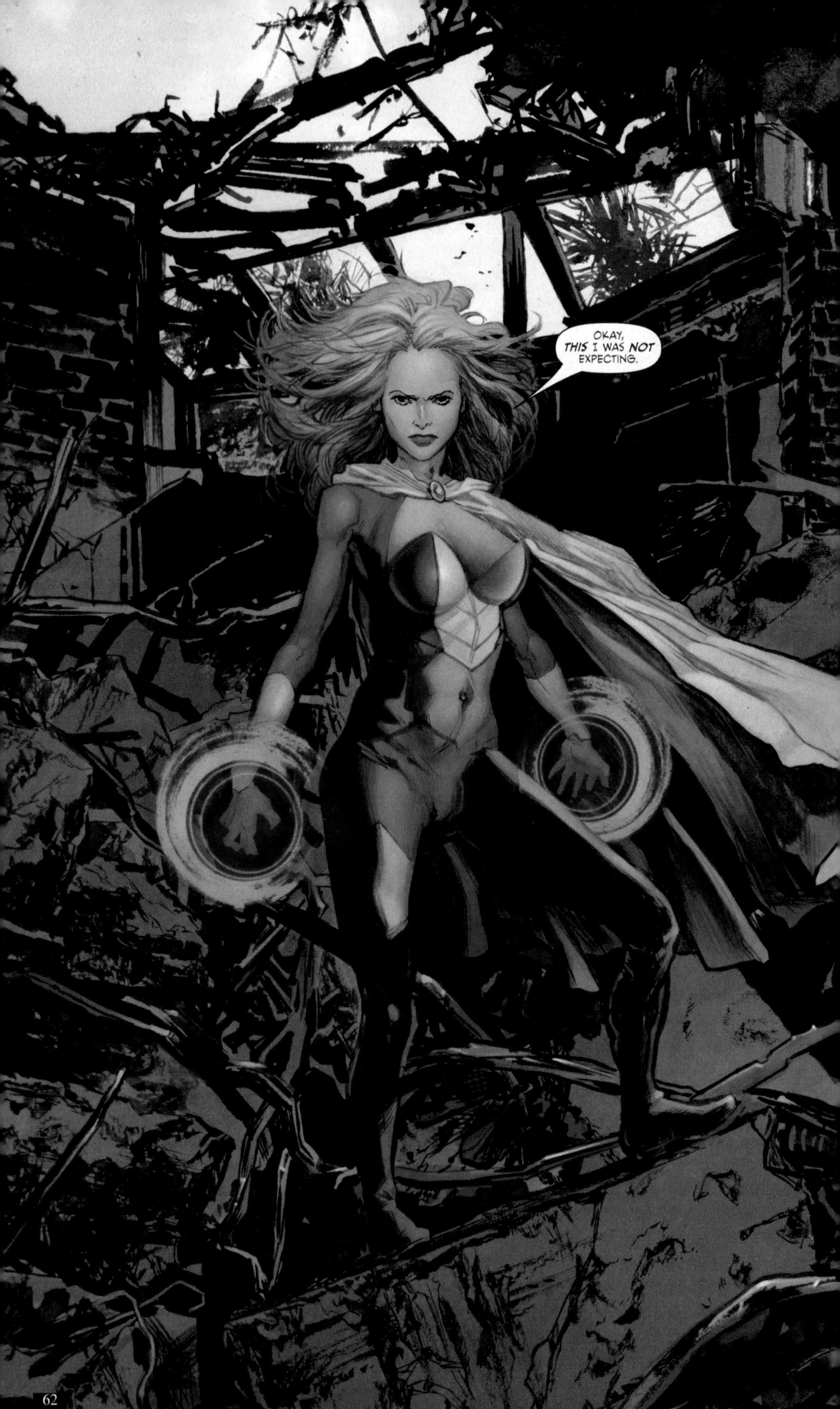
OKAY, THIS I WAS NOT EXPECTING.

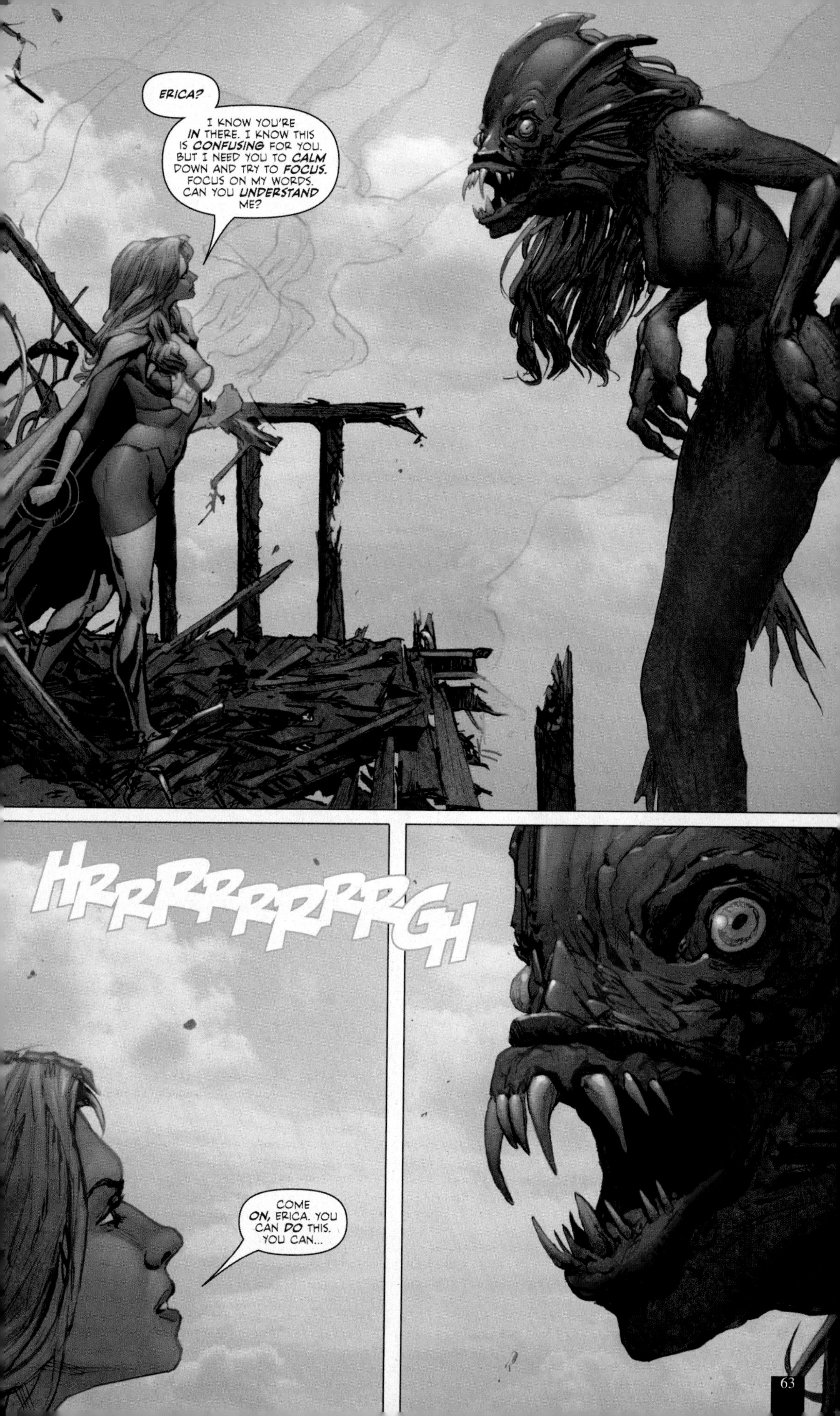
ERICA?
I KNOW YOU'RE IN THERE. I KNOW THIS IS CONFUSING FOR YOU. BUT I NEED YOU TO CALM DOWN AND TRY TO FOCUS. FOCUS ON MY WORDS. CAN YOU UNDERSTAND ME?
HRRRRRRRRGH
COME ON, ERICA. YOU CAN DO THIS. YOU CAN...

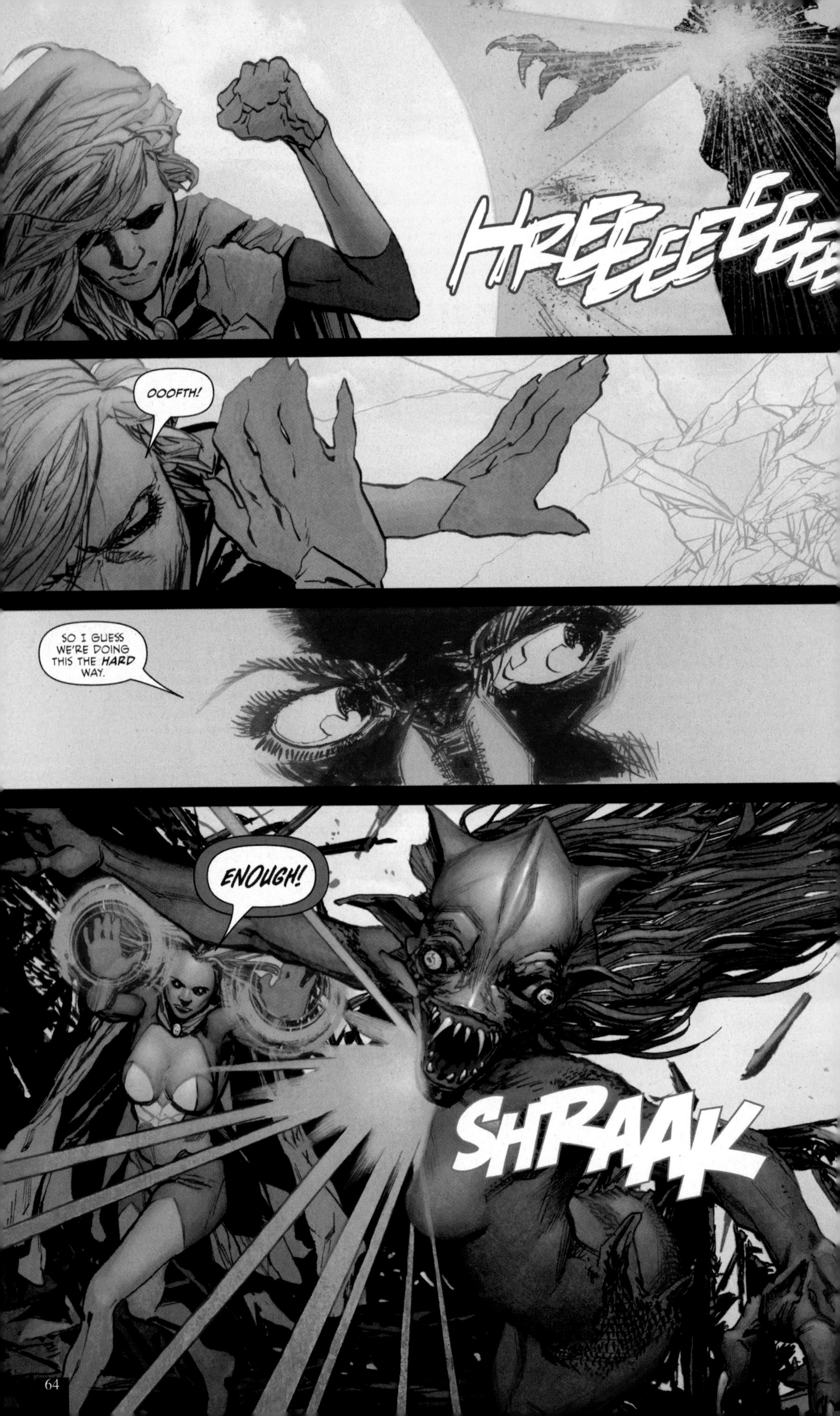
HREEEEEEEEEE
OOOFTH!
SO I GUESS WE'RE DOING THIS THE HARD WAY.
ENOUGH!
SHRAAK

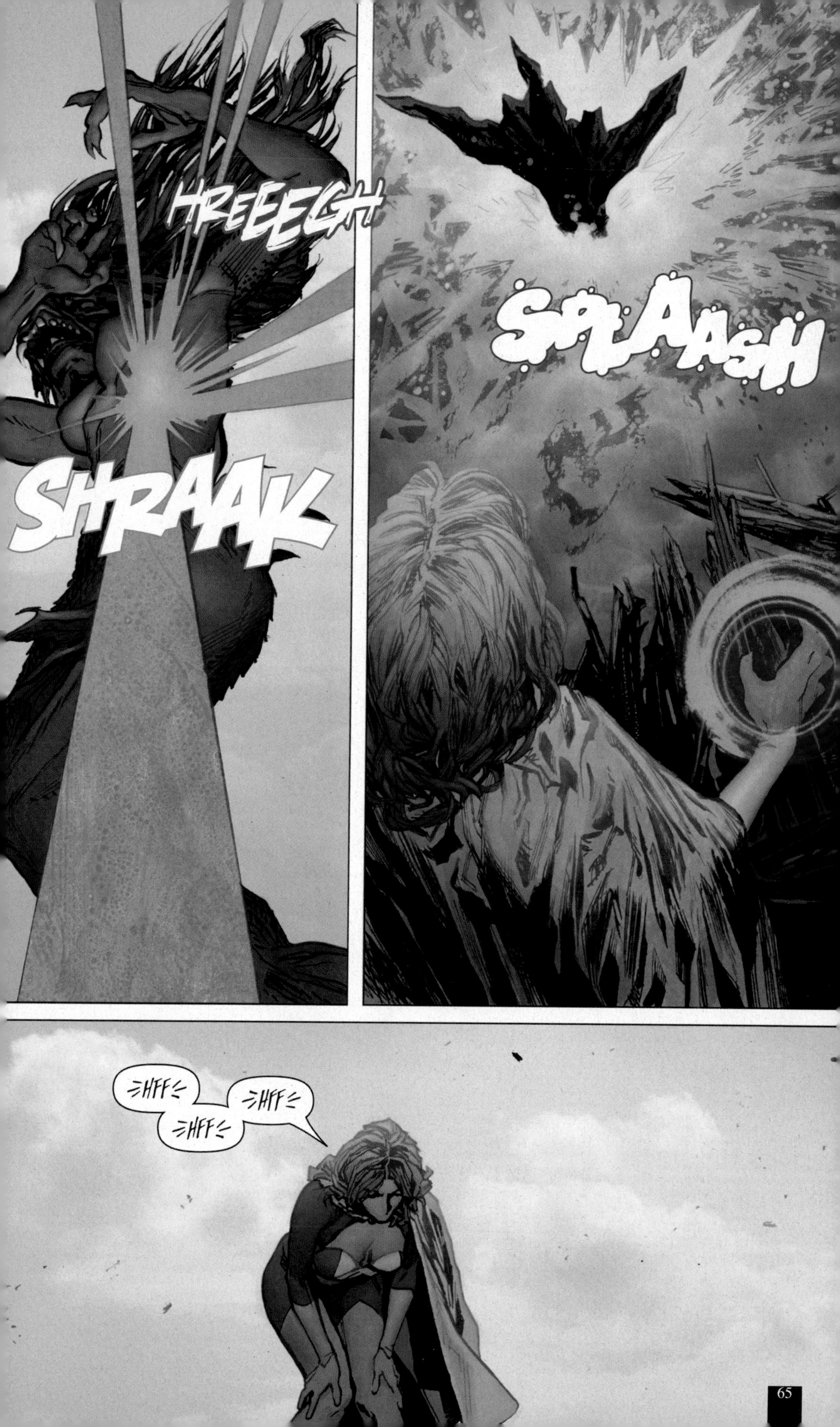
HREEEGH
SHRAAK
SPLAASH
HFF
HFF
HFF

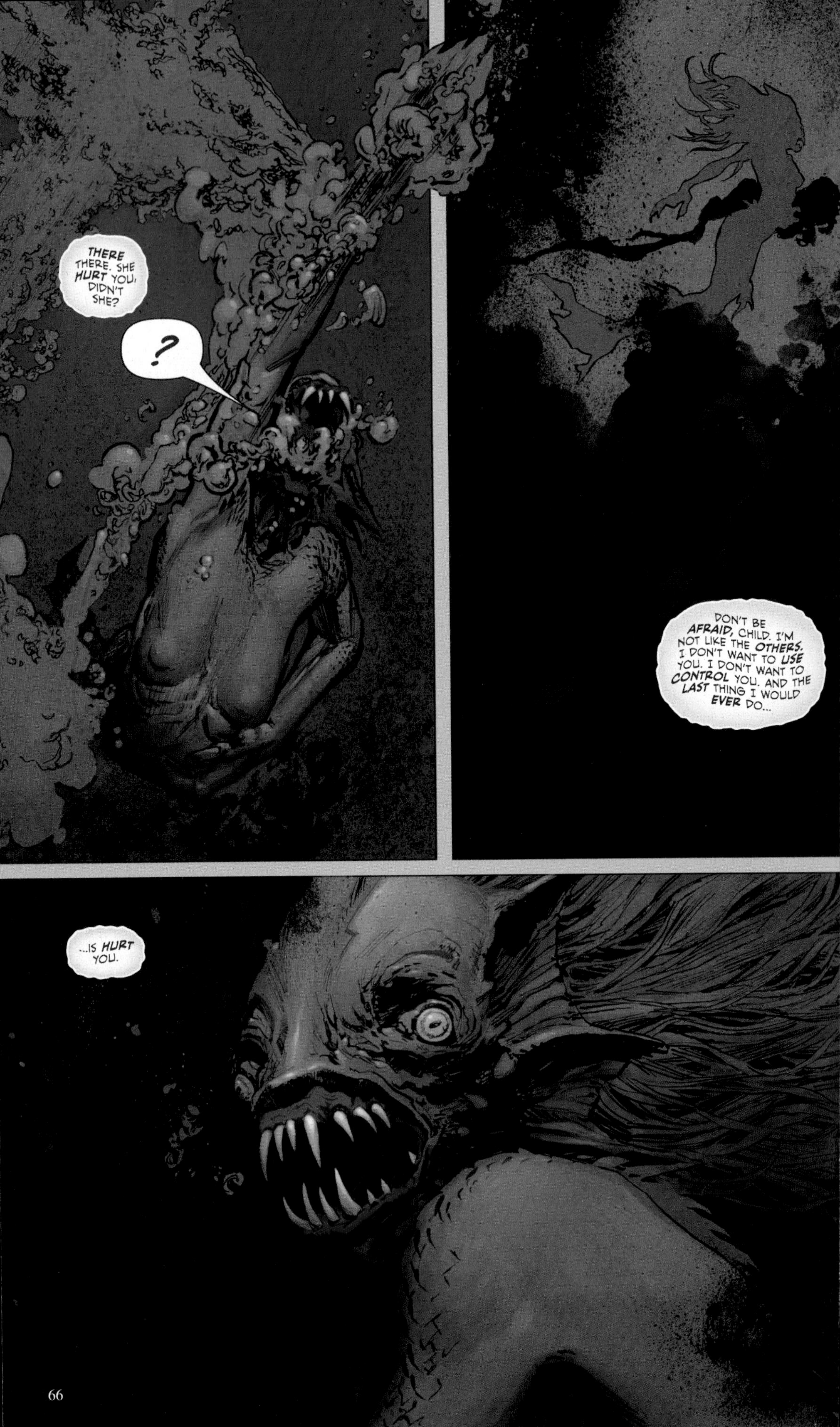
THERE THERE. SHE HURT YOU, DIDN'T SHE?
?
DON'T BE AFRAID, CHILD. I'M NOT LIKE THE OTHERS. I DON'T WANT TO USE YOU. I DON'T WANT TO CONTROL YOU. AND THE LAST THING I WOULD EVER DO...
...IS HURT YOU.

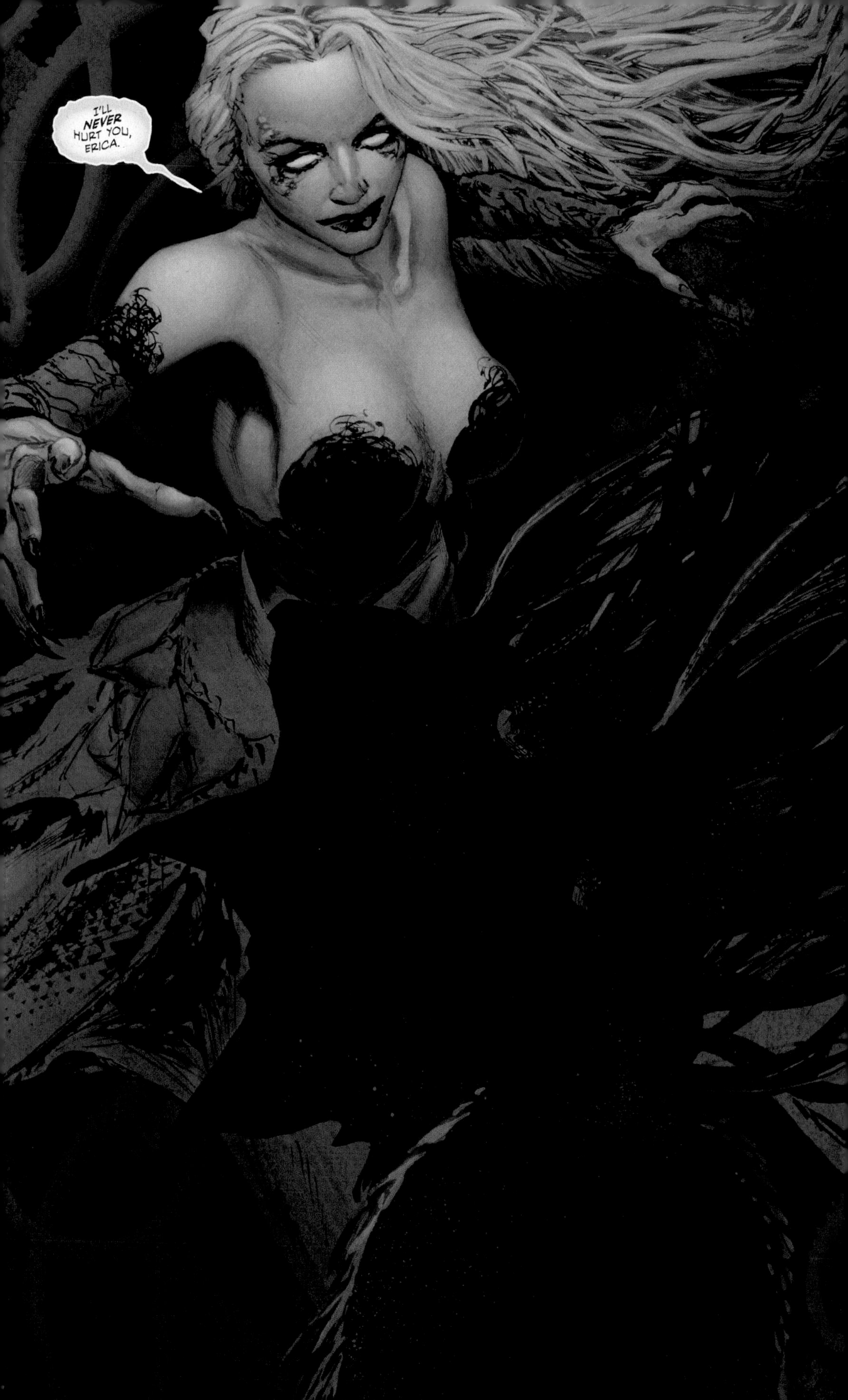
I'LL NEVER HURT YOU, ERICA.

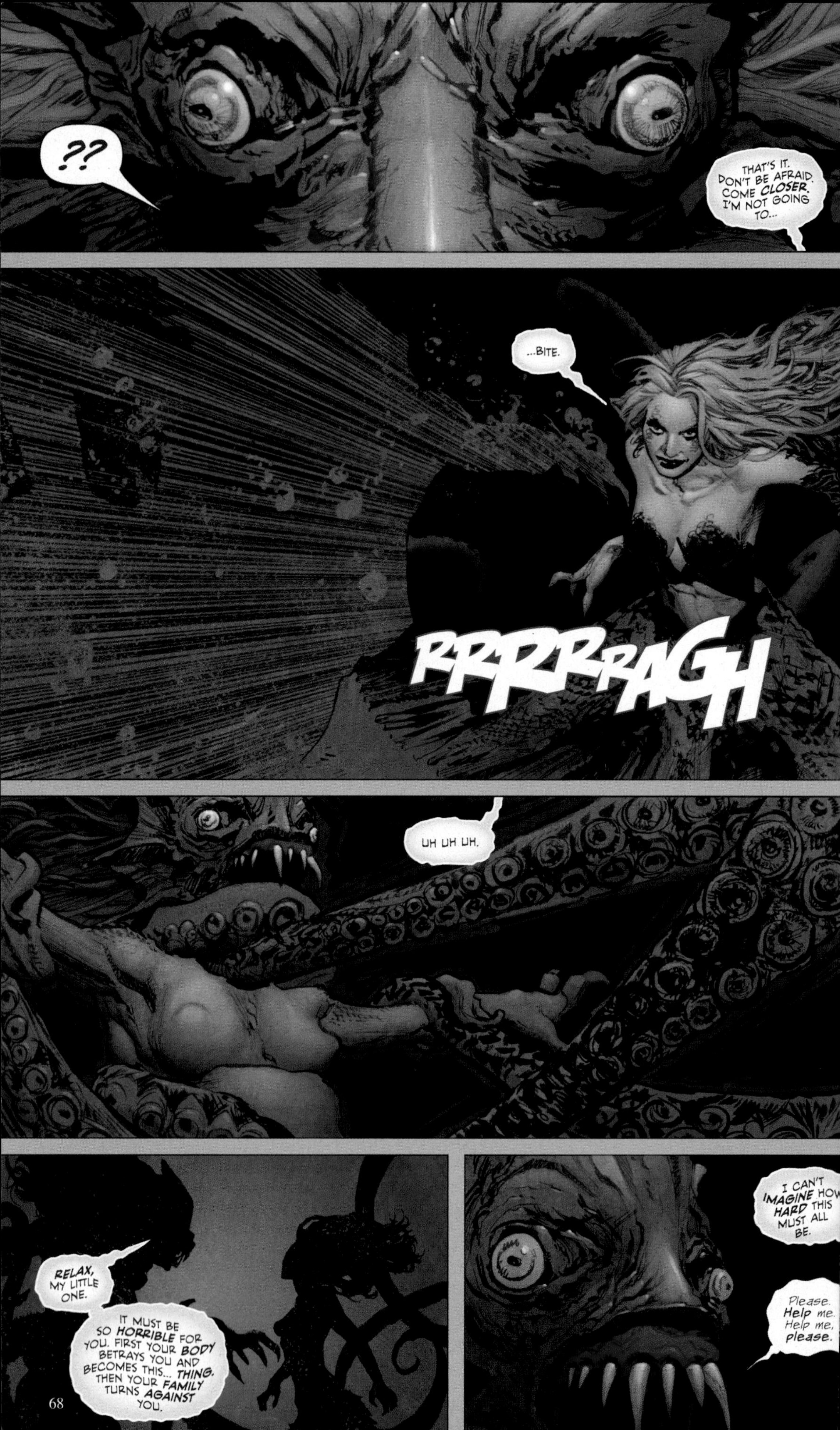
??
THAT'S IT. DON'T BE AFRAID. COME CLOSER. I'M NOT GOING TO...
...BITE.
RRRRRAGH
UH UH UH.
RELAX, MY LITTLE ONE.
IT MUST BE SO HORRIBLE FOR YOU. FIRST YOUR BODY BETRAYS YOU AND BECOMES THIS... THING. THEN YOUR FAMILY TURNS AGAINST YOU.
I CAN'T IMAGINE HOW HARD THIS MUST ALL BE.
Please. Help me. Help me, please.

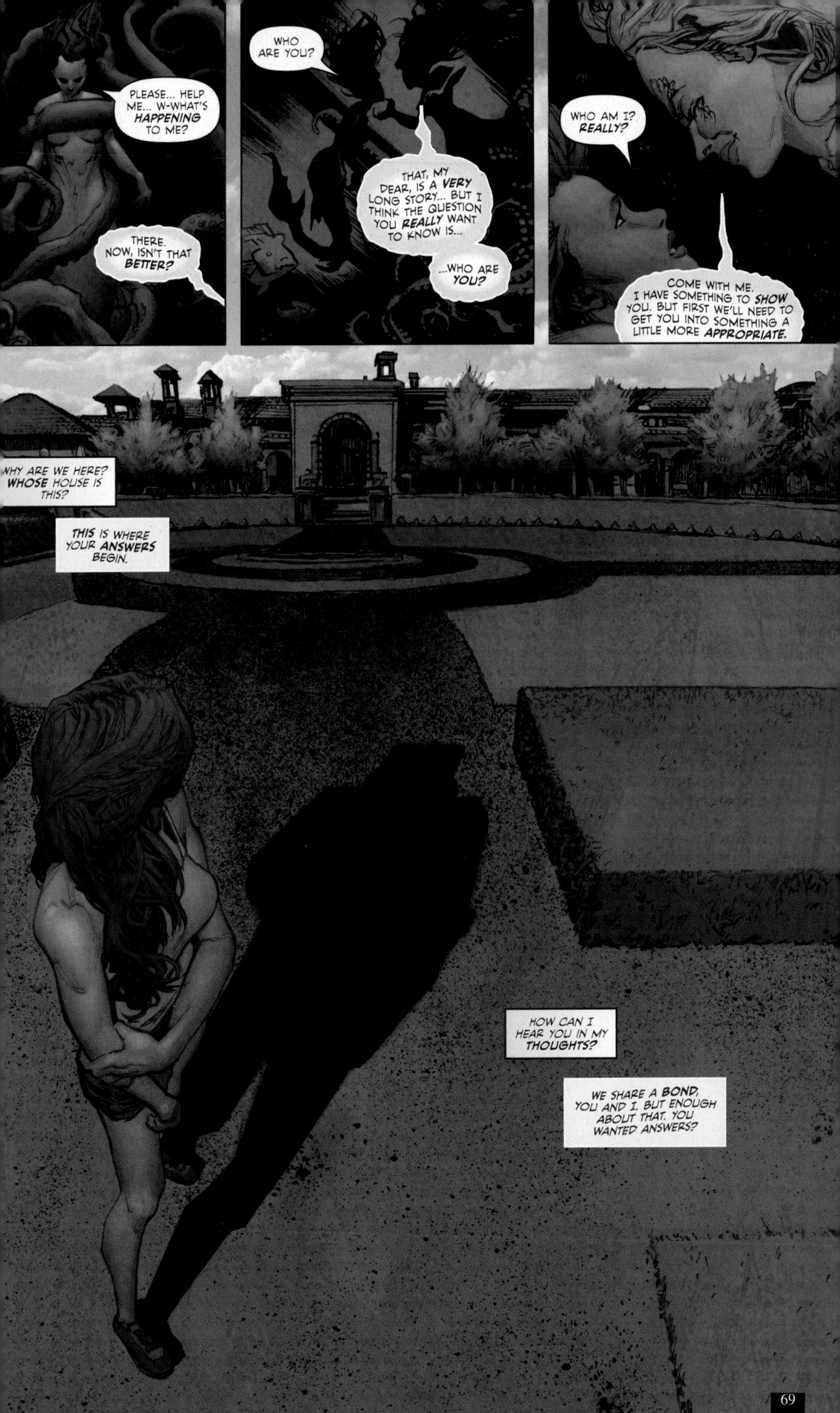
PLEASE... HELP ME... W-WHAT'S HAPPENING TO ME?
THERE. NOW, ISN'T THAT BETTER?
WHO ARE YOU?
THAT, MY DEAR, IS A VERY LONG STORY... BUT I THINK THE QUESTION YOU REALLY WANT TO KNOW IS...
...WHO ARE YOU?
WHO AM I? REALLY?
COME WITH ME. I HAVE SOMETHING TO SHOW YOU. BUT FIRST WE'LL NEED TO GET YOU INTO SOMETHING A LITTLE MORE APPROPRIATE.
WHY ARE WE HERE? WHOSE HOUSE IS THIS?
THIS IS WHERE YOUR ANSWERS BEGIN.
HOW CAN I HEAR YOU IN MY THOUGHTS?
WE SHARE A BOND, YOU AND I. BUT ENOUGH ABOUT THAT. YOU WANTED ANSWERS?

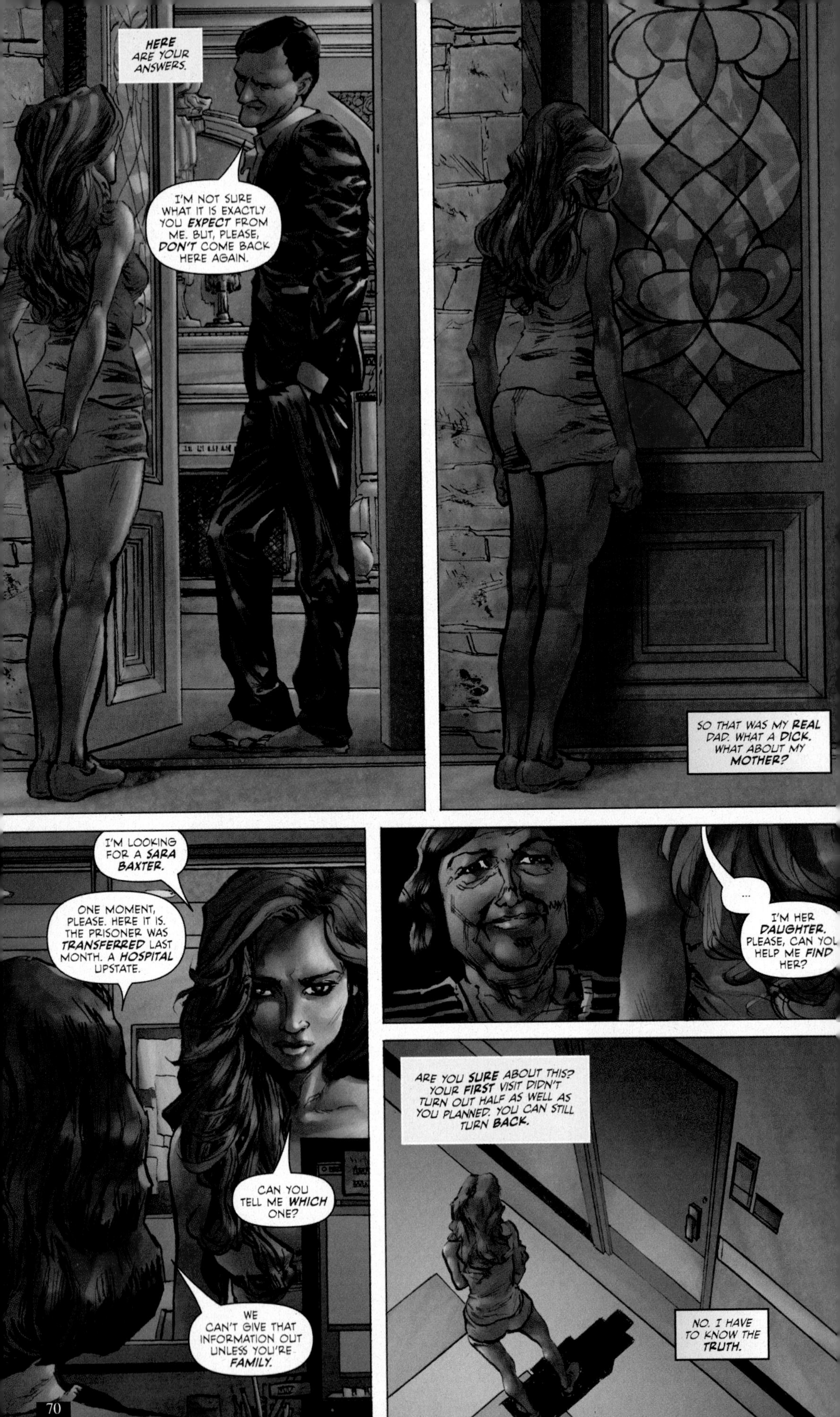
HERE ARE YOUR ANSWERS.
I'M NOT SURE WHAT IT IS EXACTLY YOU EXPECT FROM ME. BUT, PLEASE, DON'T COME BACK HERE AGAIN.
SO THAT WAS MY REAL DAD. WHAT A DICK. WHAT ABOUT MY MOTHER?
I'M LOOKING FOR A SARA BAXTER.
ONE MOMENT, PLEASE. HERE IT IS. THE PRISONER WAS TRANSFERRED LAST MONTH. A HOSPITAL UPSTATE.
CAN YOU TELL ME WHICH ONE?
WE CAN'T GIVE THAT INFORMATION OUT UNLESS YOU'RE FAMILY.
...
I'M HER DAUGHTER. PLEASE, CAN YOU HELP ME FIND HER?
ARE YOU SURE ABOUT THIS? YOUR FIRST VISIT DIDN'T TURN OUT HALF AS WELL AS YOU PLANNED. YOU CAN STILL TURN BACK.
NO. I HAVE TO KNOW THE TRUTH.

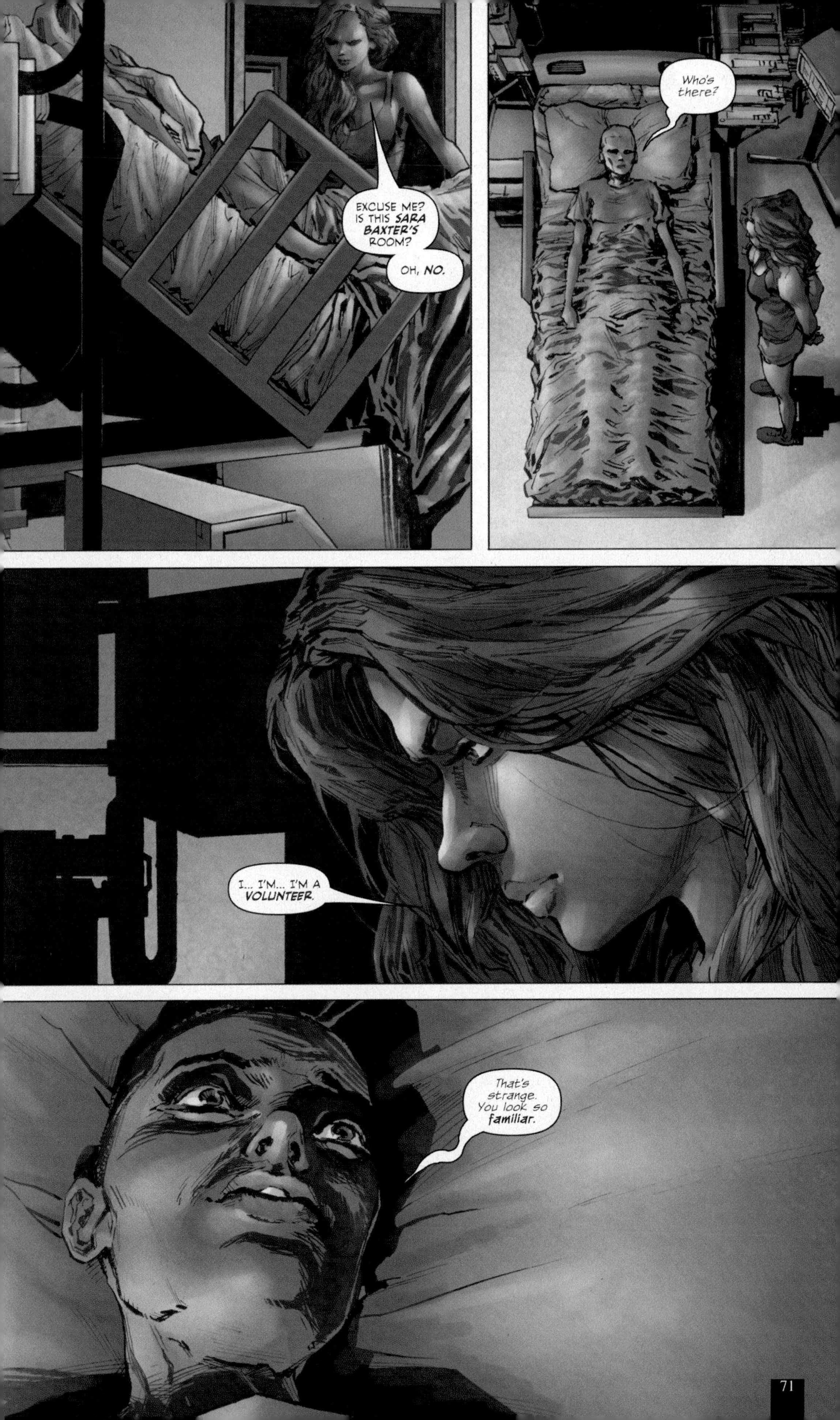
EXCUSE ME? IS THIS SARA BAXTER'S ROOM?
OH, NO.
Who's there?
I... I'M... I'M A VOLUNTEER.
That's strange. You look so familiar.

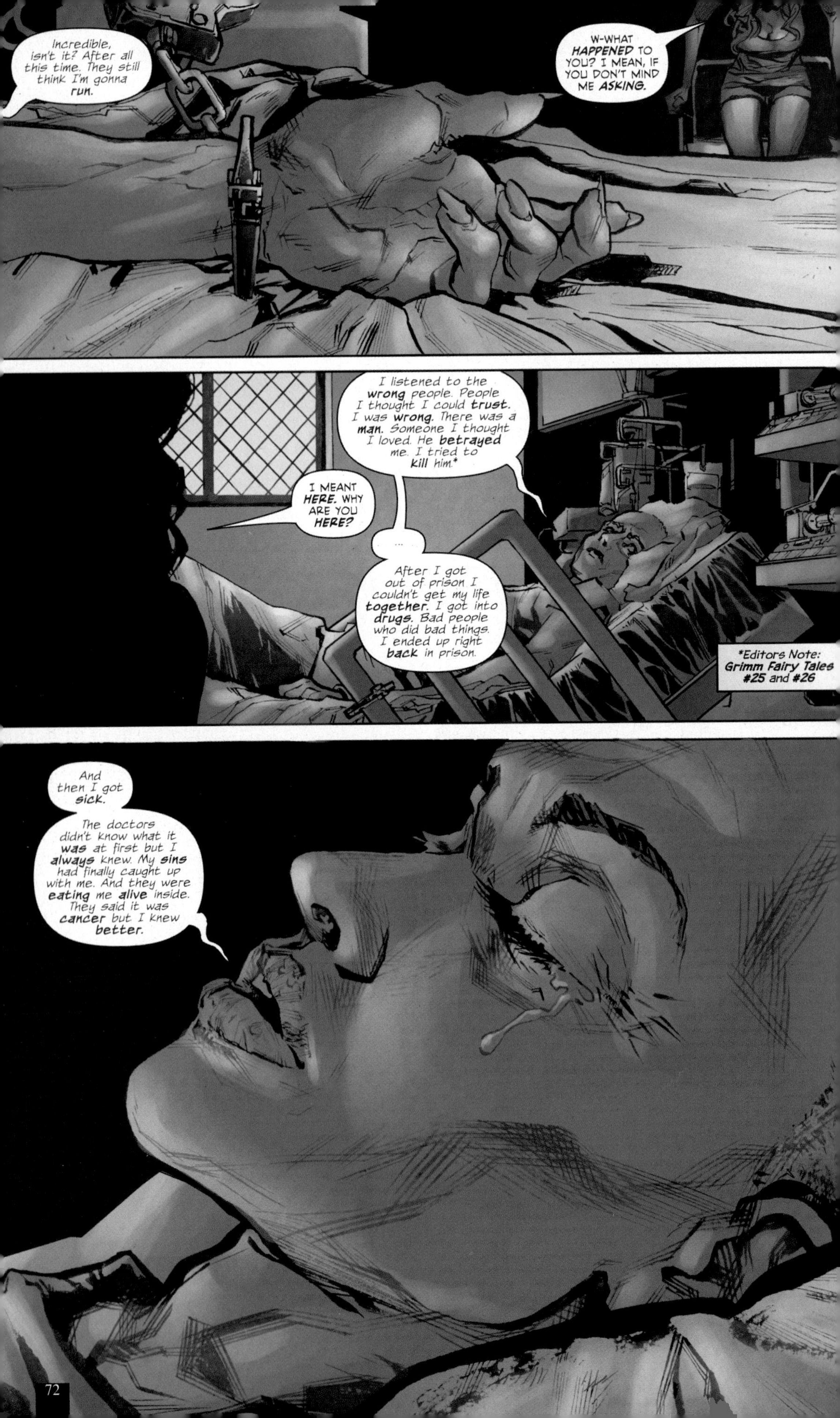

Incredible, isn't it? After all this time. They still think I'm gonna run.
W-WHAT HAPPENED TO YOU? I MEAN, IF YOU DON'T MIND ME ASKING.
I listened to the wrong people. People I thought I could trust. I was wrong. There was a man. Someone I thought I loved. He betrayed me. I tried to kill him.*
I MEANT HERE. WHY ARE YOU HERE?
...
After I got out of prison I couldn't get my life together. I got into drugs. Bad people who did bad things. I ended up right back in prison.
*Editors Note: Grimm Fairy Tales #25 and #26
And then I got sick.
The doctors didn't know what it was at first but I always knew. My sins had finally caught up with me. And they were eating me alive inside. They said it was cancer but I knew better.

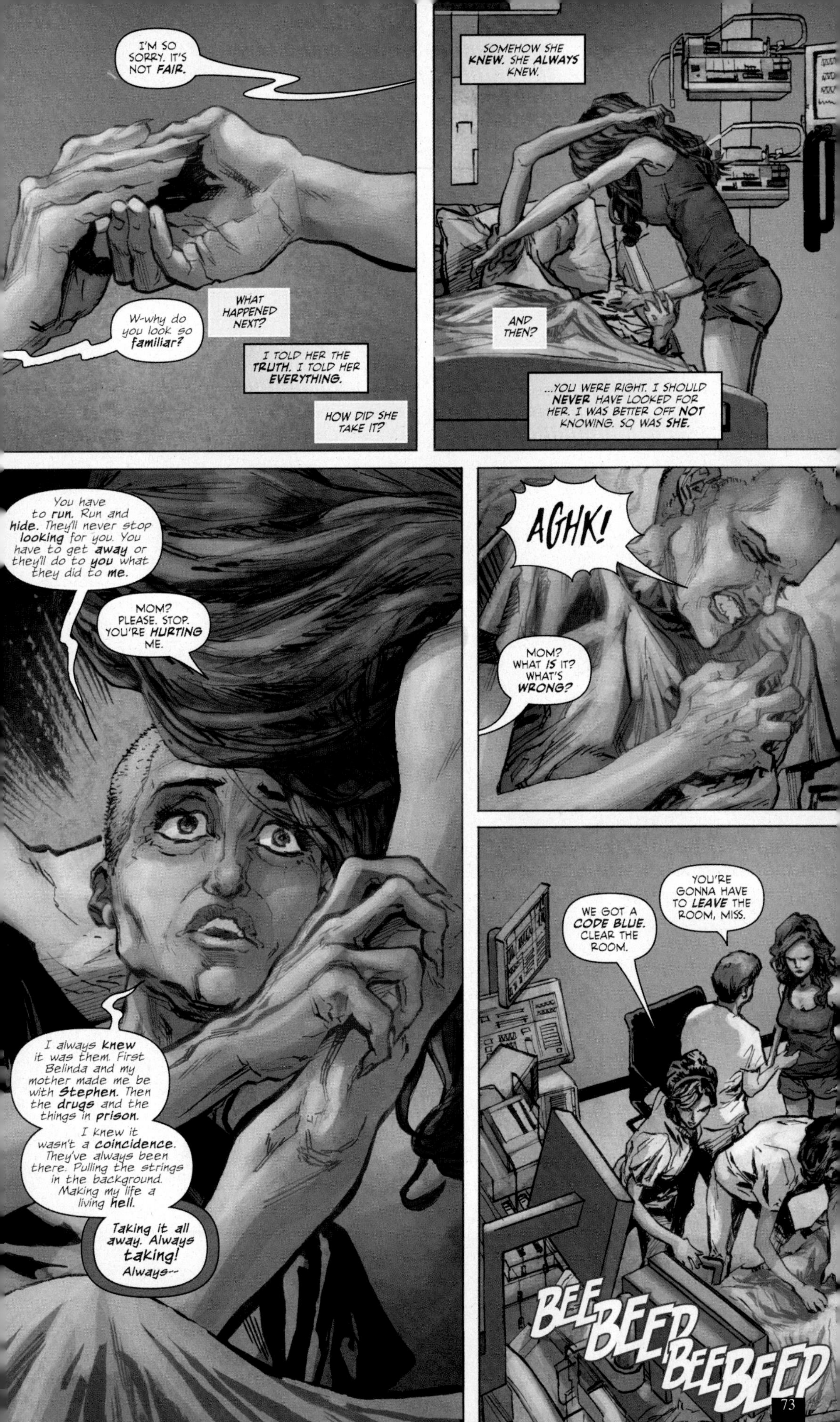
I'M SO SORRY. IT'S NOT FAIR.
W-why do you look so familiar?
WHAT HAPPENED NEXT?
I TOLD HER THE TRUTH. I TOLD HER EVERYTHING.
HOW DID SHE TAKE IT?
SOMEHOW SHE KNEW. SHE ALWAYS KNEW.
AND THEN?
...YOU WERE RIGHT. I SHOULD NEVER HAVE LOOKED FOR HER. I WAS BETTER OFF NOT KNOWING. SO WAS SHE.
You have to run. Run and hide. They'll never stop looking for you. You have to get away or they'll do to you what they did to me.
MOM? PLEASE. STOP. YOU'RE HURTING ME.
I always knew it was them. First Belinda and my mother made me be with Stephen. Then the drugs and the things in prison.
I knew it wasn't a coincidence. They've always been there. Pulling the strings in the background. Making my life a living hell.
Taking it all away. Always taking! Always--
AGHK!
MOM? WHAT IS IT? WHAT'S WRONG?
WE GOT A CODE BLUE. CLEAR THE ROOM.
YOU'RE GONNA HAVE TO LEAVE THE ROOM, MISS.
BEEBEEP BEEBEEP

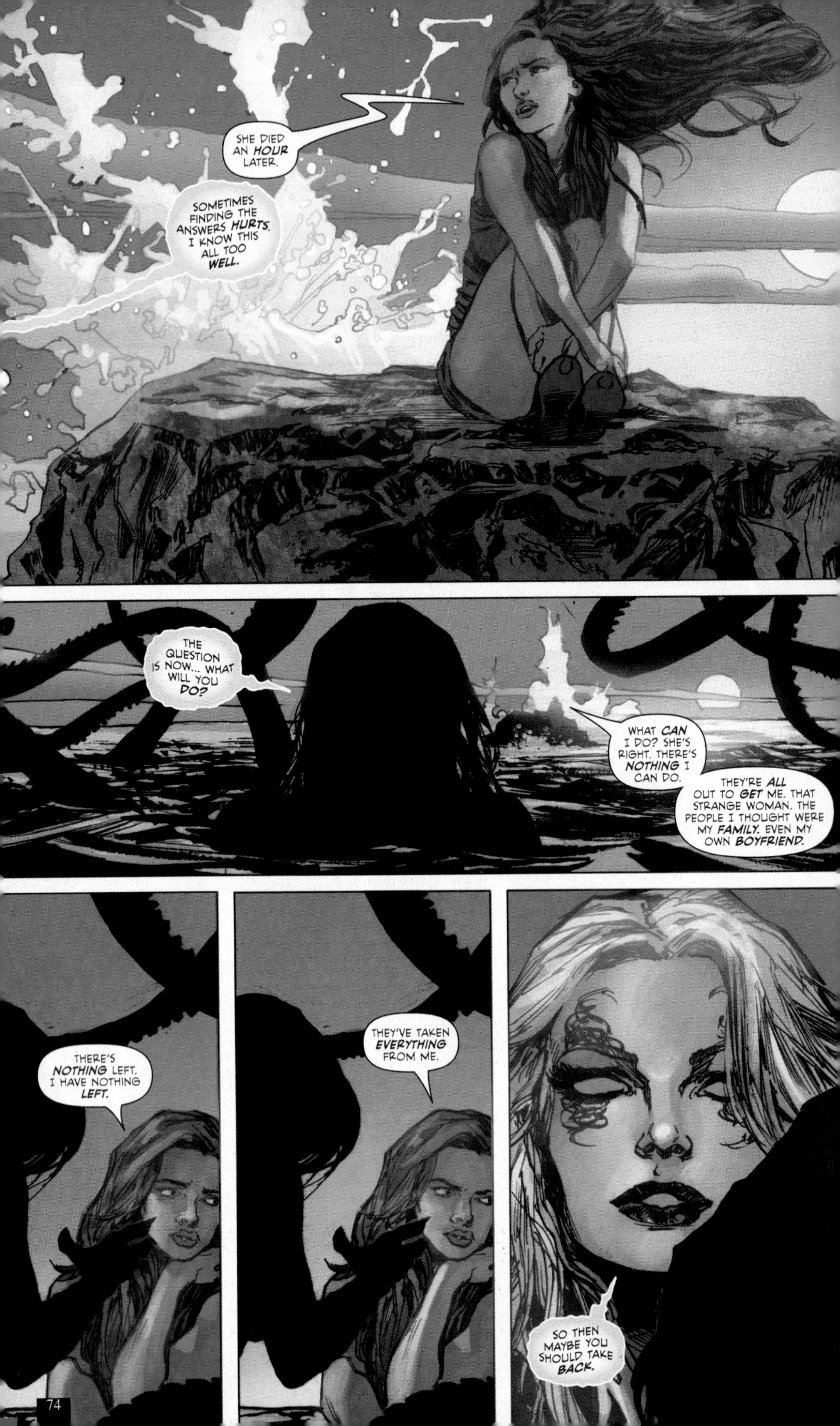

SHE DIED AN HOUR LATER.
SOMETIMES FINDING THE ANSWERS HURTS. I KNOW THIS ALL TOO WELL.
THE QUESTION IS NOW... WHAT WILL YOU DO?
WHAT CAN I DO? SHE'S RIGHT. THERE'S NOTHING I CAN DO.
THEY'RE ALL OUT TO GET ME. THAT STRANGE WOMAN. THE PEOPLE I THOUGHT WERE MY FAMILY. EVEN MY OWN BOYFRIEND.
THERE'S NOTHING LEFT. I HAVE NOTHING LEFT.
THEY'VE TAKEN EVERYTHING FROM ME.
SO THEN MAYBE YOU SHOULD TAKE BACK.

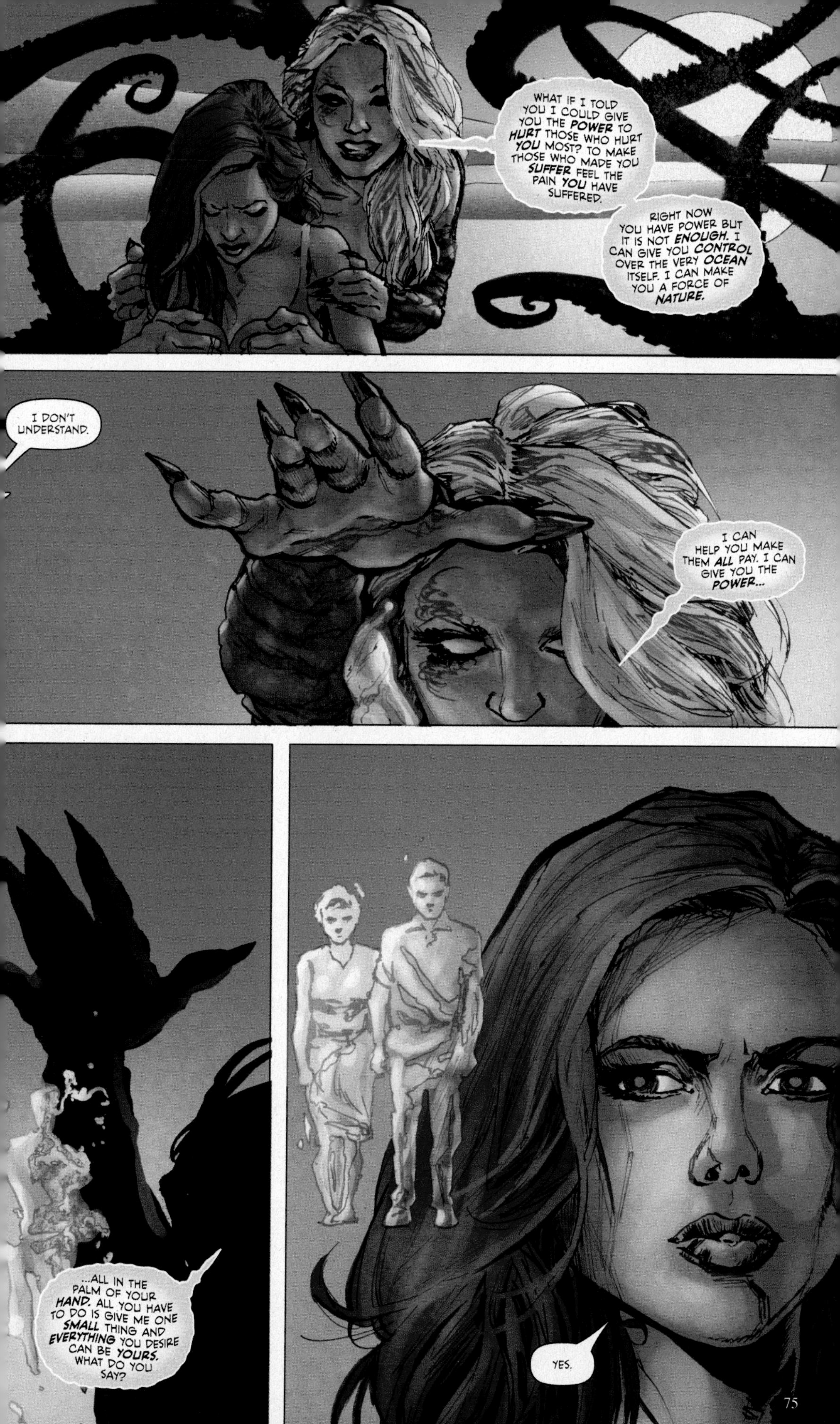
WHAT IF I TOLD YOU I COULD GIVE YOU THE POWER TO HURT THOSE WHO HURT YOU MOST? TO MAKE THOSE WHO MADE YOU SUFFER FEEL THE PAIN YOU HAVE SUFFERED.
RIGHT NOW YOU HAVE POWER BUT IT IS NOT ENOUGH. I CAN GIVE YOU CONTROL OVER THE VERY OCEAN ITSELF. I CAN MAKE YOU A FORCE OF NATURE.
I DON'T UNDERSTAND.
I CAN HELP YOU MAKE THEM ALL PAY. I CAN GIVE YOU THE POWER...
...ALL IN THE PALM OF YOUR HAND. ALL YOU HAVE TO DO IS GIVE ME ONE SMALL THING AND EVERYTHING YOU DESIRE CAN BE YOURS. WHAT DO YOU SAY?
YES.

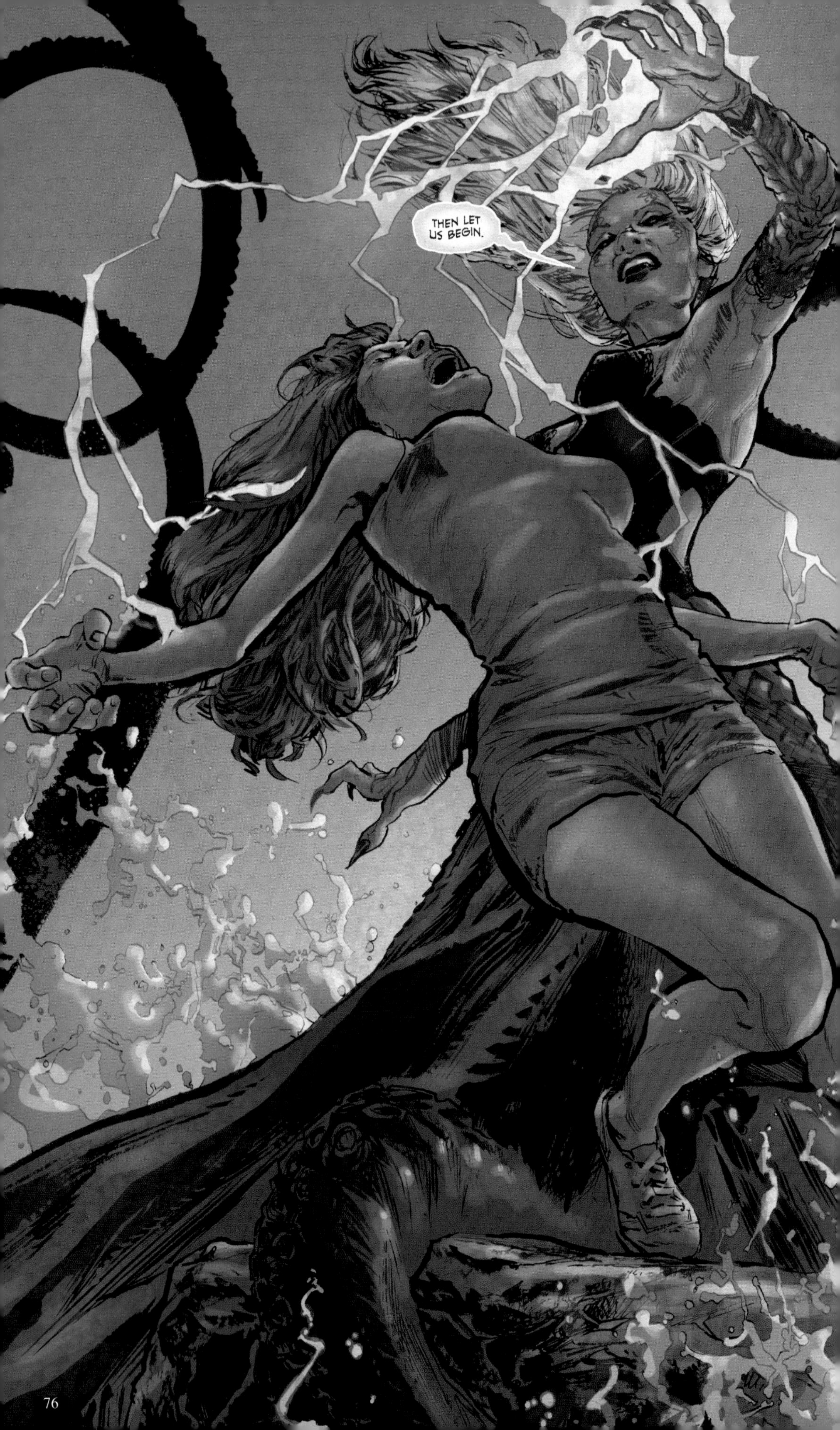
THEN LET US BEGIN.

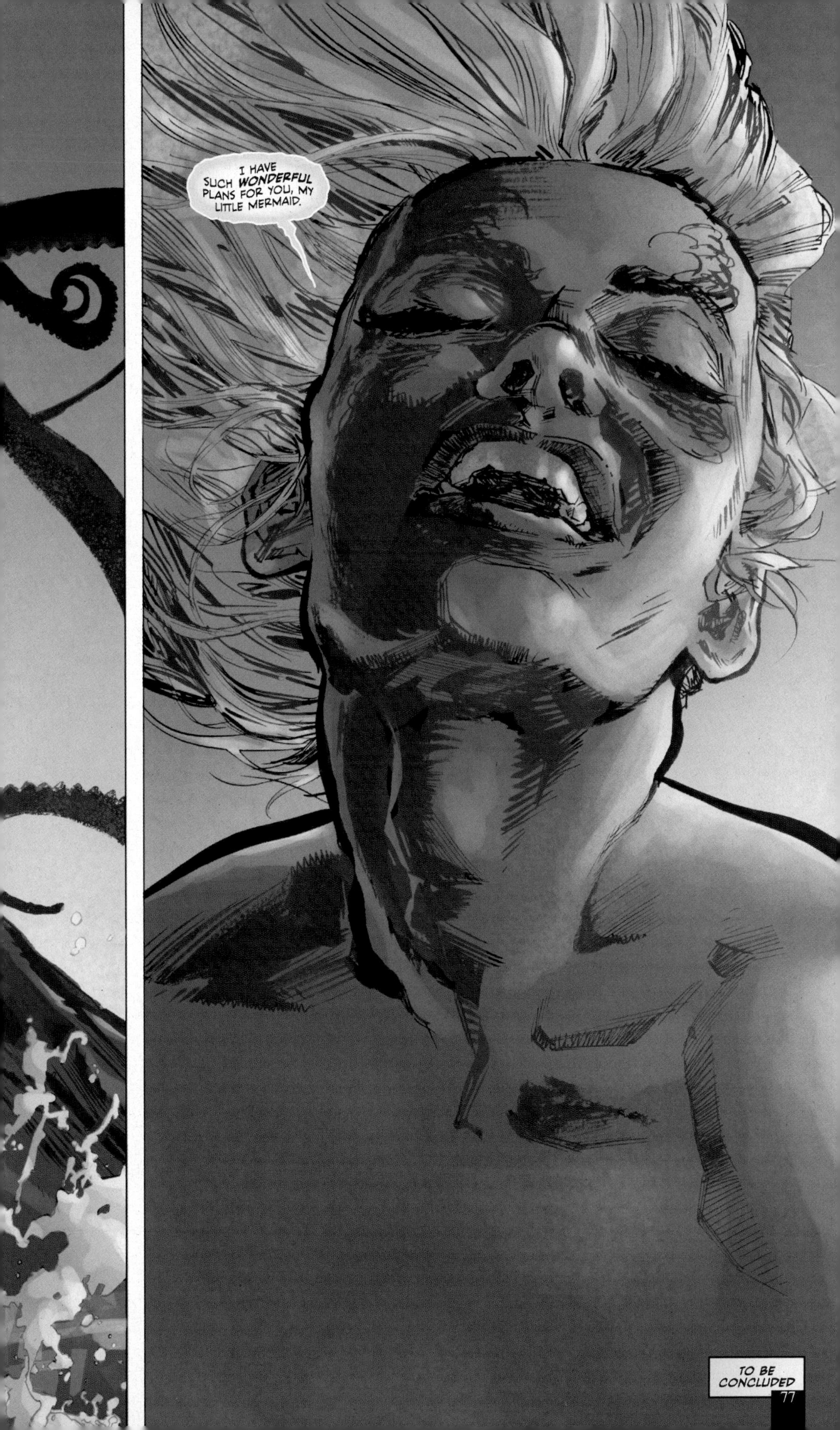
I HAVE SUCH WONDERFUL PLANS FOR YOU, MY LITTLE MERMAID.
TO BE CONCLUDED

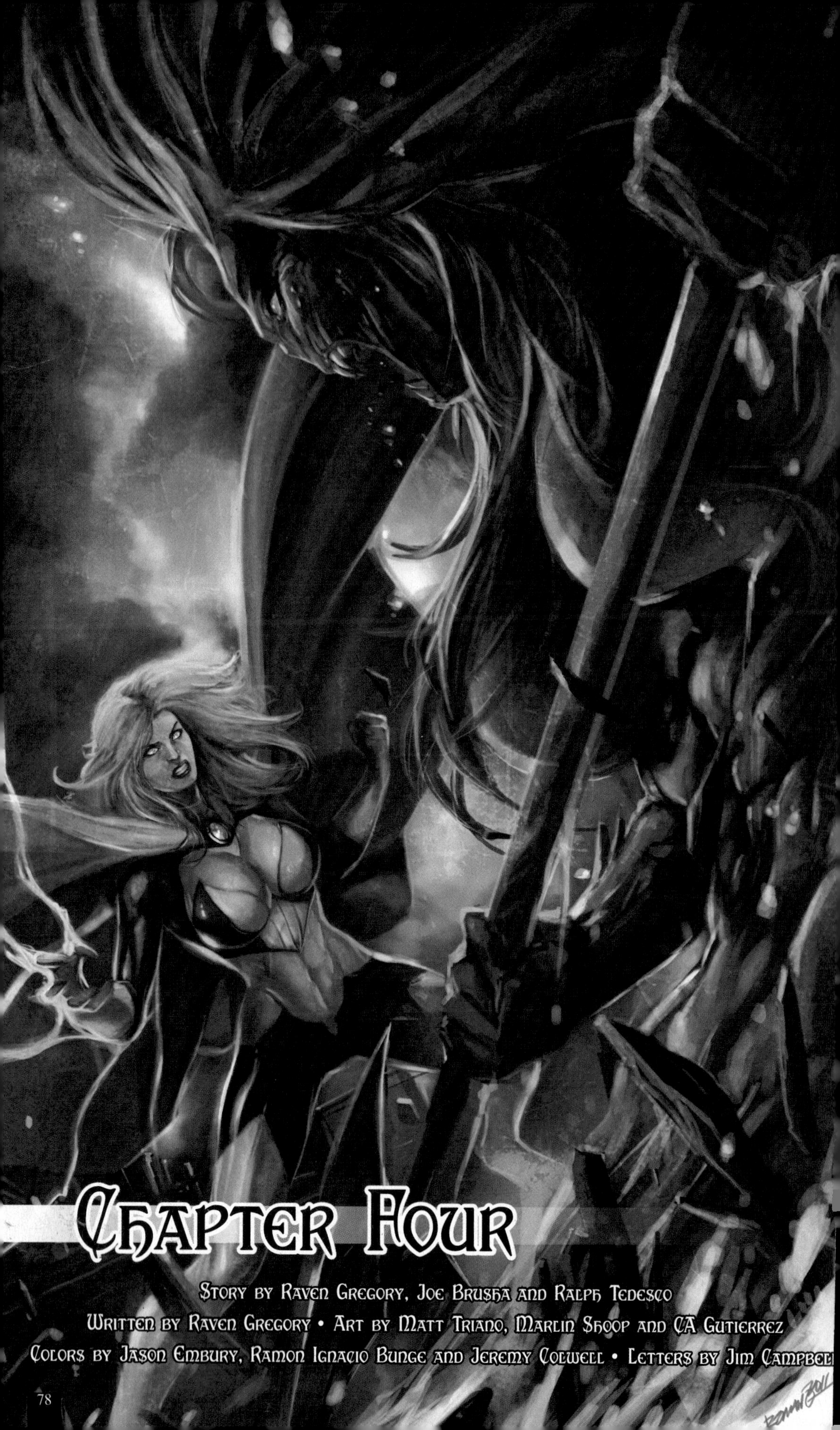

Chapter Four

Story by Raven Gregory, Joe Brusha and Ralph Tedesco

Written by Raven Gregory • Art by Matt Triano, Marlin Shoop and CA Gutierrez

Colors by Jason Embury, Ramon Ignacio Bunge and Jeremy Colwell • Letters by Jim Campbel

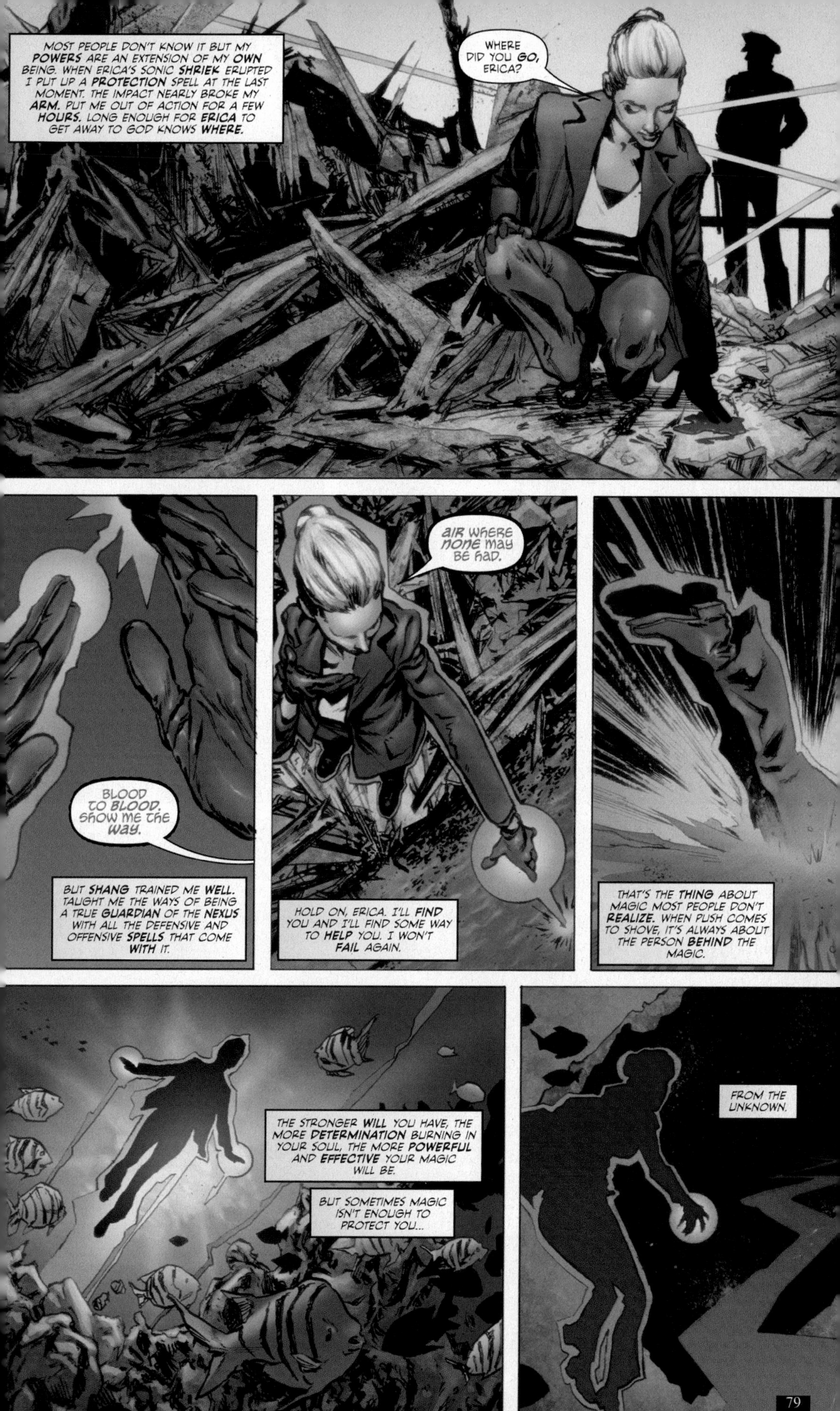

MOST PEOPLE DON'T KNOW IT BUT MY POWERS ARE AN EXTENSION OF MY OWN BEING. WHEN ERICA'S SONIC SHRIEK ERUPTED I PUT UP A PROTECTION SPELL AT THE LAST MOMENT. THE IMPACT NEARLY BROKE MY ARM. PUT ME OUT OF ACTION FOR A FEW HOURS. LONG ENOUGH FOR ERICA TO GET AWAY TO GOD KNOWS WHERE.
WHERE DID YOU GO, ERICA?
BLOOD TO BLOOD. SHOW ME THE WAY.
BUT SHANG TRAINED ME WELL. TAUGHT ME THE WAYS OF BEING A TRUE GUARDIAN OF THE NEXUS WITH ALL THE DEFENSIVE AND OFFENSIVE SPELLS THAT COME WITH IT.
AIR WHERE NONE MAY BE HAD.
HOLD ON, ERICA. I'LL FIND YOU AND I'LL FIND SOME WAY TO HELP YOU. I WON'T FAIL AGAIN.
THAT'S THE THING ABOUT MAGIC MOST PEOPLE DON'T REALIZE. WHEN PUSH COMES TO SHOVE, IT'S ALWAYS ABOUT THE PERSON BEHIND THE MAGIC.
THE STRONGER WILL YOU HAVE, THE MORE DETERMINATION BURNING IN YOUR SOUL, THE MORE POWERFUL AND EFFECTIVE YOUR MAGIC WILL BE.
BUT SOMETIMES MAGIC ISN'T ENOUGH TO PROTECT YOU...
FROM THE UNKNOWN.

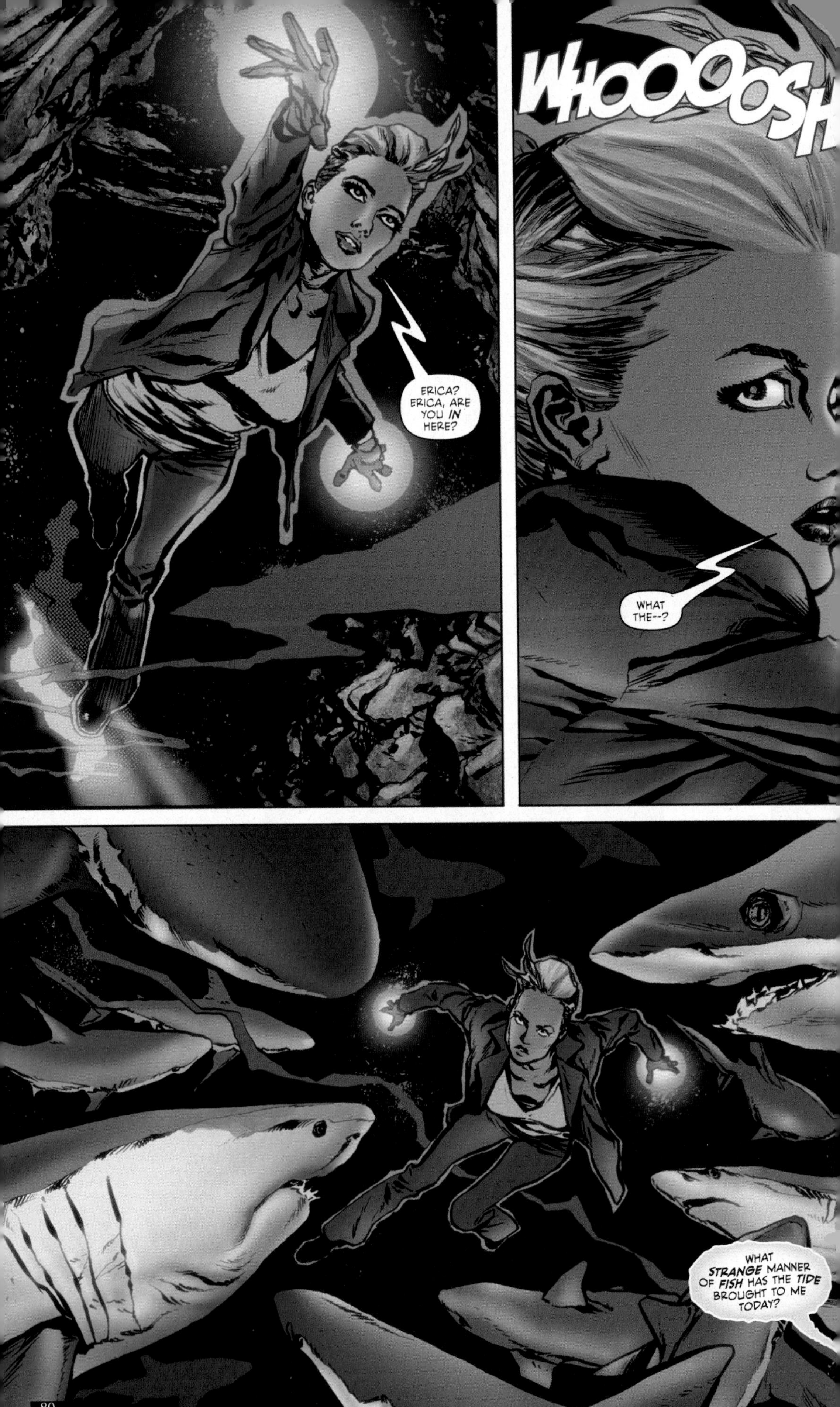
ERICA? ERICA, ARE YOU IN HERE?
WHOOOOSH
WHAT THE--?
WHAT STRANGE MANNER OF FISH HAS THE TIDE BROUGHT TO ME TODAY?

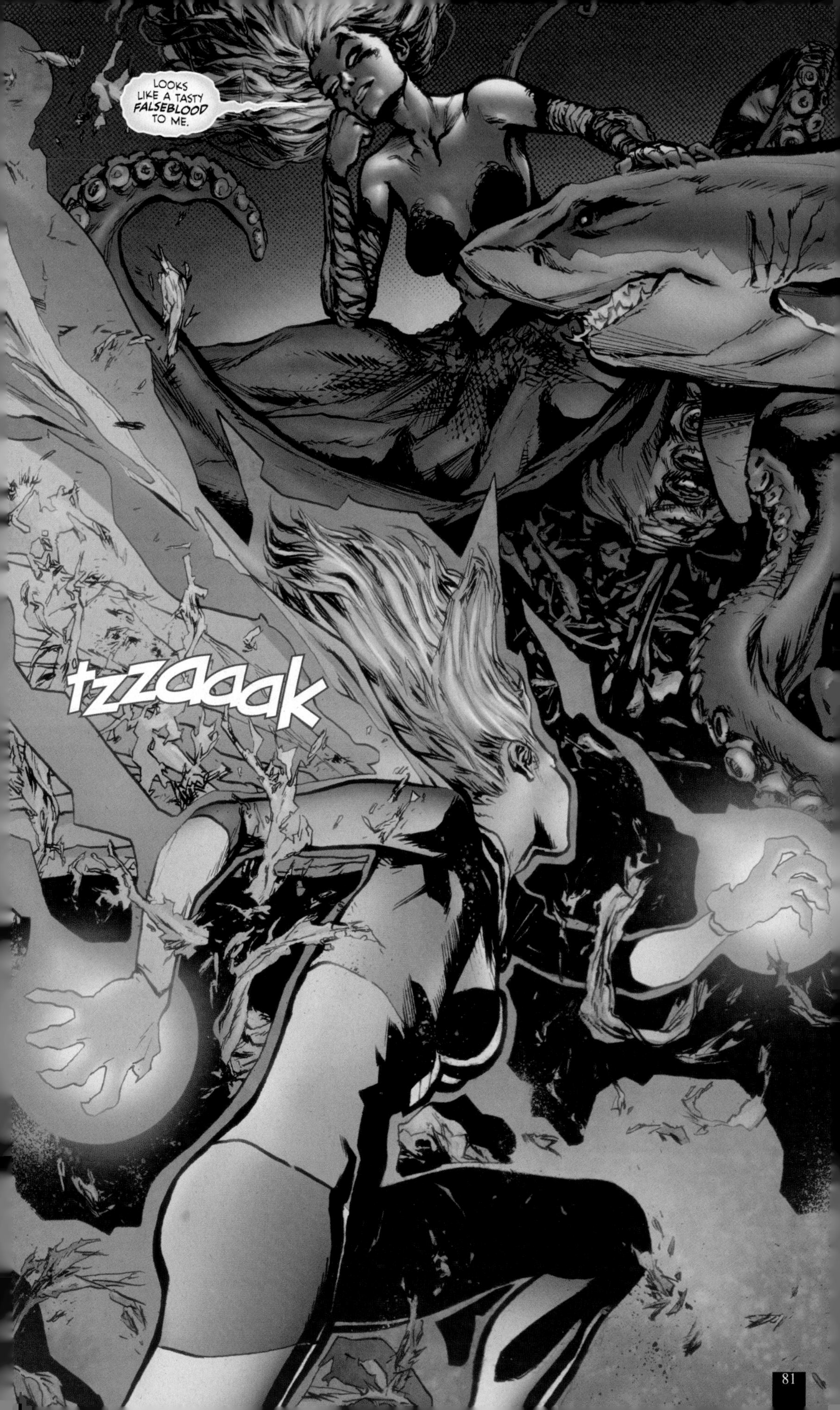
LOOKS LIKE A TASTY FALSEBLOOD TO ME.
tzzaaak

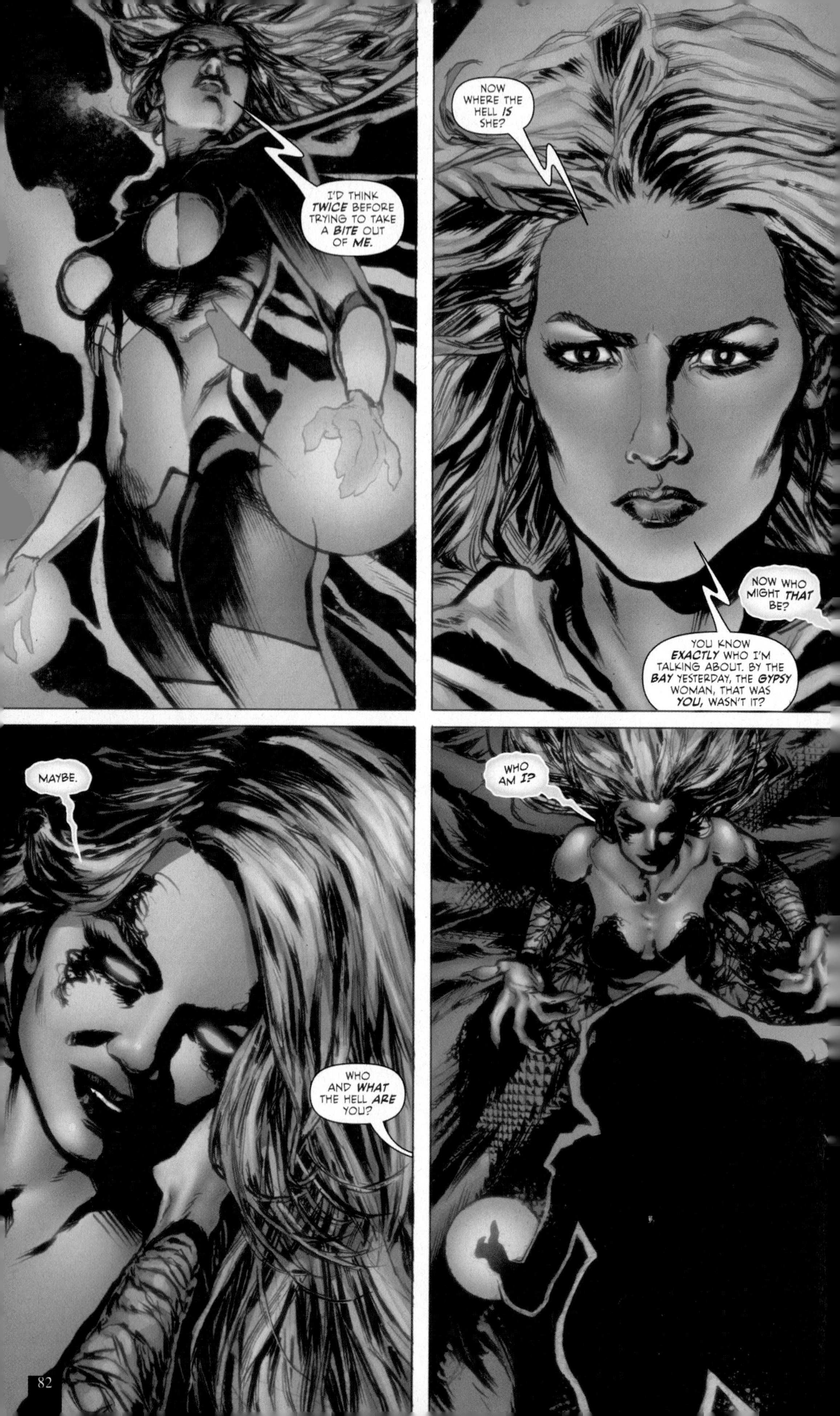
I'D THINK TWICE BEFORE TRYING TO TAKE A BITE OUT OF ME.
NOW WHERE THE HELL IS SHE?
NOW WHO MIGHT THAT BE?
YOU KNOW EXACTLY WHO I'M TALKING ABOUT. BY THE BAY YESTERDAY, THE GYPSY WOMAN, THAT WAS YOU, WASN'T IT?
MAYBE.
WHO AND WHAT THE HELL ARE YOU?
WHO AM I?

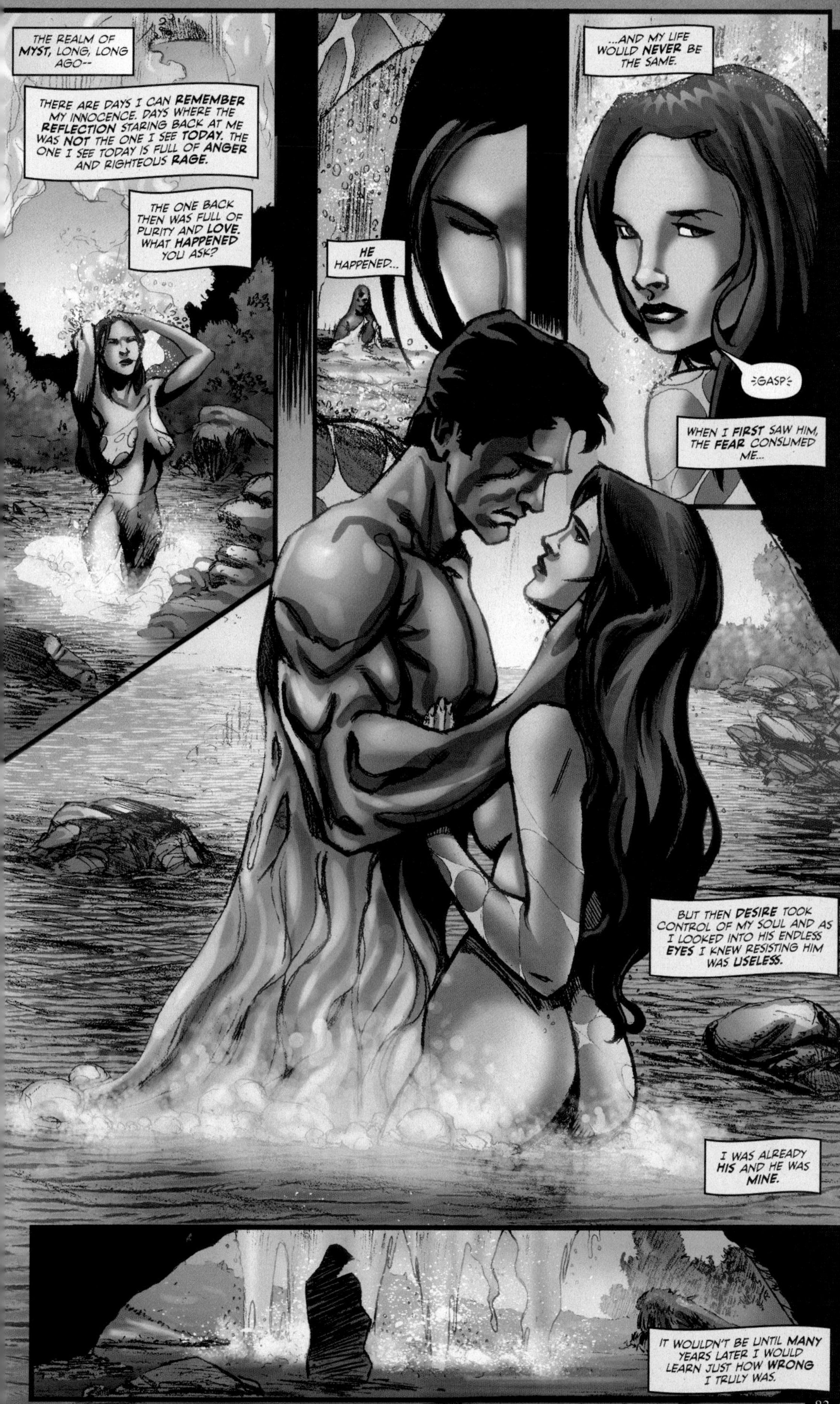
THE REALM OF MYST, LONG, LONG AGO--
THERE ARE DAYS I CAN REMEMBER MY INNOCENCE. DAYS WHERE THE REFLECTION STARING BACK AT ME WAS NOT THE ONE I SEE TODAY. THE ONE I SEE TODAY IS FULL OF ANGER AND RIGHTEOUS RAGE.
THE ONE BACK THEN WAS FULL OF PURITY AND LOVE. WHAT HAPPENED YOU ASK?
HE HAPPENED...
...AND MY LIFE WOULD NEVER BE THE SAME.
GASP
WHEN I FIRST SAW HIM, THE FEAR CONSUMED ME...
BUT THEN DESIRE TOOK CONTROL OF MY SOUL AND AS I LOOKED INTO HIS ENDLESS EYES I KNEW RESISTING HIM WAS USELESS.
I WAS ALREADY HIS AND HE WAS MINE.
IT WOULDN'T BE UNTIL MANY YEARS LATER I WOULD LEARN JUST HOW WRONG I TRULY WAS.

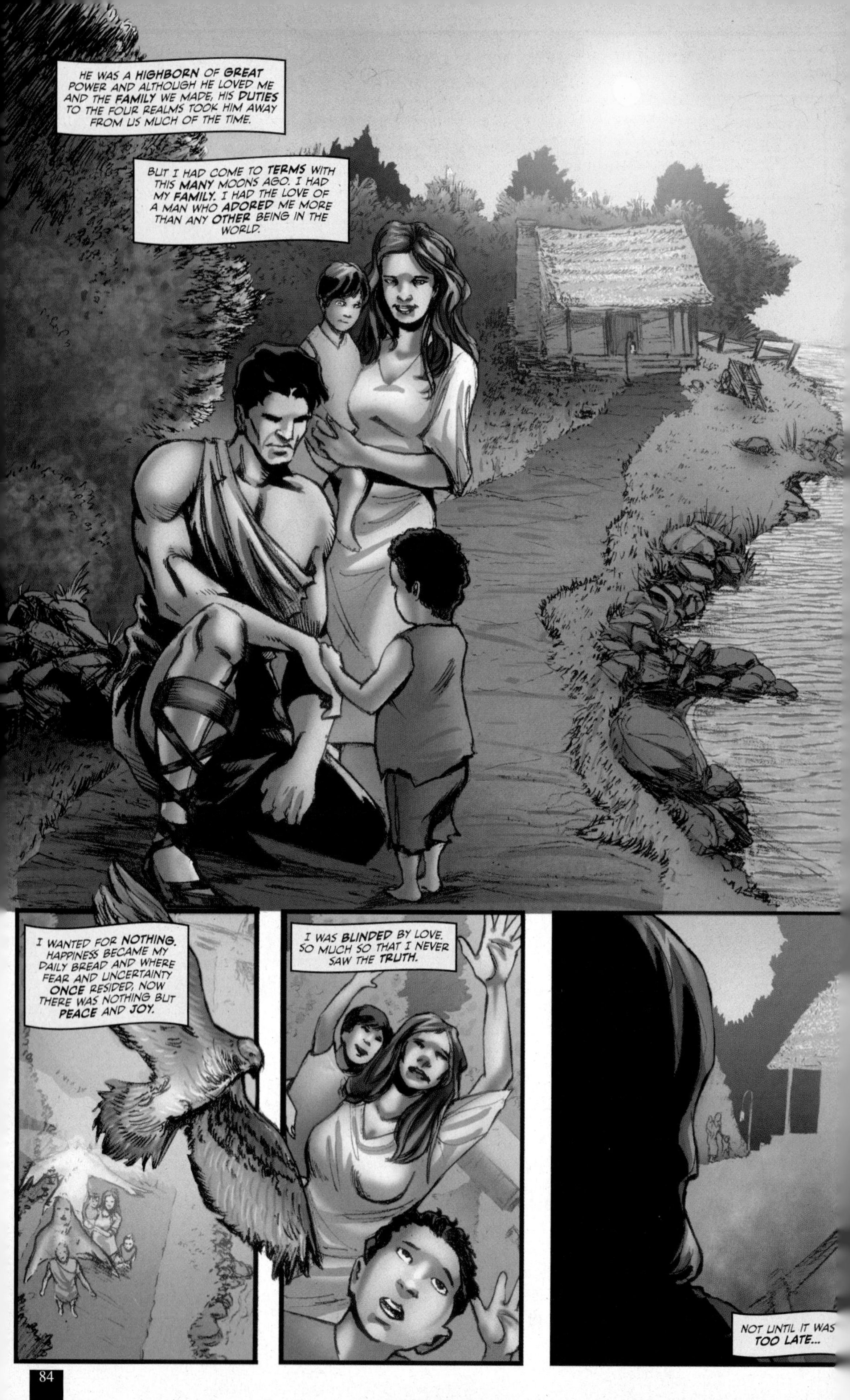
HE WAS A HIGHBORN OF GREAT POWER AND ALTHOUGH HE LOVED ME AND THE FAMILY WE MADE, HIS DUTIES TO THE FOUR REALMS TOOK HIM AWAY FROM US MUCH OF THE TIME.
BUT I HAD COME TO TERMS WITH THIS MANY MOONS AGO. I HAD MY FAMILY. I HAD THE LOVE OF A MAN WHO ADORED ME MORE THAN ANY OTHER BEING IN THE WORLD.
I WANTED FOR NOTHING. HAPPINESS BECAME MY DAILY BREAD AND WHERE FEAR AND UNCERTAINTY ONCE RESIDED, NOW THERE WAS NOTHING BUT PEACE AND JOY.
I WAS BLINDED BY LOVE. SO MUCH SO THAT I NEVER SAW THE TRUTH.
NOT UNTIL IT WAS TOO LATE...

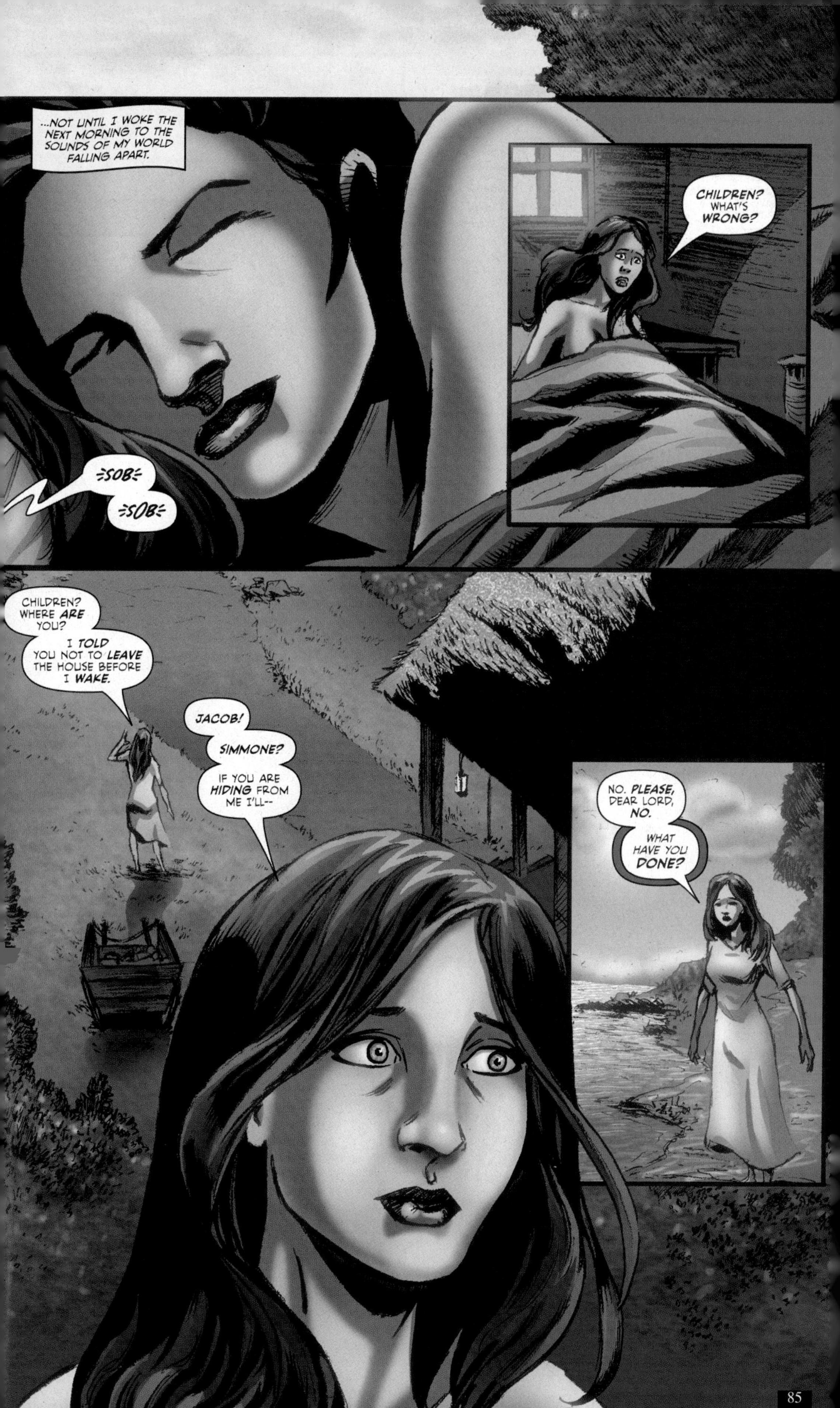
...NOT UNTIL I WOKE THE NEXT MORNING TO THE SOUNDS OF MY WORLD FALLING APART.
CHILDREN? WHAT'S WRONG?
=SOB=
=SOB=
CHILDREN? WHERE ARE YOU?
I TOLD YOU NOT TO LEAVE THE HOUSE BEFORE I WAKE.
JACOB!
SIMMONE?
IF YOU ARE HIDING FROM ME I'LL--
NO. PLEASE, DEAR LORD, NO.
WHAT HAVE YOU DONE?

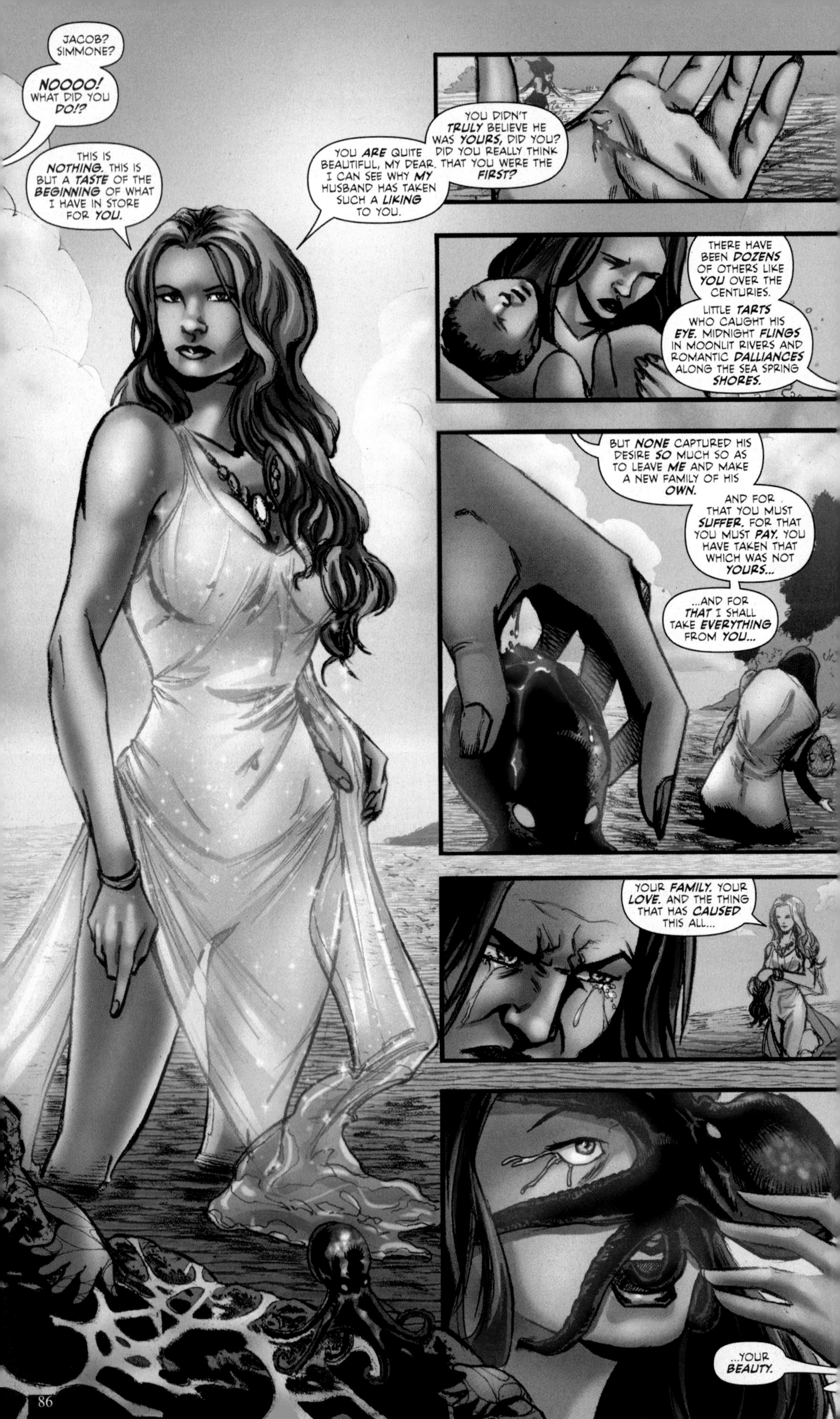
JACOB? SIMMONE?
NOOOO! WHAT DID YOU DO!?
THIS IS NOTHING. THIS IS BUT A TASTE OF THE BEGINNING OF WHAT I HAVE IN STORE FOR YOU.
YOU ARE QUITE BEAUTIFUL, MY DEAR. I CAN SEE WHY MY HUSBAND HAS TAKEN SUCH A LIKING TO YOU.
YOU DIDN'T TRULY BELIEVE HE WAS YOURS, DID YOU? DID YOU REALLY THINK THAT YOU WERE THE FIRST?
THERE HAVE BEEN DOZENS OF OTHERS LIKE YOU OVER THE CENTURIES.
LITTLE TARTS WHO CAUGHT HIS EYE. MIDNIGHT FLINGS IN MOONLIT RIVERS AND ROMANTIC DALLIANCES ALONG THE SEA SPRING SHORES.
BUT NONE CAPTURED HIS DESIRE SO MUCH SO AS TO LEAVE ME AND MAKE A NEW FAMILY OF HIS OWN.
AND FOR THAT YOU MUST SUFFER. FOR THAT YOU MUST PAY. YOU HAVE TAKEN THAT WHICH WAS NOT YOURS...
...AND FOR THAT I SHALL TAKE EVERYTHING FROM YOU...
YOUR FAMILY. YOUR LOVE. AND THE THING THAT HAS CAUSED THIS ALL...
...YOUR BEAUTY.

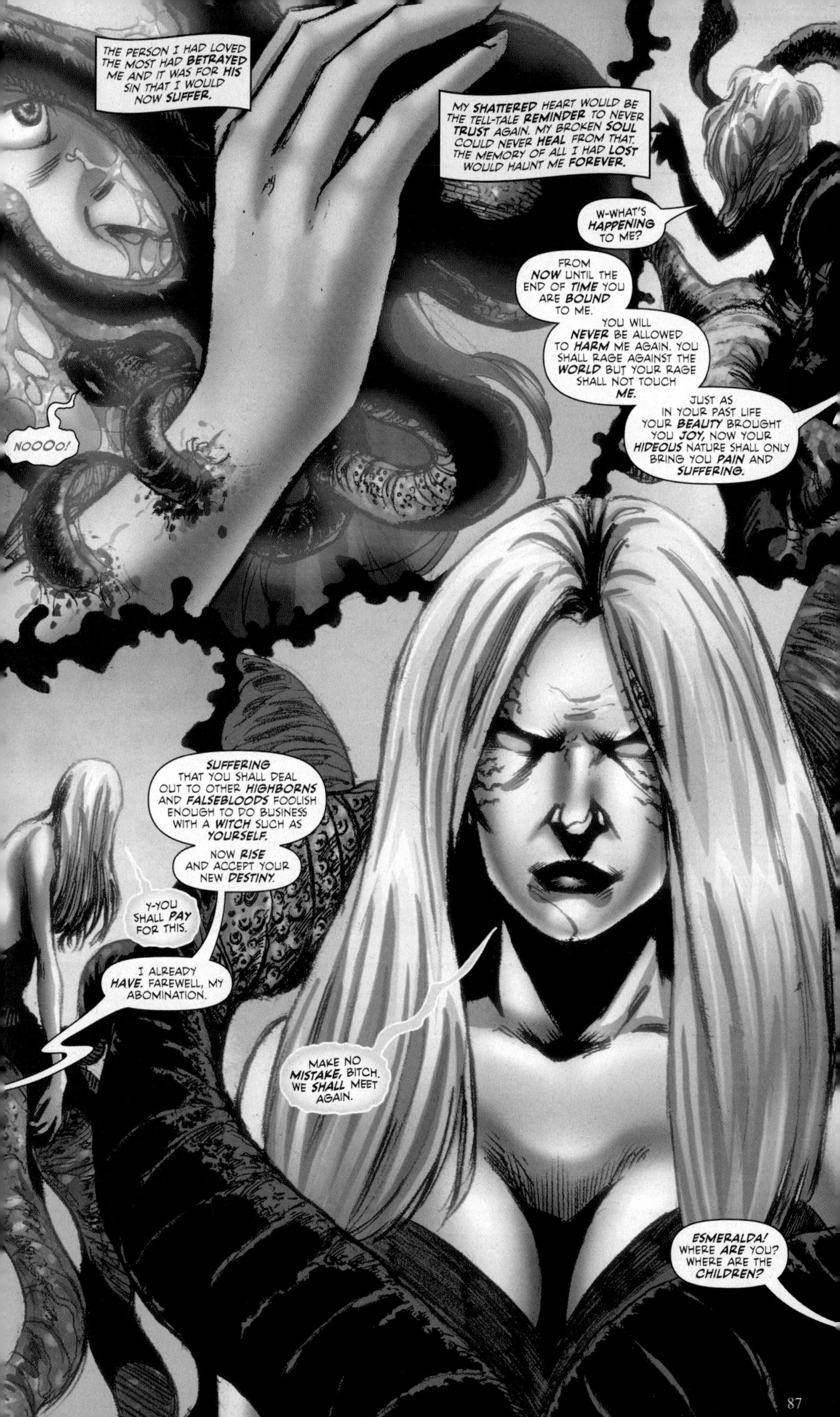
THE PERSON I HAD LOVED THE MOST HAD BETRAYED ME AND IT WAS FOR HIS SIN THAT I WOULD NOW SUFFER.
MY SHATTERED HEART WOULD BE THE TELL-TALE REMINDER TO NEVER TRUST AGAIN. MY BROKEN SOUL COULD NEVER HEAL FROM THAT. THE MEMORY OF ALL I HAD LOST WOULD HAUNT ME FOREVER.
W-WHAT'S HAPPENING TO ME?
FROM NOW UNTIL THE END OF TIME YOU ARE BOUND TO ME.
YOU WILL NEVER BE ALLOWED TO HARM ME AGAIN. YOU SHALL RAGE AGAINST THE WORLD BUT YOUR RAGE SHALL NOT TOUCH ME.
NOOOO!
JUST AS IN YOUR PAST LIFE YOUR BEAUTY BROUGHT YOU JOY, NOW YOUR HIDEOUS NATURE SHALL ONLY BRING YOU PAIN AND SUFFERING.
SUFFERING THAT YOU SHALL DEAL OUT TO OTHER HIGHBORNS AND FALSEBLOODS FOOLISH ENOUGH TO DO BUSINESS WITH A WITCH SUCH AS YOURSELF.
NOW RISE AND ACCEPT YOUR NEW DESTINY.
Y-YOU SHALL PAY FOR THIS.
I ALREADY HAVE. FAREWELL, MY ABOMINATION.
MAKE NO MISTAKE, BITCH. WE SHALL MEET AGAIN.
ESMERALDA! WHERE ARE YOU? WHERE ARE THE CHILDREN?

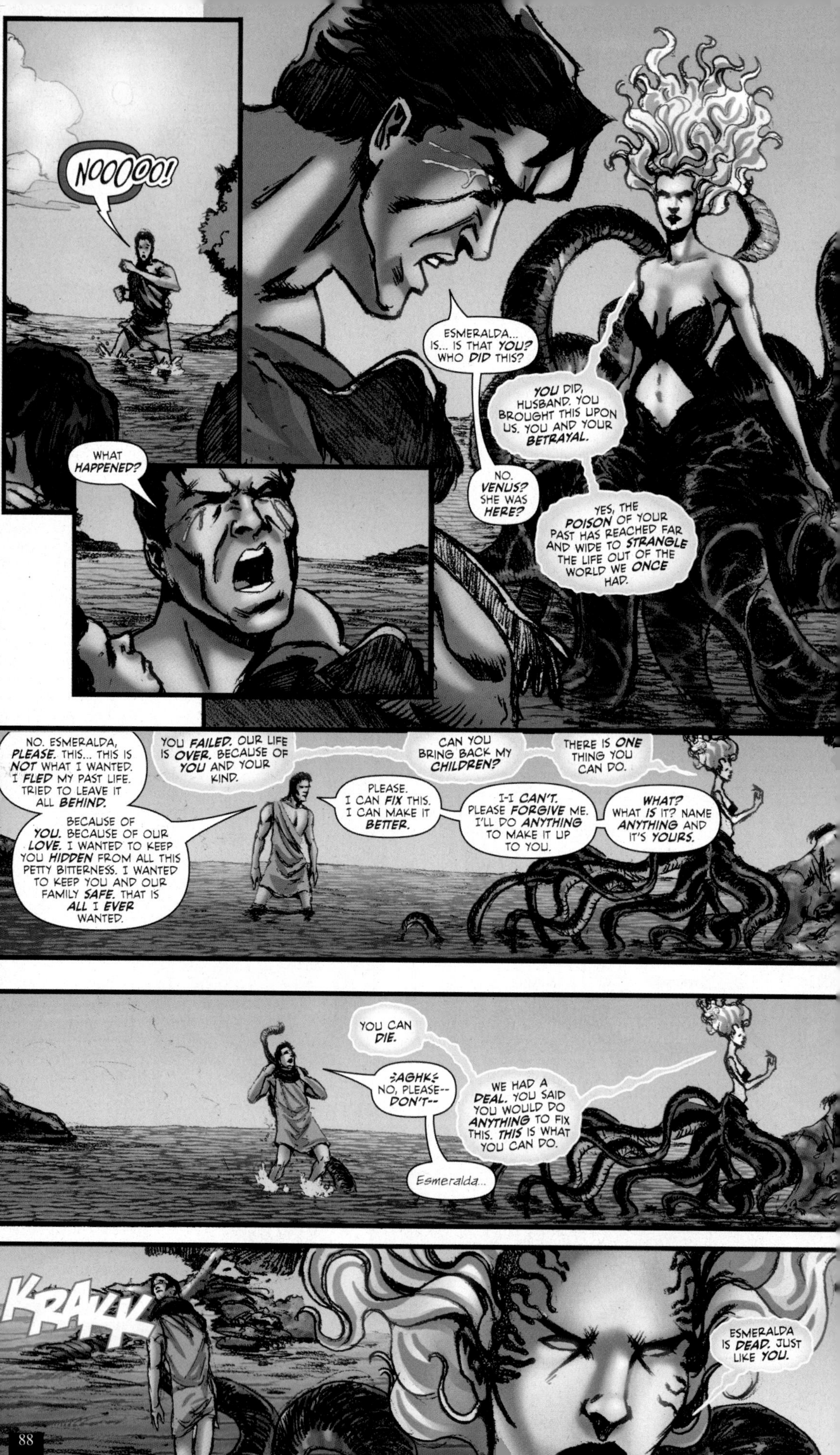
NOOOOO!
WHAT HAPPENED?
ESMERALDA... IS... IS THAT YOU? WHO DID THIS?
YOU DID, HUSBAND. YOU BROUGHT THIS UPON US. YOU AND YOUR BETRAYAL.
NO. VENUS? SHE WAS HERE?
YES, THE POISON OF YOUR PAST HAS REACHED FAR AND WIDE TO STRANGLE THE LIFE OUT OF THE WORLD WE ONCE HAD.
NO. ESMERALDA, PLEASE. THIS... THIS IS NOT WHAT I WANTED. I FLED MY PAST LIFE. TRIED TO LEAVE IT ALL BEHIND.
BECAUSE OF YOU. BECAUSE OF OUR LOVE. I WANTED TO KEEP YOU HIDDEN FROM ALL THIS PETTY BITTERNESS. I WANTED TO KEEP YOU AND OUR FAMILY SAFE. THAT IS ALL I EVER WANTED.
YOU FAILED. OUR LIFE IS OVER. BECAUSE OF YOU AND YOUR KIND.
PLEASE. I CAN FIX THIS. I CAN MAKE IT BETTER.
CAN YOU BRING BACK MY CHILDREN?
I-I CAN'T. PLEASE FORGIVE ME. I'LL DO ANYTHING TO MAKE IT UP TO YOU.
THERE IS ONE THING YOU CAN DO.
WHAT? WHAT IS IT? NAME ANYTHING AND IT'S YOURS.
YOU CAN DIE.
AGHK NO, PLEASE-- DON'T--
WE HAD A DEAL. YOU SAID YOU WOULD DO ANYTHING TO FIX THIS. THIS IS WHAT YOU CAN DO.
Esmeralda...
KRAKK
ESMERALDA IS DEAD. JUST LIKE YOU.

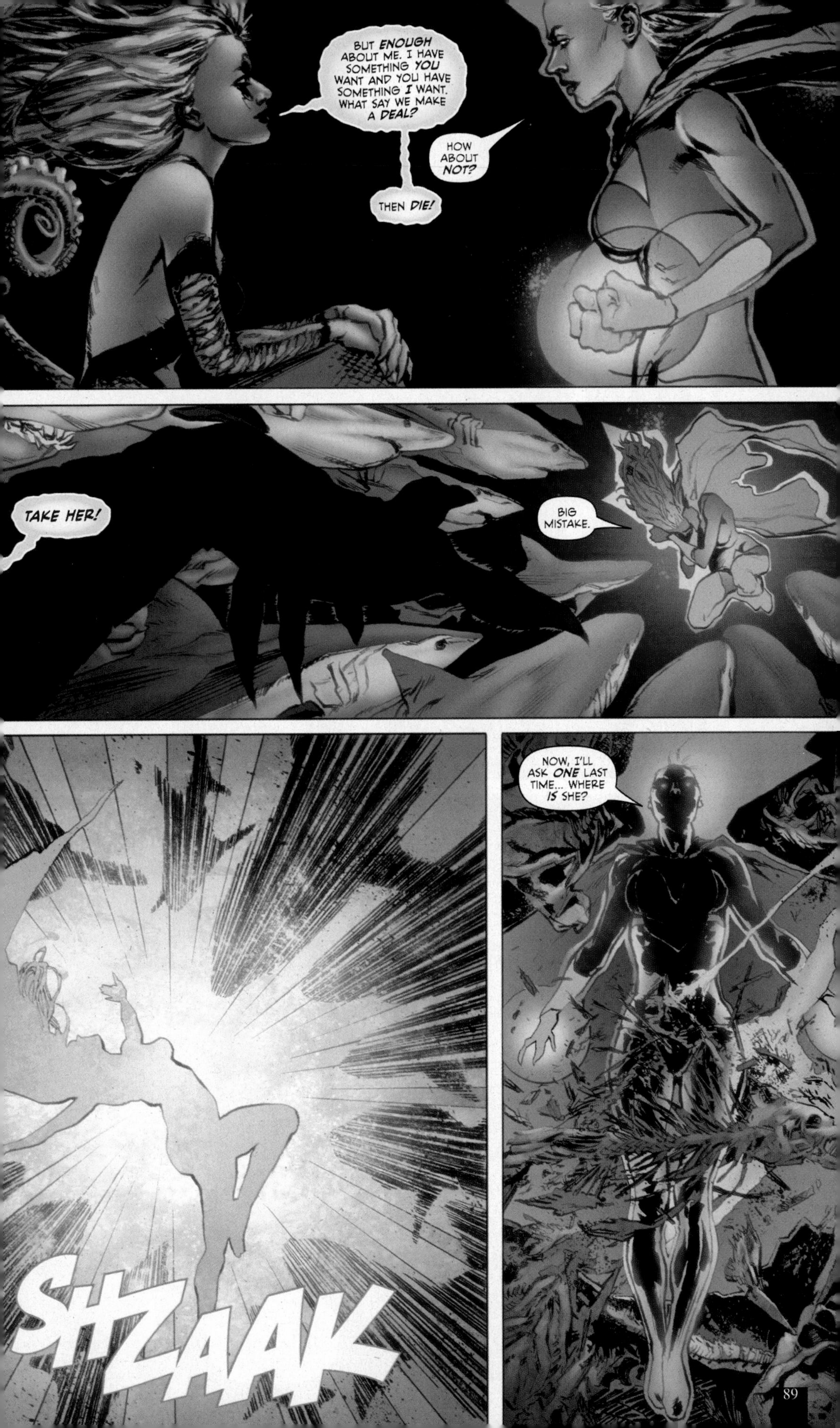
BUT ENOUGH ABOUT ME. I HAVE SOMETHING YOU WANT AND YOU HAVE SOMETHING I WANT. WHAT SAY WE MAKE A DEAL?
HOW ABOUT NOT?
THEN DIE!
TAKE HER!
BIG MISTAKE.
SHZAAK
NOW, I'LL ASK ONE LAST TIME... WHERE IS SHE?

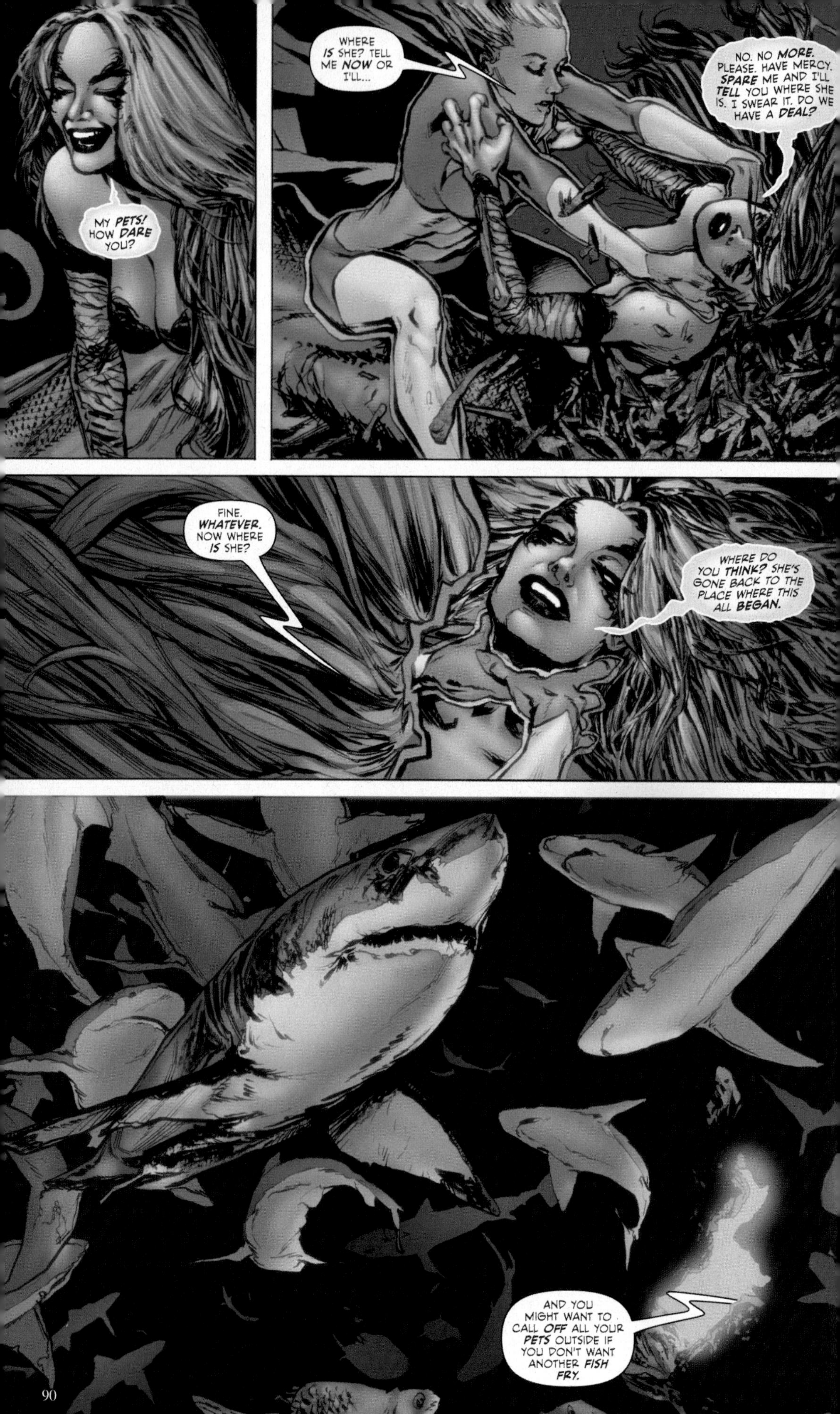
MY PETS! HOW DARE YOU?
WHERE IS SHE? TELL ME NOW OR I'LL...
NO. NO MORE. PLEASE. HAVE MERCY. SPARE ME AND I'LL TELL YOU WHERE SHE IS. I SWEAR IT. DO WE HAVE A DEAL?
FINE. WHATEVER. NOW WHERE IS SHE?
WHERE DO YOU THINK? SHE'S GONE BACK TO THE PLACE WHERE THIS ALL BEGAN.
AND YOU MIGHT WANT TO CALL OFF ALL YOUR PETS OUTSIDE IF YOU DON'T WANT ANOTHER FISH FRY.

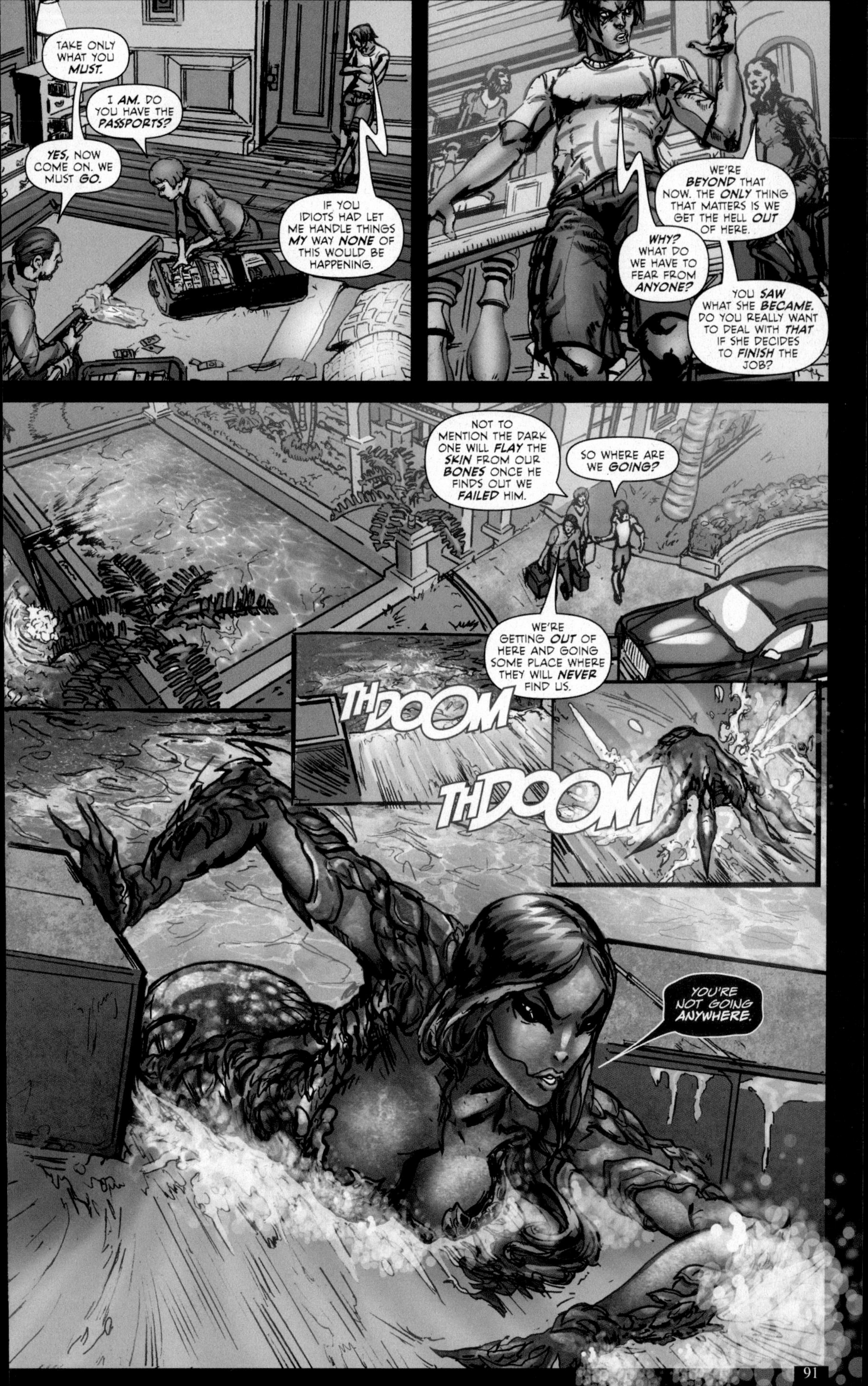

TAKE ONLY WHAT YOU MUST.
I AM. DO YOU HAVE THE PASSPORTS?
YES, NOW COME ON. WE MUST GO.
IF YOU IDIOTS HAD LET ME HANDLE THINGS MY WAY NONE OF THIS WOULD BE HAPPENING.
WE'RE BEYOND THAT NOW. THE ONLY THING THAT MATTERS IS WE GET THE HELL OUT OF HERE.
WHY? WHAT DO WE HAVE TO FEAR FROM ANYONE?
YOU SAW WHAT SHE BECAME. DO YOU REALLY WANT TO DEAL WITH THAT IF SHE DECIDES TO FINISH THE JOB?
NOT TO MENTION THE DARK ONE WILL FLAY THE SKIN FROM OUR BONES ONCE HE FINDS OUT WE FAILED HIM.
SO WHERE ARE WE GOING?
WE'RE GETTING OUT OF HERE AND GOING SOME PLACE WHERE THEY WILL NEVER FIND US.
THDOOM
THDOOM
YOU'RE NOT GOING ANYWHERE.

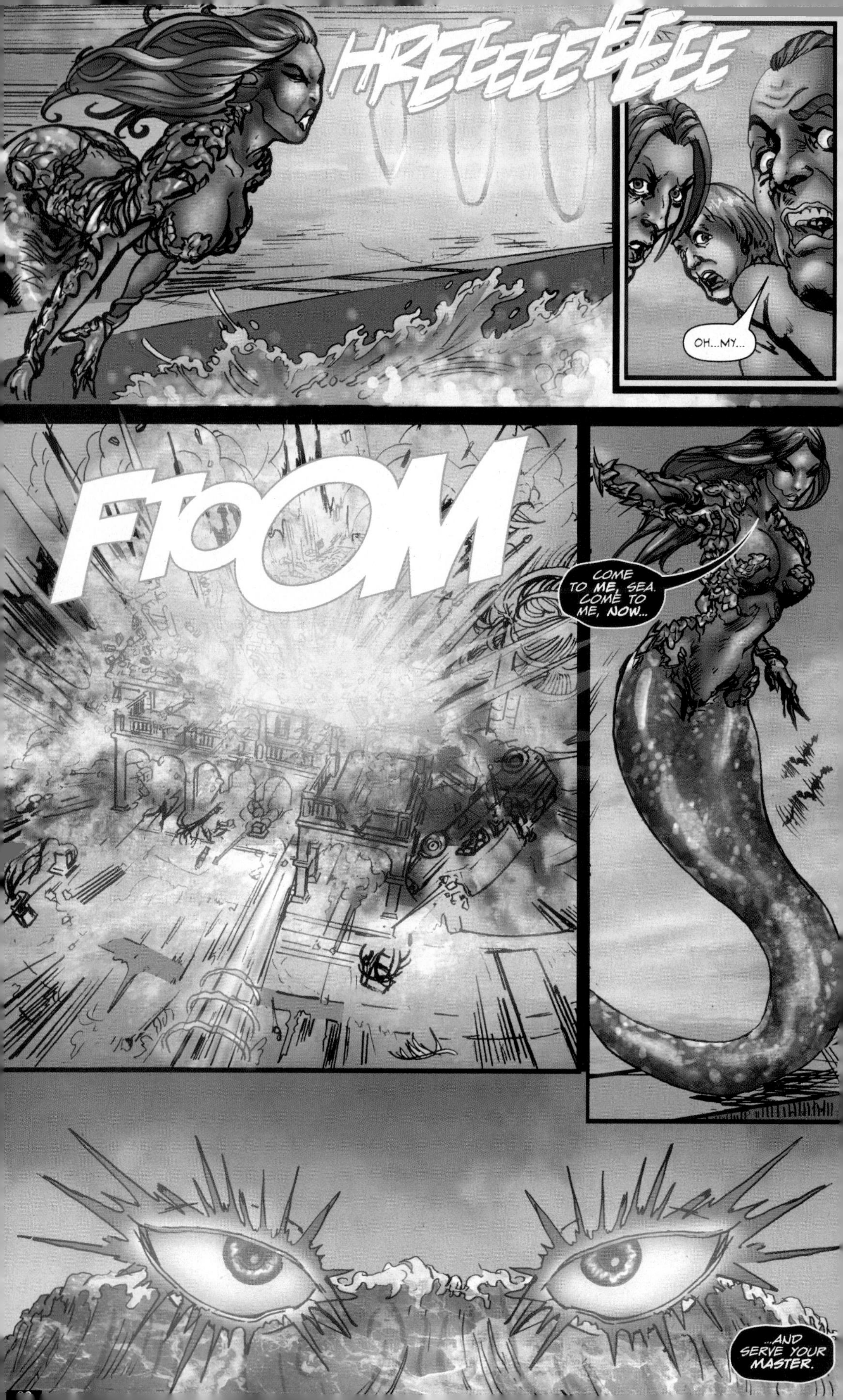
HREEEEEEEEEE
OH...MY...
FTOOM
COME TO ME, SEA. COME TO ME, NOW...
...AND SERVE YOUR MASTER.

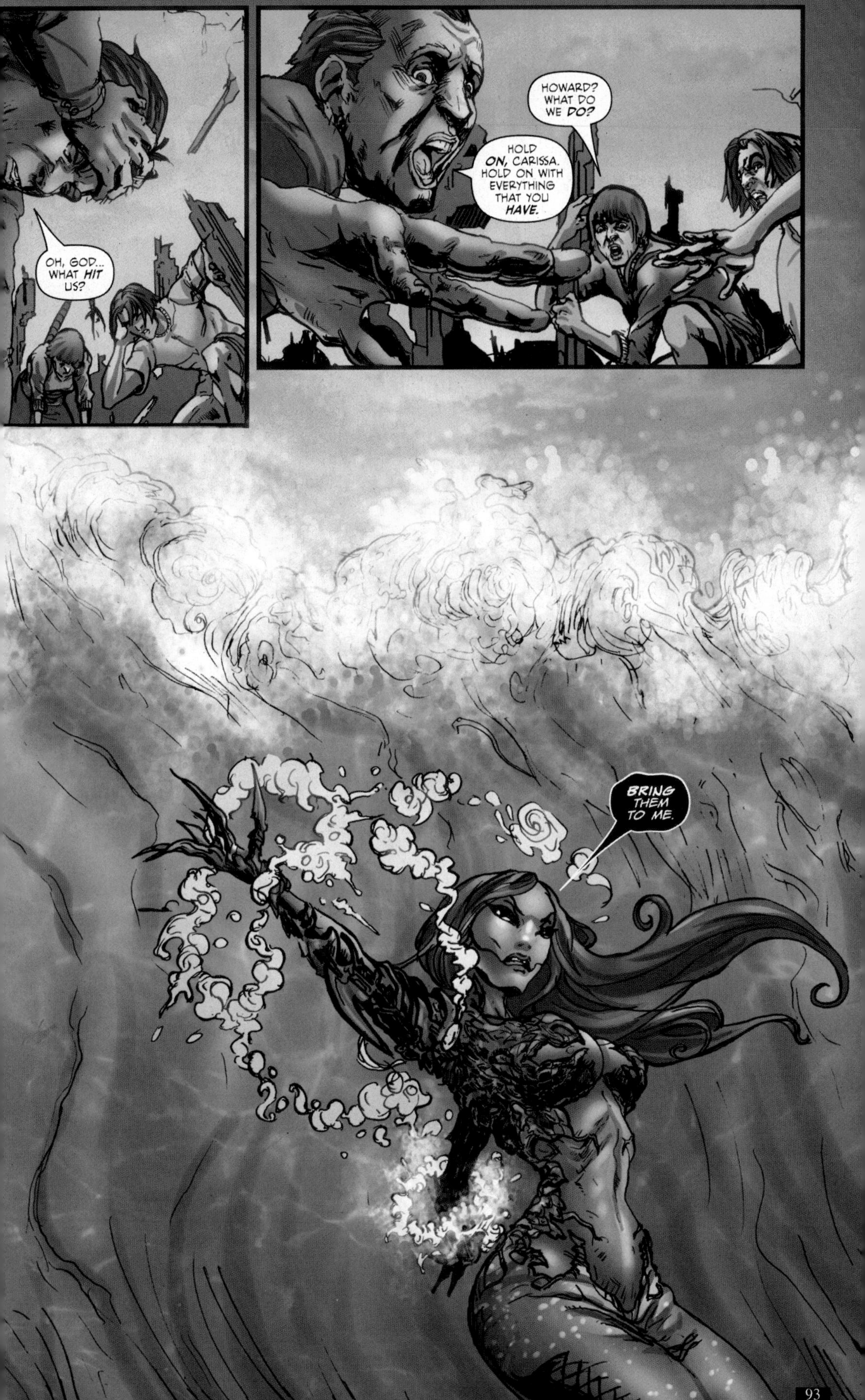
OH, GOD... WHAT HIT US?
HOWARD? WHAT DO WE DO?
HOLD ON, CARISSA. HOLD ON WITH EVERYTHING THAT YOU HAVE.
BRING THEM TO ME.

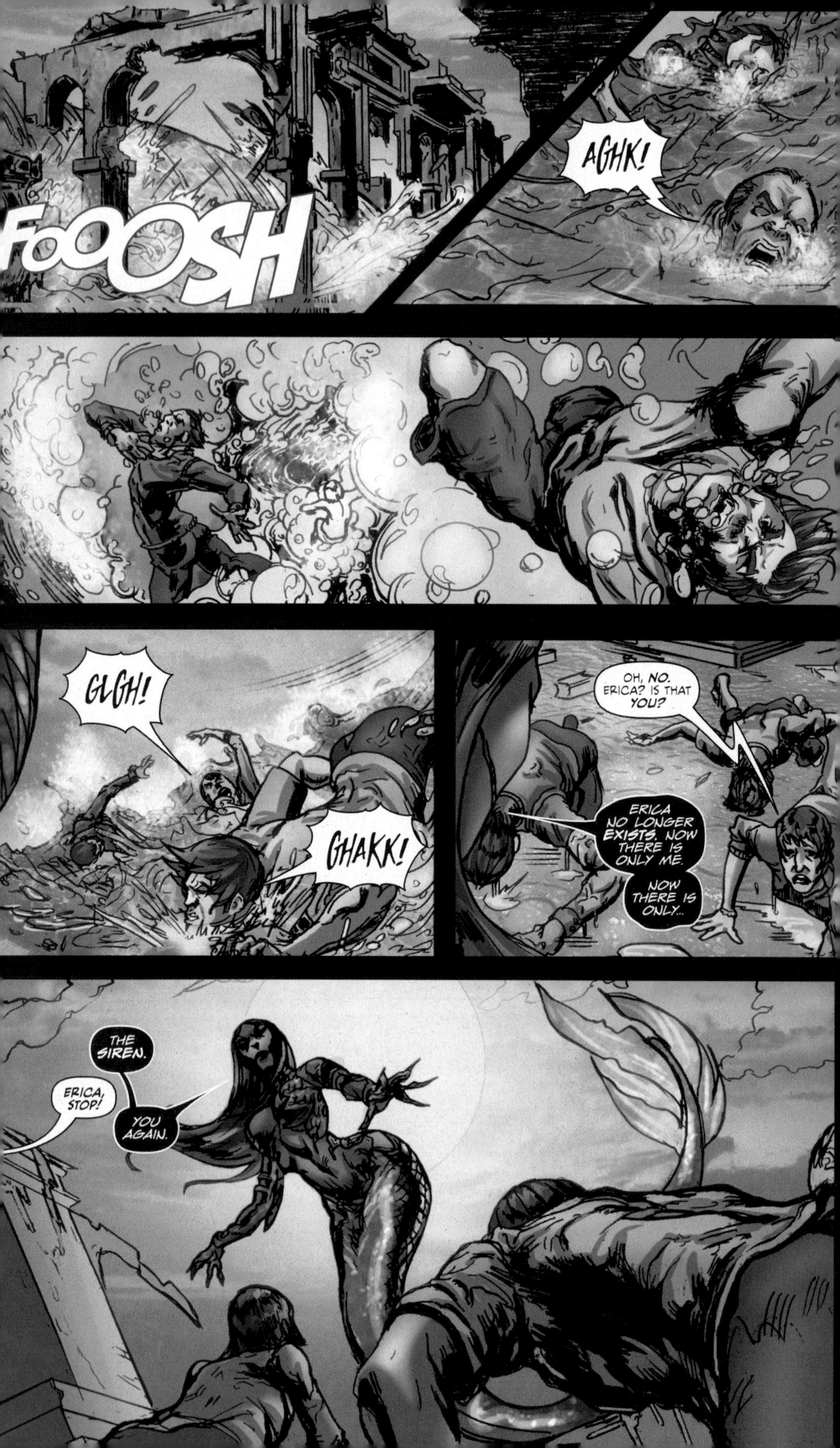
FOOOSH
AGHK!
GLGH!
GHAKK!
OH, NO. ERICA? IS THAT YOU?
ERICA NO LONGER EXISTS. NOW THERE IS ONLY ME.
NOW THERE IS ONLY...
THE SIREN.
ERICA, STOP!
YOU AGAIN.

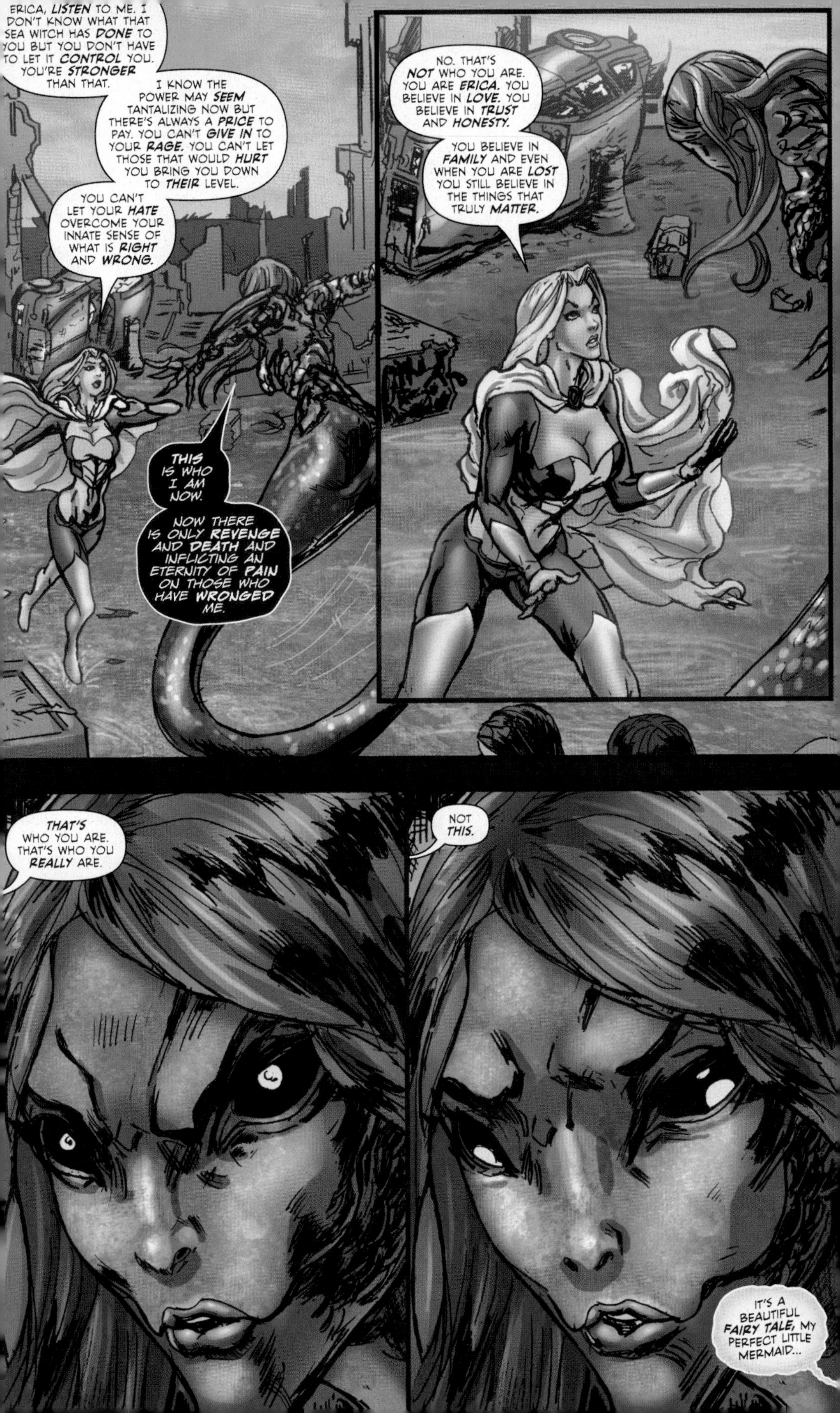
ERICA, LISTEN TO ME. I DON'T KNOW WHAT THAT SEA WITCH HAS DONE TO YOU BUT YOU DON'T HAVE TO LET IT CONTROL YOU. YOU'RE STRONGER THAN THAT.
I KNOW THE POWER MAY SEEM TANTALIZING NOW BUT THERE'S ALWAYS A PRICE TO PAY. YOU CAN'T GIVE IN TO YOUR RAGE. YOU CAN'T LET THOSE THAT WOULD HURT YOU BRING YOU DOWN TO THEIR LEVEL.
YOU CAN'T LET YOUR HATE OVERCOME YOUR INNATE SENSE OF WHAT IS RIGHT AND WRONG.
THIS IS WHO I AM NOW.
NOW THERE IS ONLY REVENGE AND DEATH AND INFLICTING AN ETERNITY OF PAIN ON THOSE WHO HAVE WRONGED ME.
NO. THAT'S NOT WHO YOU ARE. YOU ARE ERICA. YOU BELIEVE IN LOVE. YOU BELIEVE IN TRUST AND HONESTY.
YOU BELIEVE IN FAMILY AND EVEN WHEN YOU ARE LOST YOU STILL BELIEVE IN THE THINGS THAT TRULY MATTER.
THAT'S WHO YOU ARE. THAT'S WHO YOU REALLY ARE.
NOT THIS.
IT'S A BEAUTIFUL FAIRY TALE, MY PERFECT LITTLE MERMAID...

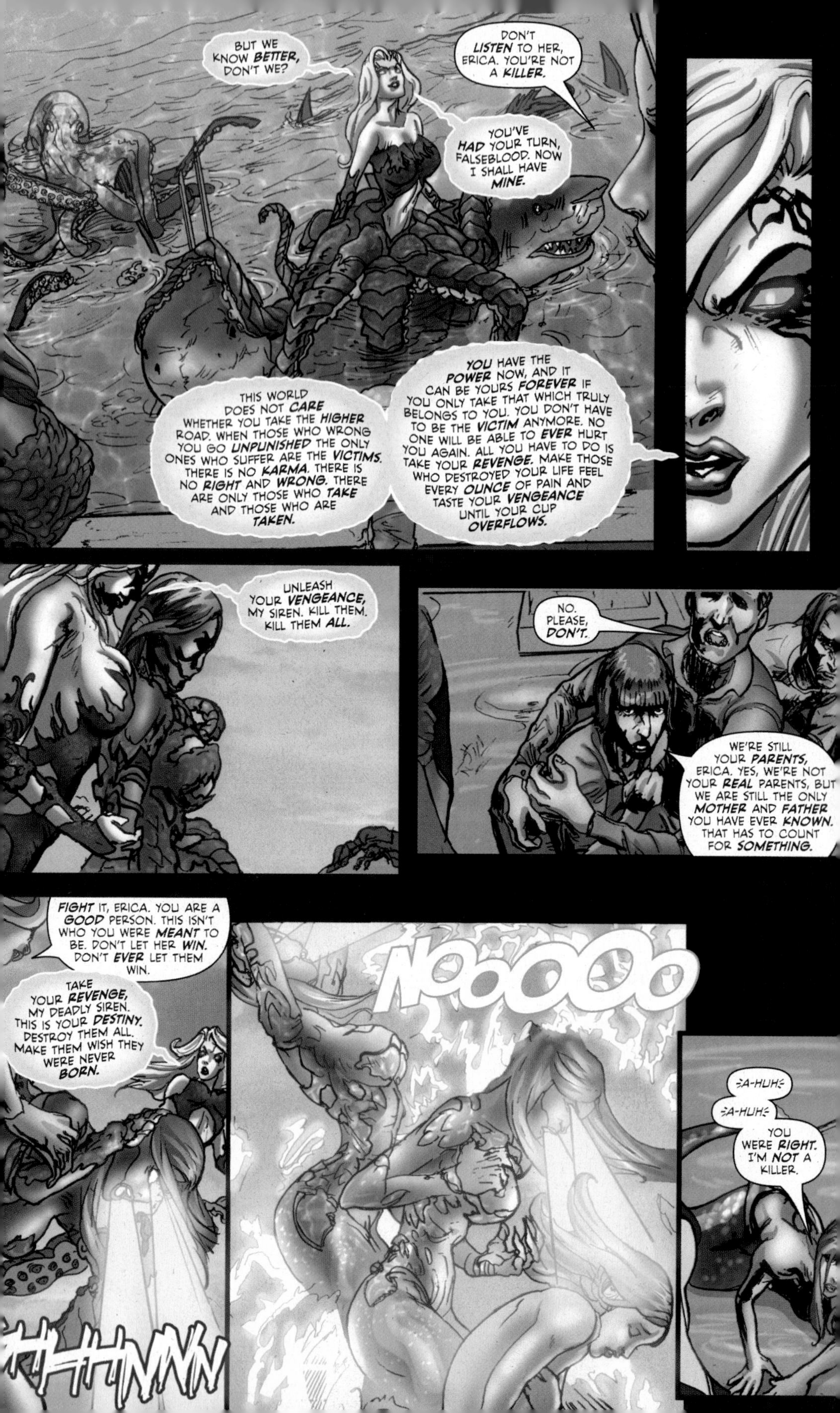

BUT WE KNOW BETTER, DON'T WE?
DON'T LISTEN TO HER, ERICA. YOU'RE NOT A KILLER.
YOU'VE HAD YOUR TURN, FALSEBLOOD. NOW I SHALL HAVE MINE.
THIS WORLD DOES NOT CARE WHETHER YOU TAKE THE HIGHER ROAD. WHEN THOSE WHO WRONG YOU GO UNPUNISHED THE ONLY ONES WHO SUFFER ARE THE VICTIMS. THERE IS NO KARMA. THERE IS NO RIGHT AND WRONG. THERE ARE ONLY THOSE WHO TAKE AND THOSE WHO ARE TAKEN.
YOU HAVE THE POWER NOW, AND IT CAN BE YOURS FOREVER IF YOU ONLY TAKE THAT WHICH TRULY BELONGS TO YOU. YOU DON'T HAVE TO BE THE VICTIM ANYMORE. NO ONE WILL BE ABLE TO EVER HURT YOU AGAIN. ALL YOU HAVE TO DO IS TAKE YOUR REVENGE. MAKE THOSE WHO DESTROYED YOUR LIFE FEEL EVERY OUNCE OF PAIN AND TASTE YOUR VENGEANCE UNTIL YOUR CUP OVERFLOWS.
UNLEASH YOUR VENGEANCE, MY SIREN. KILL THEM. KILL THEM ALL.
NO. PLEASE, DON'T.
WE'RE STILL YOUR PARENTS, ERICA. YES, WE'RE NOT YOUR REAL PARENTS, BUT WE ARE STILL THE ONLY MOTHER AND FATHER YOU HAVE EVER KNOWN. THAT HAS TO COUNT FOR SOMETHING.
FIGHT IT, ERICA. YOU ARE A GOOD PERSON. THIS ISN'T WHO YOU WERE MEANT TO BE. DON'T LET HER WIN. DON'T EVER LET THEM WIN.
TAKE YOUR REVENGE, MY DEADLY SIREN. THIS IS YOUR DESTINY. DESTROY THEM ALL. MAKE THEM WISH THEY WERE NEVER BORN.
HHHNNN
NOOOOOO
A-HUH
A-HUH
YOU WERE RIGHT. I'M NOT A KILLER.

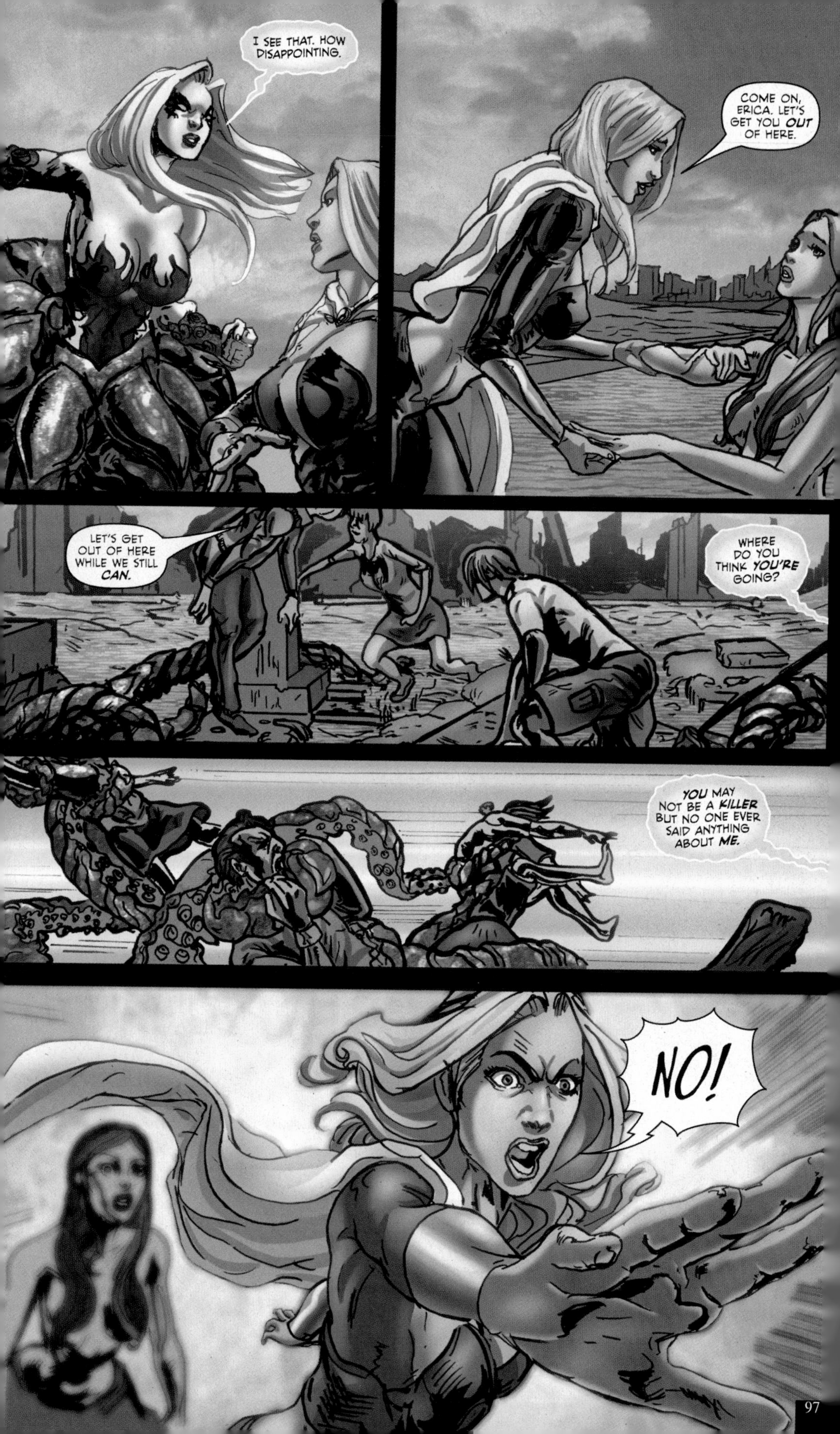
I SEE THAT. HOW DISAPPOINTING.
COME ON, ERICA. LET'S GET YOU OUT OF HERE.
LET'S GET OUT OF HERE WHILE WE STILL CAN.
WHERE DO YOU THINK YOU'RE GOING?
YOU MAY NOT BE A KILLER BUT NO ONE EVER SAID ANYTHING ABOUT ME.
NO!

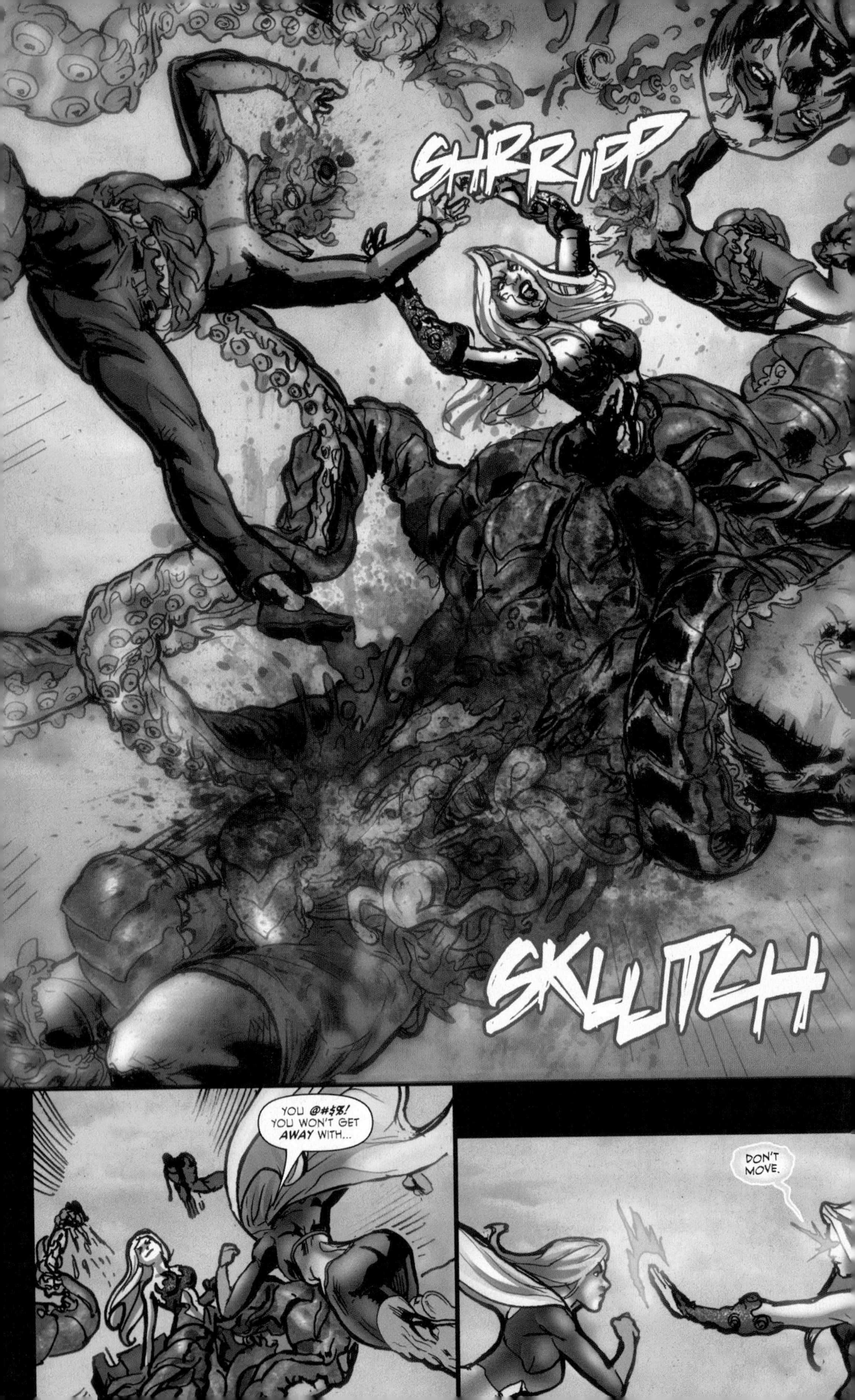
SHRRIPP
SKLLITCH
YOU @#$%! YOU WON'T GET AWAY WITH...
DON'T MOVE.

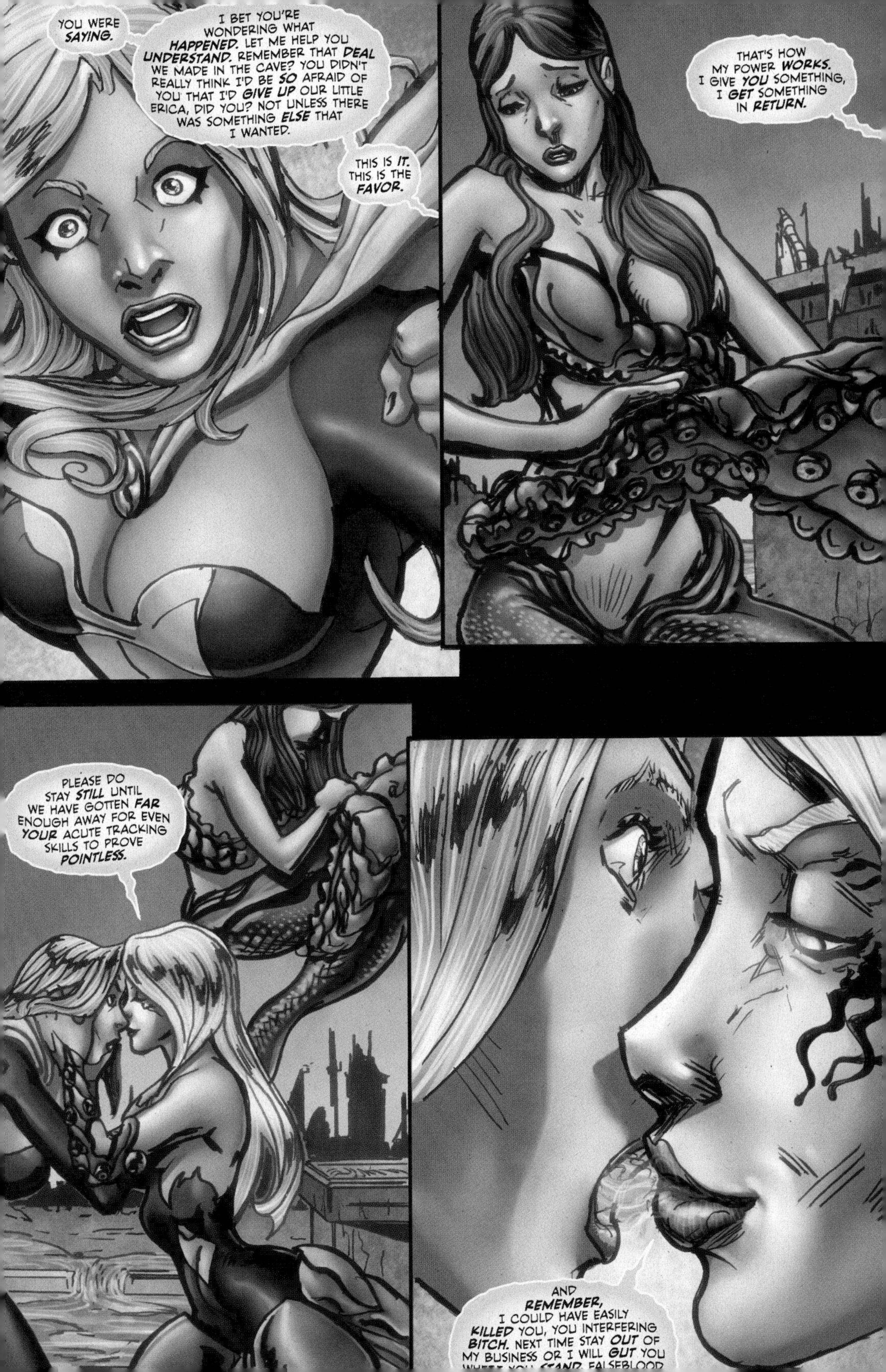

YOU WERE SAYING.
I BET YOU'RE WONDERING WHAT HAPPENED. LET ME HELP YOU UNDERSTAND. REMEMBER THAT DEAL WE MADE IN THE CAVE? YOU DIDN'T REALLY THINK I'D BE SO AFRAID OF YOU THAT I'D GIVE UP OUR LITTLE ERICA, DID YOU? NOT UNLESS THERE WAS SOMETHING ELSE THAT I WANTED.
THIS IS IT. THIS IS THE FAVOR.
THAT'S HOW MY POWER WORKS. I GIVE YOU SOMETHING, I GET SOMETHING IN RETURN.
PLEASE DO STAY STILL UNTIL WE HAVE GOTTEN FAR ENOUGH AWAY FOR EVEN YOUR ACUTE TRACKING SKILLS TO PROVE POINTLESS.
AND REMEMBER, I COULD HAVE EASILY KILLED YOU, YOU INTERFERING BITCH. NEXT TIME STAY OUT OF MY BUSINESS OR I WILL GUT YOU

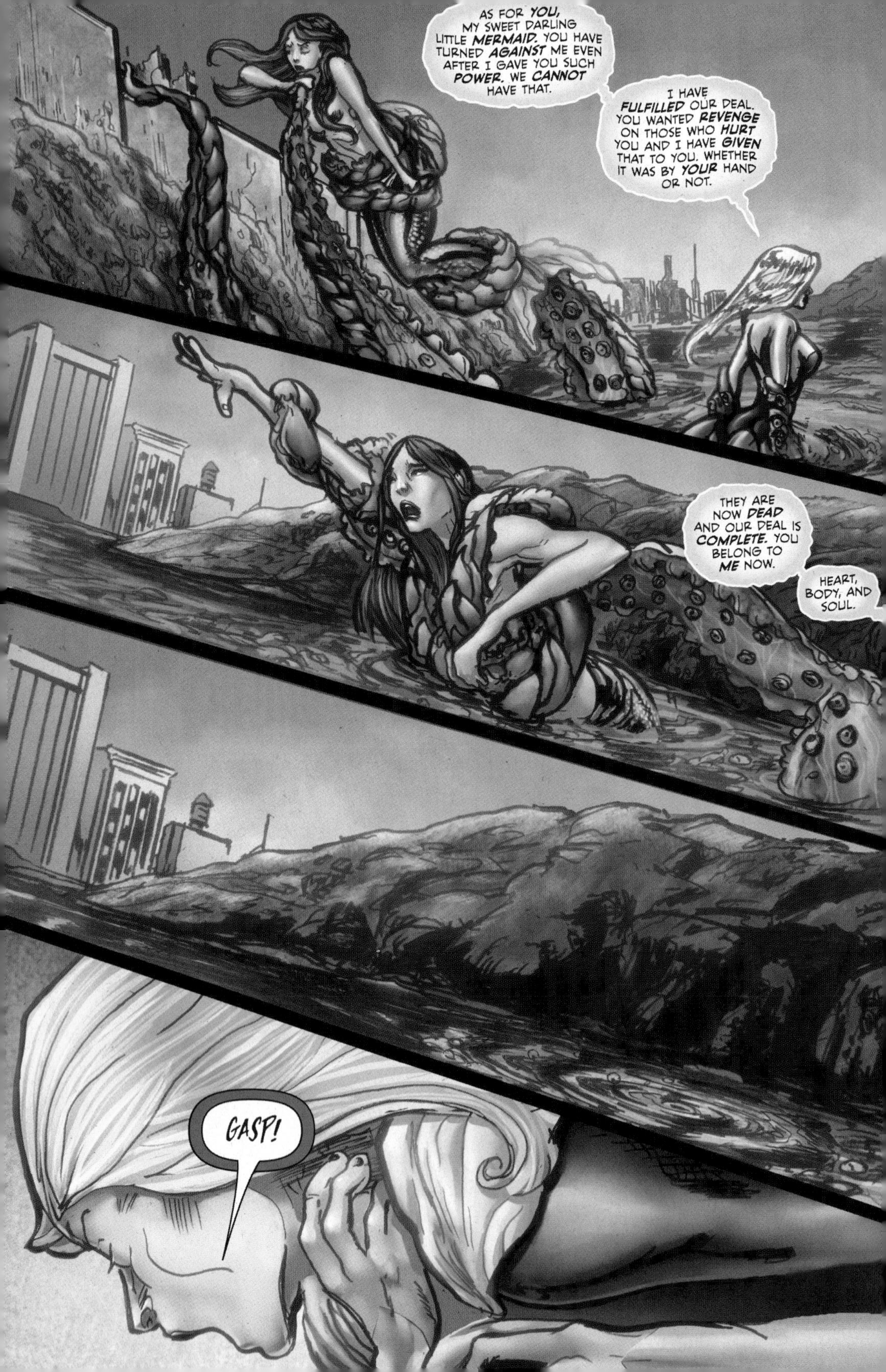
AS FOR YOU, MY SWEET DARLING LITTLE MERMAID. YOU HAVE TURNED AGAINST ME EVEN AFTER I GAVE YOU SUCH POWER. WE CANNOT HAVE THAT.
I HAVE FULFILLED OUR DEAL. YOU WANTED REVENGE ON THOSE WHO HURT YOU AND I HAVE GIVEN THAT TO YOU. WHETHER IT WAS BY YOUR HAND OR NOT.
THEY ARE NOW DEAD AND OUR DEAL IS COMPLETE. YOU BELONG TO ME NOW.
HEART, BODY, AND SOUL.
GASP!

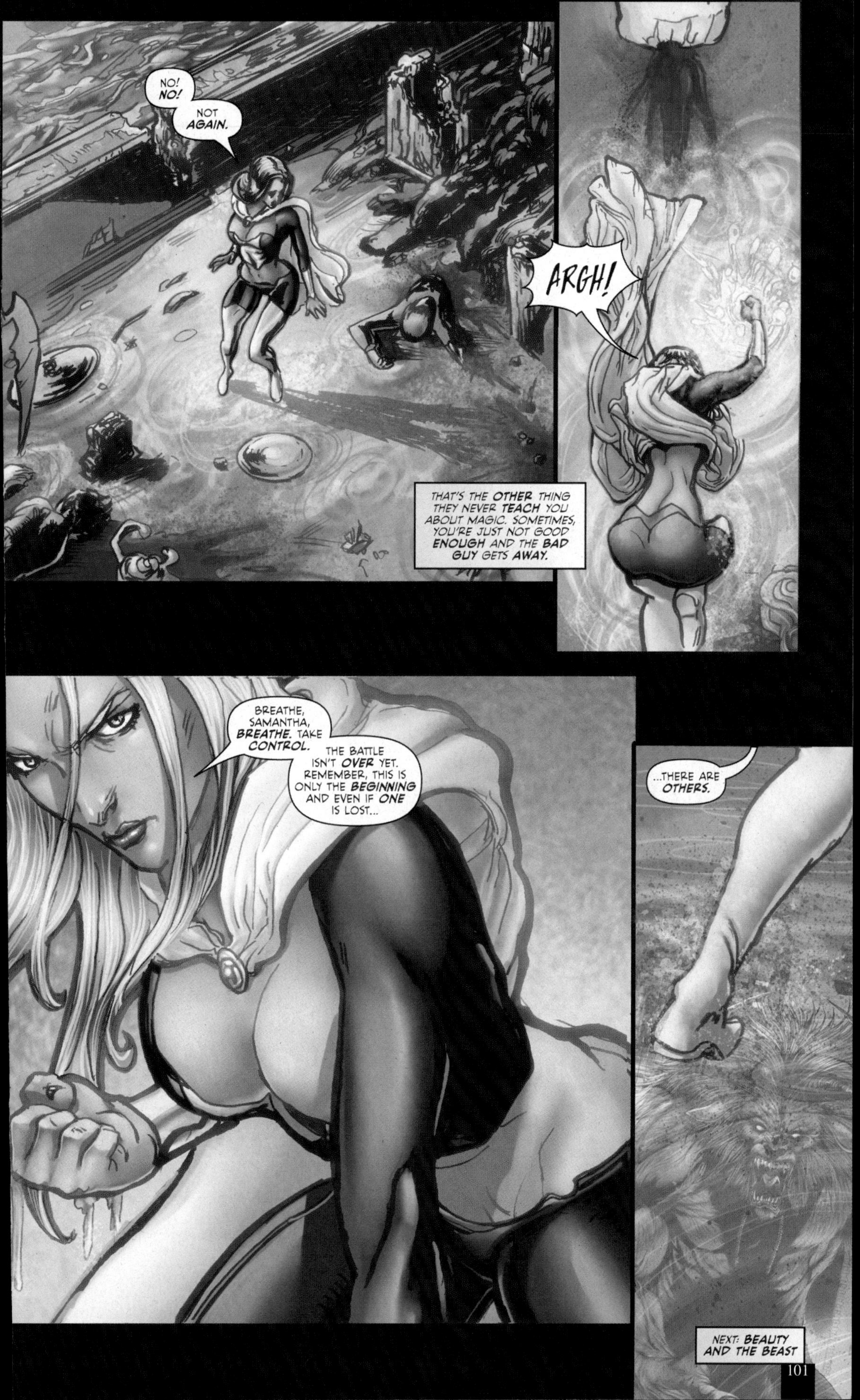
NO! NO!
NOT AGAIN.
ARGH!
THAT'S THE OTHER THING THEY NEVER TEACH YOU ABOUT MAGIC. SOMETIMES, YOU'RE JUST NOT GOOD ENOUGH AND THE BAD GUY GETS AWAY.
BREATHE, SAMANTHA, BREATHE. TAKE CONTROL.
THE BATTLE ISN'T OVER YET. REMEMBER, THIS IS ONLY THE BEGINNING AND EVEN IF ONE IS LOST...
...THERE ARE OTHERS.
NEXT: BEAUTY AND THE BEAST

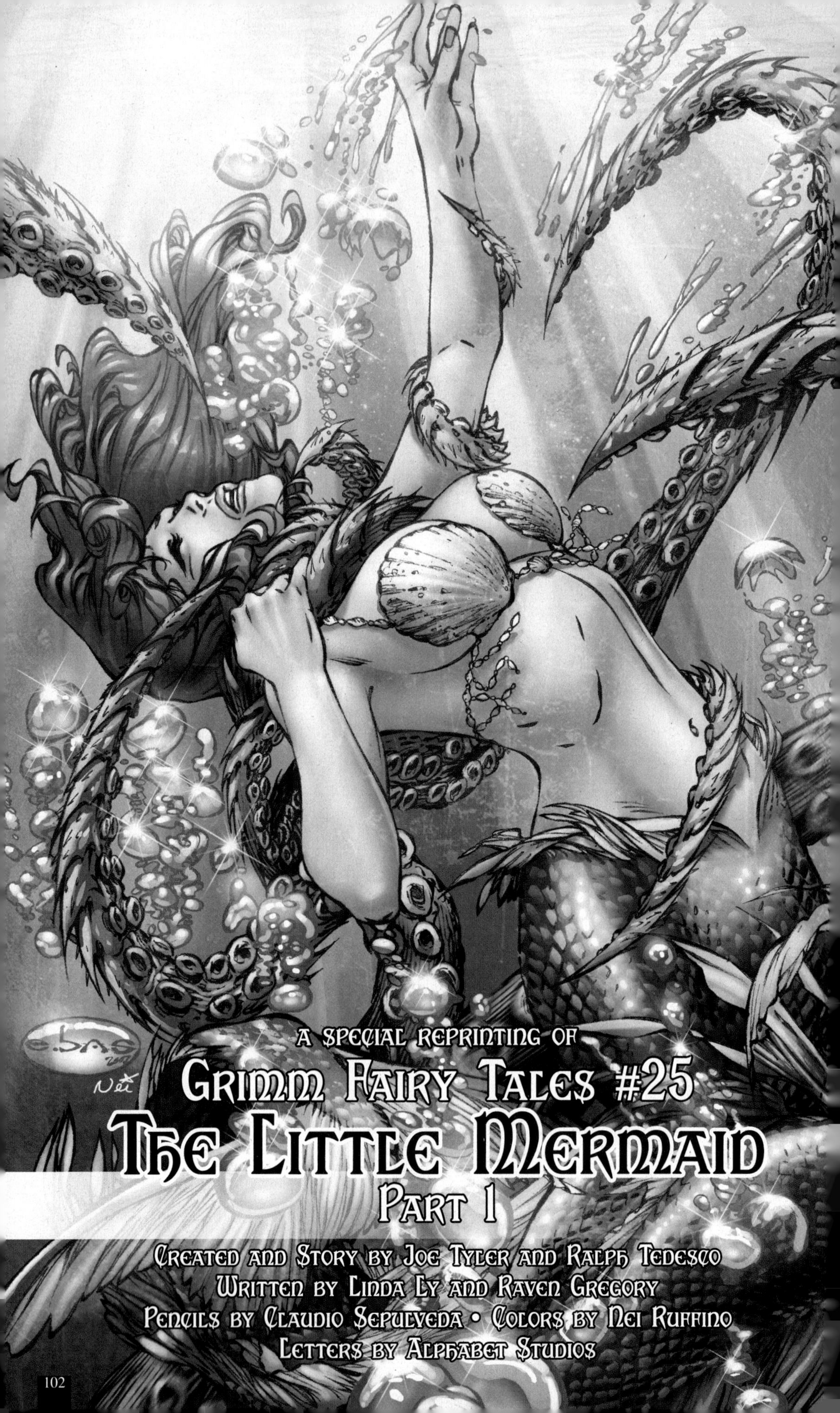

A SPECIAL REPRINTING OF

GRIMM FAIRY TALES #25
THE LITTLE MERMAID
PART 1

Created and Story by Joe Tyler and Ralph Tedesco
Written by Linda Ly and Raven Gregory
Pencils by Claudio Sepulveda • Colors by Nei Ruffino
Letters by Alphabet Studios

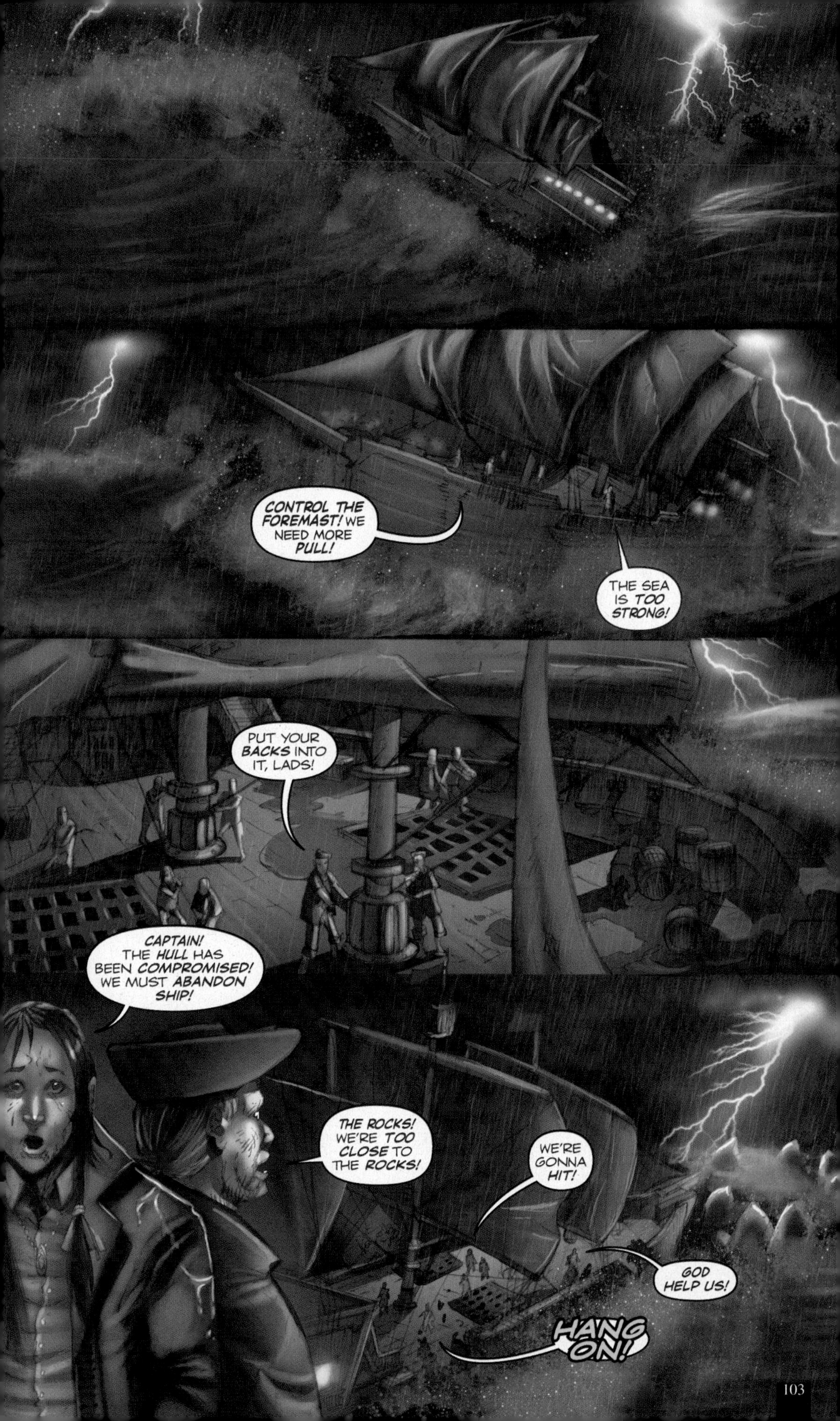
CONTROL THE FOREMAST! WE NEED MORE PULL!
THE SEA IS TOO STRONG!
PUT YOUR BACKS INTO IT, LADS!
CAPTAIN! THE HULL HAS BEEN COMPROMISED! WE MUST ABANDON SHIP!
THE ROCKS! WE'RE TOO CLOSE TO THE ROCKS!
WE'RE GONNA HIT!
GOD HELP US!
HANG ON!

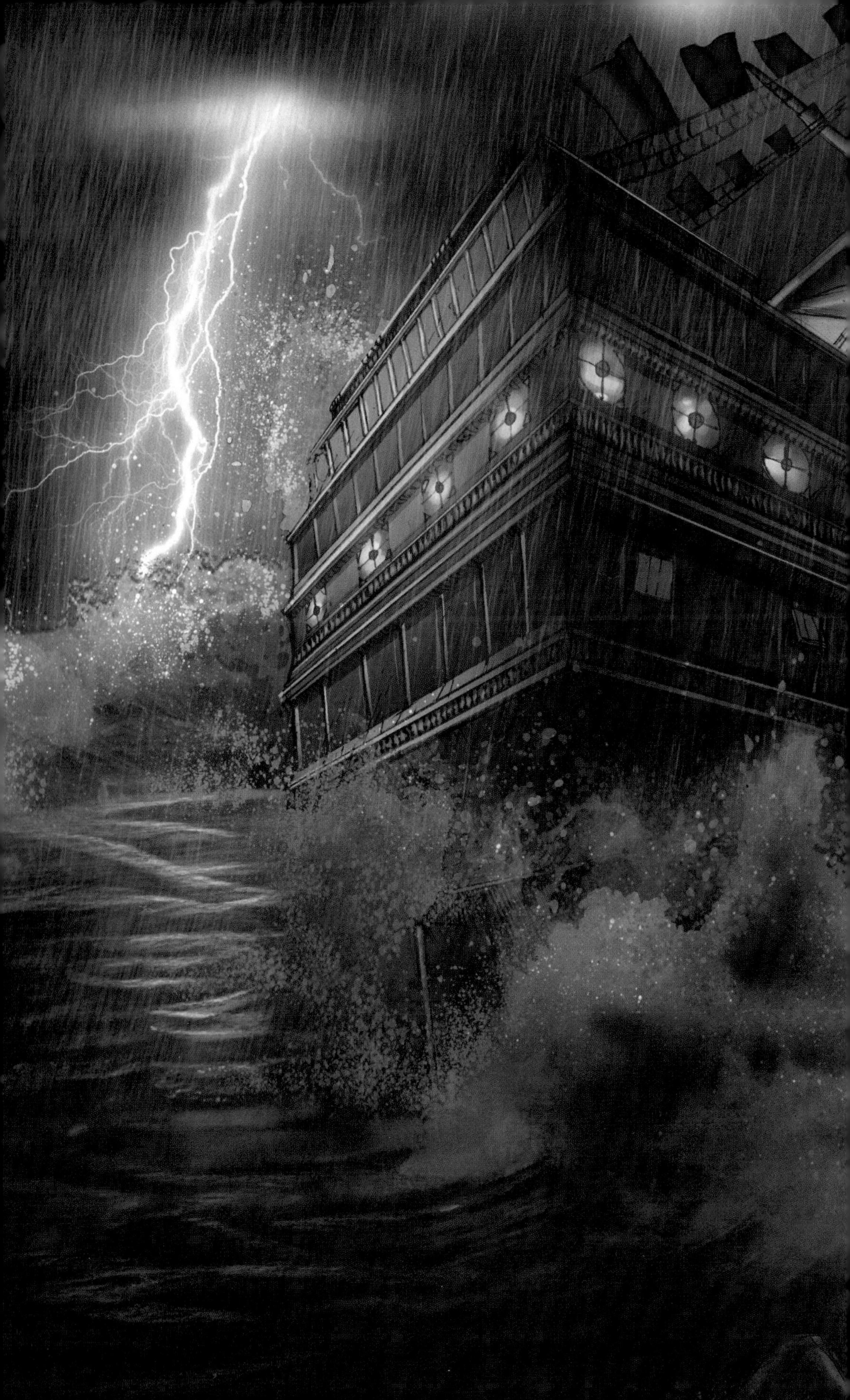

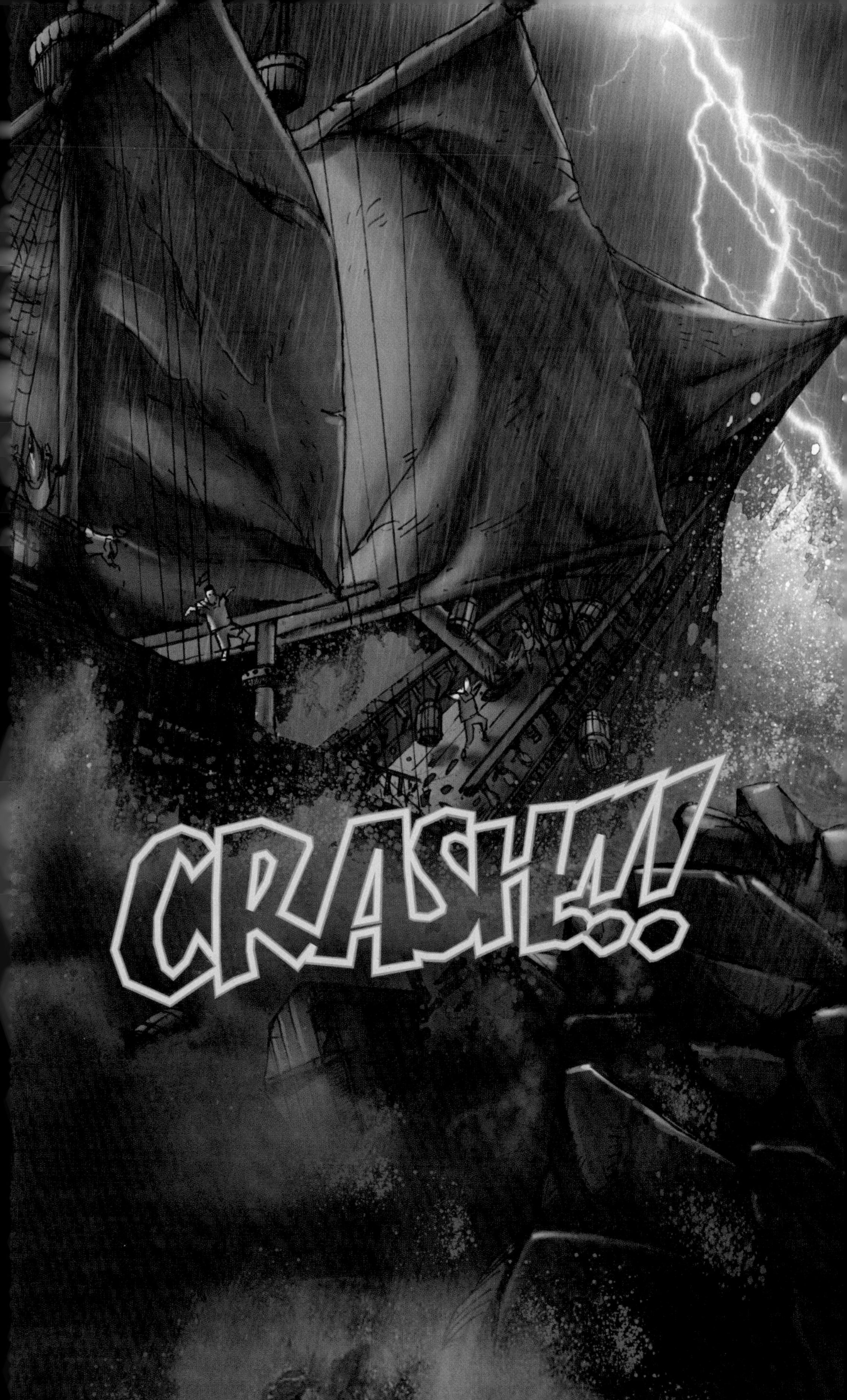
CRASH!!

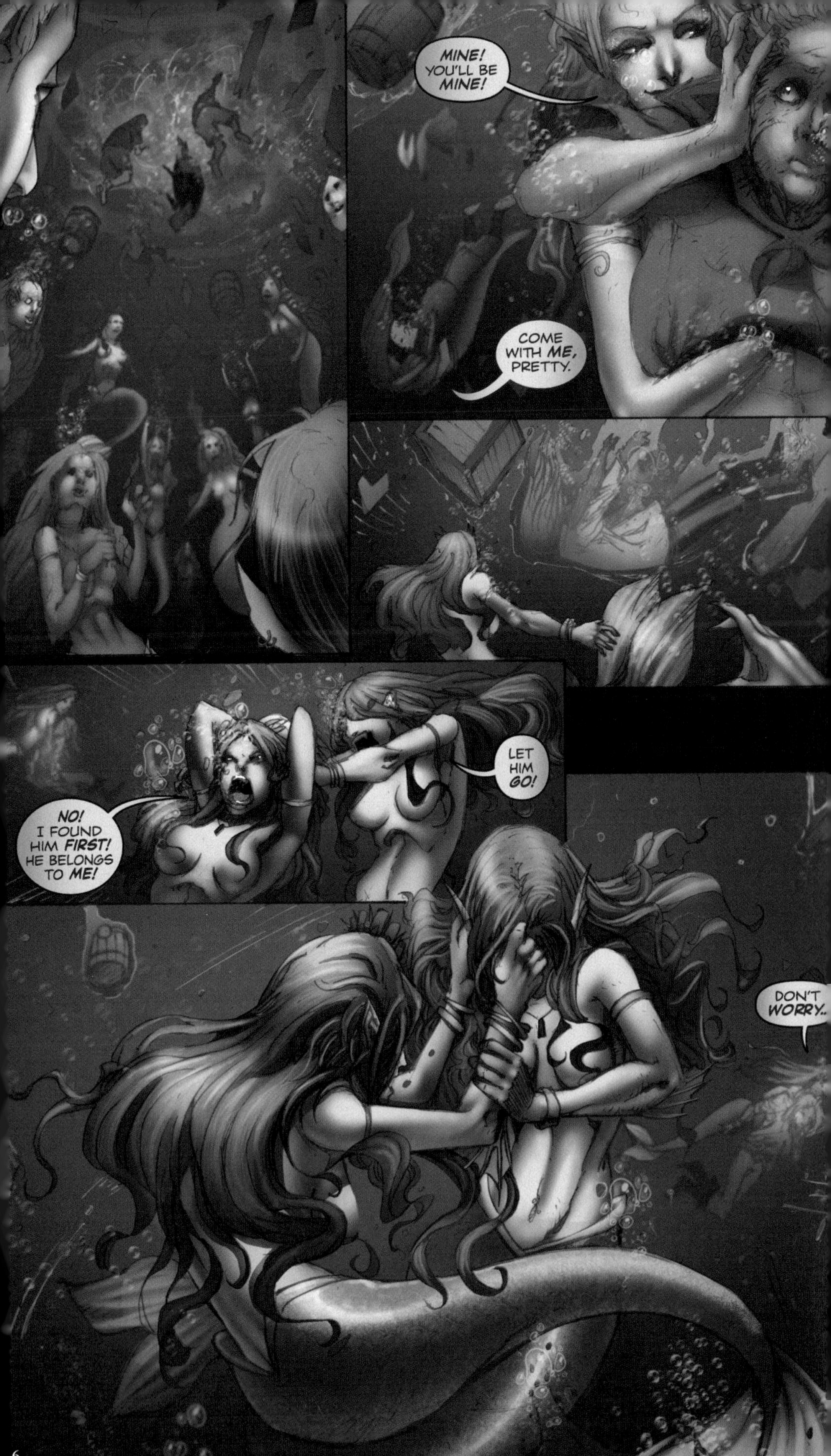
MINE! YOU'LL BE MINE!
COME WITH ME, PRETTY.
LET HIM GO!
NO! I FOUND HIM FIRST! HE BELONGS TO ME!
DON'T WORRY..

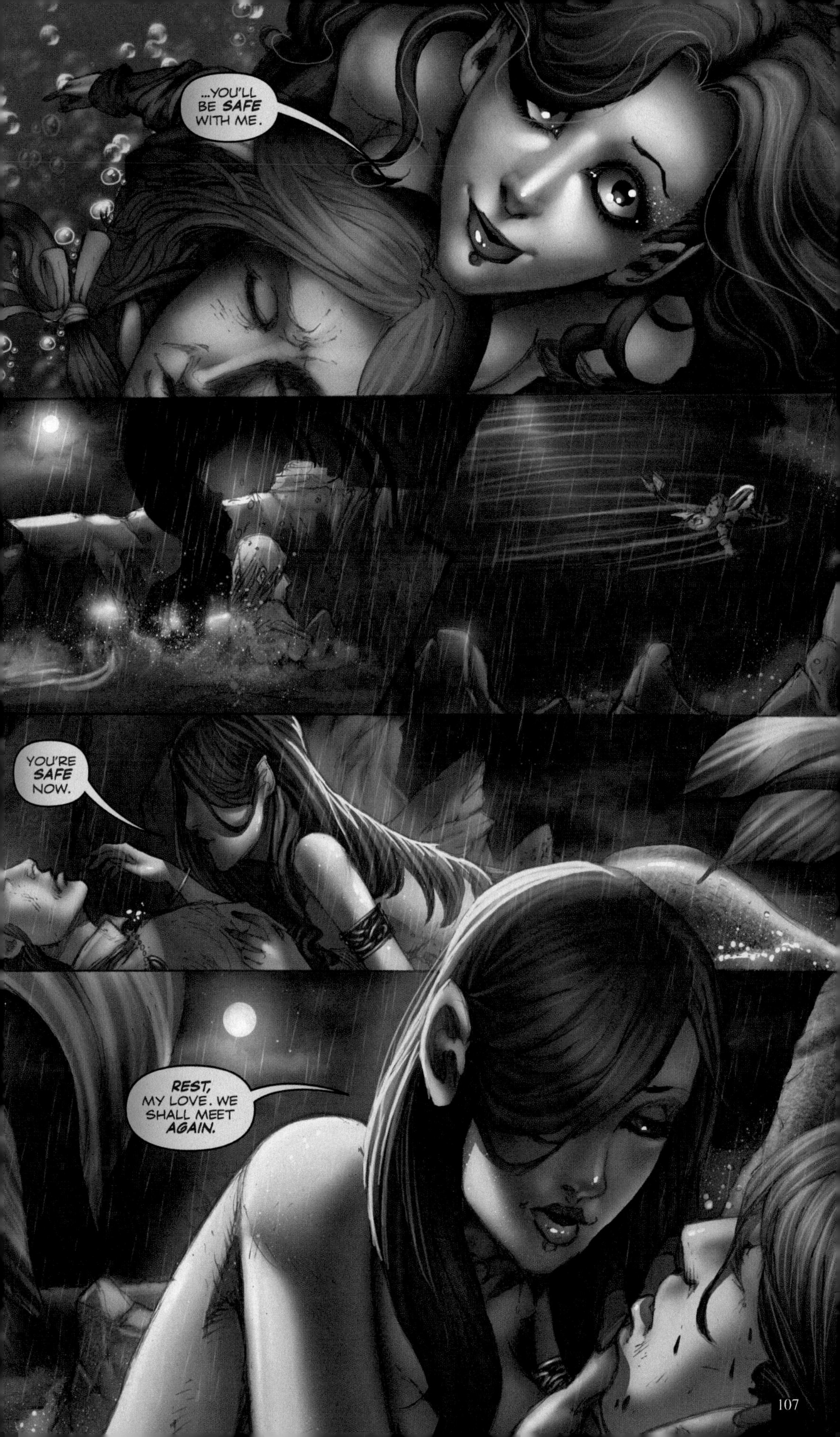
...YOU'LL BE SAFE WITH ME.
YOU'RE SAFE NOW.
REST, MY LOVE. WE SHALL MEET AGAIN.

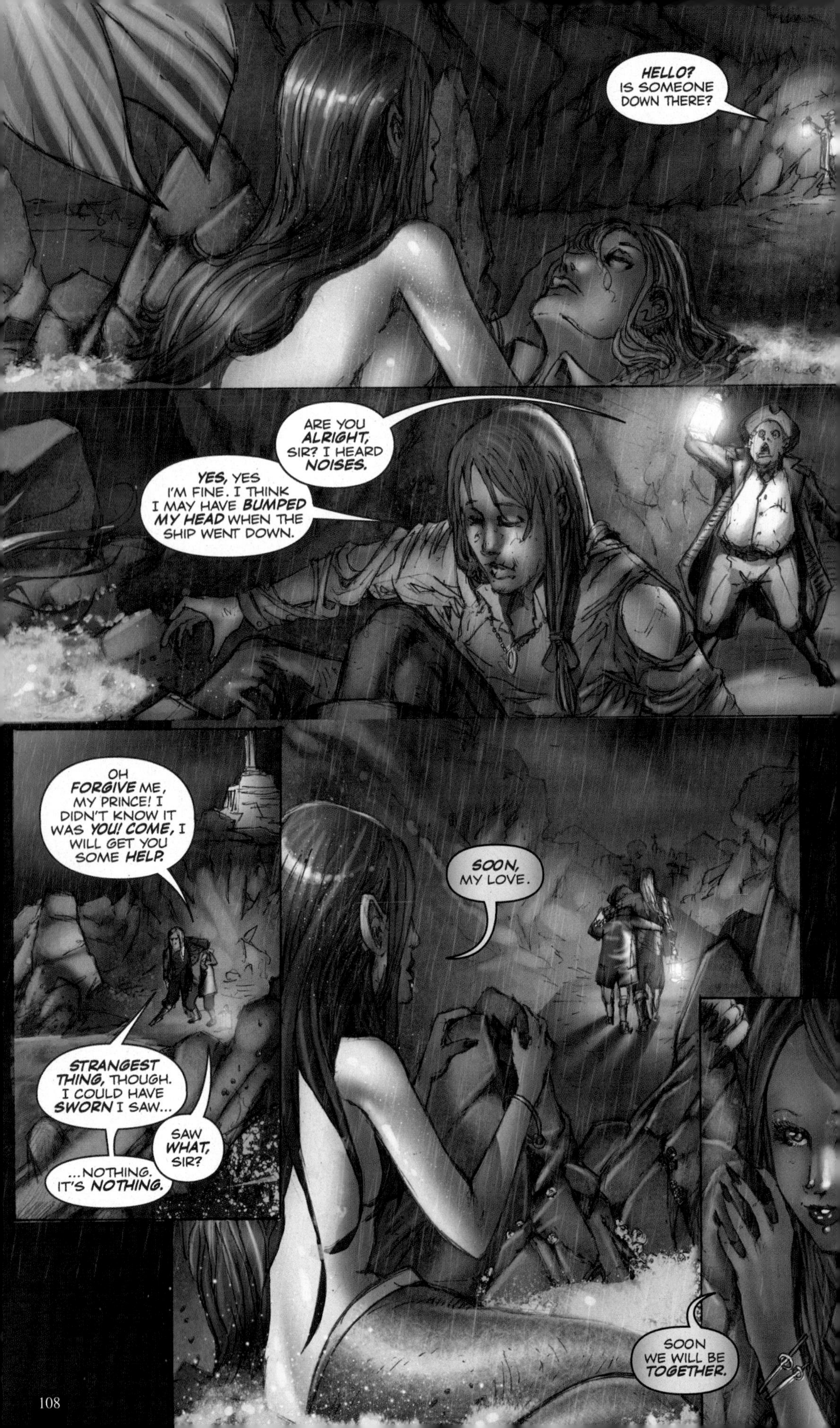
HELLO? IS SOMEONE DOWN THERE?
ARE YOU ALRIGHT, SIR? I HEARD NOISES.
YES, YES I'M FINE. I THINK I MAY HAVE BUMPED MY HEAD WHEN THE SHIP WENT DOWN.
OH FORGIVE ME, MY PRINCE! I DIDN'T KNOW IT WAS YOU! COME, I WILL GET YOU SOME HELP.
STRANGEST THING, THOUGH. I COULD HAVE SWORN I SAW...
SAW WHAT, SIR?
...NOTHING. IT'S NOTHING.
SOON, MY LOVE.
SOON WE WILL BE TOGETHER.

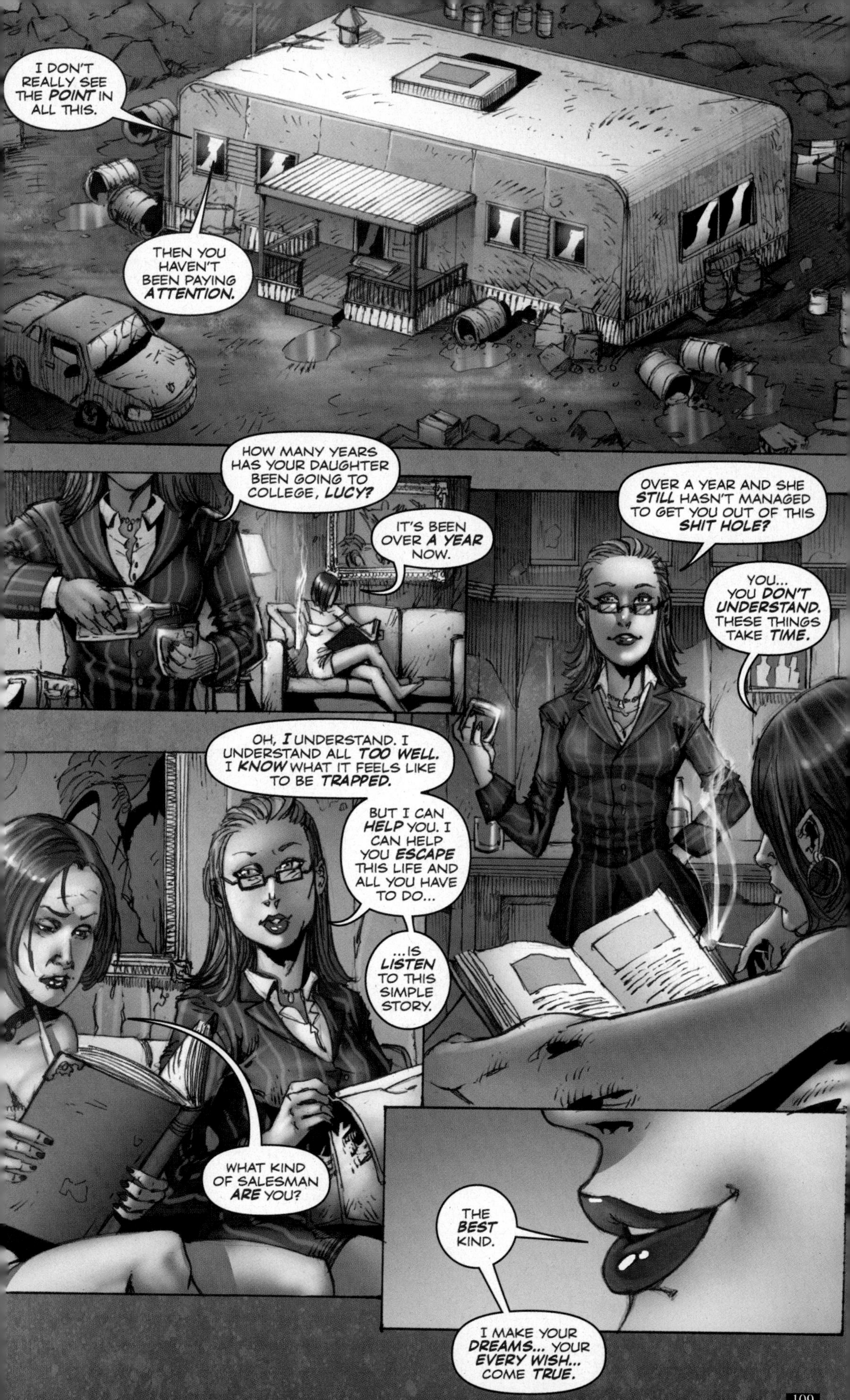

I DON'T REALLY SEE THE POINT IN ALL THIS.
THEN YOU HAVEN'T BEEN PAYING ATTENTION.
HOW MANY YEARS HAS YOUR DAUGHTER BEEN GOING TO COLLEGE, LUCY?
IT'S BEEN OVER A YEAR NOW.
OVER A YEAR AND SHE STILL HASN'T MANAGED TO GET YOU OUT OF THIS SHIT HOLE?
YOU... YOU DON'T UNDERSTAND. THESE THINGS TAKE TIME.
OH, I UNDERSTAND. I UNDERSTAND ALL TOO WELL. I KNOW WHAT IT FEELS LIKE TO BE TRAPPED.
BUT I CAN HELP YOU. I CAN HELP YOU ESCAPE THIS LIFE AND ALL YOU HAVE TO DO...
...IS LISTEN TO THIS SIMPLE STORY.
WHAT KIND OF SALESMAN ARE YOU?
THE BEST KIND.
I MAKE YOUR DREAMS... YOUR EVERY WISH... COME TRUE.

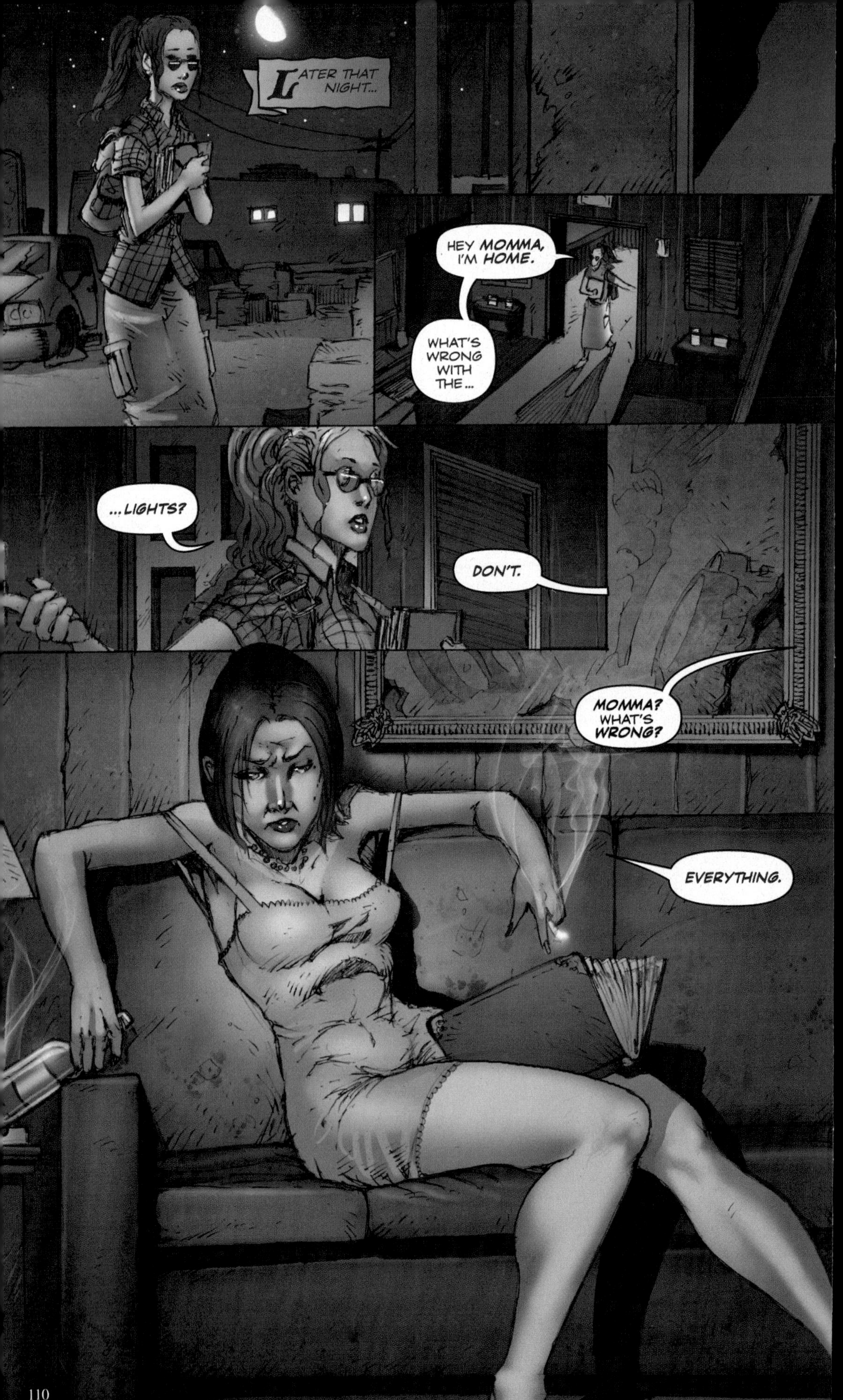
LATER THAT NIGHT...
HEY MOMMA, I'M HOME.
WHAT'S WRONG WITH THE...
...LIGHTS?
DON'T.
MOMMA? WHAT'S WRONG?
EVERYTHING.

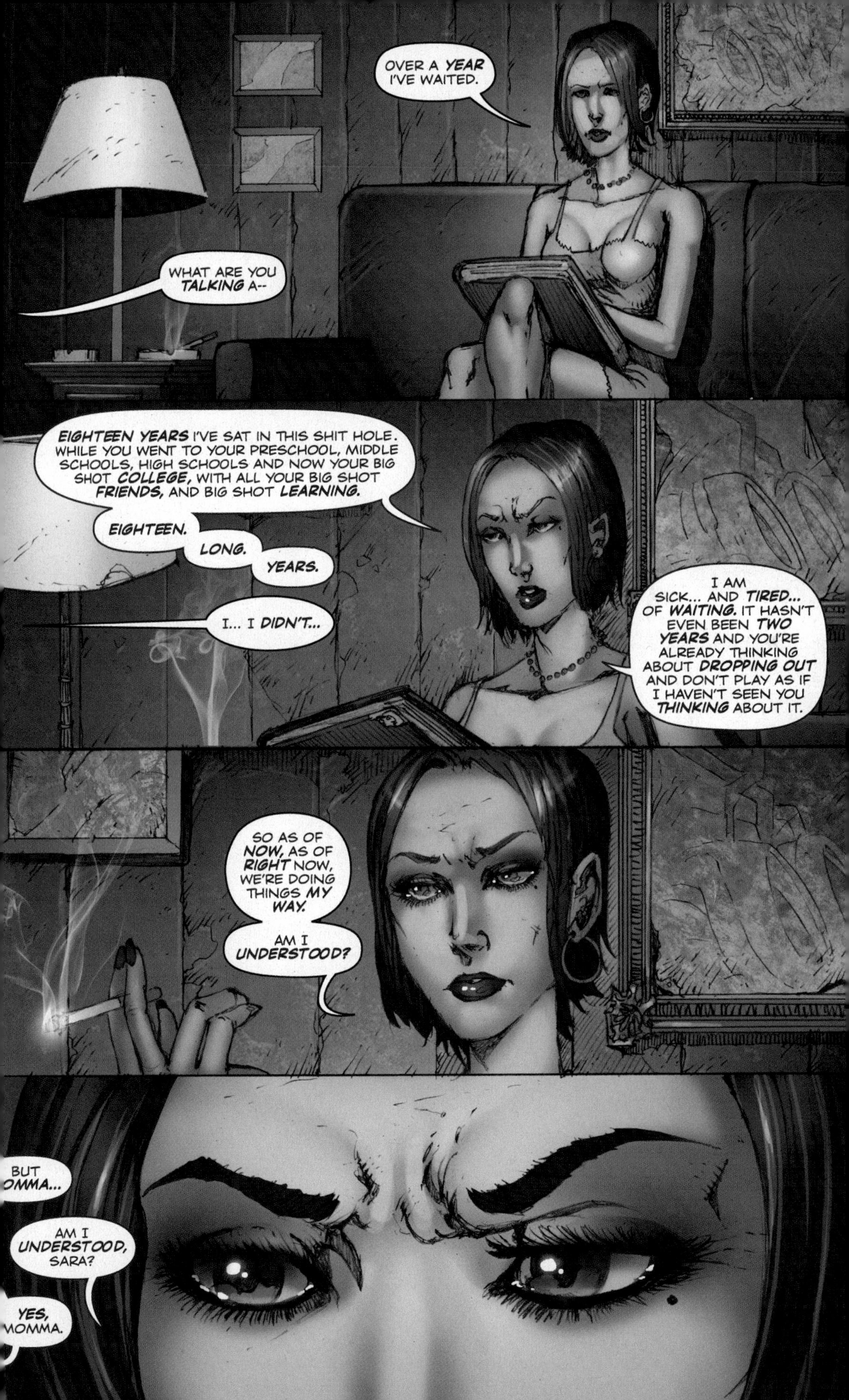
OVER A YEAR I'VE WAITED.
WHAT ARE YOU TALKING A--
EIGHTEEN YEARS I'VE SAT IN THIS SHIT HOLE. WHILE YOU WENT TO YOUR PRESCHOOL, MIDDLE SCHOOLS, HIGH SCHOOLS AND NOW YOUR BIG SHOT COLLEGE, WITH ALL YOUR BIG SHOT FRIENDS, AND BIG SHOT LEARNING.
EIGHTEEN.
LONG.
YEARS.
I... I DIDN'T...
I AM SICK... AND TIRED... OF WAITING. IT HASN'T EVEN BEEN TWO YEARS AND YOU'RE ALREADY THINKING ABOUT DROPPING OUT AND DON'T PLAY AS IF I HAVEN'T SEEN YOU THINKING ABOUT IT.
SO AS OF NOW, AS OF RIGHT NOW, WE'RE DOING THINGS MY WAY.
AM I UNDERSTOOD?
BUT OMMA...
AM I UNDERSTOOD, SARA?
YES, MOMMA.

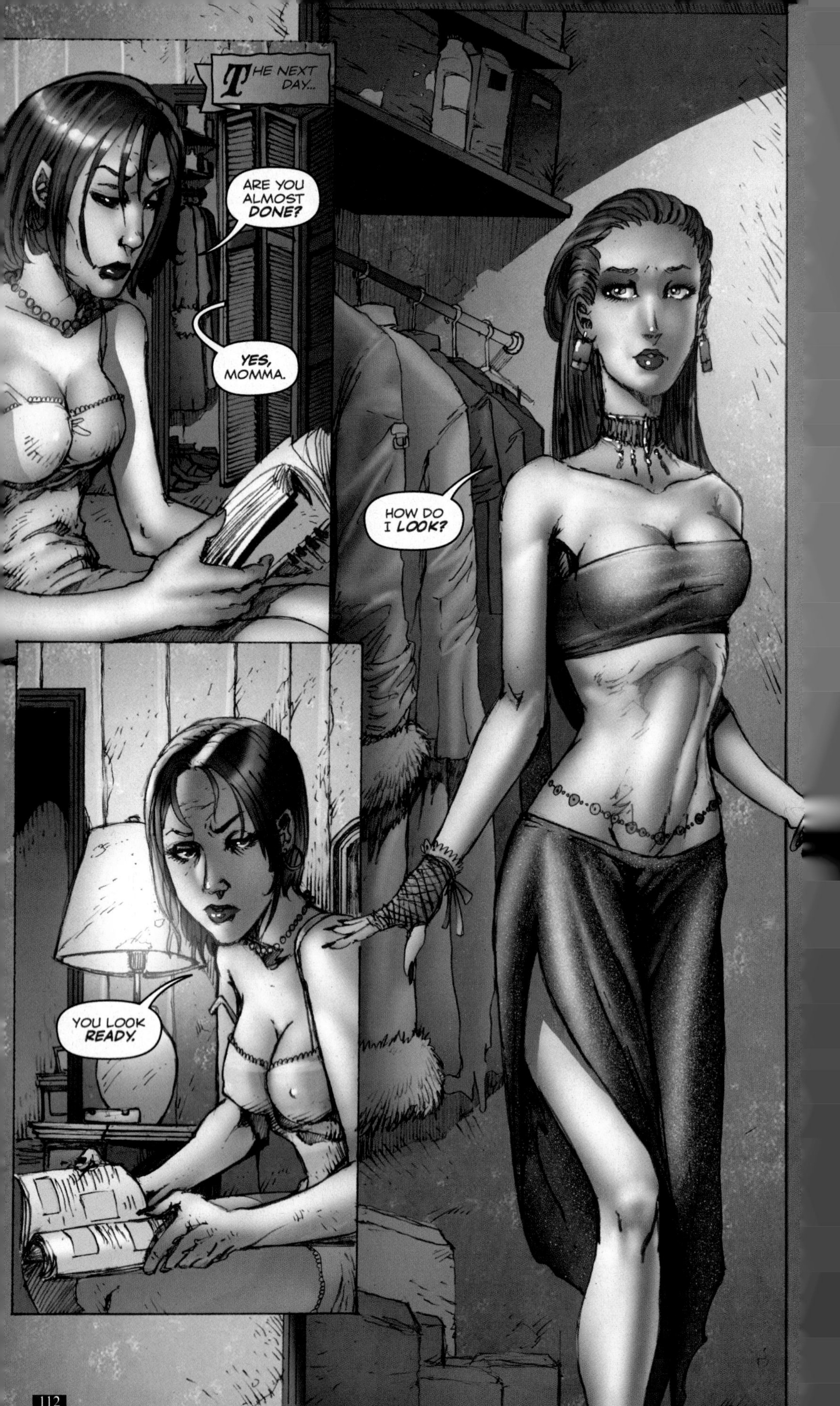
THE NEXT DAY...
ARE YOU ALMOST DONE?
YES, MOMMA.
HOW DO I LOOK?
YOU LOOK READY.

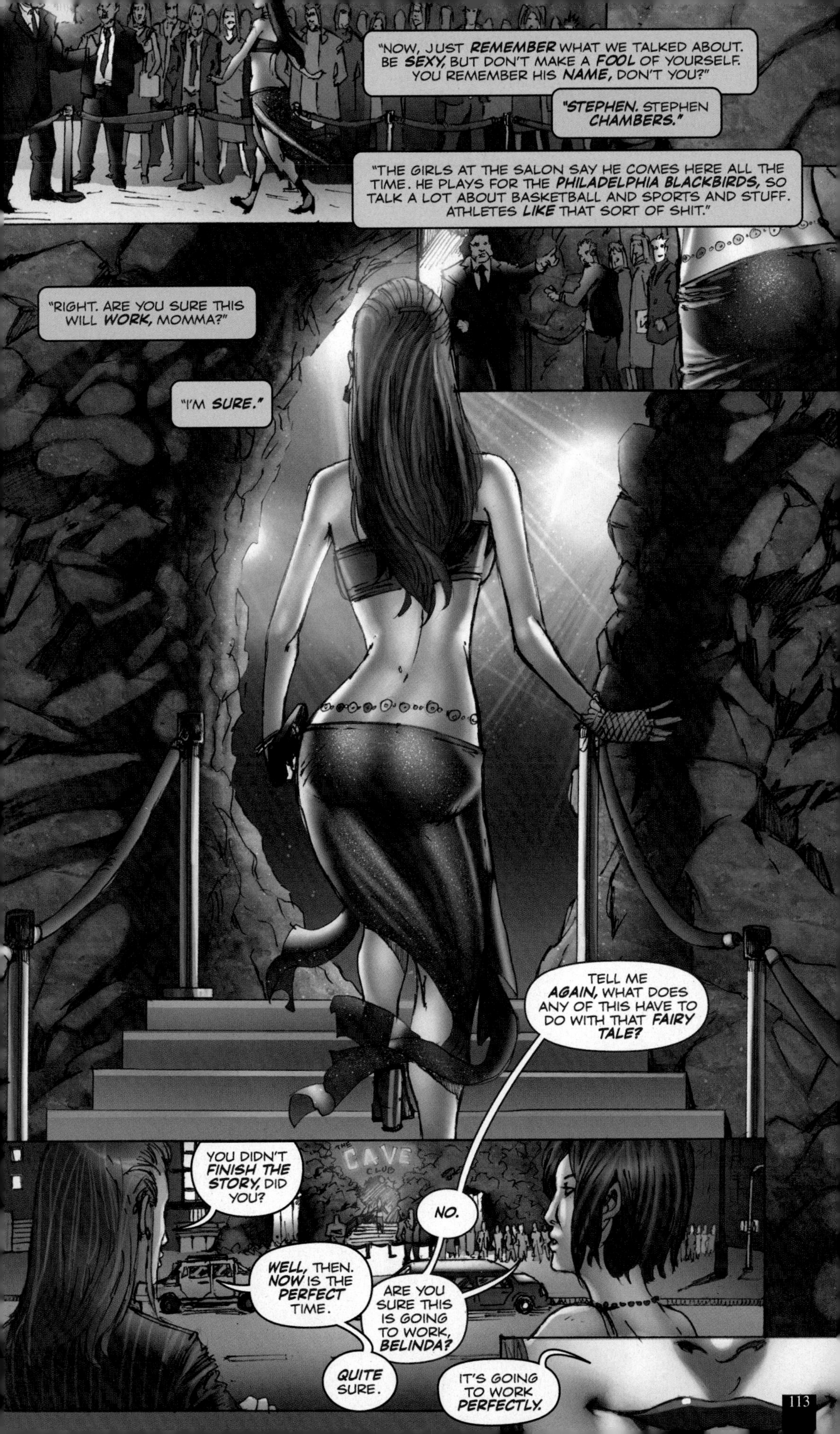
"NOW, JUST REMEMBER WHAT WE TALKED ABOUT. BE SEXY, BUT DON'T MAKE A FOOL OF YOURSELF. YOU REMEMBER HIS NAME, DON'T YOU?"
"STEPHEN. STEPHEN CHAMBERS."
"THE GIRLS AT THE SALON SAY HE COMES HERE ALL THE TIME. HE PLAYS FOR THE PHILADELPHIA BLACKBIRDS, SO TALK A LOT ABOUT BASKETBALL AND SPORTS AND STUFF. ATHLETES LIKE THAT SORT OF SHIT."
"RIGHT. ARE YOU SURE THIS WILL WORK, MOMMA?"
"I'M SURE."
TELL ME AGAIN, WHAT DOES ANY OF THIS HAVE TO DO WITH THAT FAIRY TALE?
THE CAVE CLUB
YOU DIDN'T FINISH THE STORY, DID YOU?
NO.
WELL, THEN. NOW IS THE PERFECT TIME.
ARE YOU SURE THIS IS GOING TO WORK, BELINDA?
QUITE SURE.
IT'S GOING TO WORK PERFECTLY.

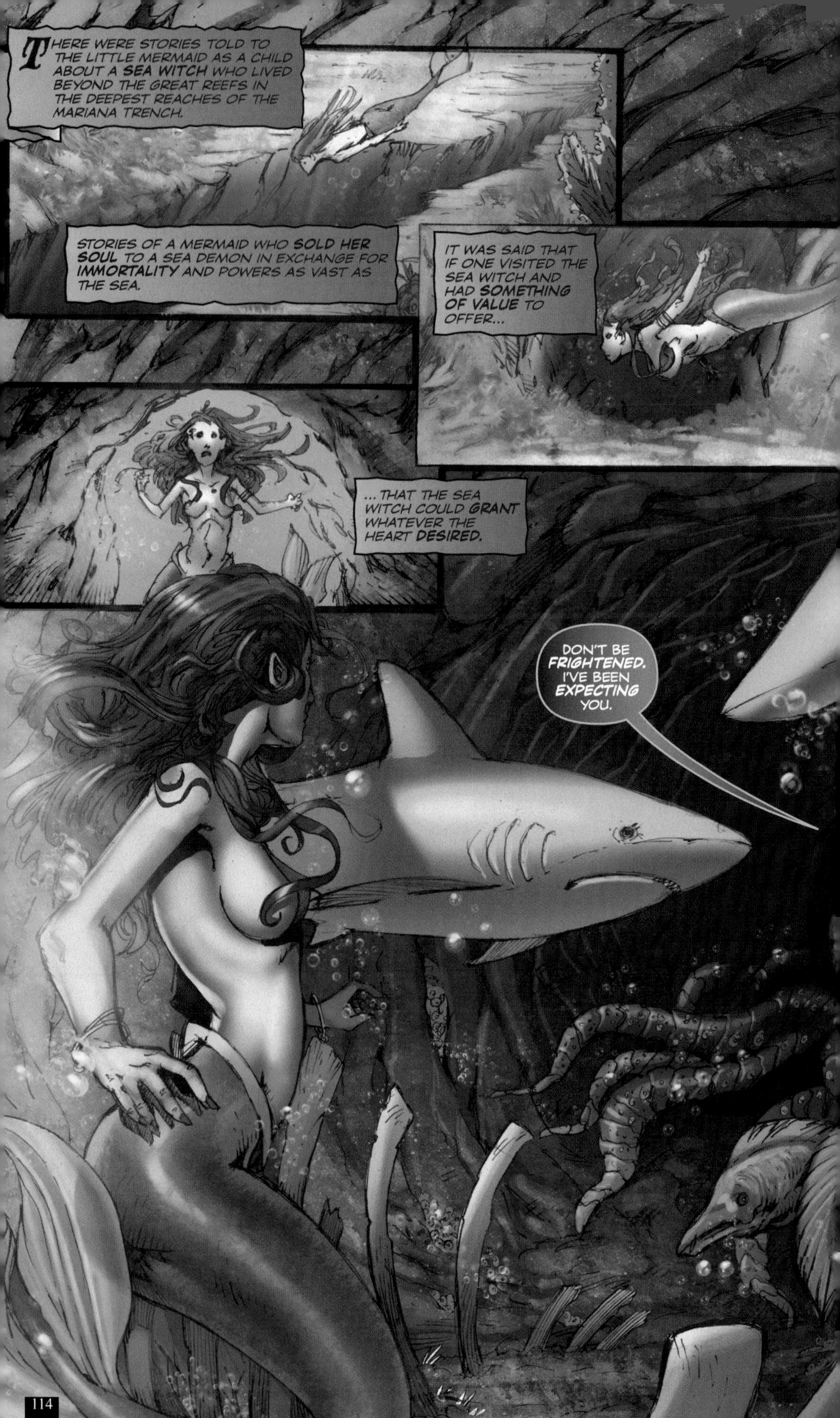
THERE WERE STORIES TOLD TO THE LITTLE MERMAID AS A CHILD ABOUT A SEA WITCH WHO LIVED BEYOND THE GREAT REEFS IN THE DEEPEST REACHES OF THE MARIANA TRENCH.
STORIES OF A MERMAID WHO SOLD HER SOUL TO A SEA DEMON IN EXCHANGE FOR IMMORTALITY AND POWERS AS VAST AS THE SEA.
IT WAS SAID THAT IF ONE VISITED THE SEA WITCH AND HAD SOMETHING OF VALUE TO OFFER...
...THAT THE SEA WITCH COULD GRANT WHATEVER THE HEART DESIRED.
DON'T BE FRIGHTENED. I'VE BEEN EXPECTING YOU.

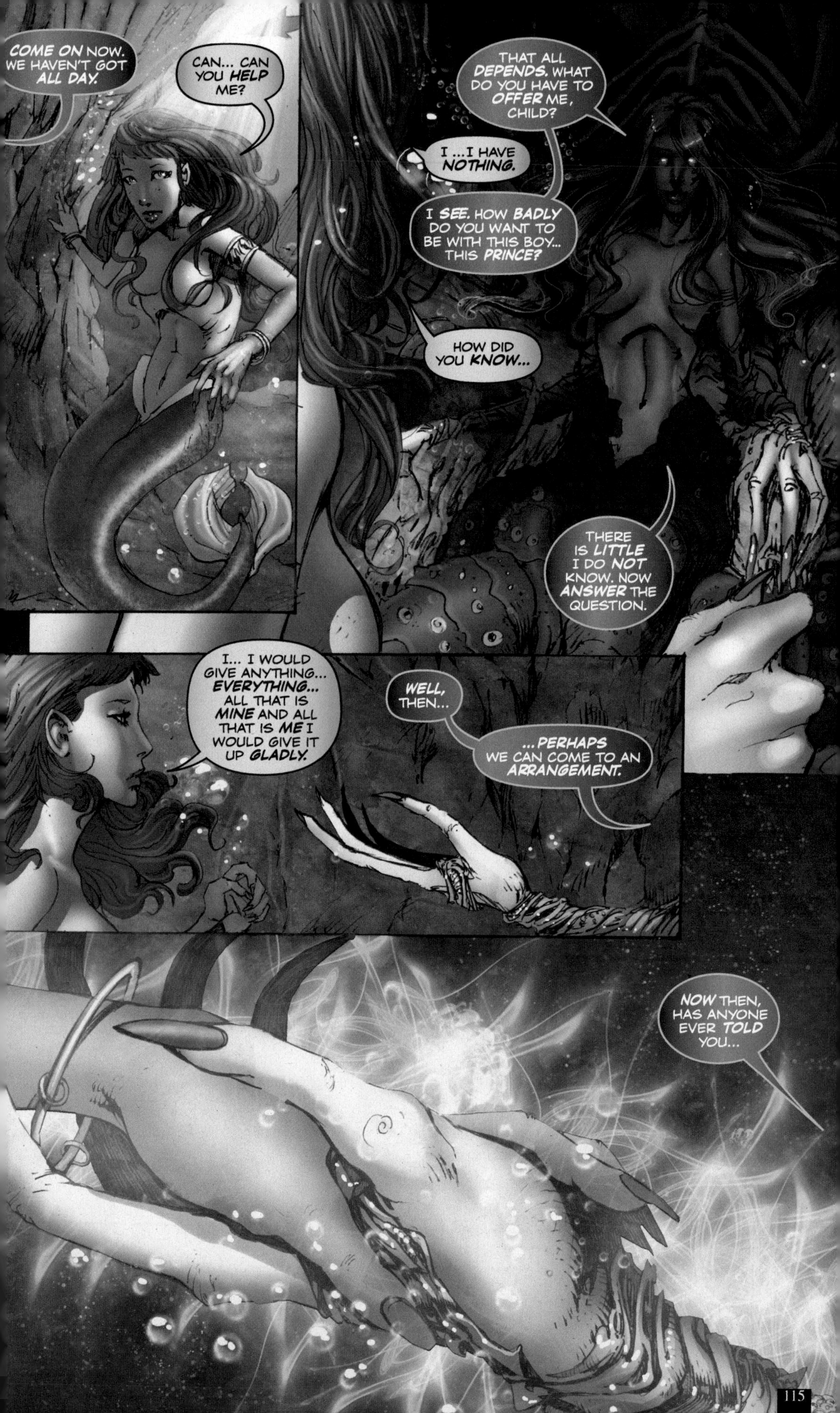
COME ON NOW. WE HAVEN'T GOT ALL DAY.
CAN... CAN YOU HELP ME?
THAT ALL DEPENDS. WHAT DO YOU HAVE TO OFFER ME, CHILD?
I ...I HAVE NOTHING.
I SEE. HOW BADLY DO YOU WANT TO BE WITH THIS BOY... THIS PRINCE?
HOW DID YOU KNOW...
THERE IS LITTLE I DO NOT KNOW. NOW ANSWER THE QUESTION.
I... I WOULD GIVE ANYTHING... EVERYTHING... ALL THAT IS MINE AND ALL THAT IS ME I WOULD GIVE IT UP GLADLY.
WELL, THEN...
...PERHAPS WE CAN COME TO AN ARRANGEMENT.
NOW THEN, HAS ANYONE EVER TOLD YOU...

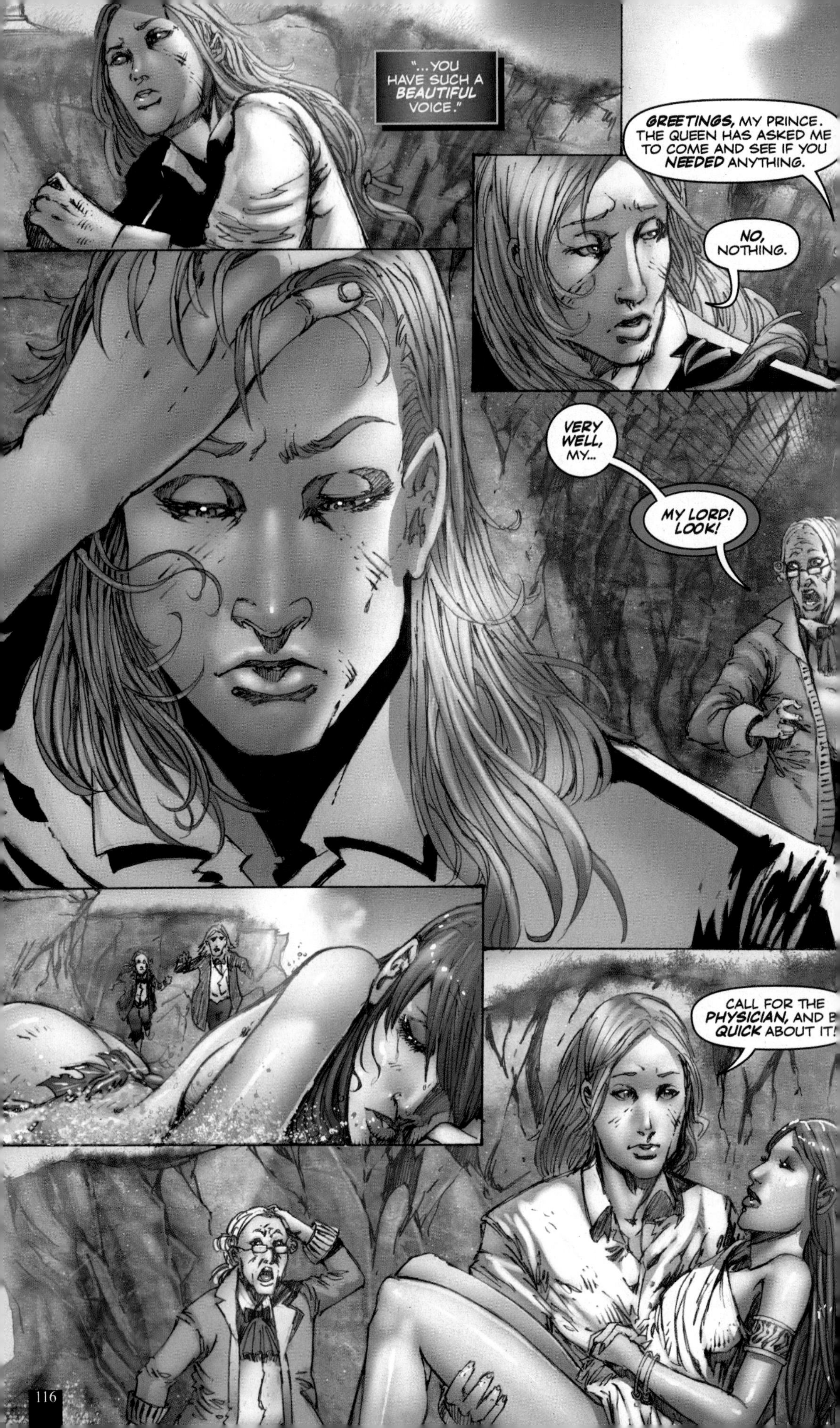
"...YOU HAVE SUCH A BEAUTIFUL VOICE."
GREETINGS, MY PRINCE. THE QUEEN HAS ASKED ME TO COME AND SEE IF YOU NEEDED ANYTHING.
NO, NOTHING.
VERY WELL, MY...
MY LORD! LOOK!
CALL FOR THE PHYSICIAN, AND B QUICK ABOUT IT!

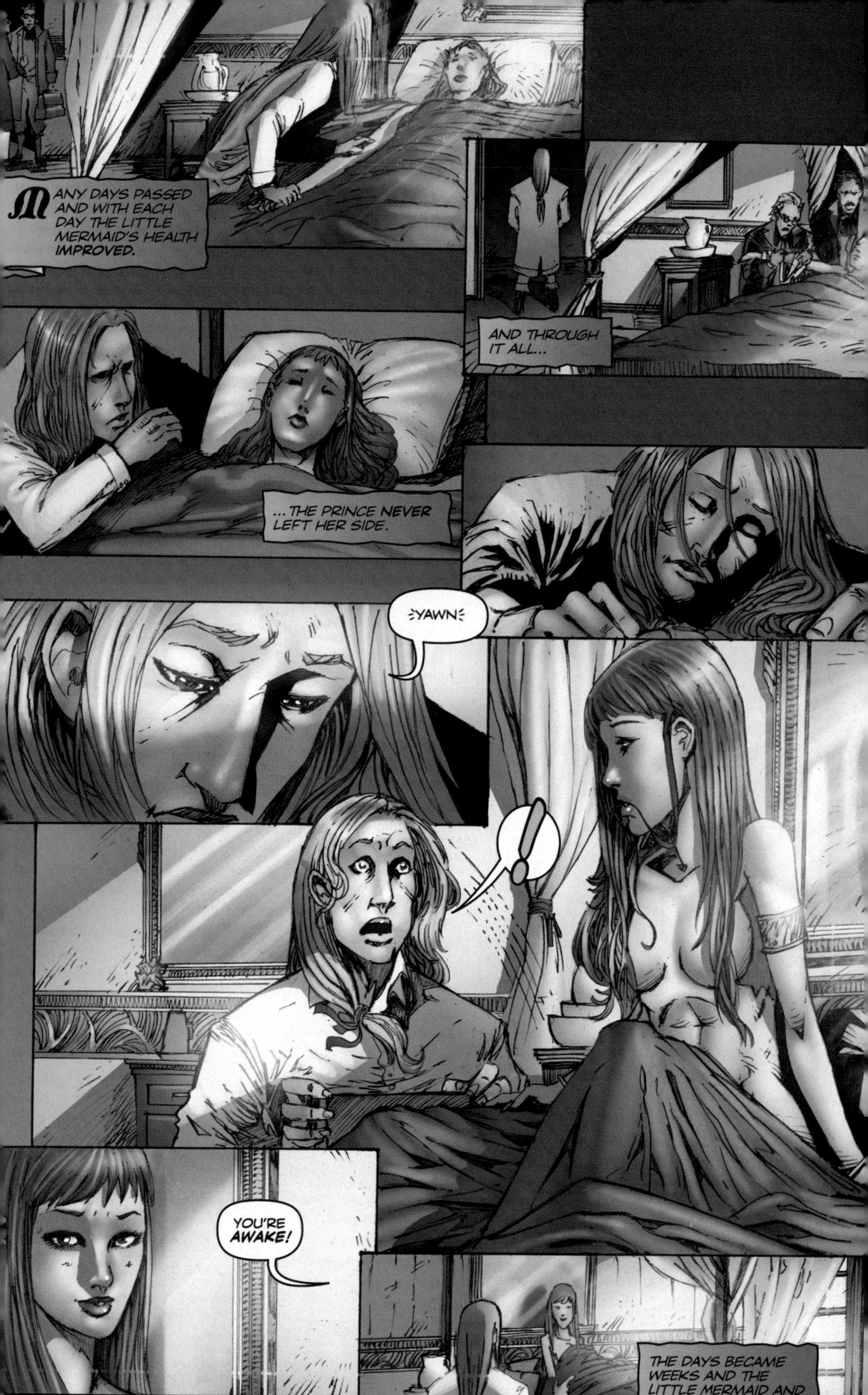
MANY DAYS PASSED AND WITH EACH DAY THE LITTLE MERMAID'S HEALTH IMPROVED.
AND THROUGH IT ALL...
...THE PRINCE NEVER LEFT HER SIDE.
YAWN
!
YOU'RE AWAKE!
THE DAYS BECAME WEEKS AND THE LITTLE MERMAID AND THE PRINCE BECAME CLOSER AND CLOSER AS TIME PASSED BY.

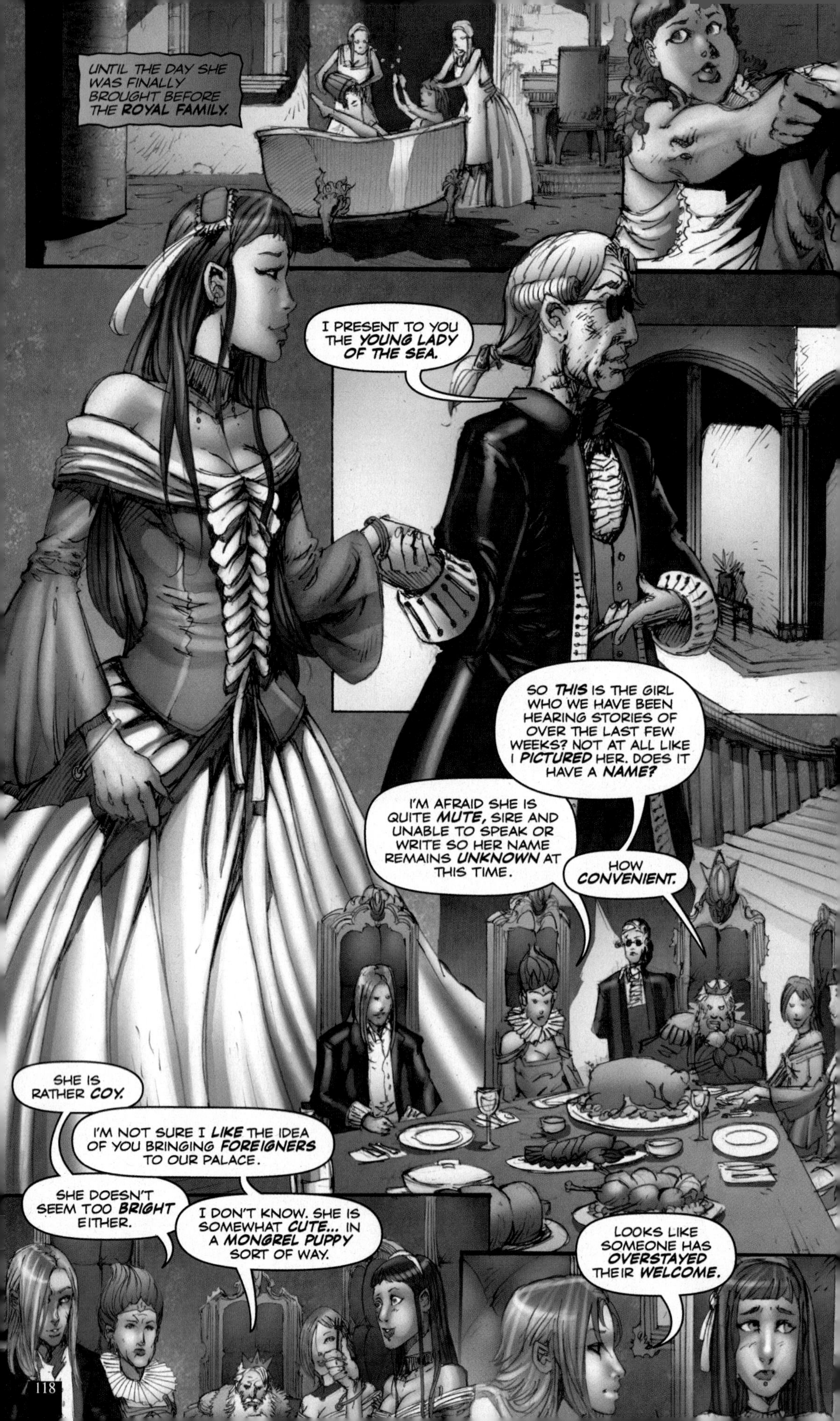

UNTIL THE DAY SHE WAS FINALLY BROUGHT BEFORE THE ROYAL FAMILY.
I PRESENT TO YOU THE YOUNG LADY OF THE SEA.
SO THIS IS THE GIRL WHO WE HAVE BEEN HEARING STORIES OF OVER THE LAST FEW WEEKS? NOT AT ALL LIKE I PICTURED HER. DOES IT HAVE A NAME?
I'M AFRAID SHE IS QUITE MUTE, SIRE AND UNABLE TO SPEAK OR WRITE SO HER NAME REMAINS UNKNOWN AT THIS TIME.
HOW CONVENIENT.
SHE IS RATHER COY.
I'M NOT SURE I LIKE THE IDEA OF YOU BRINGING FOREIGNERS TO OUR PALACE.
SHE DOESN'T SEEM TOO BRIGHT EITHER.
I DON'T KNOW. SHE IS SOMEWHAT CUTE... IN A MONGREL PUPPY SORT OF WAY.
LOOKS LIKE SOMEONE HAS OVERSTAYED THEIR WELCOME.

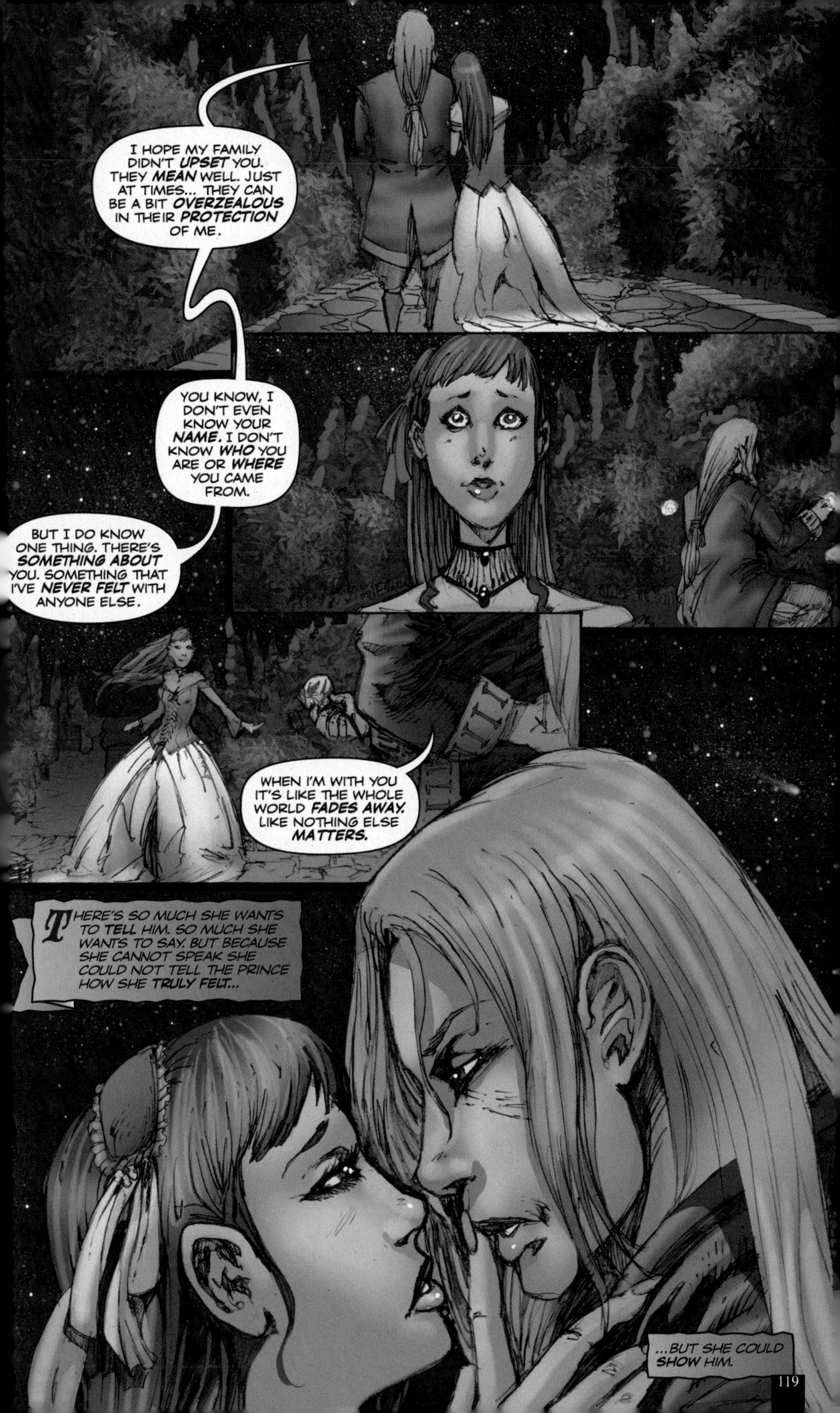
I HOPE MY FAMILY DIDN'T UPSET YOU. THEY MEAN WELL. JUST AT TIMES... THEY CAN BE A BIT OVERZEALOUS IN THEIR PROTECTION OF ME.
YOU KNOW, I DON'T EVEN KNOW YOUR NAME. I DON'T KNOW WHO YOU ARE OR WHERE YOU CAME FROM.
BUT I DO KNOW ONE THING. THERE'S SOMETHING ABOUT YOU. SOMETHING THAT I'VE NEVER FELT WITH ANYONE ELSE.
WHEN I'M WITH YOU IT'S LIKE THE WHOLE WORLD FADES AWAY. LIKE NOTHING ELSE MATTERS.
THERE'S SO MUCH SHE WANTS TO TELL HIM. SO MUCH SHE WANTS TO SAY. BUT BECAUSE SHE CANNOT SPEAK SHE COULD NOT TELL THE PRINCE HOW SHE TRULY FELT...
...BUT SHE COULD SHOW HIM.

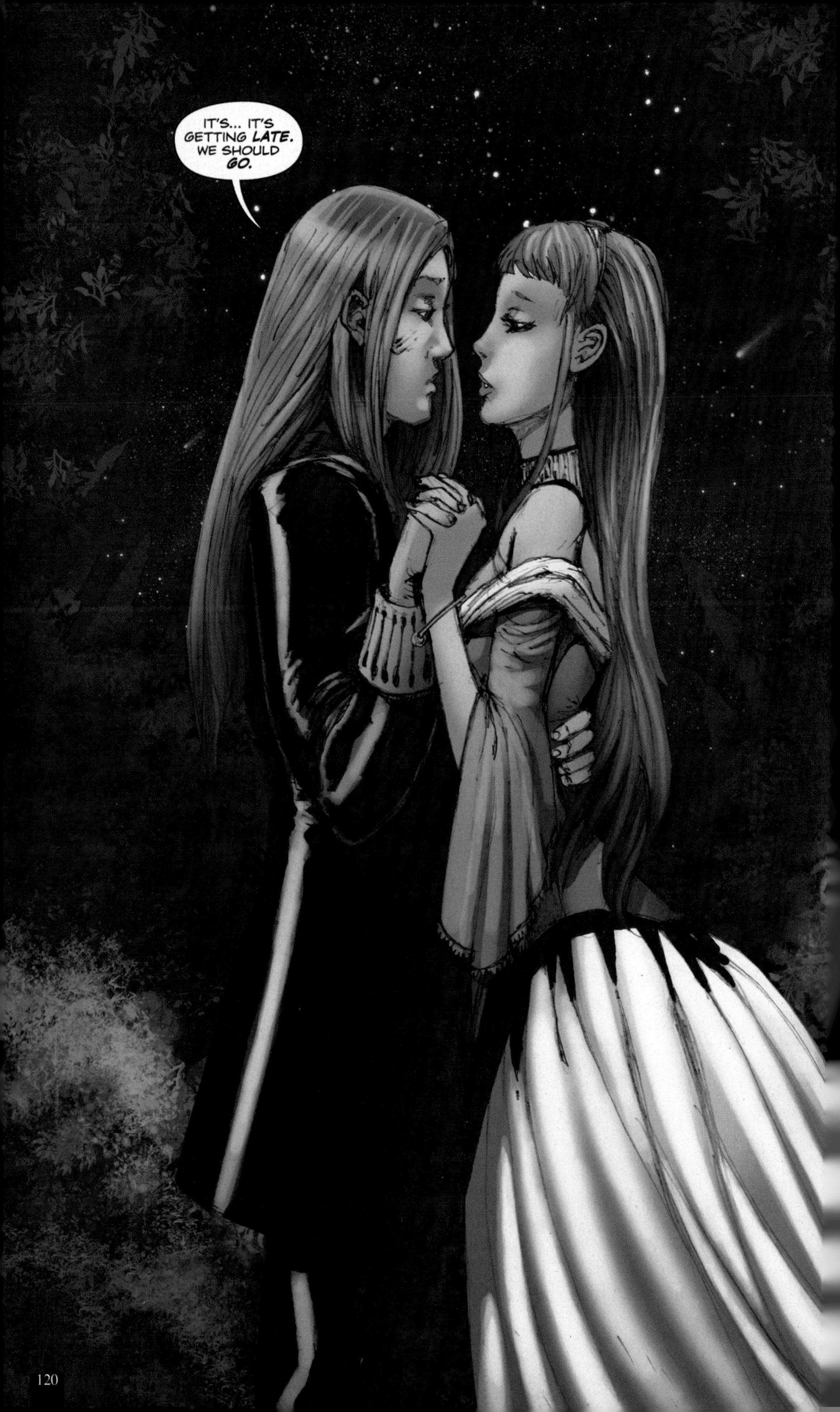
IT'S... IT'S GETTING LATE. WE SHOULD GO.

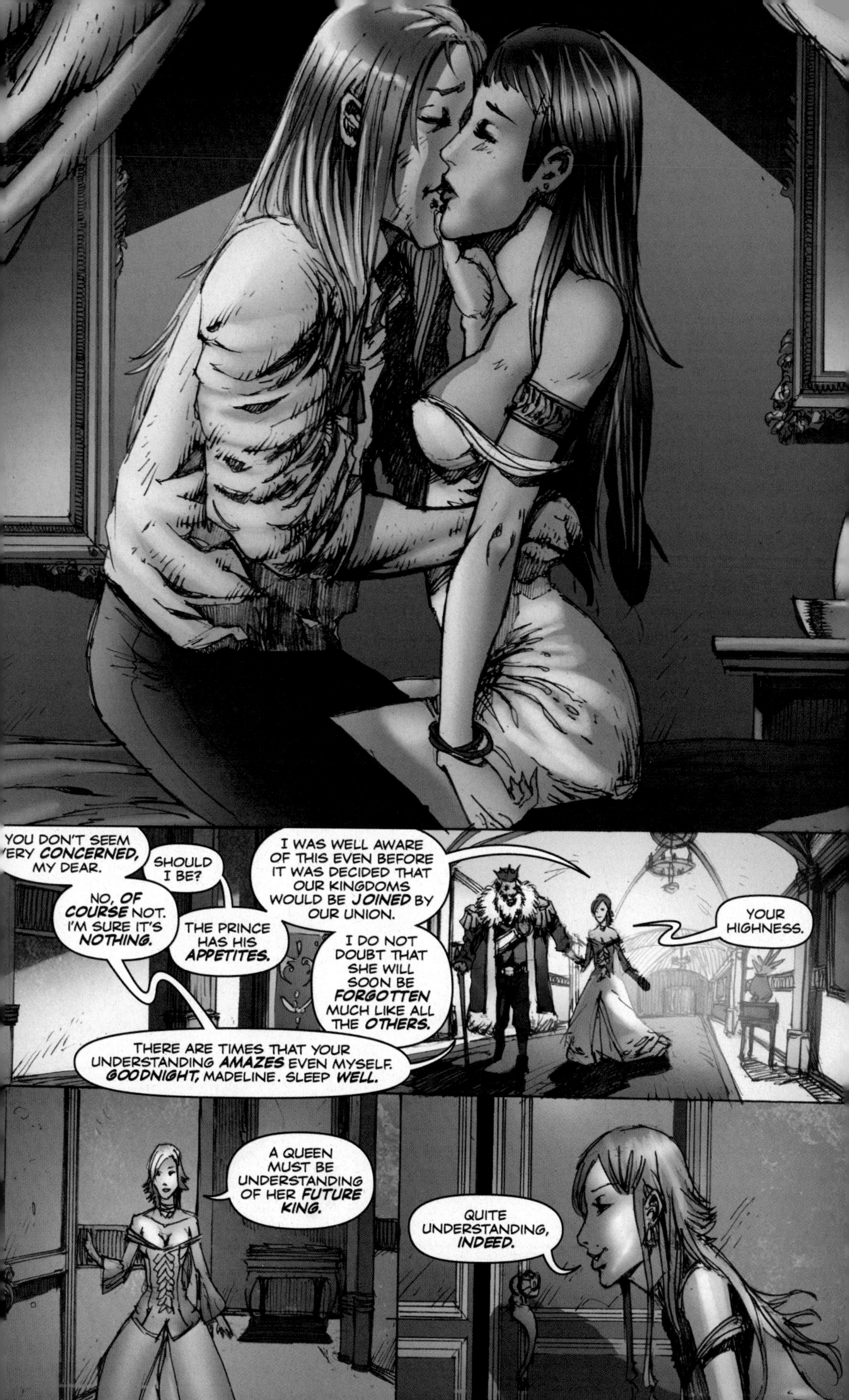

YOU DON'T SEEM ERY CONCERNED, MY DEAR.
SHOULD I BE?
NO, OF COURSE NOT. I'M SURE IT'S NOTHING.
THE PRINCE HAS HIS APPETITES.
I WAS WELL AWARE OF THIS EVEN BEFORE IT WAS DECIDED THAT OUR KINGDOMS WOULD BE JOINED BY OUR UNION.
I DO NOT DOUBT THAT SHE WILL SOON BE FORGOTTEN MUCH LIKE ALL THE OTHERS.
YOUR HIGHNESS.
THERE ARE TIMES THAT YOUR UNDERSTANDING AMAZES EVEN MYSELF. GOODNIGHT, MADELINE. SLEEP WELL.
A QUEEN MUST BE UNDERSTANDING OF HER FUTURE KING.
QUITE UNDERSTANDING, INDEED.

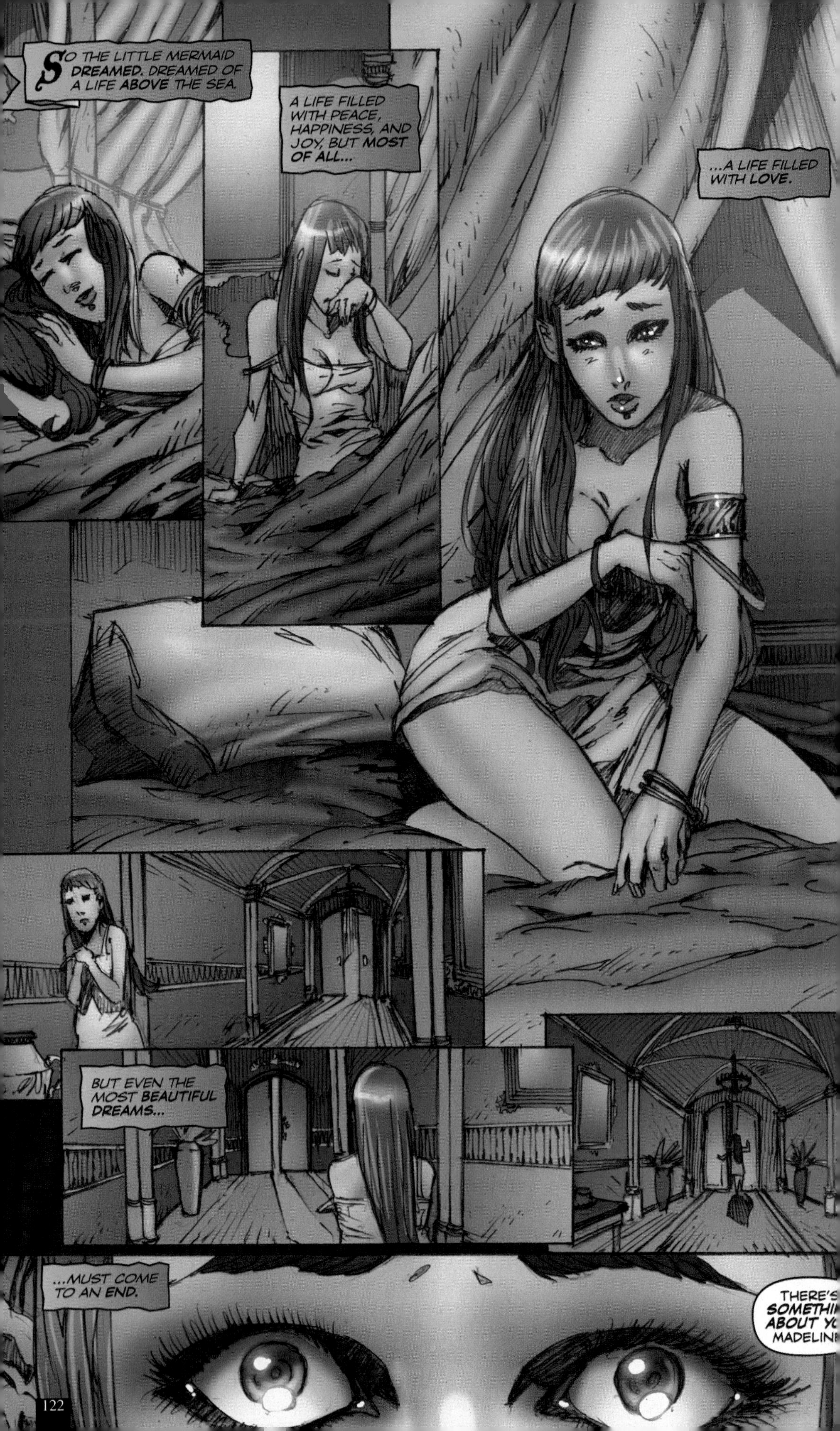

SO THE LITTLE MERMAID DREAMED. DREAMED OF A LIFE ABOVE THE SEA.
A LIFE FILLED WITH PEACE, HAPPINESS, AND JOY, BUT MOST OF ALL...
...A LIFE FILLED WITH LOVE.
BUT EVEN THE MOST BEAUTIFUL DREAMS...
...MUST COME TO AN END.

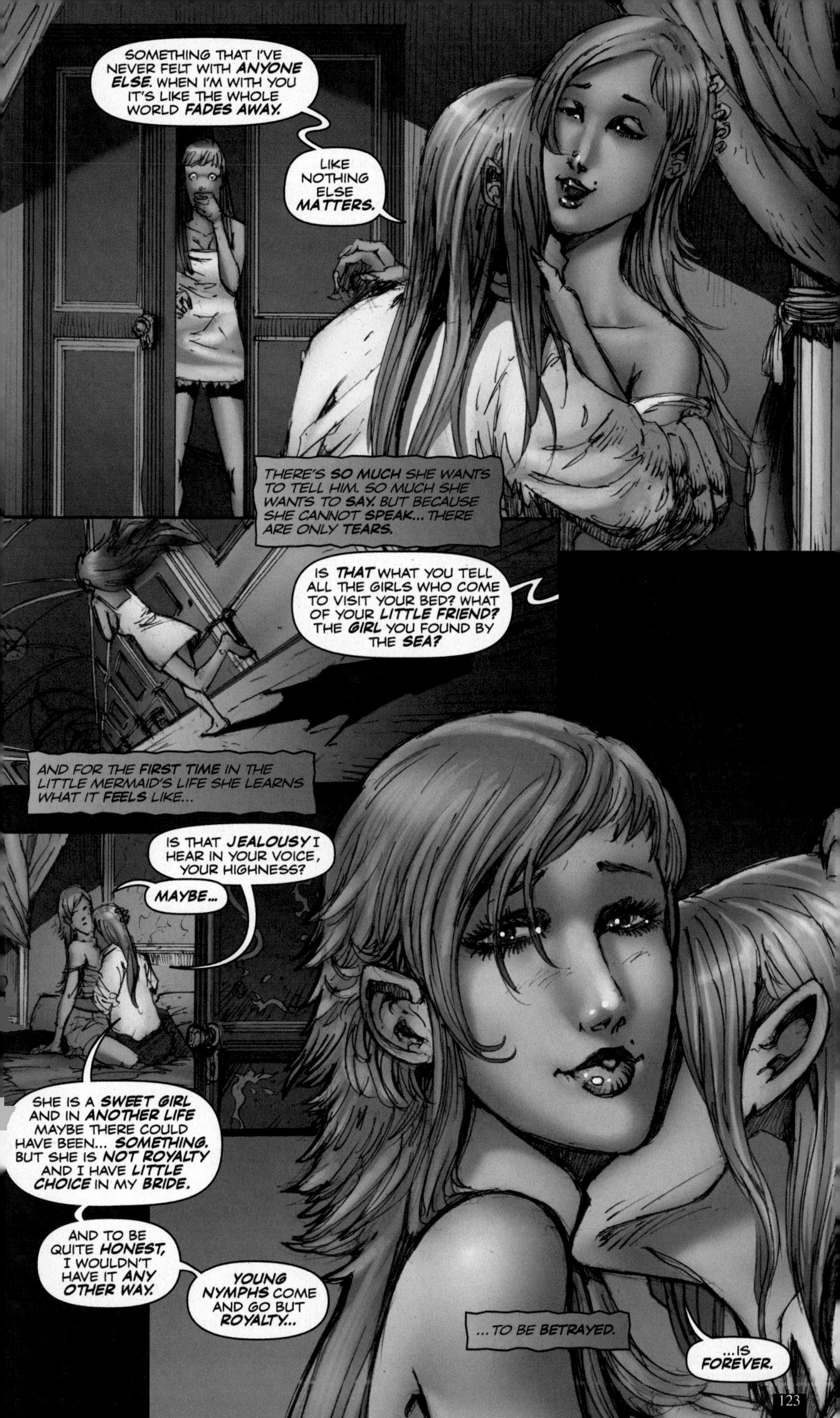
SOMETHING THAT I'VE NEVER FELT WITH ANYONE ELSE. WHEN I'M WITH YOU IT'S LIKE THE WHOLE WORLD FADES AWAY.
LIKE NOTHING ELSE MATTERS.
THERE'S SO MUCH SHE WANTS TO TELL HIM. SO MUCH SHE WANTS TO SAY. BUT BECAUSE SHE CANNOT SPEAK... THERE ARE ONLY TEARS.
IS THAT WHAT YOU TELL ALL THE GIRLS WHO COME TO VISIT YOUR BED? WHAT OF YOUR LITTLE FRIEND? THE GIRL YOU FOUND BY THE SEA?
AND FOR THE FIRST TIME IN THE LITTLE MERMAID'S LIFE SHE LEARNS WHAT IT FEELS LIKE...
IS THAT JEALOUSY I HEAR IN YOUR VOICE, YOUR HIGHNESS?
MAYBE...
SHE IS A SWEET GIRL AND IN ANOTHER LIFE MAYBE THERE COULD HAVE BEEN... SOMETHING. BUT SHE IS NOT ROYALTY AND I HAVE LITTLE CHOICE IN MY BRIDE.
AND TO BE QUITE HONEST, I WOULDN'T HAVE IT ANY OTHER WAY.
YOUNG NYMPHS COME AND GO BUT ROYALTY...
...TO BE BETRAYED.
...IS FOREVER.

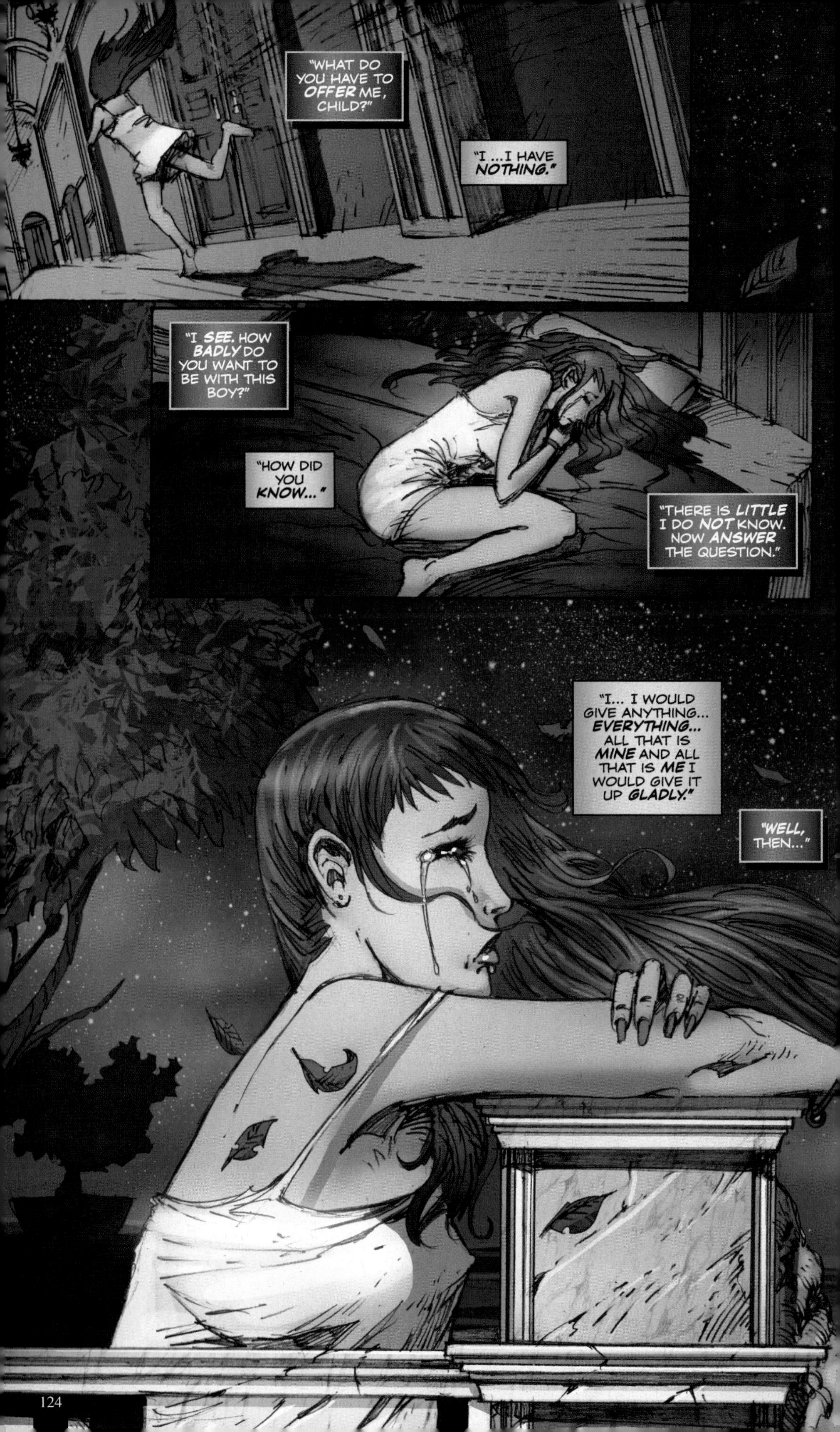
"WHAT DO YOU HAVE TO OFFER ME, CHILD?"
"I ...I HAVE NOTHING."
"I SEE. HOW BADLY DO YOU WANT TO BE WITH THIS BOY?"
"HOW DID YOU KNOW..."
"THERE IS LITTLE I DO NOT KNOW. NOW ANSWER THE QUESTION."
"I... I WOULD GIVE ANYTHING... EVERYTHING... ALL THAT IS MINE AND ALL THAT IS ME I WOULD GIVE IT UP GLADLY."
"WELL, THEN..."

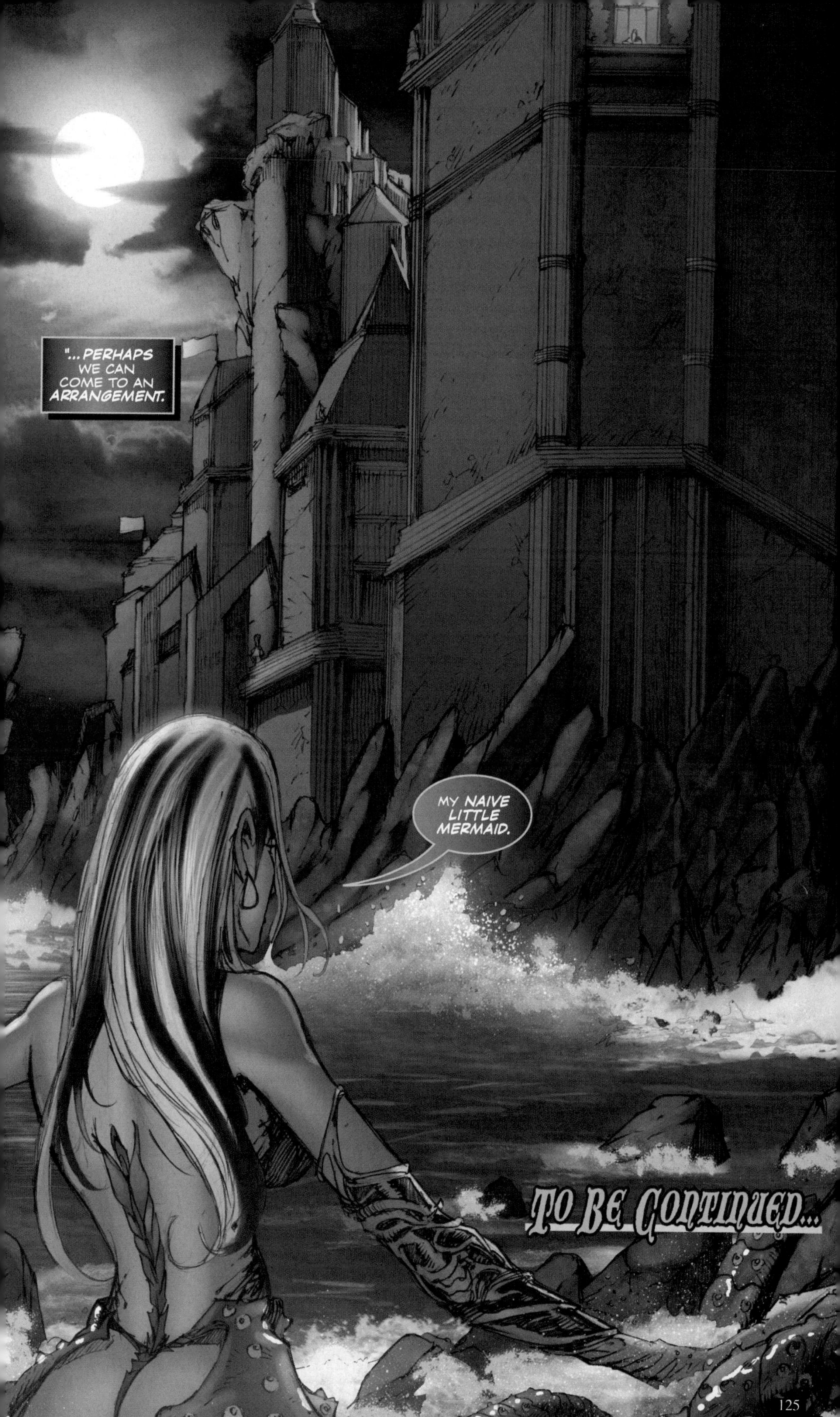
WE CAN COME TO AN ARRANGEMENT.
"...PERHAPS WE CAN COME TO AN ARRANGEMENT.
MY NAIVE LITTLE MERMAID.
TO BE CONTINUED...

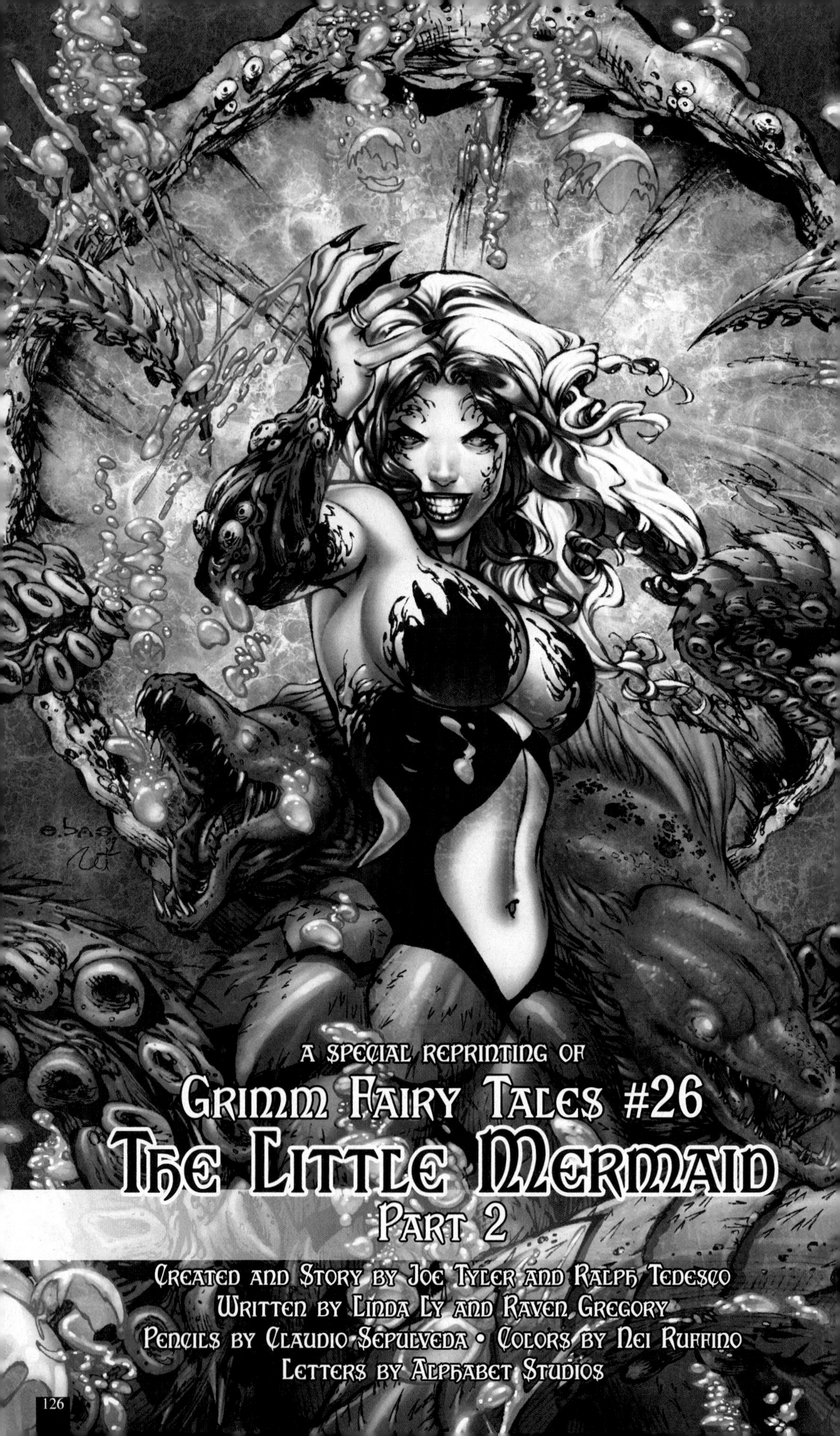

A SPECIAL REPRINTING OF

GRIMM FAIRY TALES #26

THE LITTLE MERMAID

PART 2

Created and Story by Joe Tyler and Ralph Tedesco
Written by Linda Ly and Raven Gregory
Pencils by Claudio Sepulveda • Colors by Nei Ruffino
Letters by Alphabet Studios

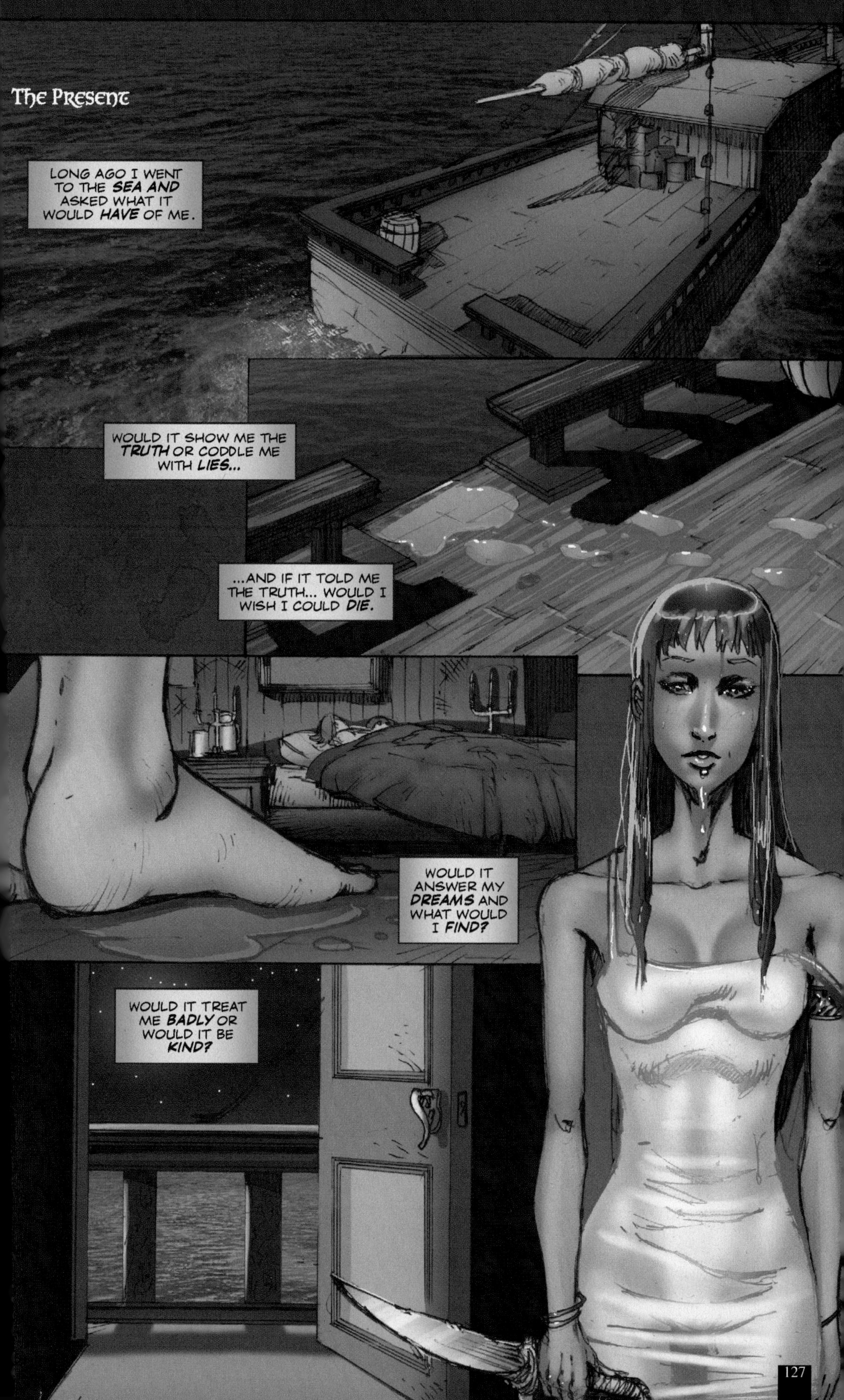
The Present
LONG AGO I WENT TO THE SEA AND ASKED WHAT IT WOULD HAVE OF ME.
WOULD IT SHOW ME THE TRUTH OR CODDLE ME WITH LIES...
...AND IF IT TOLD ME THE TRUTH... WOULD I WISH I COULD DIE.
WOULD IT ANSWER MY DREAMS AND WHAT WOULD I FIND?
WOULD IT TREAT ME BADLY OR WOULD IT BE KIND?

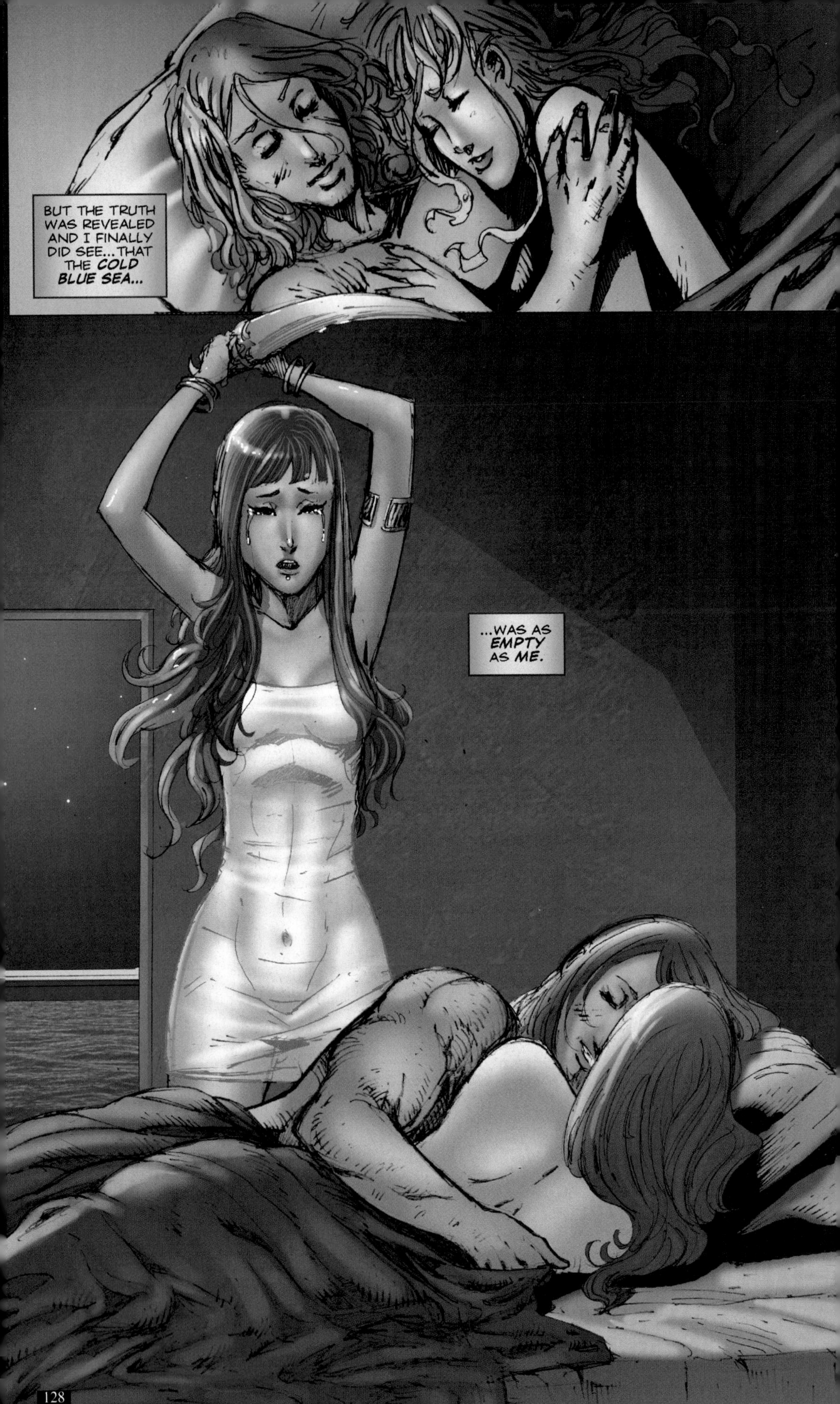
BUT THE TRUTH WAS REVEALED AND I FINALLY DID SEE...THAT THE *COLD BLUE SEA...*
...WAS AS *EMPTY* AS *ME.*

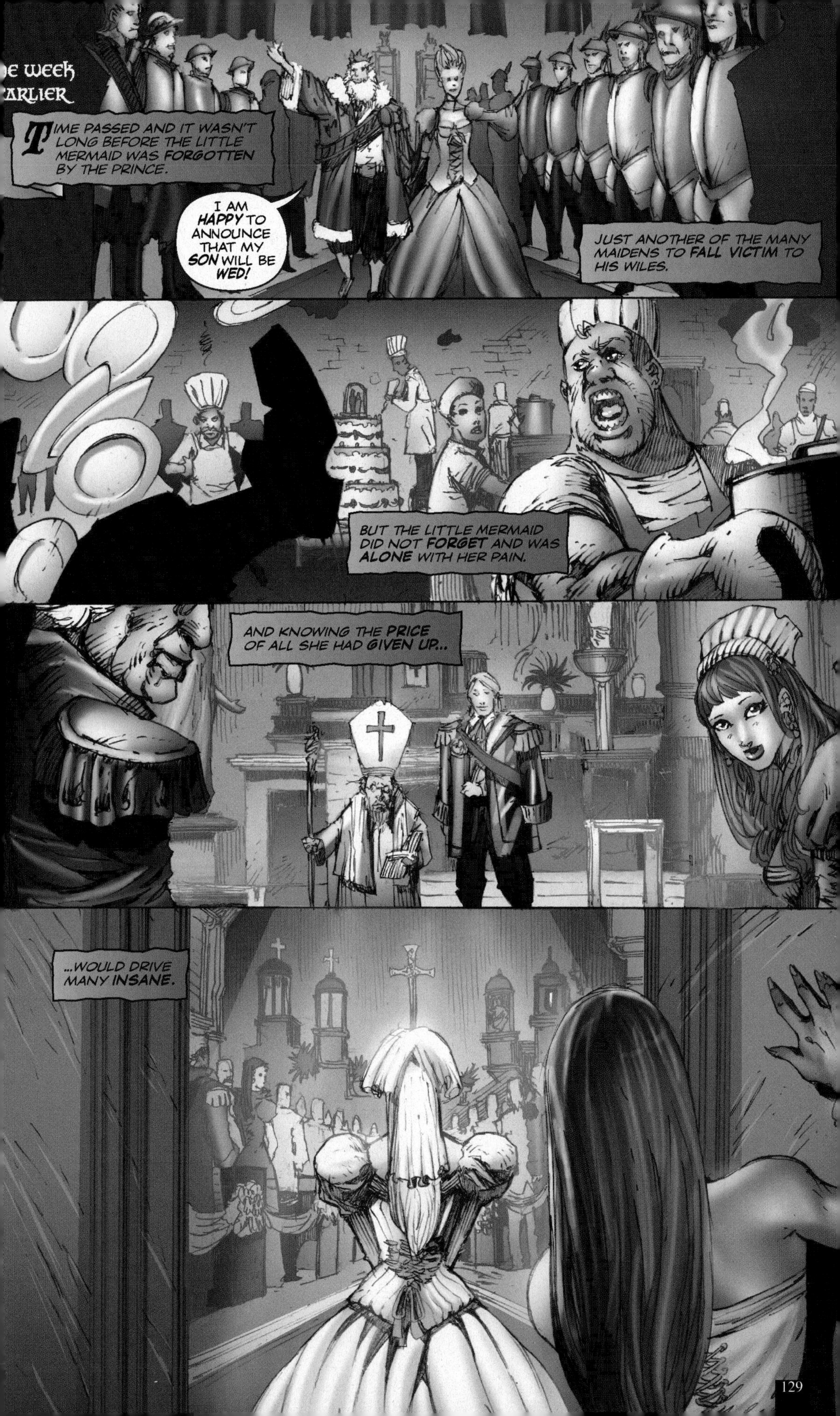

E WEEK
ARLIER
TIME PASSED AND IT WASN'T LONG BEFORE THE LITTLE MERMAID WAS FORGOTTEN BY THE PRINCE.
I AM HAPPY TO ANNOUNCE THAT MY SON WILL BE WED!
JUST ANOTHER OF THE MANY MAIDENS TO FALL VICTIM TO HIS WILES.
BUT THE LITTLE MERMAID DID NOT FORGET AND WAS ALONE WITH HER PAIN.
AND KNOWING THE PRICE OF ALL SHE HAD GIVEN UP...
...WOULD DRIVE MANY INSANE.

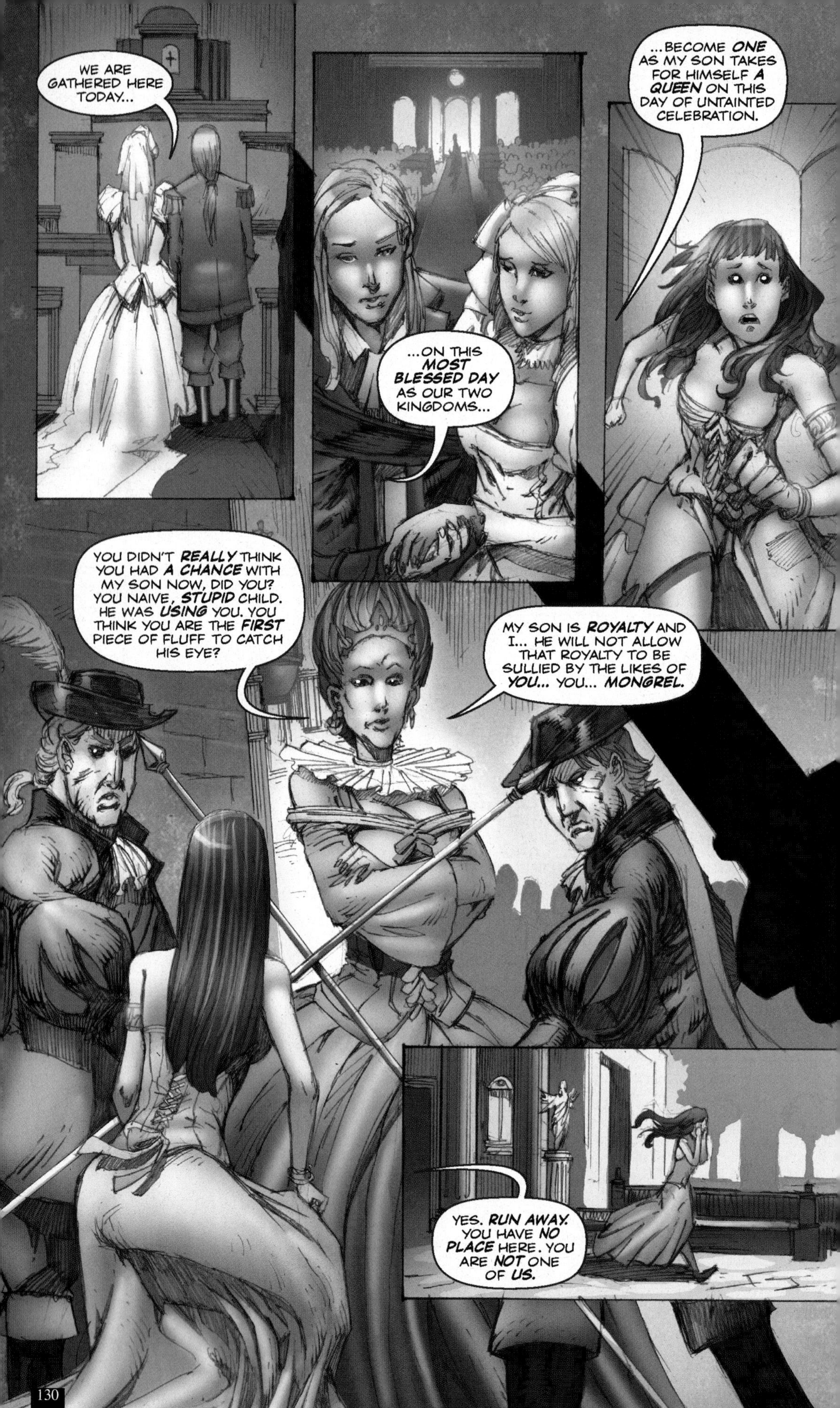
WE ARE GATHERED HERE TODAY...
...ON THIS MOST BLESSED DAY AS OUR TWO KINGDOMS...
...BECOME ONE AS MY SON TAKES FOR HIMSELF A QUEEN ON THIS DAY OF UNTAINTED CELEBRATION.
YOU DIDN'T REALLY THINK YOU HAD A CHANCE WITH MY SON NOW, DID YOU? YOU NAIVE, STUPID CHILD. HE WAS USING YOU. YOU THINK YOU ARE THE FIRST PIECE OF FLUFF TO CATCH HIS EYE?
MY SON IS ROYALTY AND I... HE WILL NOT ALLOW THAT ROYALTY TO BE SULLIED BY THE LIKES OF YOU... YOU... MONGREL.
YES. RUN AWAY. YOU HAVE NO PLACE HERE. YOU ARE NOT ONE OF US.

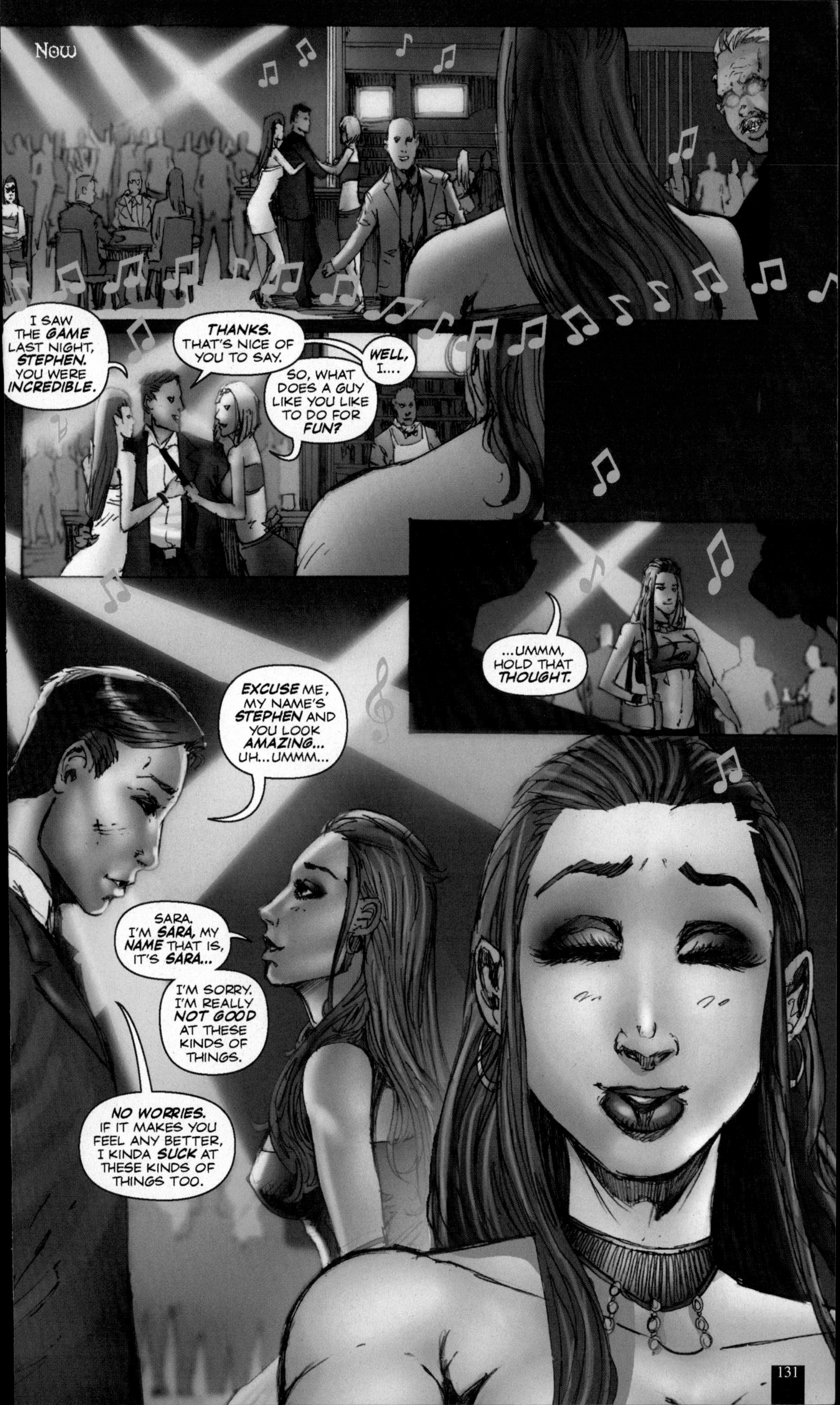

Now
I SAW THE GAME LAST NIGHT, STEPHEN. YOU WERE INCREDIBLE.
THANKS. THAT'S NICE OF YOU TO SAY.
SO, WHAT DOES A GUY LIKE YOU LIKE TO DO FOR FUN?
WELL, I....
...UMMM, HOLD THAT THOUGHT.
EXCUSE ME, MY NAME'S STEPHEN AND YOU LOOK AMAZING... UH...UMMM...
SARA. I'M SARA, MY NAME THAT IS, IT'S SARA...
I'M SORRY. I'M REALLY NOT GOOD AT THESE KINDS OF THINGS.
NO WORRIES. IF IT MAKES YOU FEEL ANY BETTER, I KINDA SUCK AT THESE KINDS OF THINGS TOO.

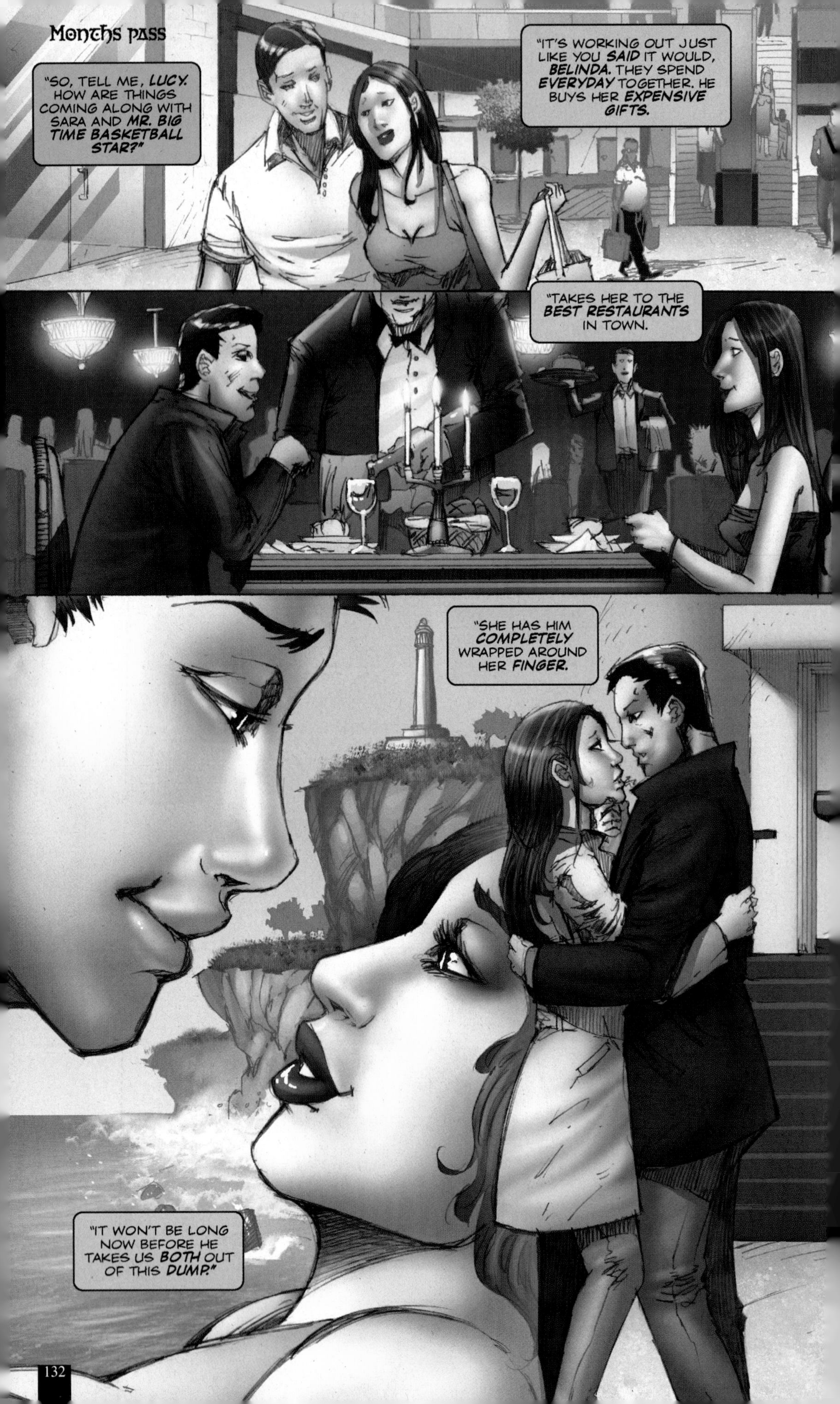
Months pass
"SO, TELL ME, LUCY. HOW ARE THINGS COMING ALONG WITH SARA AND MR. BIG TIME BASKETBALL STAR?"
"IT'S WORKING OUT JUST LIKE YOU SAID IT WOULD, BELINDA. THEY SPEND EVERYDAY TOGETHER. HE BUYS HER EXPENSIVE GIFTS.
"TAKES HER TO THE BEST RESTAURANTS IN TOWN.
"SHE HAS HIM COMPLETELY WRAPPED AROUND HER FINGER.
"IT WON'T BE LONG NOW BEFORE HE TAKES US BOTH OUT OF THIS DUMP."

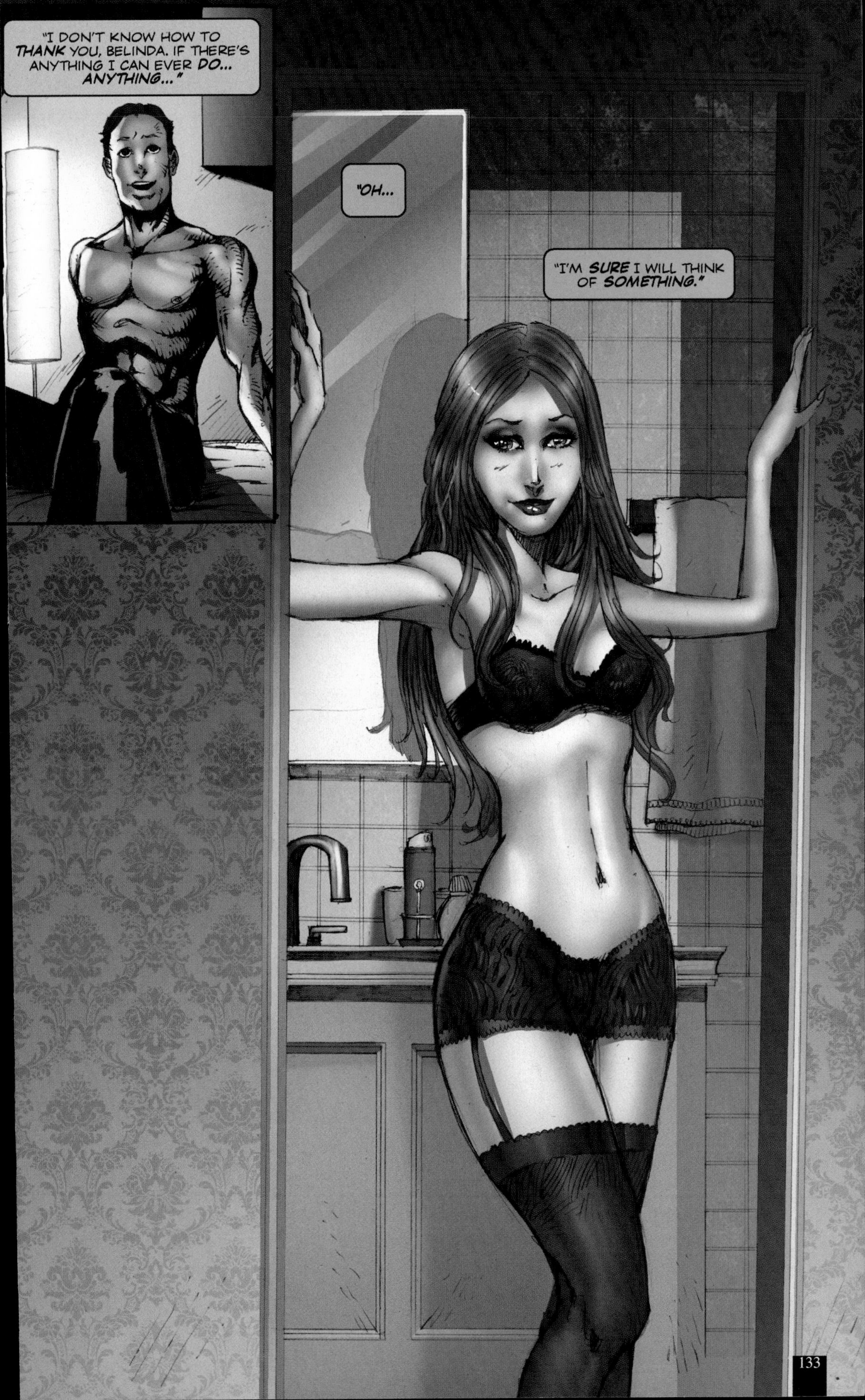
"I DON'T KNOW HOW TO THANK YOU, BELINDA. IF THERE'S ANYTHING I CAN EVER DO... ANYTHING..."
"OH...
"I'M SURE I WILL THINK OF SOMETHING."

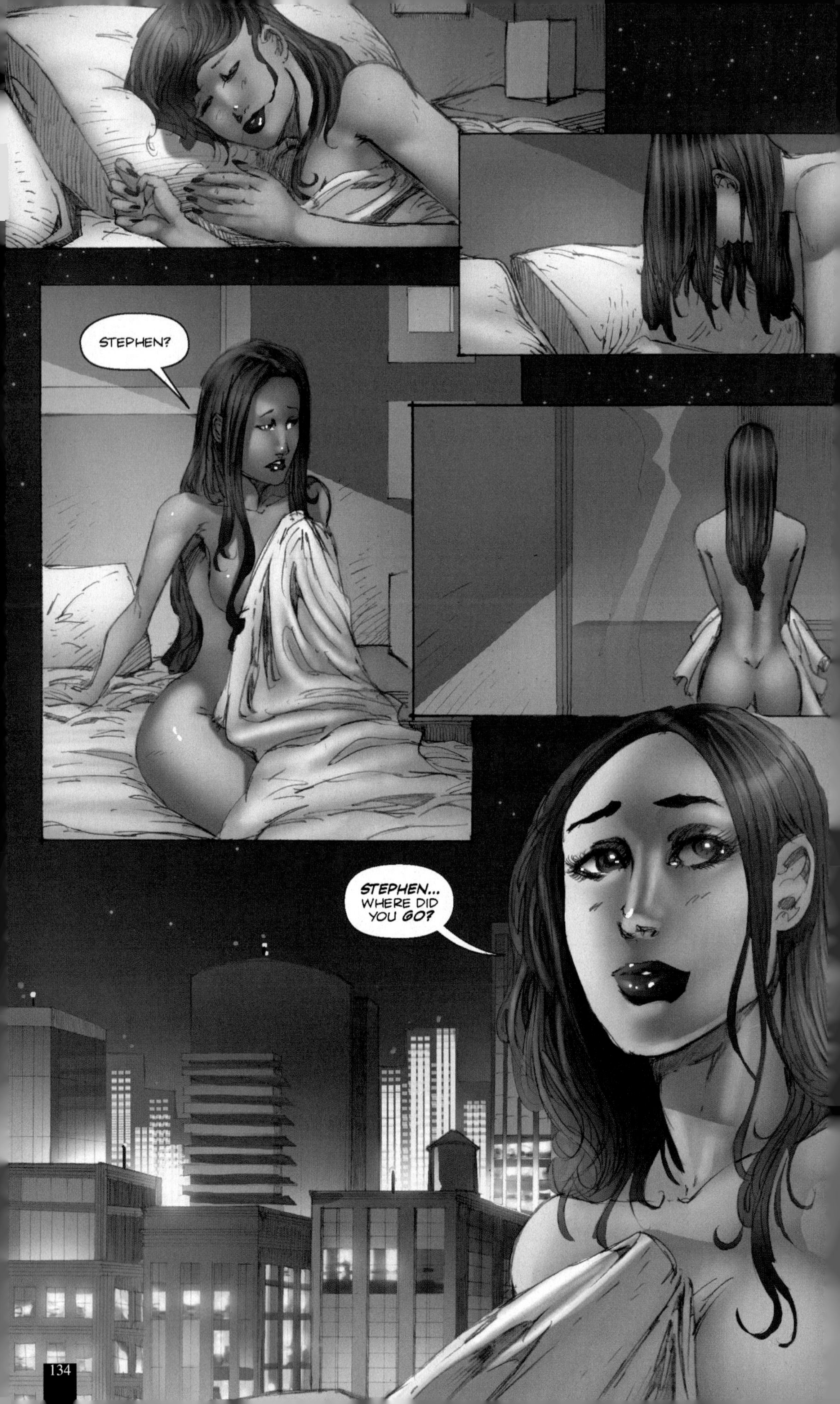
STEPHEN?
STEPHEN... WHERE DID YOU GO?

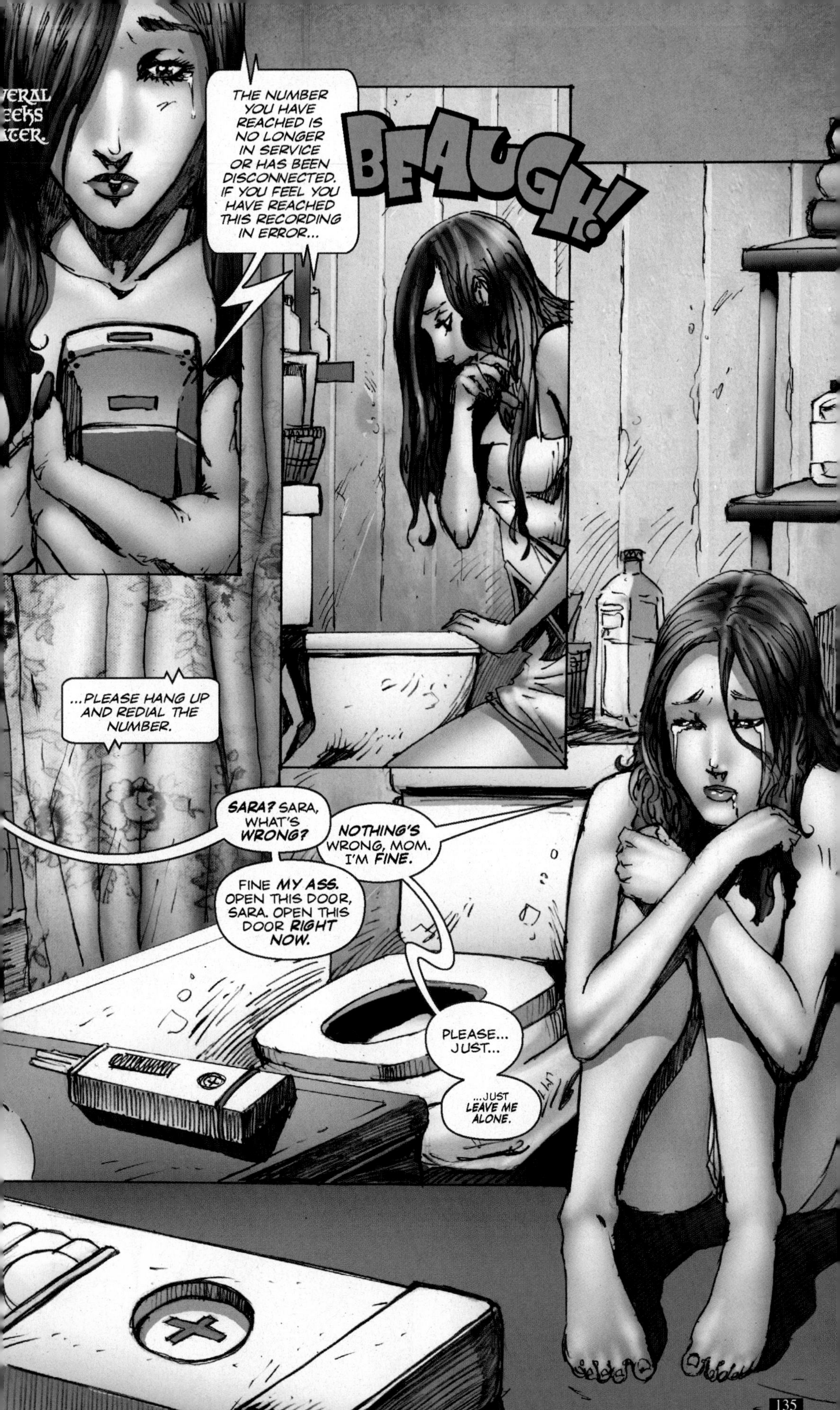

...VERAL ...EEKS ...ATER.
THE NUMBER YOU HAVE REACHED IS NO LONGER IN SERVICE OR HAS BEEN DISCONNECTED. IF YOU FEEL YOU HAVE REACHED THIS RECORDING IN ERROR...
BEAUGH!
...PLEASE HANG UP AND REDIAL THE NUMBER.
SARA? SARA, WHAT'S WRONG?
NOTHING'S WRONG, MOM. I'M FINE.
FINE MY ASS. OPEN THIS DOOR, SARA. OPEN THIS DOOR RIGHT NOW.
PLEASE... JUST...
...JUST LEAVE ME ALONE.

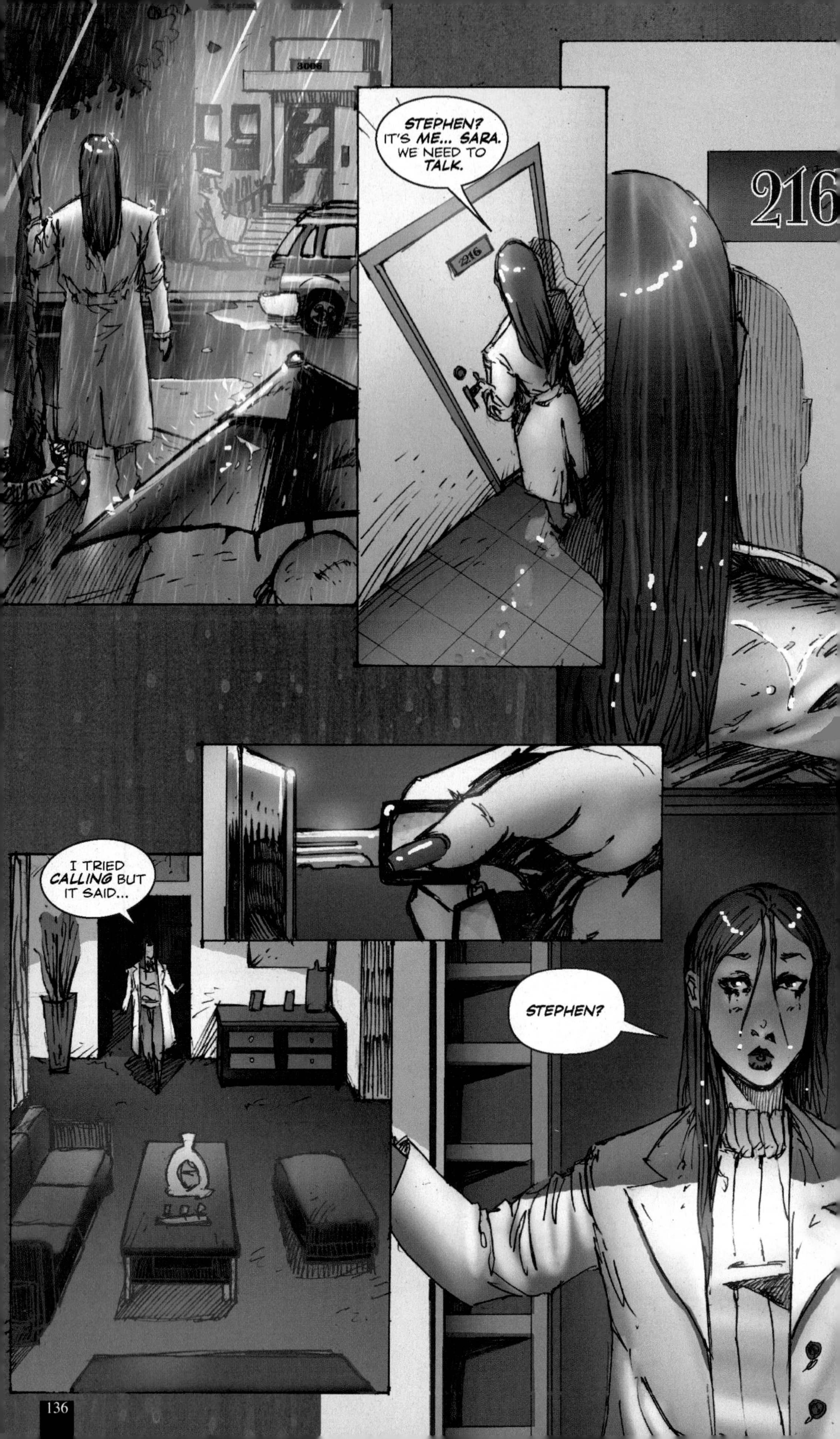
3006
STEPHEN? IT'S ME... SARA. WE NEED TO TALK.
216
216
I TRIED CALLING BUT IT SAID...
STEPHEN?

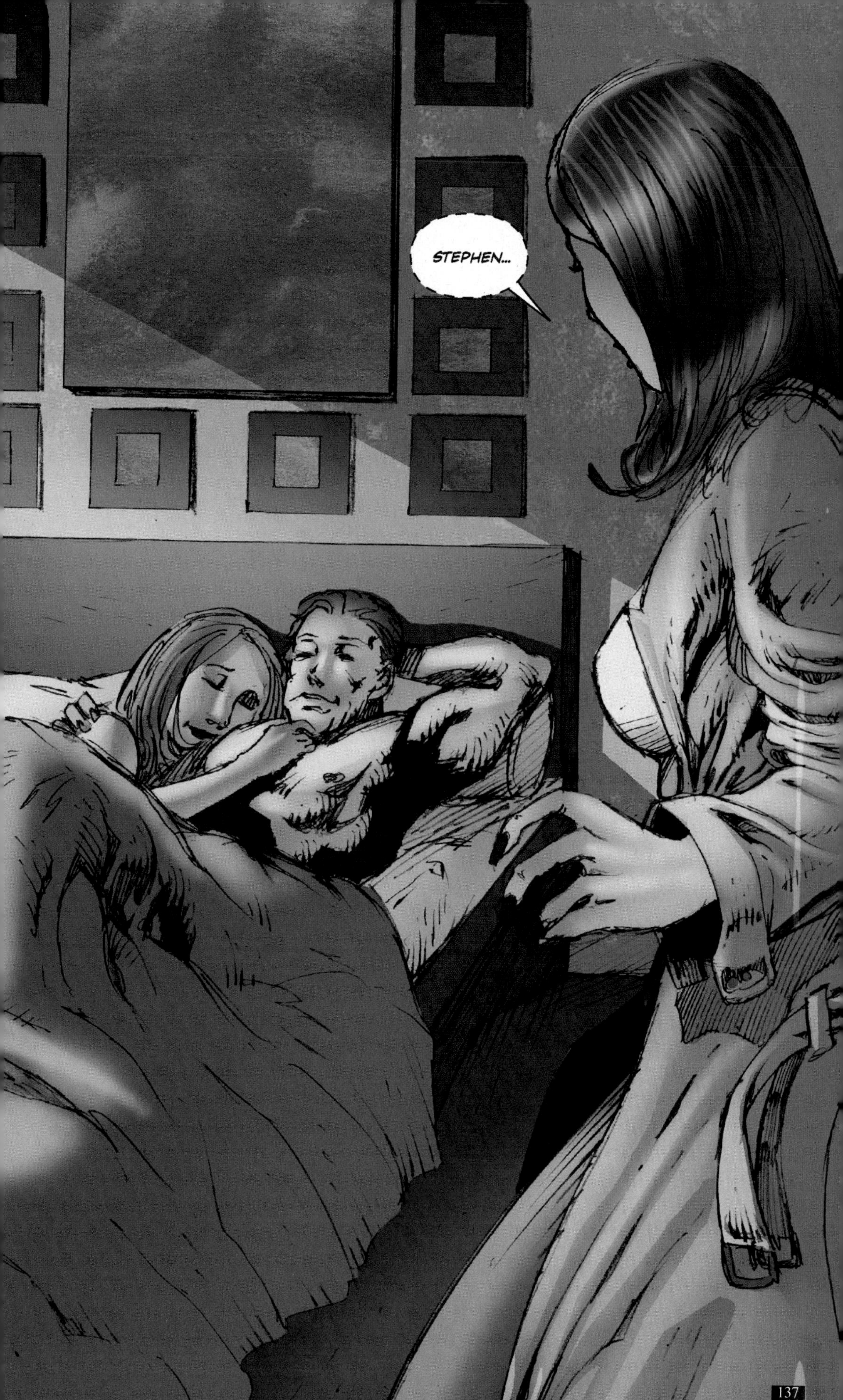
STEPHEN...

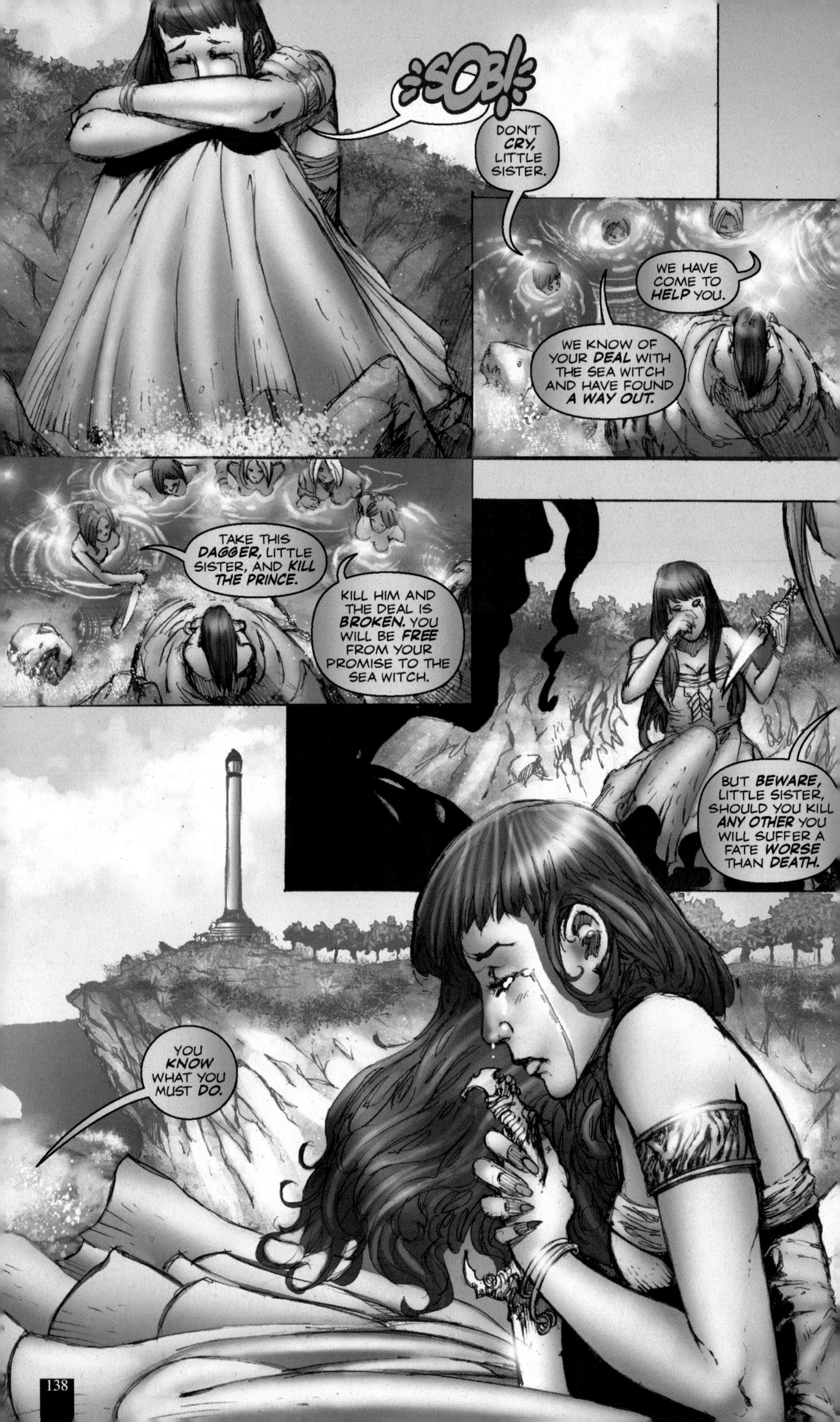
SOB!
DON'T CRY, LITTLE SISTER.
WE HAVE COME TO HELP YOU.
WE KNOW OF YOUR DEAL WITH THE SEA WITCH AND HAVE FOUND A WAY OUT.
TAKE THIS DAGGER, LITTLE SISTER, AND KILL THE PRINCE.
KILL HIM AND THE DEAL IS BROKEN. YOU WILL BE FREE FROM YOUR PROMISE TO THE SEA WITCH.
BUT BEWARE, LITTLE SISTER, SHOULD YOU KILL ANY OTHER YOU WILL SUFFER A FATE WORSE THAN DEATH.
YOU KNOW WHAT YOU MUST DO.

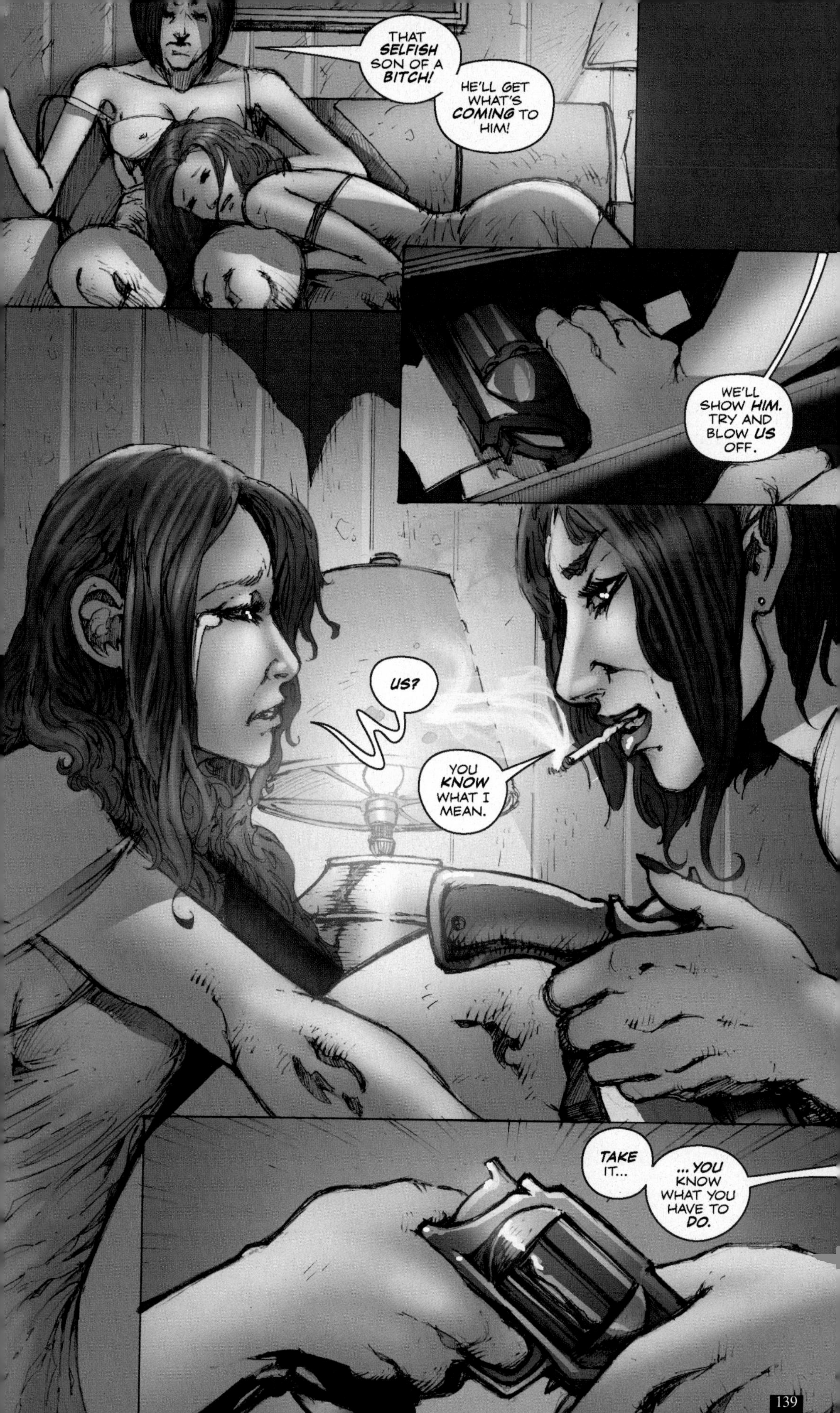

THAT SELFISH SON OF A BITCH!
HE'LL GET WHAT'S COMING TO HIM!
WE'LL SHOW HIM. TRY AND BLOW US OFF.
US?
YOU KNOW WHAT I MEAN.
TAKE IT...
...YOU KNOW WHAT YOU HAVE TO DO.

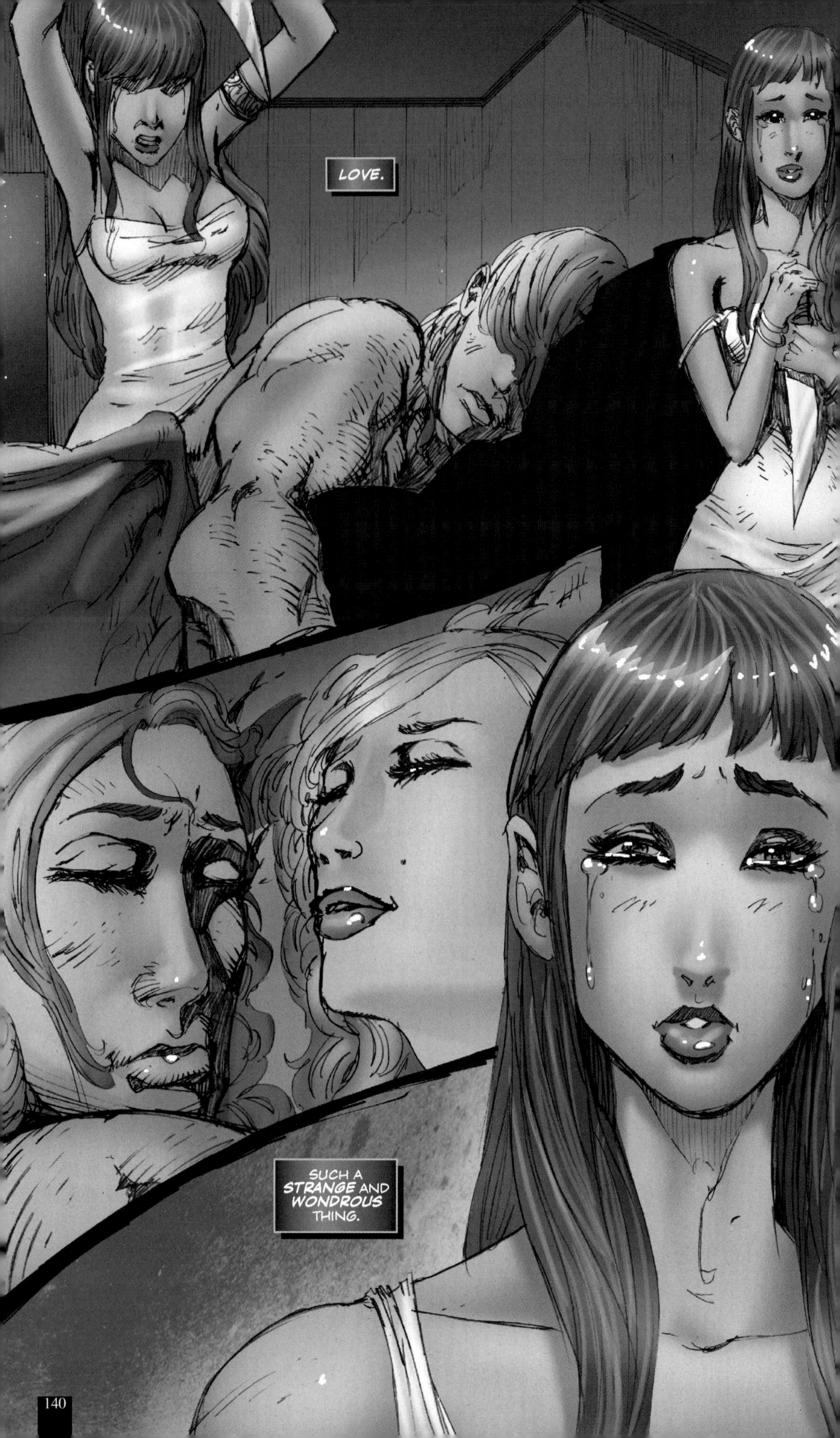
LOVE.
SUCH A STRANGE AND WONDROUS THING.

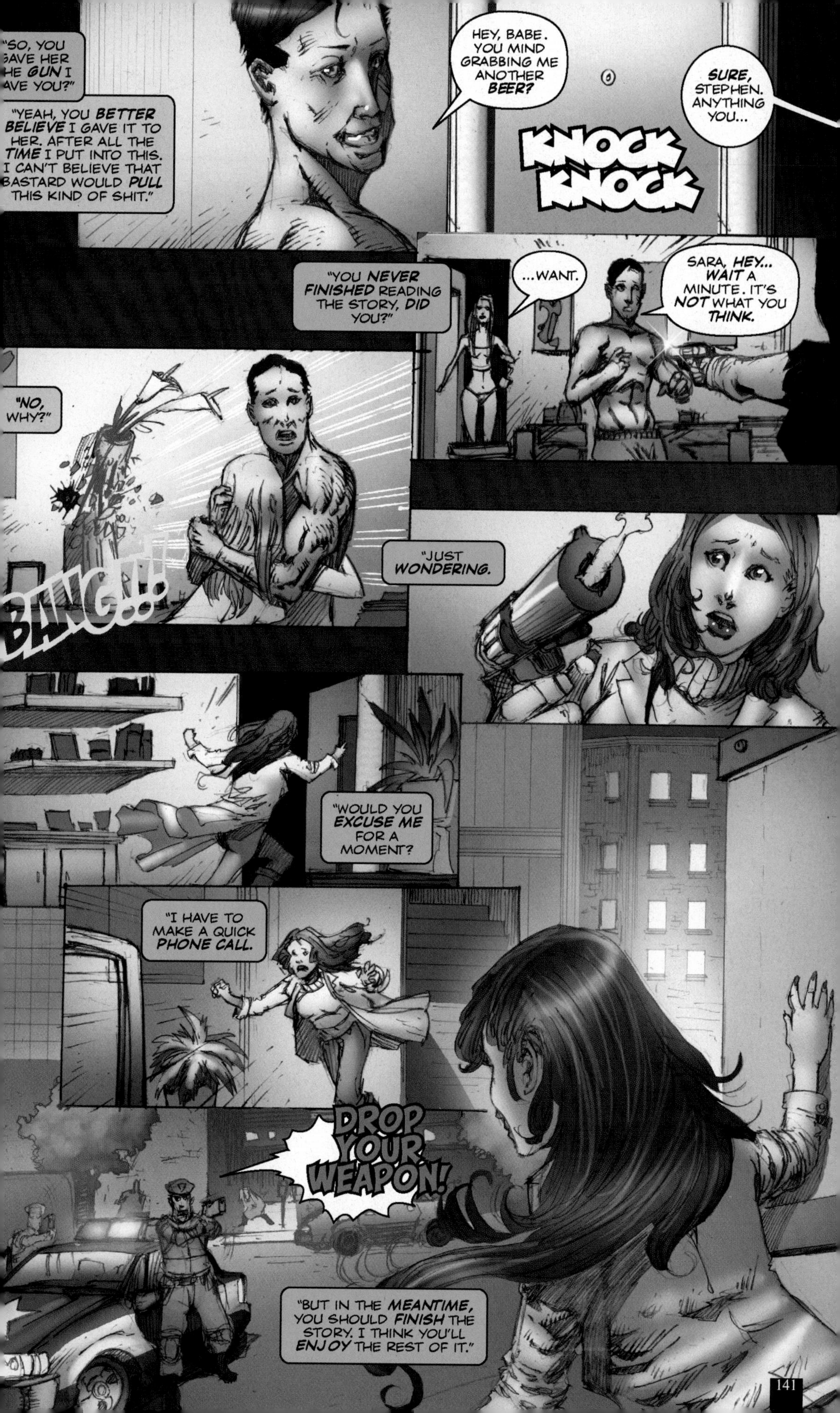
"SO, YOU GAVE HER THE GUN I GAVE YOU?"
"YEAH, YOU BETTER BELIEVE I GAVE IT TO HER. AFTER ALL THE TIME I PUT INTO THIS. I CAN'T BELIEVE THAT BASTARD WOULD PULL THIS KIND OF SHIT."
HEY, BABE. YOU MIND GRABBING ME ANOTHER BEER?
SURE, STEPHEN. ANYTHING YOU...
KNOCK KNOCK
"YOU NEVER FINISHED READING THE STORY, DID YOU?"
...WANT.
SARA, HEY... WAIT A MINUTE. IT'S NOT WHAT YOU THINK.
"NO, WHY?"
BANG!!!
"JUST WONDERING.
"WOULD YOU EXCUSE ME FOR A MOMENT?
"I HAVE TO MAKE A QUICK PHONE CALL.
DROP YOUR WEAPON!
"BUT IN THE MEANTIME, YOU SHOULD FINISH THE STORY. I THINK YOU'LL ENJOY THE REST OF IT."

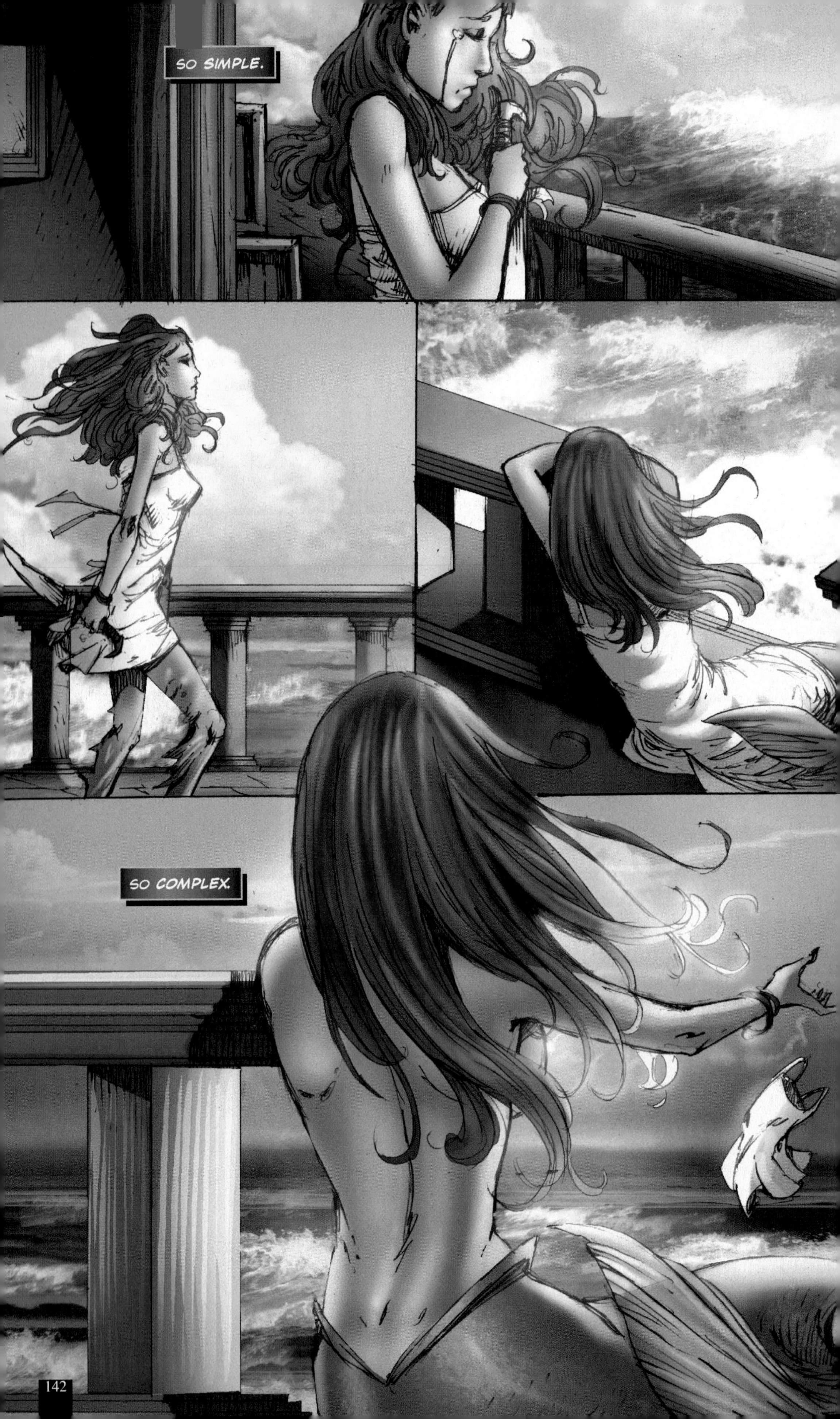
SO SIMPLE.
SO COMPLEX.

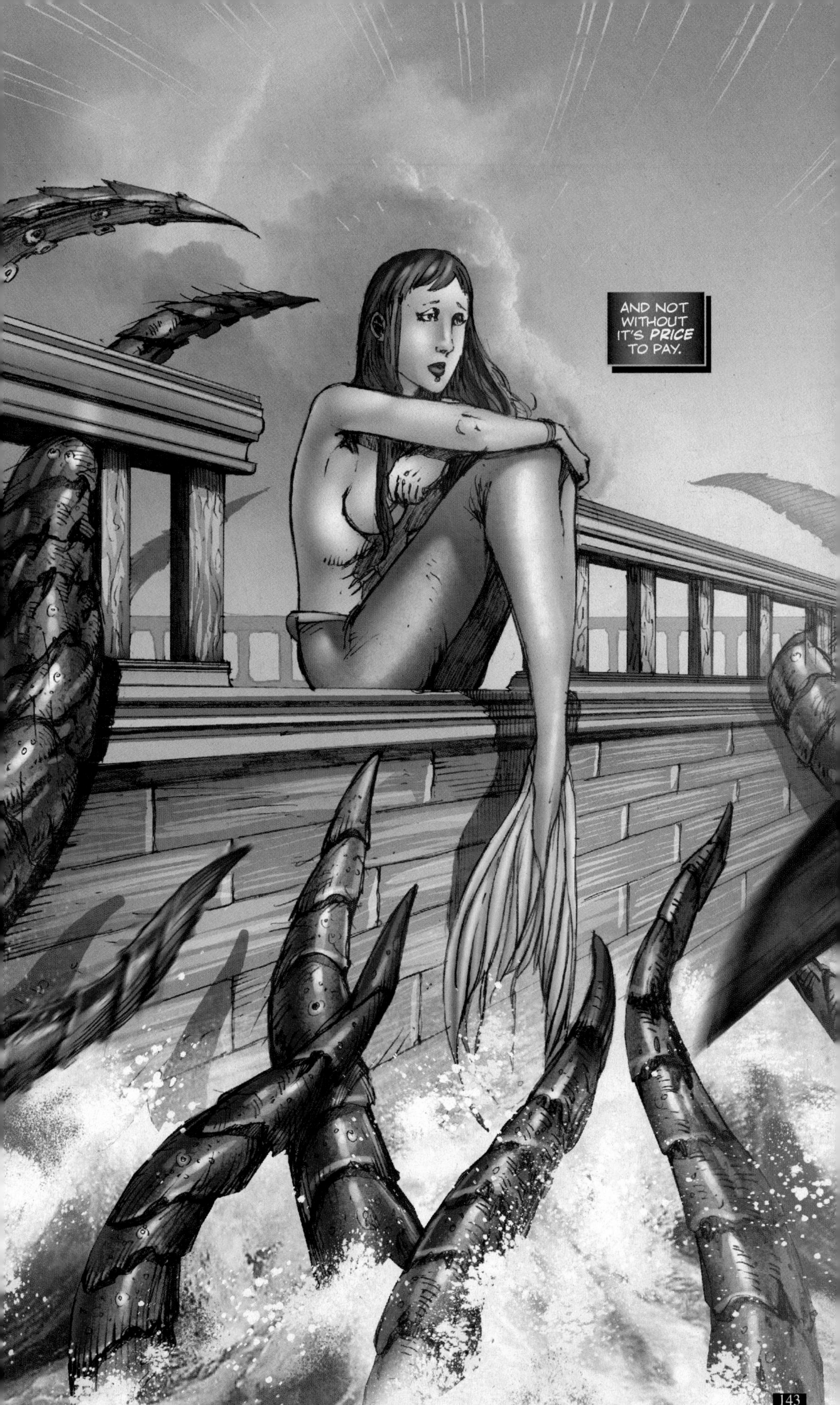
AND NOT WITHOUT IT'S PRICE TO PAY.

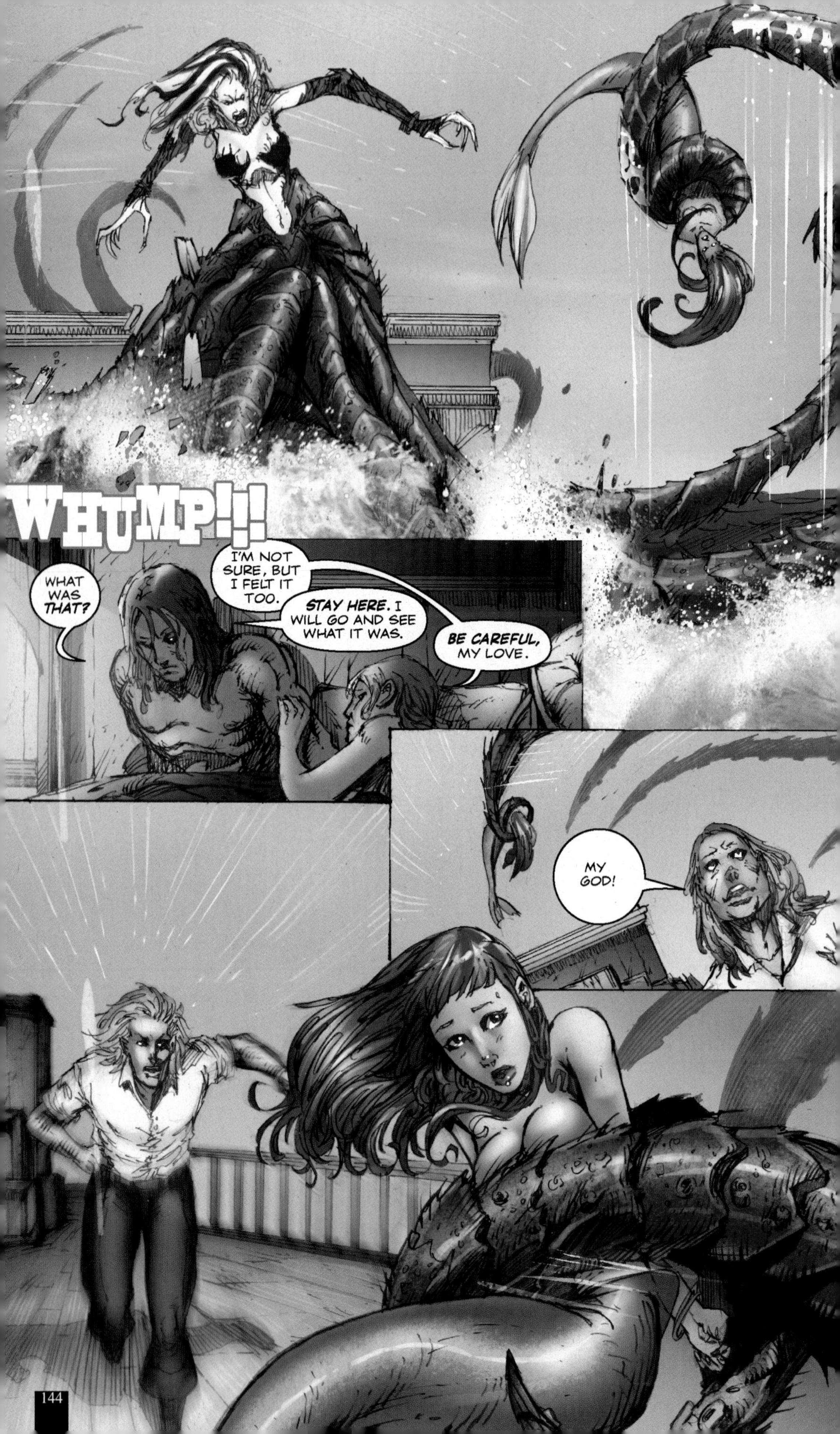

WHUMP!!!
WHAT WAS THAT?
I'M NOT SURE, BUT I FELT IT TOO.
STAY HERE. I WILL GO AND SEE WHAT IT WAS.
BE CAREFUL, MY LOVE.
MY GOD!

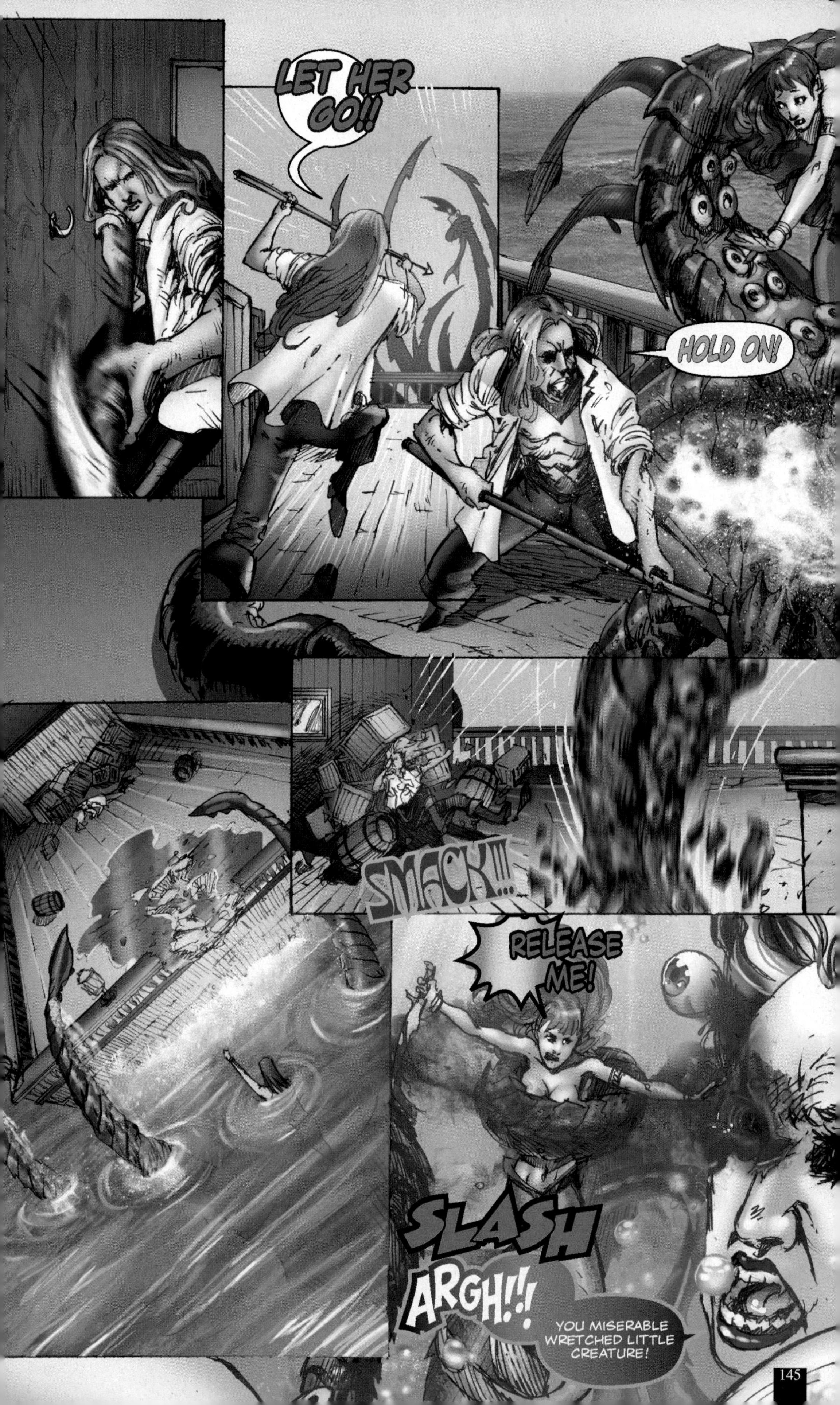
LET HER GO!!
HOLD ON!
SMACK!!!
RELEASE ME!
SLASH
ARGH!!!
YOU MISERABLE WRETCHED LITTLE CREATURE!

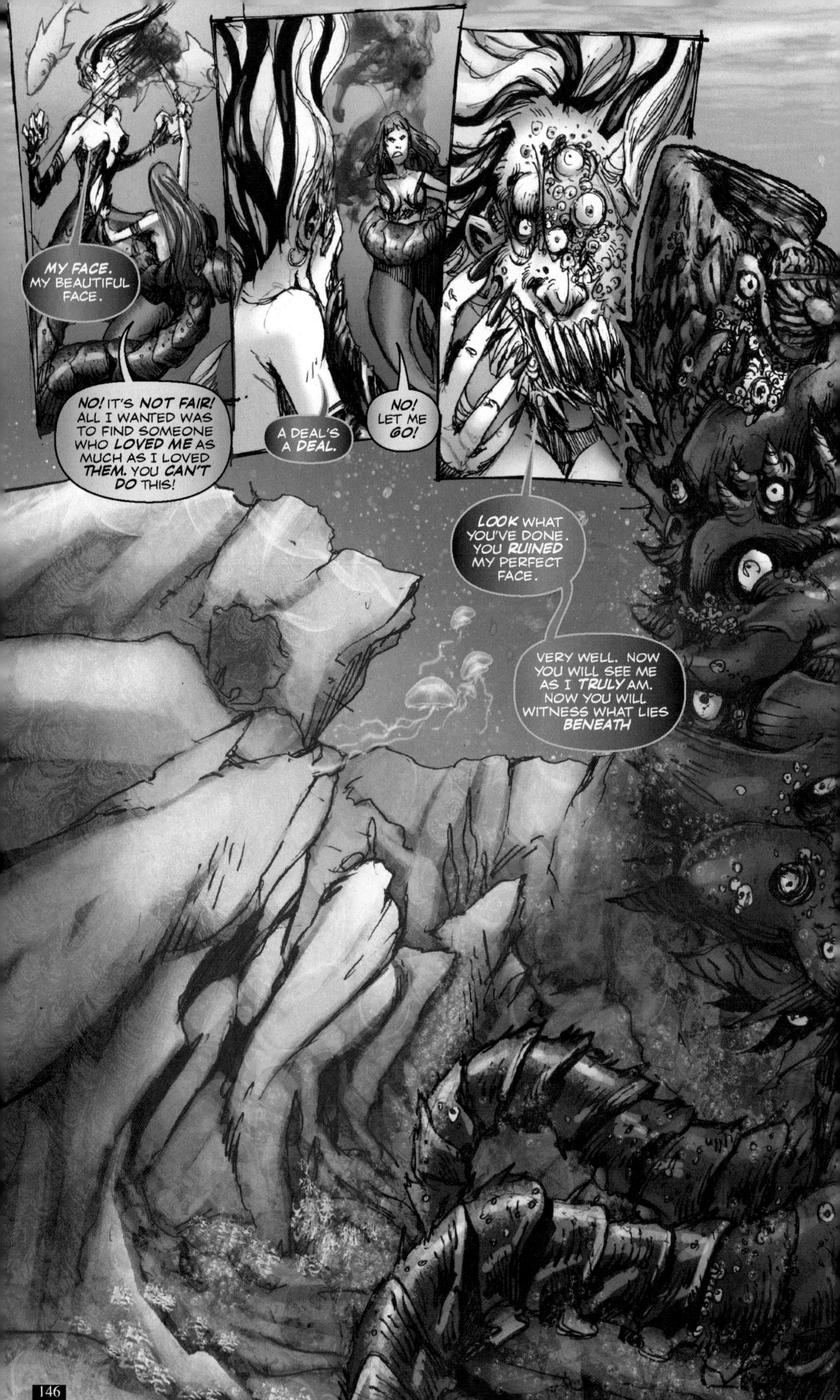
MY FACE. MY BEAUTIFUL FACE.
NO! IT'S NOT FAIR! ALL I WANTED WAS TO FIND SOMEONE WHO LOVED ME AS MUCH AS I LOVED THEM. YOU CAN'T DO THIS!
A DEAL'S A DEAL.
NO! LET ME GO!
LOOK WHAT YOU'VE DONE. YOU RUINED MY PERFECT FACE.
VERY WELL. NOW YOU WILL SEE ME AS I TRULY AM. NOW YOU WILL WITNESS WHAT LIES BENEATH

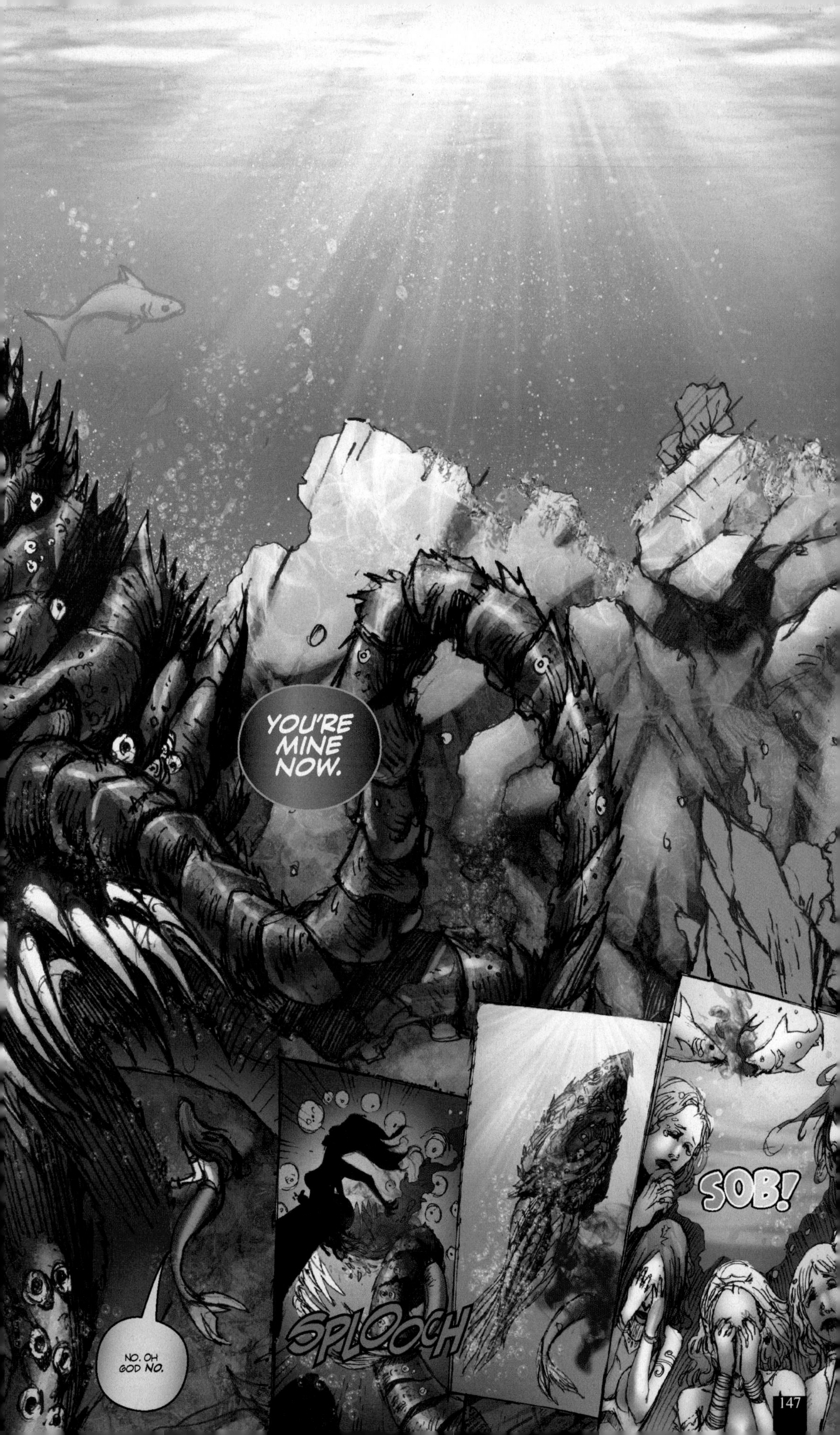
YOU'RE MINE NOW.
NO. OH GOD NO.
SPLOOCH
SOB!

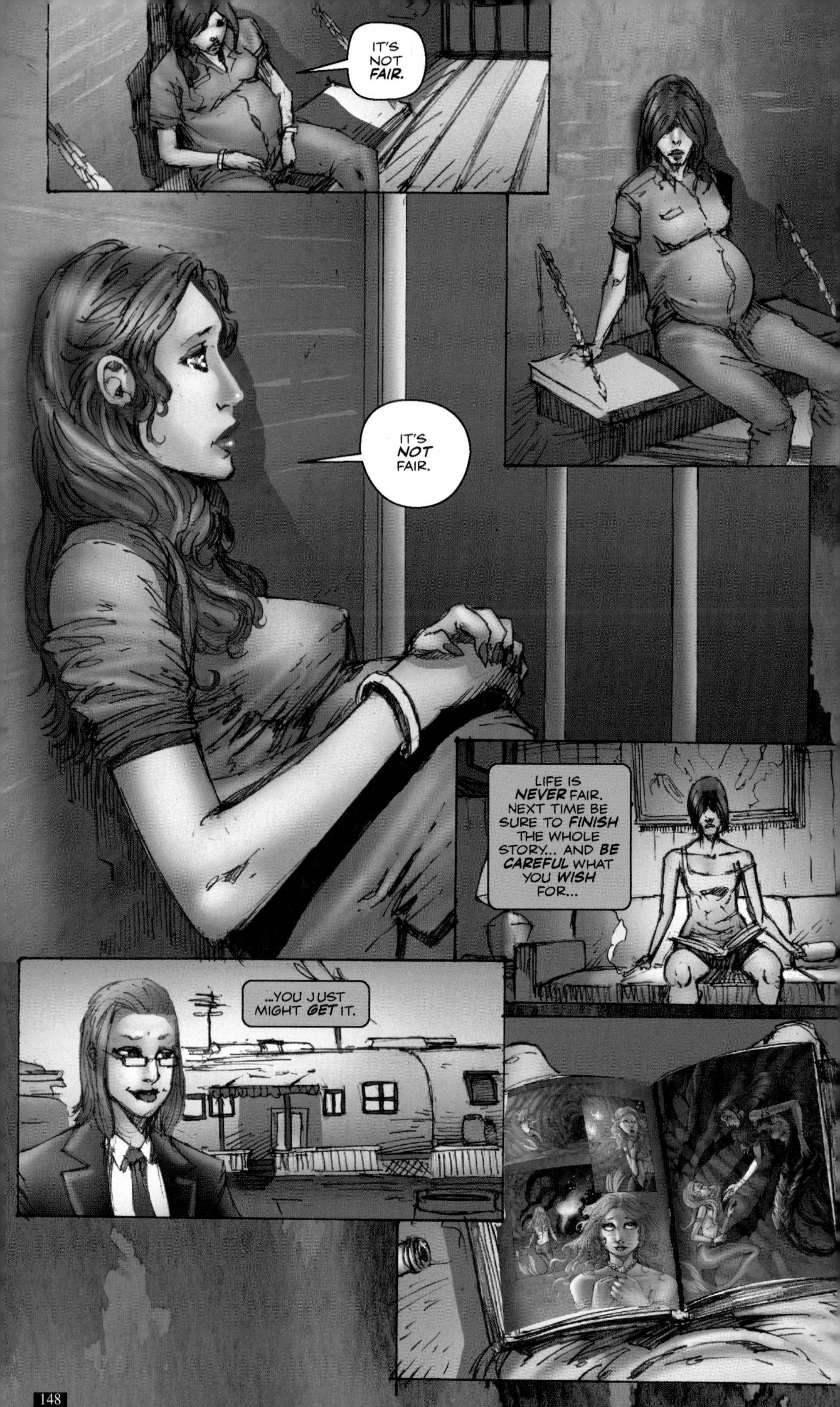
IT'S NOT **FAIR.**
IT'S **NOT** FAIR.
LIFE IS **NEVER** FAIR. NEXT TIME BE SURE TO **FINISH** THE WHOLE STORY... AND **BE CAREFUL** WHAT YOU **WISH** FOR...
...YOU JUST MIGHT **GET** IT.

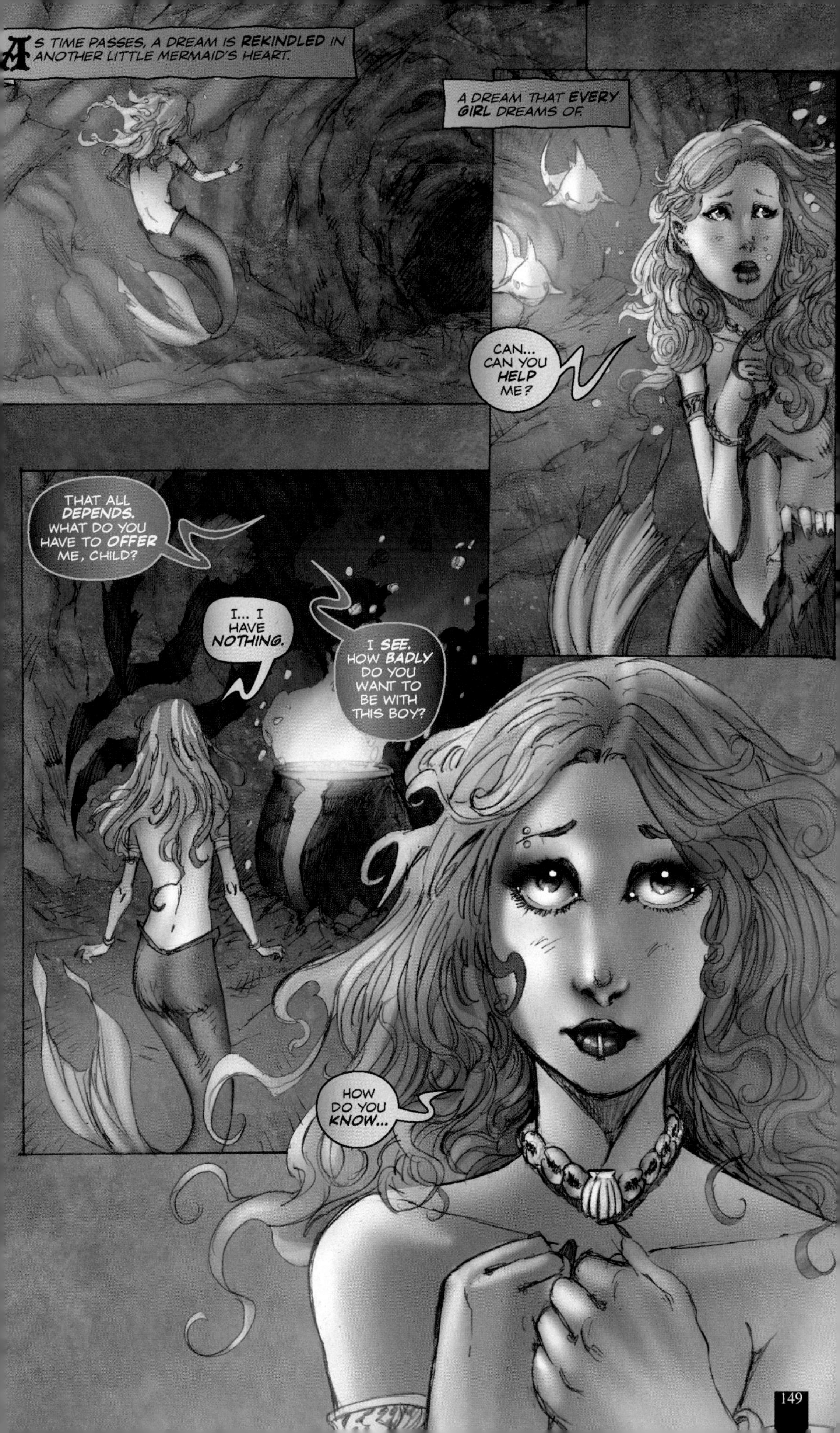
AS TIME PASSES, A DREAM IS **REKINDLED** IN ANOTHER LITTLE MERMAID'S HEART.
A DREAM THAT **EVERY GIRL** DREAMS OF.
CAN... CAN YOU **HELP** ME?
THAT ALL **DEPENDS.** WHAT DO YOU HAVE TO **OFFER** ME, CHILD?
I... I HAVE **NOTHING.**
I **SEE.** HOW **BADLY** DO YOU WANT TO BE WITH THIS BOY?
HOW DO YOU **KNOW...**

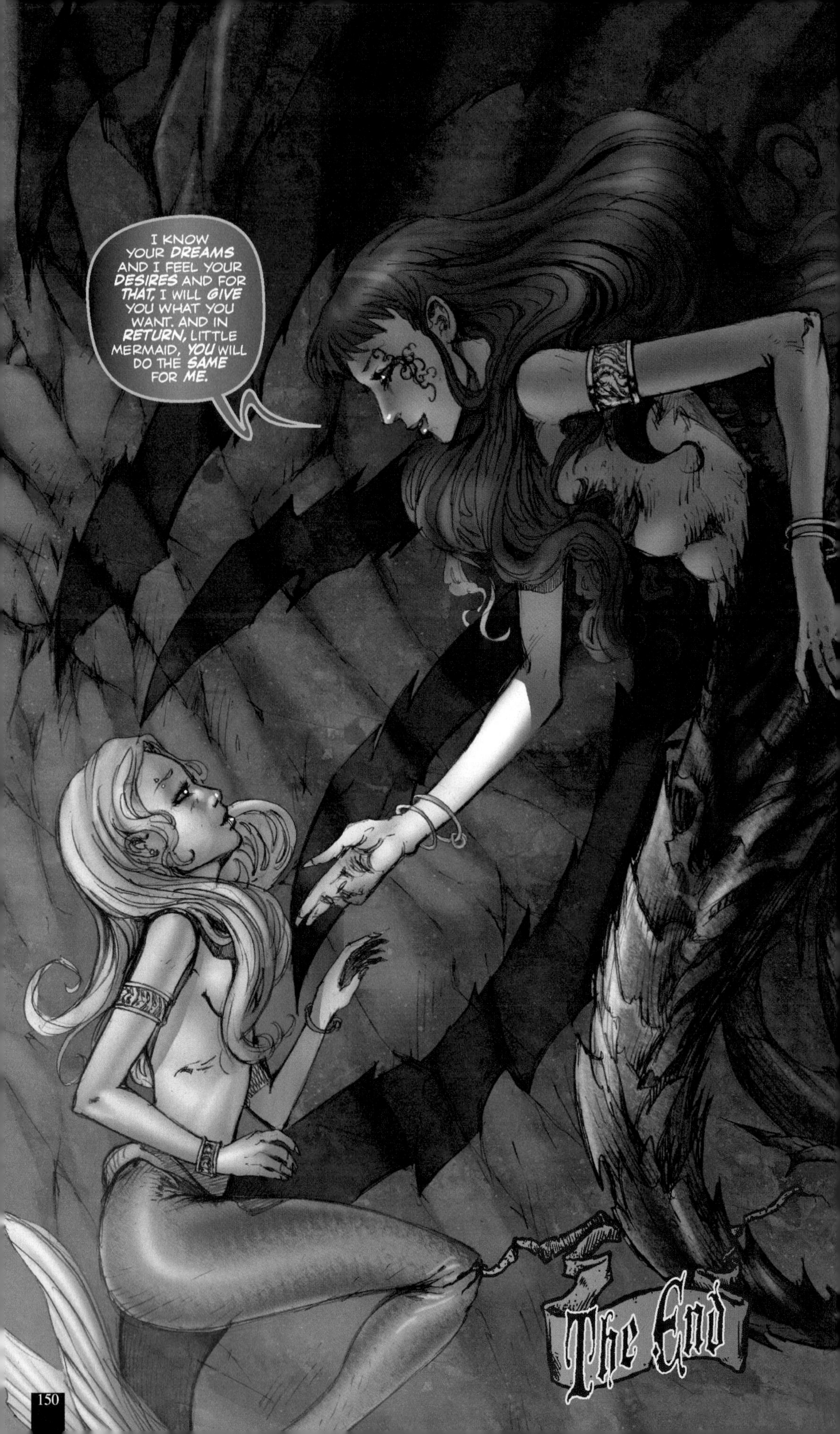
I KNOW YOUR DREAMS AND I FEEL YOUR DESIRES AND FOR THAT, I WILL GIVE YOU WHAT YOU WANT. AND IN RETURN, LITTLE MERMAID, YOU WILL DO THE SAME FOR ME.
The End

Grimm Fairy Tales
Myths & Legends

Cover Gallery

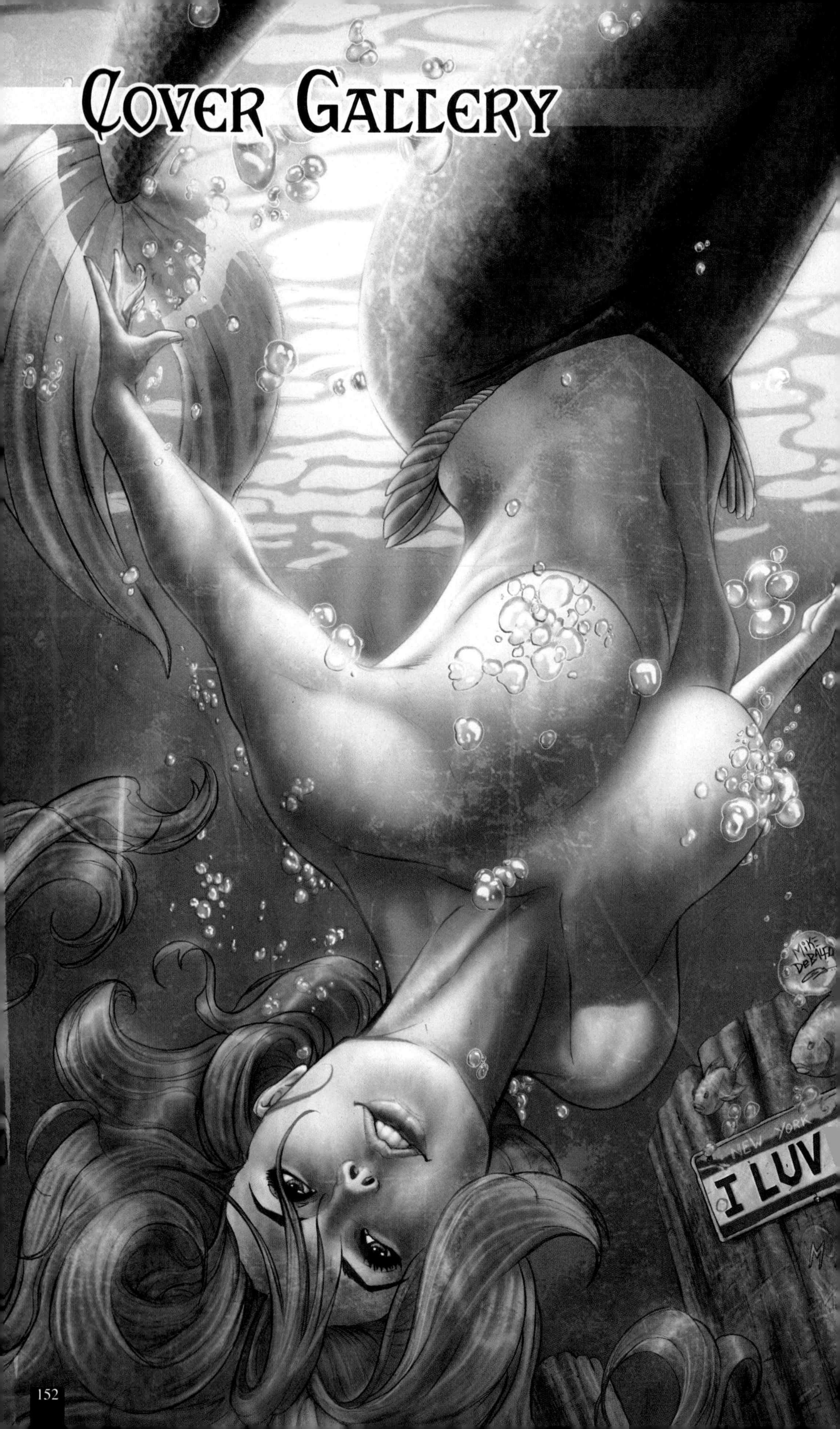
MIKE DEBALFO
NEW YORK
I LUV

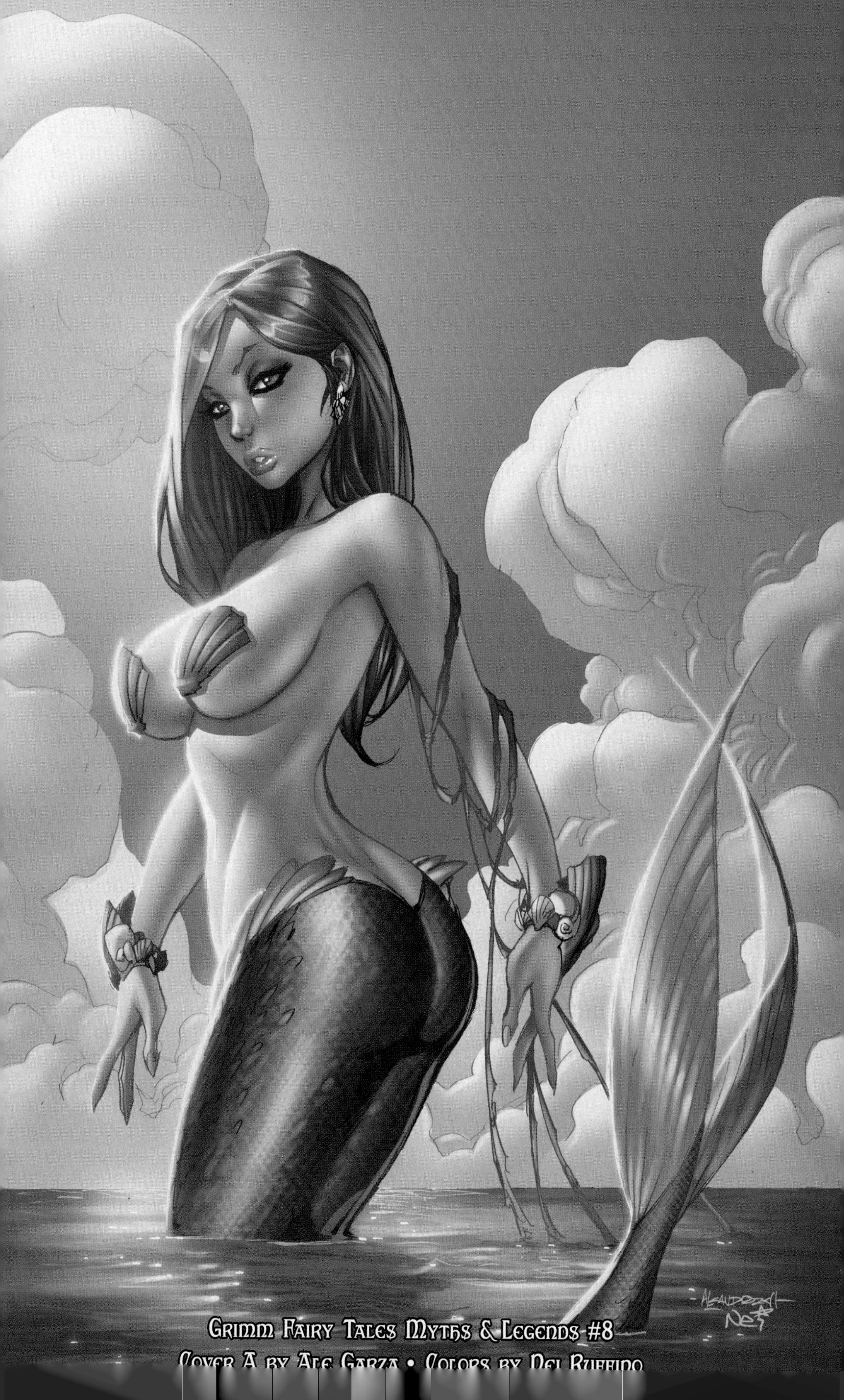

Grimm Fairy Tales Myths & Legends #8
Cover A by Ale Garza • Colors by Nei Ruffino

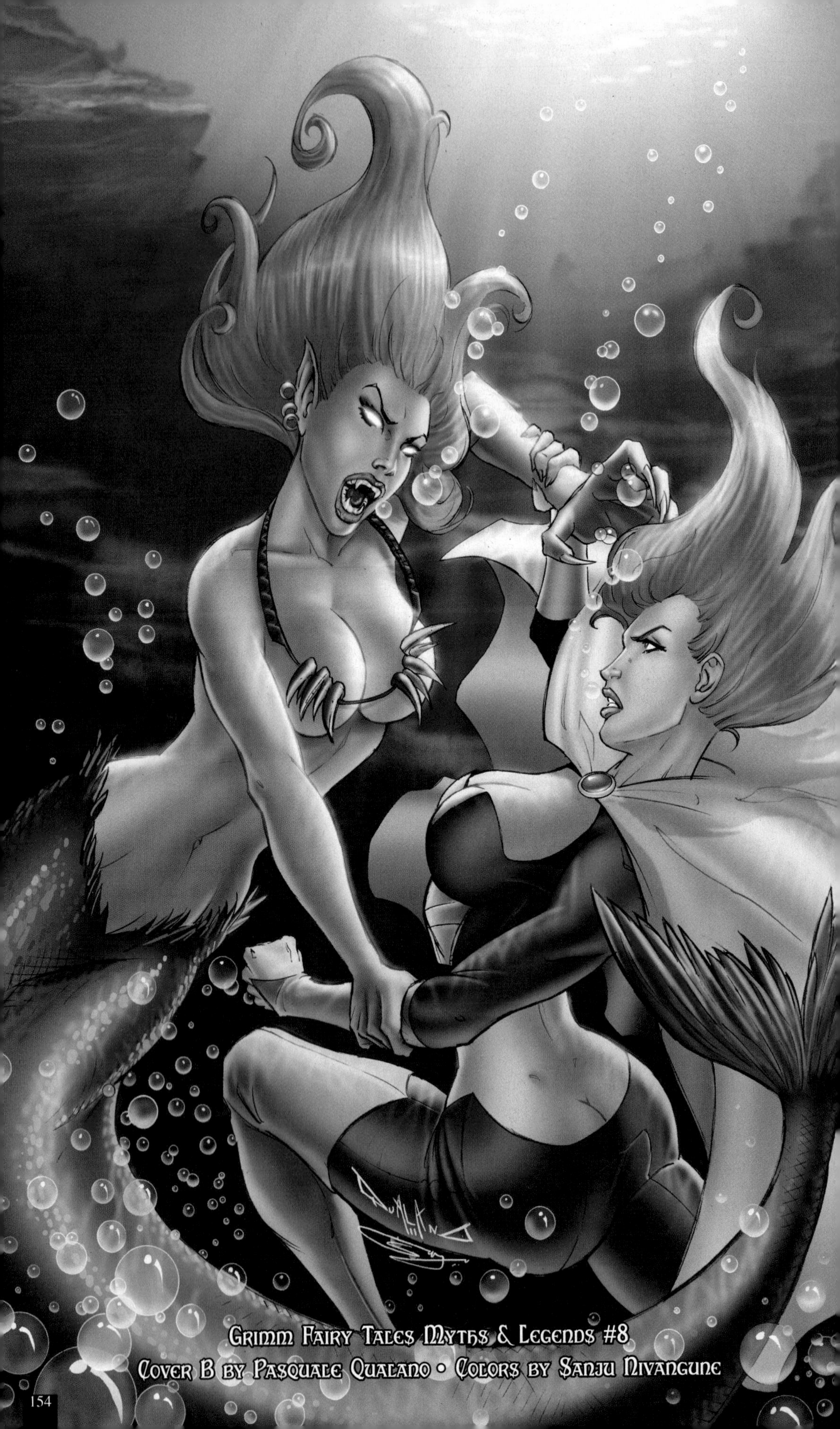

Grimm Fairy Tales Myths & Legends #8
Cover B by Pasquale Qualano • Colors by Sanju Nivangune

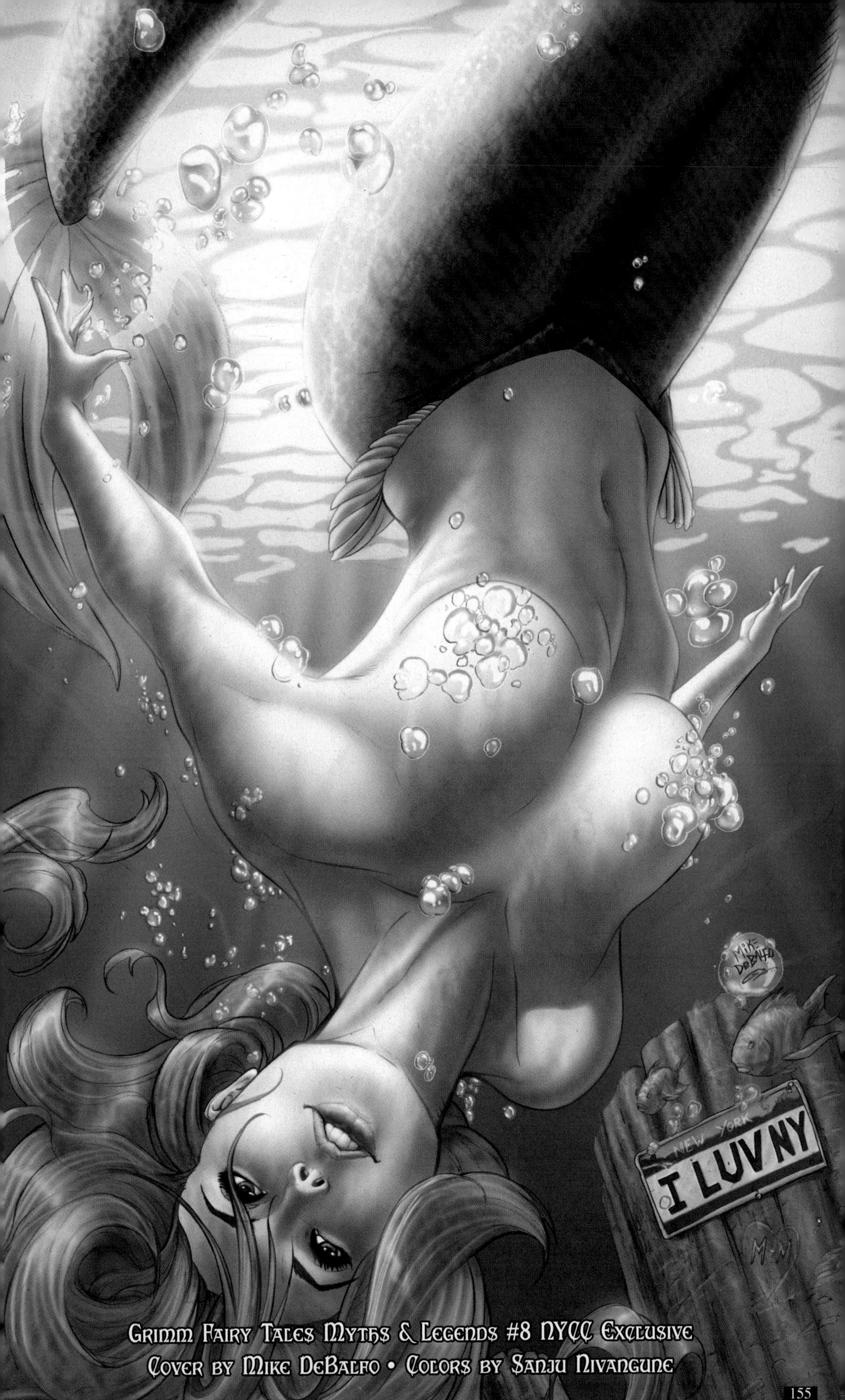
NEW YORK
I LUVNY

Grimm Fairy Tales Myths & Legends #8 NYCC Exclusive
Cover by Mike DeBalfo • Colors by Sanju Nivangune

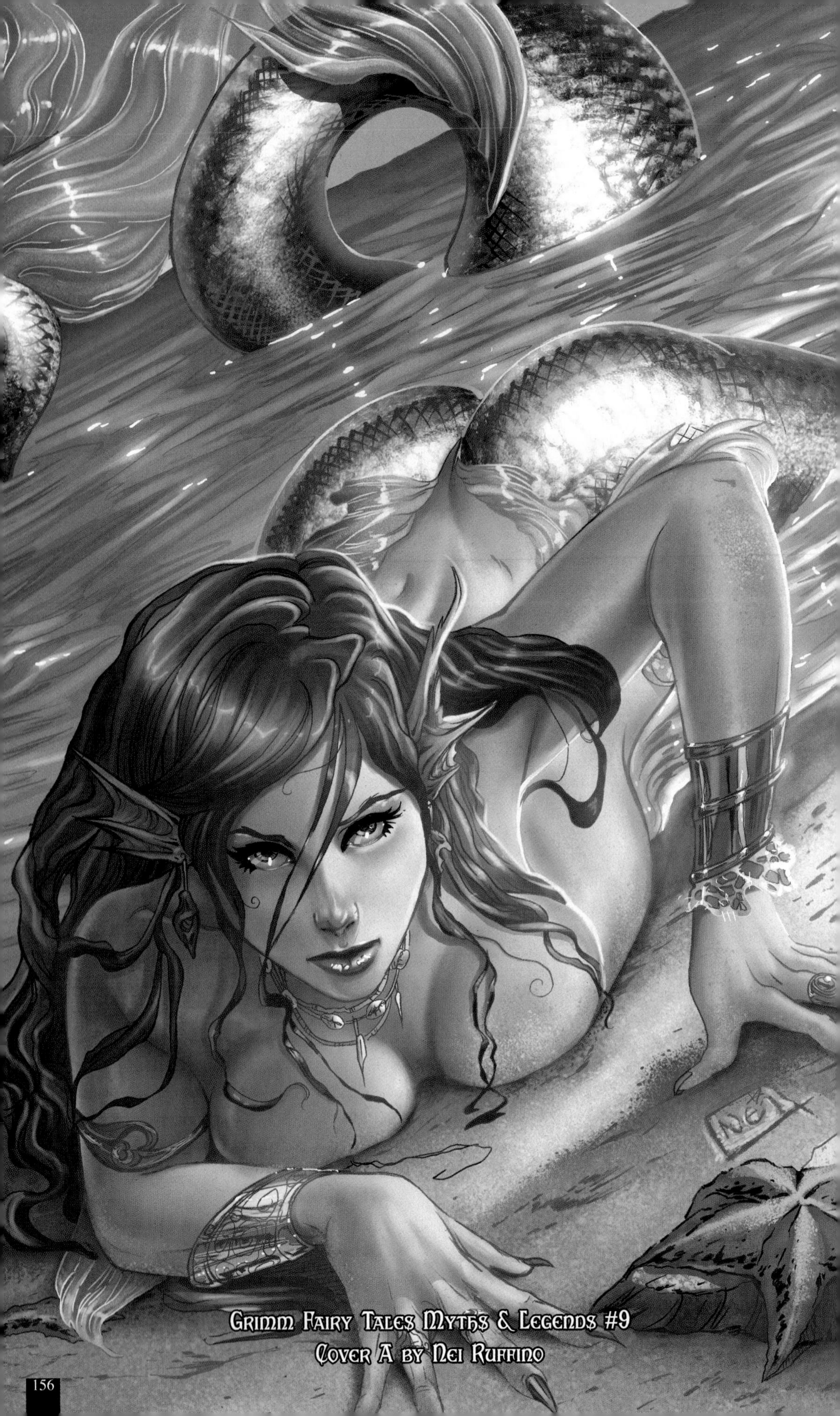

Grimm Fairy Tales Myths & Legends #9
Cover A by Nei Ruffino

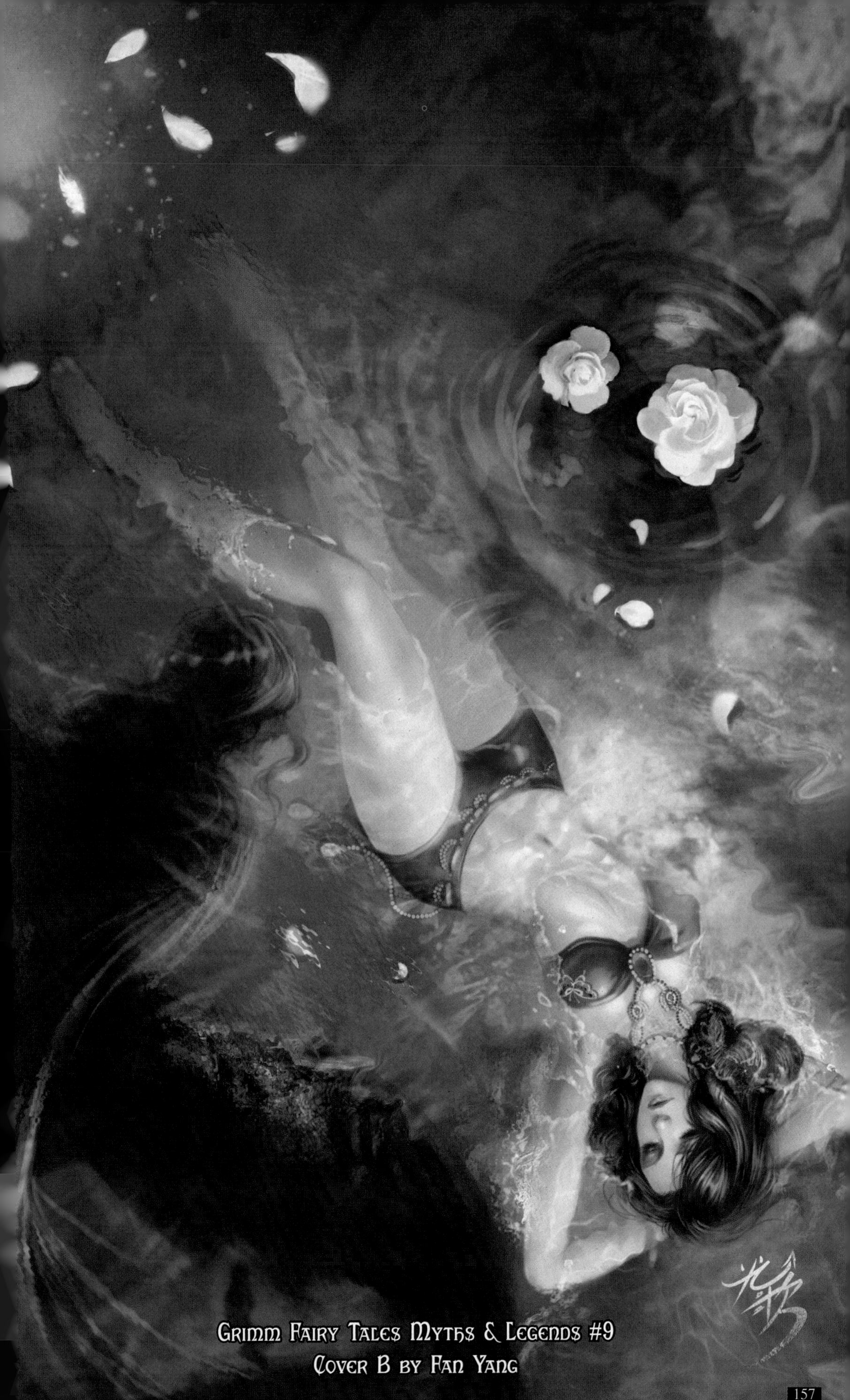

Grimm Fairy Tales Myths & Legends #9
Cover B by Fan Yang

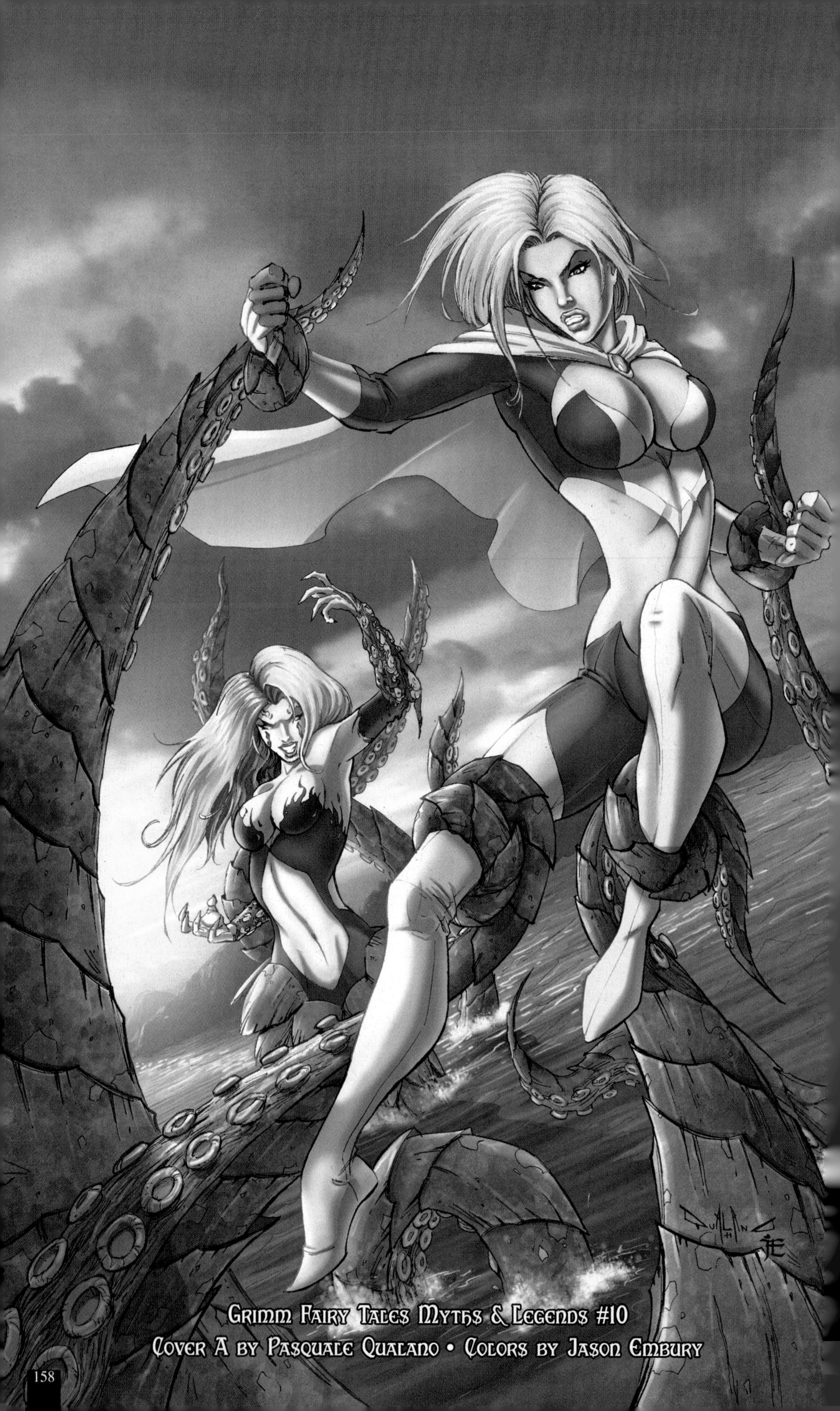

Grimm Fairy Tales Myths & Legends #10
Cover A by Pasquale Qualano • Colors by Jason Embury

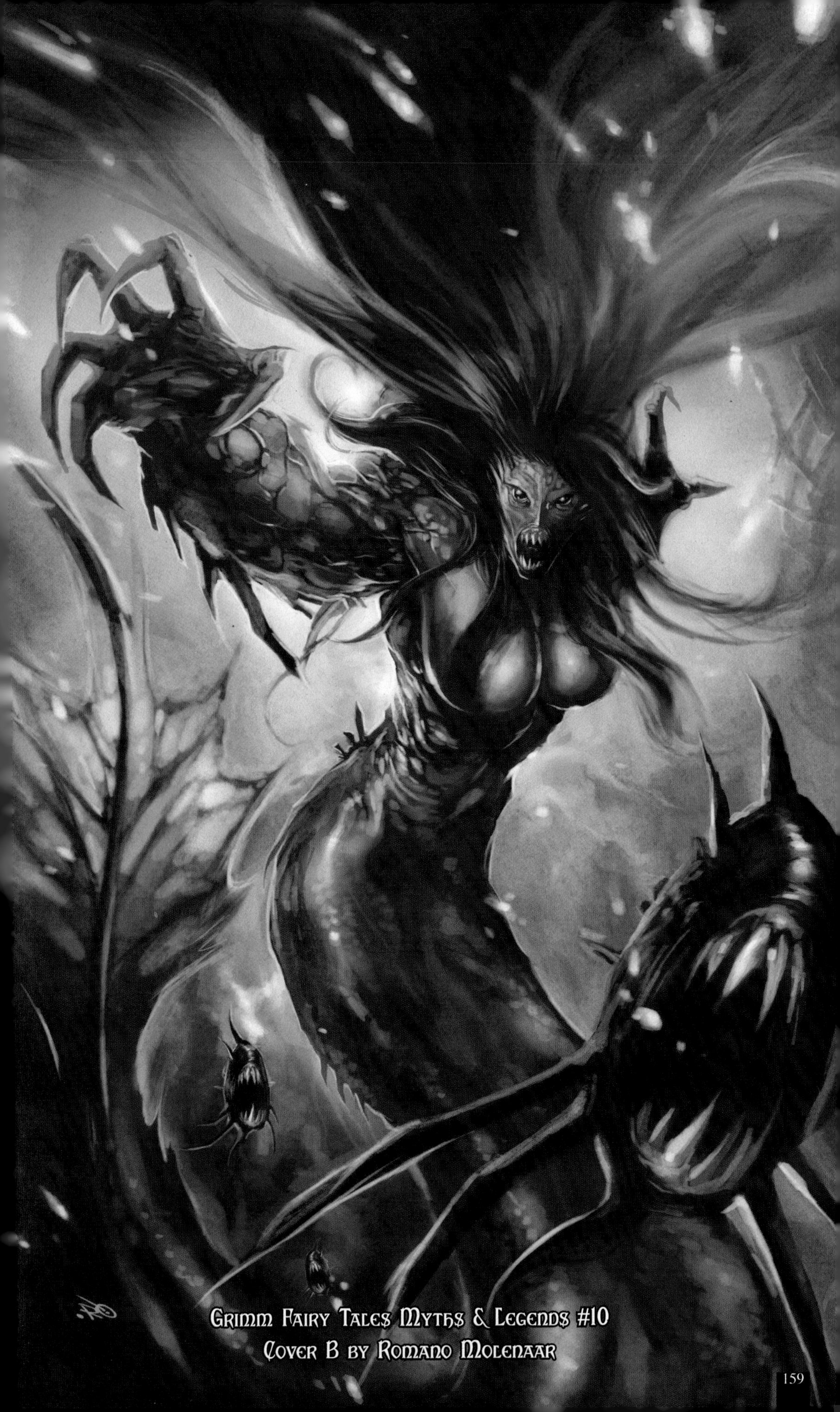

Grimm Fairy Tales Myths & Legends #10
Cover B by Romano Molenaar

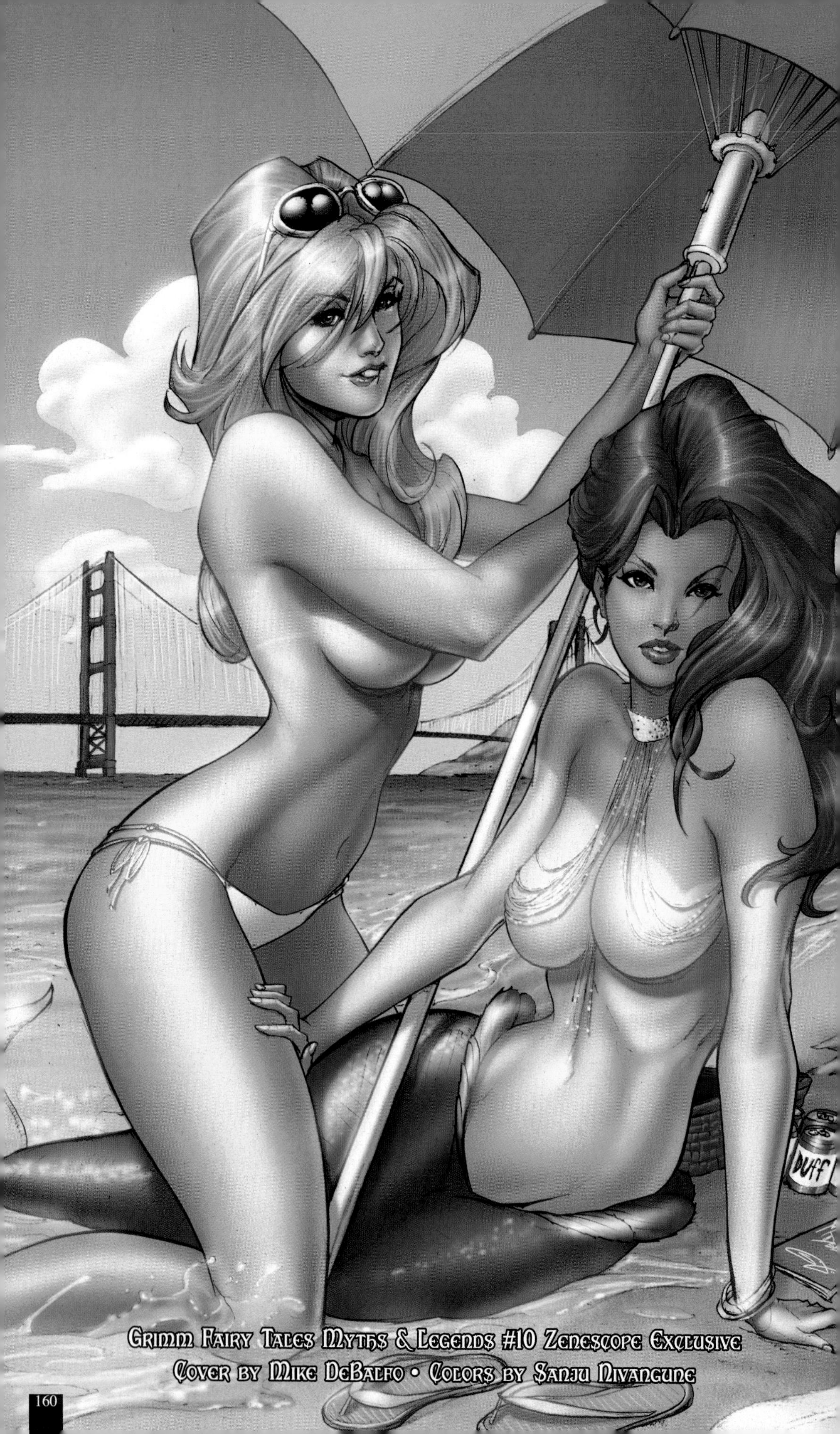
DUFF

Grimm Fairy Tales Myths & Legends #10 Zenescope Exclusive
Cover by Mike DeBalfo • Colors by Sanju Nivangune

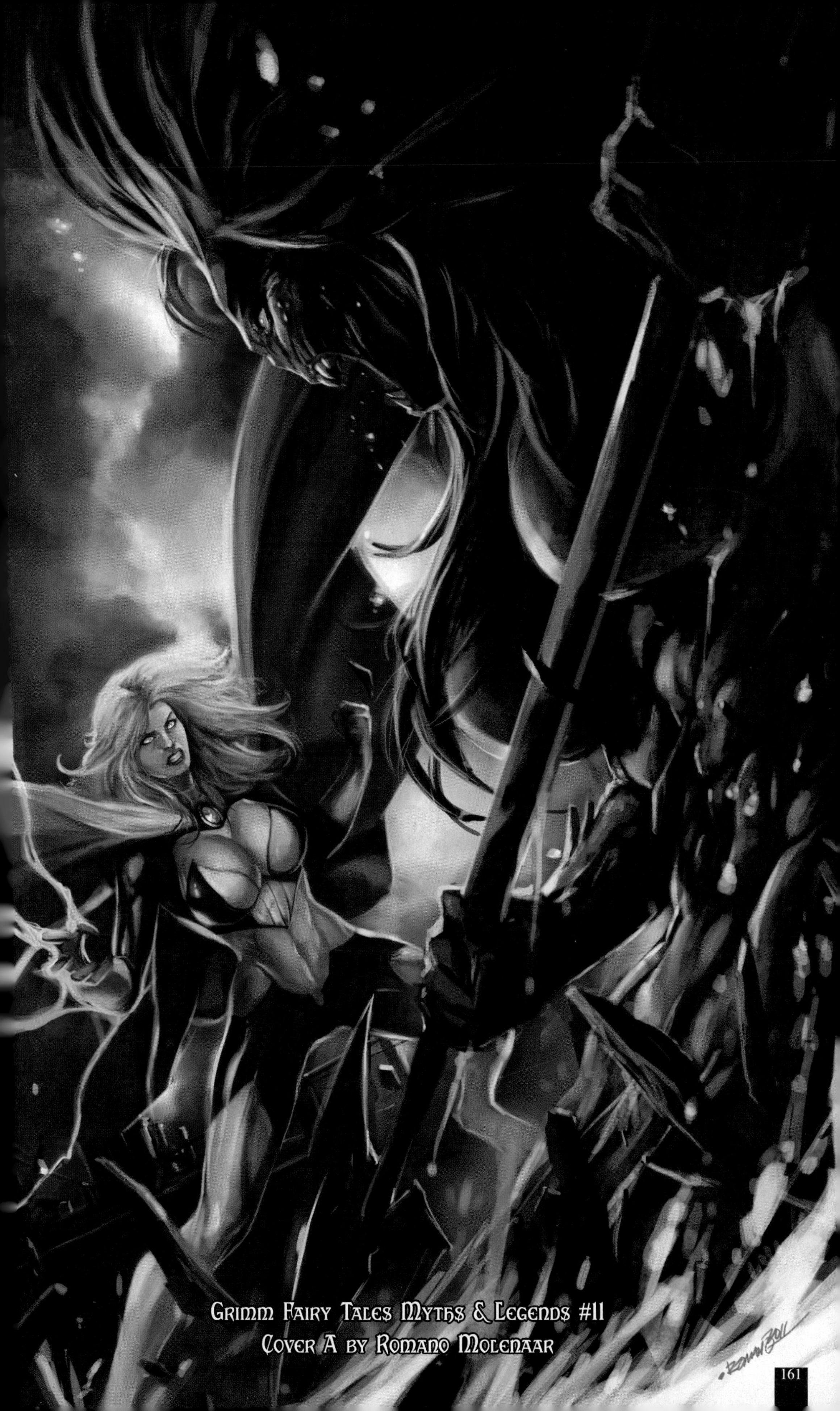

Grimm Fairy Tales Myths & Legends #11
Cover A by Romano Molenaar

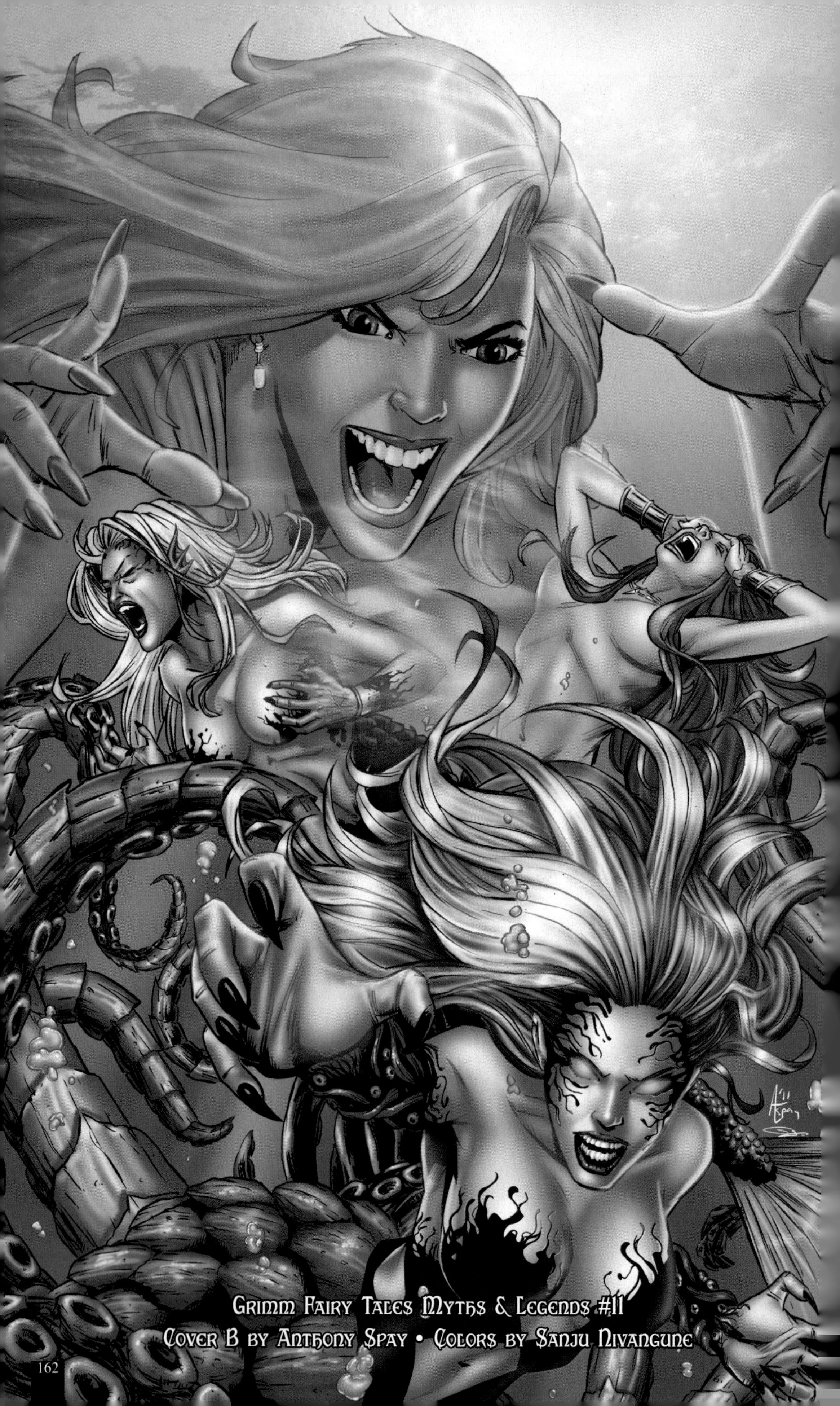

Grimm Fairy Tales Myths & Legends #11
Cover B by Anthony Spay • Colors by Sanju Nivangune

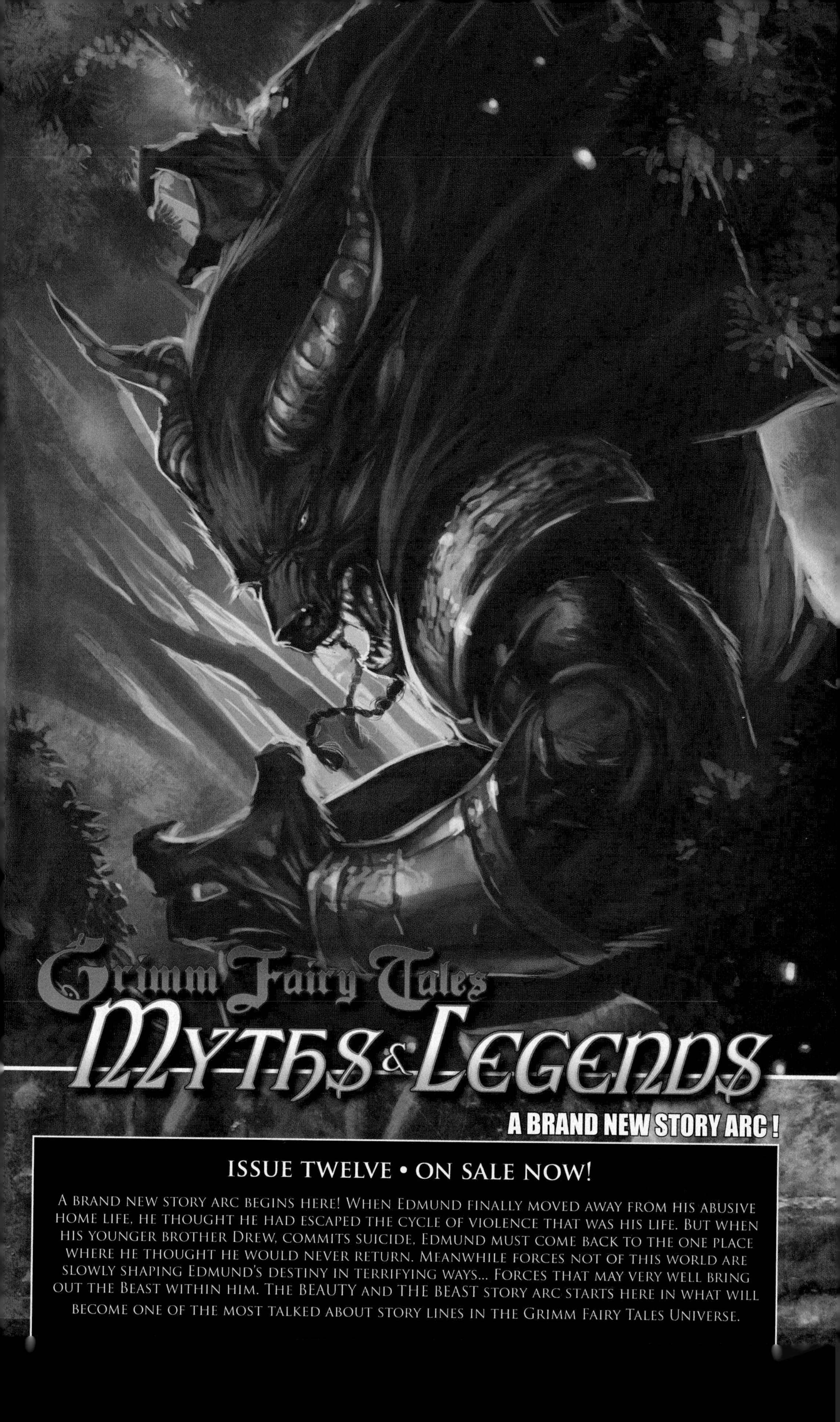
Grimm Fairy Tales
Myths & Legends
A BRAND NEW STORY ARC !
ISSUE TWELVE • ON SALE NOW!
A brand new story arc begins here! When Edmund finally moved away from his abusive home life, he thought he had escaped the cycle of violence that was his life. But when his younger brother Drew, commits suicide, Edmund must come back to the one place where he thought he would never return. Meanwhile forces not of this world are slowly shaping Edmund's destiny in terrifying ways... Forces that may very well bring out the Beast within him. The BEAUTY and THE BEAST story arc starts here in what will become one of the most talked about story lines in the Grimm Fairy Tales Universe.

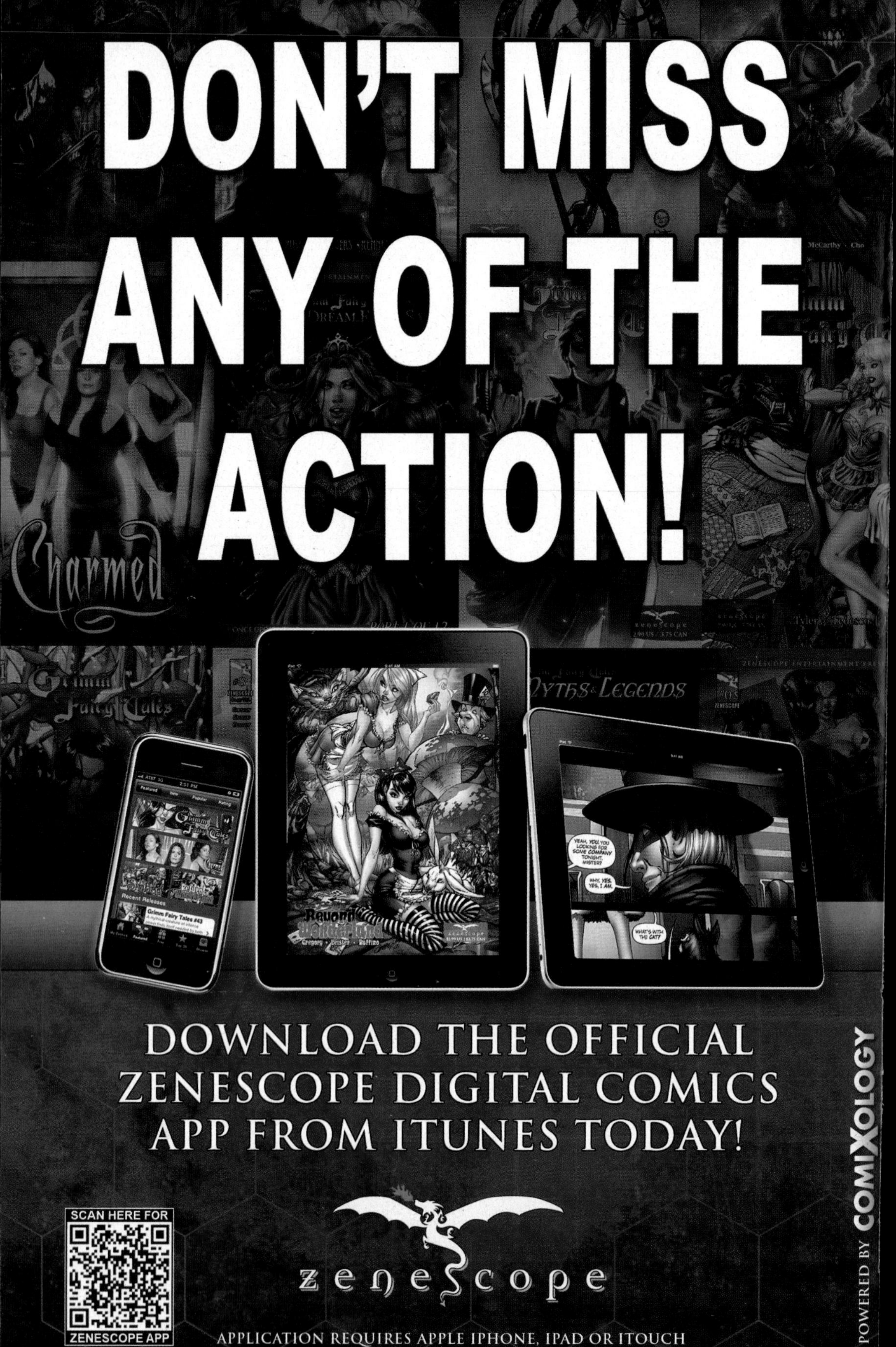
DON'T MISS ANY OF THE ACTION!
Charmed
DOWNLOAD THE OFFICIAL ZENESCOPE DIGITAL COMICS APP FROM ITUNES TODAY!
SCAN HERE FOR
ZENESCOPE APP
zenescope
APPLICATION REQUIRES APPLE IPHONE, IPAD OR ITOUCH
POWERED BY COMIXOLOGY

ENTER THE GRIMM FAIRY TALES UNIVERSE WITH THESE EPIC TRADE COLLECTIONS!

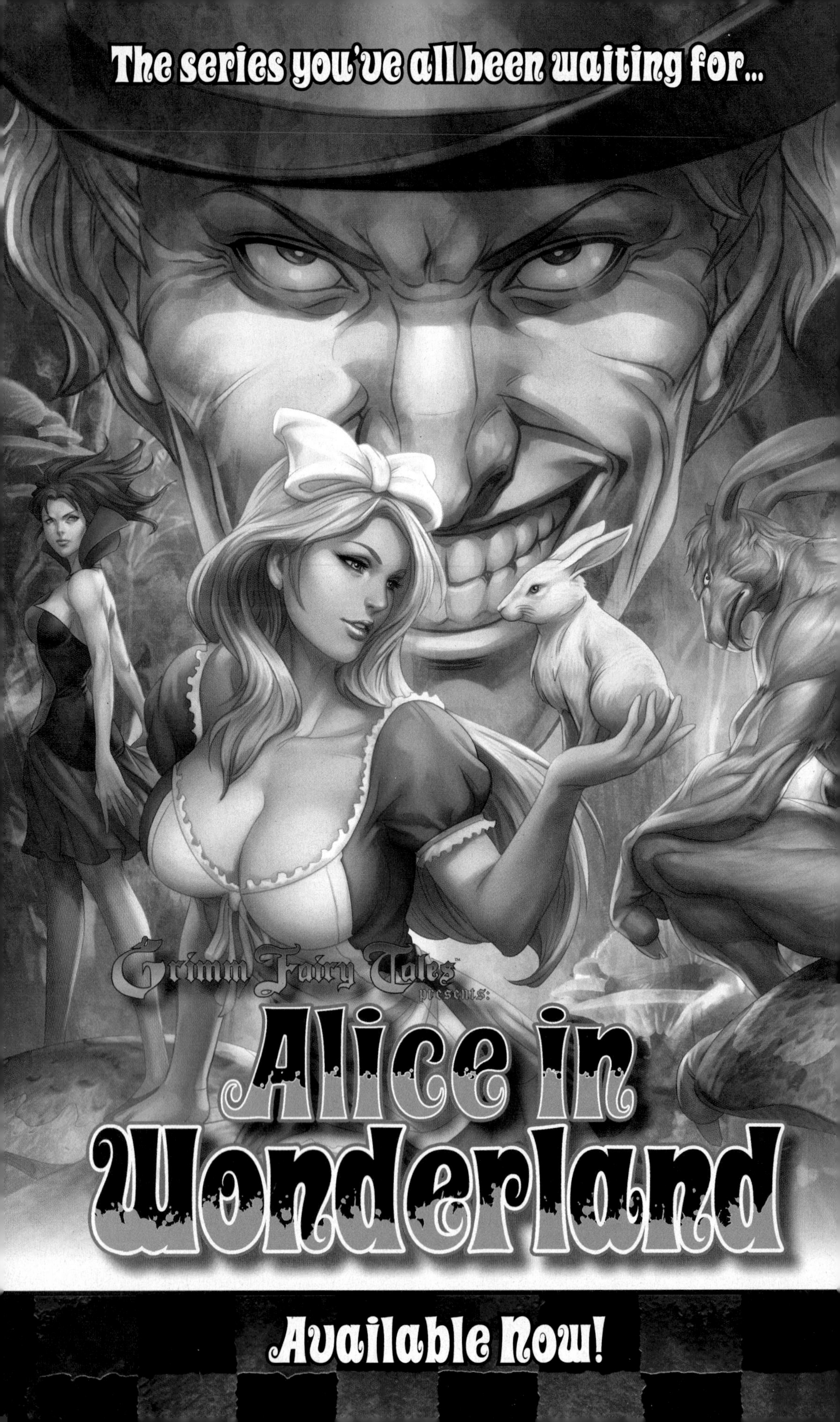
The series you've all been waiting for...
Grimm Fairy Tales™ presents:
Alice in Wonderland
Available Now!

Grimm Fairy Tales
Myths & Legends